THE
ORGANIC
GARDEN
BOOK

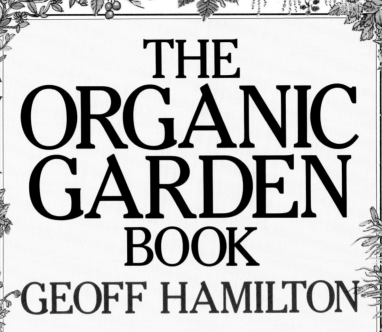

THE
ORGANIC
GARDEN
BOOK

GEOFF HAMILTON

CROWN PUBLISHERS, INC.
NEW YORK

· SENIOR EDITOR ·
Jemima Dunne
· SENIOR ART EDITOR ·
Neville Graham

· EDITORS ·
Sophie Mitchell
Tim Hammond
· ART EDITOR ·
Derek Coombes
· DESIGNER ·
Joanna Martin

· MANAGING EDITOR ·
Daphne Razazan

· AMERICAN EDITOR ·
Marjorie Dietz

Published in 1987 in the United States of America
by Crown Publishers, Inc., 225 Park Avenue South,
New York, New York 10003
and represented in Canada by
the Canadian MANDA Group

Originally published in Great Britain in 1987
by Dorling Kindersley Limited, London

Manufactured in Italy

**Library of Congress Cataloguing-in-Publication
Data**

Hamilton, Geoff.
  The organic garden book.

  1. Organic gardening. I. Title.
SB453.5.H36   1987   635.9'87   86-32924
ISBN 0-517-56541-2

CONTENTS

NB *Latin plant names are given
throughout the book where they differ
from the common names.*

INTRODUCTION

Organic gardening is an emotive subject. There are those who think that organic methods of cultivation are the sole remaining way to save the planet and, at the other extreme, those who think that organic gardening is the refuge of bearded loonies in kaftans and sandals who live in grubby communes on brown rice and sunflower seeds. I believe they are neither. Fortunately, many millions of gardeners all over the world are now beginning to consider organic gardening methods and to evaluate them rationally. Even the long-sceptical scientists are having second thoughts as the public demand for chemical-free food and a safer environment increases.

I have been a professional gardener for thirty years and I have to admit that, up to ten years ago, I too was sceptical about organic gardening. Of course, it's hard to argue with the developments resulting from modern research: agricultural and horticultural science has increased yields dramatically, which has kept food prices stable for years and increased the general well-being of the population of the Western world a thousand-fold. Indeed it would be foolish to deny that science has made, and is still making, a tremendous contribution to the art of growing both productive and ornamental plants. However perfect nature's methods may be, it was never intended that the land should be as productive as we now demand. While nature may have intended one scraggy little wild carrot every yard, we demand a big fat juicy carrot every

few inches. So we have needed all our ingenuity to improve on nature's methods.

Research has helped in several ways that the organic gardener should certainly not shun: varieties of both productive and ornamental plants have been improved almost beyond recognition; quality has been enhanced by finding ways of protecting our plants against the worst of weather; yields have been improved by extending harvesting periods using glass and plastic. And, as a result of research into plants and the way in which they grow, cultivation techniques have been developed to such an extent that the Western world's larder is full to overflowing.

THE MISTAKES OF MODERN TECHNOLOGY

While modern technology cannot be condemned out of hand, there have been many mistakes. The dramatic turnaround from scarcity to plenty over the past century has been achieved at the expense of a massive and ever-increasing input of chemicals and with little thought for tomorrow.

Where corn has proved more profitable than cows, the practice of replacing organic matter on the land has died out. The result is that soils are becoming lifeless and, in many cases, simply disappearing into the sea. Larger machines have demanded larger fields and, as a result, trees and hedgerows have disappeared taking their dependent wildlife with them.

Plants need a certain level of nutrients for healthy growth so, in order to maintain these

A source of water above
A pool, however small, will attract all kinds of insects and small mammals.

Mixed planting scheme left
Mixing flowers and vegetables in the same bed can look very attractive.

levels, more and more chemical fertilizers are poured on to the land every year, filling the plants we eat with alien chemicals and polluting our waterways.

The traditional practice of mixing and rotating crops has been abandoned for short-term profit, with the result that pests and diseases build up to uncontrollable proportions. Killing them with poison sprays becomes essential and, as resistant strains of both pests and diseases develop, so more powerful chemicals have to be used. It is this aspect that is most worrying to us, the consumers of food produced in this way.

Every year, some chemical previously thought to have been safe is banned somewhere in the world. One of the early cases was the insecticide DDT. There is no doubt that it saved many thousands of lives by killing malaria-carrying mosquitoes, but it was also found to build up in the bodies of animals and birds, causing untold losses of wildlife; it was banned in most Western countries before it caused any deaths in humans. This was followed by the soil insecticide dieldrin, the selective weedkiller Ioxynil, suspected of causing birth defects, and, in most Western countries, the herbicide, trichlorophenoxy-acetic acid, or 2,4,5-T, which has been linked with cancer. Not only have these chemicals been shown to cause untold damage to wildlife, but some have also been found in alarming quantities in food, even after processing and cooking.

WHAT IS THE SOLUTION?

For anyone with a garden, the solution seems simple: grow your own produce. But the chemical industry is big business, so gardeners have, over the years, been persuaded that they too can "benefit" from research carried out by the commercial growers and farmers. After all, what is good for the professional must be good for amateurs. In fact, nothing could be further from the truth.

While we can certainly benefit in some ways from research, there is absolutely no need for the home gardener to follow commercial practices blindly. Remember the professional grows on a large scale for profit, while we do so on a small scale for pleasure. He needs all his harvest to be ready at the same time, while we want to stagger it. What's more, there is no need to sacrifice anything in terms of yield and quality. Let me give you an example.

If a farmer has twenty acres of cabbages, he can almost certainly expect an attack of cabbage white butterfly, no self-respecting butterfly could miss such an opportunity. So, to avoid the hungry caterpillars devouring the entire crop, the farmer may have no alternative but to spray. The gardener, on the other hand, has perhaps only ten or a dozen plants. And, if he is an organic gardener, they'll be interplanted with other crops and so effectively camouflaged from the butterflies, who recognize them by sight and perhaps smell. The chances are the cabbages will be missed altogether but, if a butterfly does see them and lay her eggs, there is still no need to reach for a spray. All you need to do is walk down the row occasionally, pick off the offending caterpillars and drop them into a jar of kerosene. You will get one hundred per cent control and it will cost you nothing. What's more, your cabbages will be perfectly clean and healthy. Even better, if you grow the right kind of plants in the ornamental borders and amongst the vegetables, the birds and the ground beetles will do the job for you.

A variety of vegetables above
Planting a wide range of vegetables not only produces a varied crop, but also reduces the risk of pest and disease attack.

The essential herb garden right
Always include herbs in an organic garden, as they attract many insects and have innumerable uses in the kitchen.

The same philosophy applies to fertilizers. In a natural soil there are millions of micro-organisms beavering away on our behalf, producing the nutrients that plants need for healthy growth. Look after them by feeding the soil (rather than applying chemical fertilizers to feed the plants) and they'll repay you a thousand-fold. They'll not thank you for a daily dose of paraquat.

MY EXPERIMENTS

Let's look at the other side of the coin for a moment. Ever since I started gardening, I have come across some quite extraordinary and fanciful remedies for plant ills and some cultivation techniques that stretch credibility well beyond breaking point. Moreover, organic gardening does have more than its fair share of eccentrics. And that can be off-putting. On the other hand, Christopher Columbus was held to be eccentric for saying that the world was round until he actually proved it. And that has been my solution.

Over the past ten years I have been conducting various experiments. I've tried to keep an open mind (and that has not always been easy); however outlandish the theory seemed, I've tried it under as near scientifically experimental conditions as possible. It's important to set up proper trials because, in many cases, when an organic gardener has reported complete success with a pest or disease control, he has not grown a control plot at the same time. The gardener may think, for example, that carrot fly was defeated by surrounding the rows with creosoted string, but how does any one know that there would have been an attack in any case? Unless a nearby row is attacked, the experiment proves nothing. Alas, I have tried the creosoted string method and it didn't work.

I set up trials to test the many suggested organic controls for cabbage root maggot. I grew one row with rhubarb stem underneath the plants, one row with a few mothballs, one with a layer of comfrey spread over the soil and another watered with extract of nettle leaves. In order to be as comprehensive as possible, I grew other rows treated with the chemical insecticides diazinon and bromophos. Most outlandish of all, I surrounded each plant in one of the rows with a bit of carpet underlay. And, of course, I grew a control row with no treatment at all.

The cabbage root maggot did attack; the rows with rhubarb, mothballs, comfrey and nettles all suffered, as did the control row. Those that were treated with soil insecticides were about 80 per cent free, but the row with the carpet underlay was completely unscathed. I use it every year now and it doesn't cost me anything.

I now have a row of four identical plots about 5×6.5m (15×20ft), each growing identical plants, ranging from apple trees and fruit bushes down to cauliflower, cabbages, carrots and other vegetables. One plot is treated organically, one inorganically, one traditionally using a mixture of the two methods and, of course, there is the obligatory control plot, which gets no added organic matter or chemicals at all. I thought at first that the experiments would be invalidated by having the plots so close together: wouldn't their close proximity mean that the insects would simply hop from one plot to another, that weeds could creep under the fences and microbes move through the soil?

Well, of course, that may be so, but I realized that this was the way it had to be. If the experiment was to benefit the average gardener, the organic plot would have to be able to cope with the ills sent from next door. After all, few of us are lucky enough to be completely isolated, and converting the entire street to organic gardening would take much more than gardening skills.

But, amazingly, I found not the slightest problem. Weeds tried to creep in from the next plot but I dealt with those by installing a polyethylene barrier beneath the fence. Most marvellous of all, the hover-flies attracted by the marigolds in the organic plot, ate the aphids in the next door plot as well, and the frogs nipped in and had a go at their slugs too.

THE AIM OF THIS BOOK

So, this book is the result of thirty years gardening and ten years of organic trials. I don't claim that you'll find every organic remedy you've ever heard of and you won't find any magic or mysterious folklore.

What you will discover is a mixture of traditional gardening and modern technology, all of which has been tried and tested over the years in my own garden and proved to be effective. My aim is to make a productive, beautiful, interesting and enjoyable garden that provides an alternative habitat for wildlife of all kinds, gives me a happy, healthy and absorbing occupation and provides me with food that tastes like nature intended and that I know is free from pollution. I'd like to share that with you.

THE ORGANIC WAY

THERE IS NOTHING mystical or magical about organic gardening. It is simply a way of working with nature rather than against it, of recycling natural materials to maintain soil fertility and of encouraging natural methods of pest and disease control, rather than relying on chemicals. It is in fact far less cranky than the methods employed by the chemical grower.

Organic gardening is much more than just a way of growing plants without chemical sprays and artificial fertilizers. It recognizes that the complex workings of nature have been successful in sustaining life over hundreds of millions of years, so the basic organic cultivation principles closely follow those found in the natural world. Don't be misled into thinking that these principles will have a detrimental effect on yield or quality. In fact, you are much more likely to increase both and, in doing so, you will be providing an alternative habitat for wildlife, whilst being certain that the fruit and vegetables produced in your garden are safe, flavorsome and chemical-free.

THE CHEMICAL GARDENER

The purely chemical gardener uses his soil simply as a means of anchoring plant roots and of holding artificial fertilizers to provide plant nutrients. This approach does have excellent results, in the short term.

In the long term, however, it has two disastrous consequences. Because organic matter is not replaced, the soil organisms die out; without them the soil structure breaks down and the soil becomes hard, airless and unproductive. Attempts at "force-feeding" the plants result in soft, sappy growth, which is prone to attack by all manner of pests and diseases. In order to control them, chemical pesticides are used, often with short-term success. But, in killing the pest, they also kill its natural predators so, eventually, the problem gets worse. Stronger and more poisonous pesticides have to be resorted to, and so it goes on. It is a vicious circle that, once started, is difficult to break.

THE ORGANIC GARDENER

The organic gardener has a more constructive approach based on an awareness that there is a fine balance in the natural world which allows all the species to co-exist without any one gaining dominance.

By growing a wide diversity of plants, the organic gardener will attract and build up a miniature eco-system of pests and predators so that, provided the balance isn't upset by killing them with chemicals, no species will be allowed to build up to an unacceptable level.

The soil is teeming with millions of micro-organisms which, in the course of their lives, will release those nutrients required for healthy plant growth from organic matter. So, rather than feeding the plants, the organic way is to feed the soil with natural materials and allow the plants to draw on that reservoir of nutrients as and when they want them. Plants grown this way will be stronger and more able to resist attacks by pests and diseases.

Improving on nature

Natural methods of sustaining plant growth were never intended to support the kinds of demands we make on our gardens. The technique itself is perfect, but, to produce a good crop, we have to intensify it.

The main ways of doing this are quite simple: feeding the soil and improving its texture; protecting seeds during germination; making sure that the plants have adequate water; and by vigilant control of pests and diseases.

LOOKING AFTER THE SOIL

In nature, for example, soil fertility is maintained by recycling organic matter (*see overleaf*). Gardeners, on the other hand, remove much of the organic material from the productive garden in the form of fruit and vegetables, and from the ornamental garden by weeding, pruning, mowing and cutting flowers. This organic matter has to be replaced through the compost heap, animal manure and green-manure crops. Even then, our intensive methods may need further inputs of concentrated animal and plant residues.

In nature, soil texture, aeration and drainage are maintained by the action of burrowing animals, such as worms and insects. Gardeners can improve on this by digging regularly.

SEEDING AND WATERING

In nature, many of the seeds produced never germinate, due to adverse conditions or predators. Whereas, in the garden, this no longer has to be haphazard. We can ensure that seeds and mature plants are protected and that the right amount of water is supplied in dry weather.

CONTROLLING PESTS AND DISEASES

We can improve on natural methods of pest and disease control too. We can deliberately fill our gardens with a wide diversity of plants that we know will attract and encourage the predators of the pests that threaten our cultivated plants.

THE FINAL CROP

Our plant breeders have produced varieties that are resistant to pests and diseases and that will give us bigger crops and more beautiful flowers, while thousands of years of growing experience have enabled us to come up with techniques that will outcrop nature many times over.

But, if we are to continue our success, we must stick to the rules. We may be able to manipulate nature in the short term by using chemical methods but it is folly to think that we can ever assume complete control.

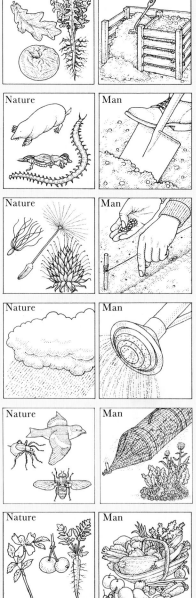

Worms pull plant remains into the upper layers of the soil. Worm casts are a valuable fertilizer.

The soil feeds the plants

GARDENING WITH NATURE

ENRICHING THE SOIL
In nature, dead or rotting vegetation and animal manure provide adequate nourishment for the soil. As man removes the crops he grows, he must add compost and manure to improve the soil.

Nature | *Man*

DIGGING
Despite the activity of burrowing animals and penetrating plant roots, untended soil is still relatively hard and compacted. Man can improve the texture by digging to allow air and water through the soil.

Nature | *Man*

SEEDING
In nature, relatively few seeds germinate because of competition from other plants and poor conditions. In the garden, most seeds will germinate as they can be given optimum conditions and spacings.

Nature | *Man*

WATERING
Plants are dependent on water for their survival. Whereas adequate rainfall cannot be guaranteed in nature, in the garden, additional water can be given to the plants in very dry weather.

Nature | *Man*

PEST CONTROL
Nature maintains its delicate balance by ensuring that pests and predators control each other's numbers. Man can encourage and assist this process while also protecting his plants using artificial means.

Nature | *Man*

THE FINAL CROP
Left to its own devices, nature would not produce a very abundant harvest, either in terms of quantity or the size of the individual foods. The harvest from cultivated ground is richer and far more varied.

Nature | *Man*

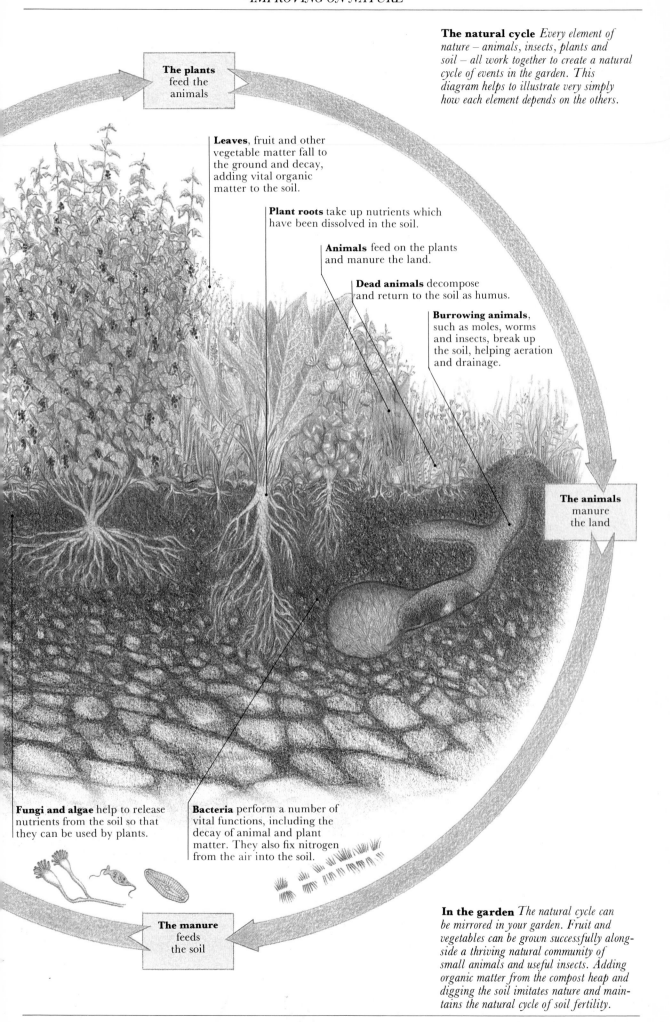

The natural cycle *Every element of nature – animals, insects, plants and soil – all work together to create a natural cycle of events in the garden. This diagram helps to illustrate very simply how each element depends on the others.*

The plants feed the animals

Leaves, fruit and other vegetable matter fall to the ground and decay, adding vital organic matter to the soil.

Plant roots take up nutrients which have been dissolved in the soil.

Animals feed on the plants and manure the land.

Dead animals decompose and return to the soil as humus.

Burrowing animals, such as moles, worms and insects, break up the soil, helping aeration and drainage.

The animals manure the land

Fungi and algae help to release nutrients from the soil so that they can be used by plants.

Bacteria perform a number of vital functions, including the decay of animal and plant matter. They also fix nitrogen from the air into the soil.

The manure feeds the soil

In the garden *The natural cycle can be mirrored in your garden. Fruit and vegetables can be grown successfully alongside a thriving natural community of small animals and useful insects. Adding organic matter from the compost heap and digging the soil imitates nature and maintains the natural cycle of soil fertility.*

THE SOIL

THE SOIL IS the basic raw material of the gardener's art. It should never be dismissed as a mere collection of mineral particles used to anchor roots, or worse still as "dirt". It is much more than that.

Certainly, its basic structure consists of rock particles broken down by frost and thaw action, wind and river flow, to produce the different textures that give us soil "types" (*see page 14*). However, a large part of its make-up is organic matter – vegetable and animal remains in various stages of decay – along with air and water, which are all essential for the support of plant and animal life. All of this provides a home for millions and millions of living organisms, such as soil fungi, algae, bacteria, insects and worms, which work to provide just the right conditions for healthy plant growth. These organisms provide the plants with food in a form they can ingest, and improve the structure of the soil by breaking it up and allowing more air to circulate.

It is perhaps in the treatment of soil, more than anywhere, that organic gardening differs from other gardening methods. The very first principle of organic gardening is to nurture and encourage this subterranean life so that it can support a much larger plant population than nature ever intended (*see also* Soil Improvement *and* Fertilizers, *pages 18-42*).

THE FORMATION OF SOIL

Soil is formed over millions of years by the physical or chemical weathering of rock. Clay soils are formed by chemical weathering, where the mineral composition of the rock is changed, usually by the action of weak acids. Other types of soil are the result of physical weathering, which does not involve any change in the chemical content of the rock, but gradually erodes it mechanically. This physical weathering may happen within the rock or externally.

In hot climates, such as those which prevail in desert areas, the widely fluctuating temperatures of day and night cause rocks to expand and contract regularly. Over a period of time the stress caused by the continual expansion and contraction leads to the physical disintegration of the rock and the formation of soil particles.

In colder conditions, like those which affected much of the world during the last Ice Age, rocks are broken down by the action of water entering cracks in the rock and freezing. As it freezes, the water expands, forcing the rock to split open. The movement of giant glaciers was responsible for the formation of soil, as it wore away fragments of the rock below, and the action of streams and rivers also serves to wear away rocks to form soil.

What is soil?

The soil in your garden is a very complex structure and its cultivation depends on many different elements. There are several different soil types which all have advantages and disadvantages. For example, the soil may be acid or alkaline; it may be heavy or light; it may drain well or badly; it may be very stony.

SOIL PROFILE

What you see in your garden is simply the surface of the soil. Soil is made up of three layers: topsoil, subsoil and the soil parent matter. Topsoil is formed over the years by the addition of organic matter that follows the decomposition of dead plants or animals (*see page 11*). It is

inhabited by a wide range of living organisms, and it is in this layer that the majority of the feeding roots of plants exist. Topsoils can be improved and deepened by the regular addition of organic matter (*see pages 18-34*).

The second layer is the subsoil, which is low in nutrients, generally contains few or no microorganisms, and is therefore inhospitable to roots. Thus, when digging deeply, it is advisable to bring to the surface only very small amounts of subsoil; these can be mixed with organic matter and will, eventually, turn into topsoil. Double digging breaks up subsoil, and improves drainage, without bringing the subsoil to the surface (*see* Basic Techniques, *page 264*).

The nature of the subsoil has a profound effect on the water-holding capacity of the soil in general. If you have very sandy or rocky subsoil, which drains very freely, you will need to increase the bulky organic matter content (*see pages 16-17*), and thus the water-holding capacity, of the topsoil. On the other hand, heavy clay subsoil, which drains poorly, may necessitate the installation of an artificial drainage system (*see* Basic Techniques, *page 262*).

The third layer – the parent material – is the original mineral from which the soil was formed. This layer is normally deep enough not to concern the gardener, but may, on high ground, be comparatively near the surface. If this is the case, try to increase the depth of the topsoil by adding organic matter to the top layer.

SOIL TYPES

There are five main soil types – clay, sand, silt, limestone and peat – and it is the nature of the original rock and the size of the mineral fragments that determine the soil type (*see page 14*). It is important to know what kind of soil you are dealing with in your garden because the way in which you manage it, the timing of cultivations and the plants you grow will depend to a large extent on the nature of the soil.

However, having said this, most soils contain a mixture of minerals. If a soil is referred to as, for example, "clay", then this indicates its major constituent. Soil mixtures are known as loams; for example, a soil made up of 50 per cent clay and silt and 50 per cent sand is a "medium loam". Similarly, a soil which contains a high proportion of sand might be described as a "sandy loam", while one which contains a relatively large amount of clay might be described as a "heavy loam".

PRACTICAL CHARACTERISTICS

Soils can also be heavy or light. A heavy soil contains a much higher proportion of clay. This type of soil has very small particles, which tend to pack together, preventing free passage of water. Heavy soil is often very difficult to work initially because it tends to be either very wet and sticky or very dry and hard. Eventually though, when it has been ameliorated by the natural drainage afforded by plant roots and the addition of organic matter, heavy soil becomes an excellent moisture- and nutrient-retaining medium. Light soils, on the other hand, are easy to dig, and warm up quickly in the spring but allow very free drainage, which has its own problems. Water and nutrients disappear through the topsoil and into the subsoil and eventually the drainage system. Light soils require constant additions of organic matter to form a topsoil that retains moisture, and generally need more applications of fertilizers than heavy soils.

ACIDITY AND ALKALINITY

Soil may also contain lime, which will cause it to be either "acid" or "alkaline", depending on the amount. The lime content will make a considerable difference to the fertility of the soil, and will govern the range of plants you can grow, as it has the ability to make some nutrients unavailable to plants (*see pages 38-9*). For a straightforward test to determine the amount of lime in the soil, see page 37.

STONES

The proportion of stones or gravel in your soil does not influence its texture classification, but may affect its fertility and drainage. Stony soil has the advantages and disadvantages of a free-draining soil (*see pages 16-17*) and it may need regular applications of bulky organic matter to improve water retention. If you are lucky enough to have a heavy topsoil and a very stony subsoil, you have the best of both worlds, with surface moisture and nutrient retention, plus good drainage of excess water.

IDENTIFYING SOIL LAYERS

If you dig a deep hole in the garden, the varying colours and textures make it easy to identify the different layers. This is a valuable exercise, because it enables you to understand the nature of your soil and therefore gives you a clue as to the best way to work it. The depth of each layer will vary considerably from one area to the next.

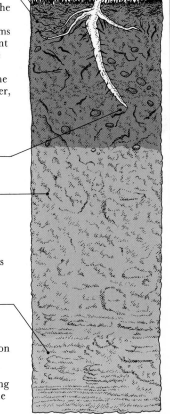

Topsoil This is the darkest layer of soil. It contains the organic matter, fungi, bacteria, insects and worms necessary for healthy plant growth. The depth of the topsoil can range from 5cm (2in) to 2m (6ft). The deeper this layer the better, because plant roots have more space to grow and take up nutrients.

Depth of root growth

Subsoil Lighter in color than topsoil because it contains no humus, this layer is largely devoid of plant nutrients. The structure of subsoil affects the drainage of the soil.

Parent matter This consists mostly of unaltered rock. It is the area least affected by any cultivation of topsoil. The depth at which this level starts depends on the underlying rock and the height of the piece of land.

Soil types

When seen together the five soil types – clay, sand, silt, peat and limestone – look different. a mixture of minerals; the soils illustrated here are as near to the pure mineral as possible. Each soil type has advantages and disadvantages, so each needs a slightly different management technique and supports different types of plants. This is discussed in more detail in *The Ornamental Garden* (*see pages 74-125*) and *The Vegetable Garden* (*see pages 132-201*).

CLAY
This is a heavy, cold soil which feels sticky when moist and hard and compacted when dry. The minute particles are less than 0.002mm in size. This means that clay does not drain easily and is difficult to work in wet conditions. However, it is possible to turn it into a very workable fertile soil (*see opposite*). Clay soils are normally well supplied with plant foods and are capable of supporting a wide variety of plants.
See page 92 for a list of plants for clay soil.

SAND
This is a dry, light soil, which will feel gritty if rubbed between the fingers. Sand particles range in size from 0.2mm, for the very finest sand, to 2mm for the coarsest. Sandy soil is easy to work and particularly good because it warms up quickly in the spring and can therefore be cultivated earlier than most soils. Because it is free-draining, nutrients tend to be lost easily so it will need supplementing with a great deal of organic matter as well as extra fertilizer.
See page 92 for a list of plants for sandy soil.

LIMESTONE (Calcareous soil)
A pale, "hungry-looking" soil, limestone often contains a high proportion of stones and flints. The large particles make it free-draining and very quick to lose nutrients and water. Often, the topsoil is rather shallow, making it unsuitable for plants with deep roots. Worse still, limestone is alkaline; in other words it contains a great deal of lime, making it inhospitable to many plants.
See page 93 for a list of plants for alkaline soil.

SILT
This type of soil is neither gritty or sticky. The soil particles are small – between 0.002mm and 0.05mm, making silt smooth and silky to the touch. When wet, it has a tendency to pack down, leaving the soil cold, heavy and badly drained, like clay. However, it is possible to improve the texture of the soil by applying liberal quantities of well-rotted compost or manure. Silt soils support the same range of plants as clay.
See page 92 for a list of plants for silt soil.

PEAT
Peat is a distinctive dark brown or gray color, and has a spongy texture. It is rich in decomposed organic matter and therefore requires little additional compost or manure. The younger brown peat is much easier to work and more fertile than the heavier, black, bog-like type. All peaty soils tend to become waterlogged, so need to be drained artificially. Peat is usually acid and therefore will need to have lime added to increase the range of plants that can be cultivated.
See page 93 for a list of plants for acid soil.

Soil management

The ideal soil has a good crumbly structure, is rich in organic matter, drains well enough to prevent the topsoil becoming waterlogged in heavy rain, and is capable of providing the nutrients needed for healthy plant growth. The various soil types described left all have their own advantages and disadvantages. Each type is in fact a mixture of different particles in varying proportions, and a short period of observation and a test will soon establish which mineral predominates. You can then use one of the following management techniques to get the best from your particular soil.

Identifying your soil type *Take a handful of soil from your garden and rub a little between your finger and thumb. Clay feels sticky and will roll into a ball that simply changes shape when pressed. Sand is coarse and gritty, while silt feels silky smooth. Limestone has a dry crumbly feel and a grayish-white color, while peat is just the reverse, black and moist.*

Clay

While clay is beset with problems initially, a little work and sound management can produce excellent results. It is certainly true that, in the early stages of cultivation, clay is not nearly as convenient to work as a light soil such as sand. When it is wet, it rapidly becomes a soggy mess of mud and, when it dries out, it sets like concrete.

Clay is a badly drained, cold and heavy soil because the spaces between each particle are too small to allow free passage of water and air, so the soil is always in danger of settling down to form a solid, airless mass. Improving the soil structure can take a few years, but a good clay soil is capable of growing far better crops than a sandy soil ever could.

DIGGING

It is best, if you can, to dig a clay soil during the autumn (*see page 263*), either at a time when there has been a little rain to soften the hard-baked soil, or when it is drying out after being soaked, but before it is hard again. In temperate climates, these times are fairly frequent, but in drier climates it calls for good organization and rapid action when the weather changes.

When heavy soil gets wet and dries out again, it expands and contracts, causing the mass of soil to crack into innumerable small clods. If water then gets into these cracks and freezes, it will force them further apart, breaking the soil down to a sowable tilth. So dig clay soils over in the autumn, leaving the surface rough and uneven through the winter to expose the maximum amount of soil surface to the elements. At the same time, you can work the organic material into the upper levels.

DRAINAGE

Because clay was broken down chemically, it's also possible to combine the particles chemically by a process known as "flocculation". If sufficient lime is added to the soil, the tiny particles of clay will bind together to form much larger crumbs, through which air, water and plant roots can freely pass. Check the requirements of the plants you wish to grow and use as much lime as you can without making conditions intolerable for them (*see page 35*). In addition, if your soil is very heavy, dig coarse grit into the soil – approximately one to two bucketfuls every square meter/yard (*see page 75*).

Raising a section of soil above its immediate surroundings will improve drainage quite considerably. To help the soil dry out and warm up: raise your ornamental beds slightly (*see page 75*) and grow your vegetables on the deep-bed system (*see page 135*). The important thing with clay is that you should never tread on it when it is wet or you'll destroy years of work. If you have to walk on it, lay boards down first.

ORGANIC MATTER

Adding plenty of bulky organic matter to a clay soil will hold the particles apart so that roots and water can pass through. After a few years, when the level of organic matter is satisfactory and the soil is filled with the roots of previous crops, clay becomes much easier to work. In fact, every plant you grow plays its part in improving the soil for the next plant generation.

Silt

The main problem with a silt soil, as with clay, is one of drainage. Of all the soils formed by grinding, silt has the smallest particles. Only the particles of clay are smaller, but they were formed by chemical action.

The size of the particles means that they tend to pack together very closely when wet, preventing the free passage of water and air through the soil. So drainage is poor and there is a danger

of the soil settling down to form an airless mass. However, if you never walk on the soil when it is wet (use boards), and condition it as recommended here, silt is perfectly manageable and will produce quite satisfactory results.

DIGGING

Silt soil should be cultivated only when it is dry enough not to stick to your boots. Conditions underfoot permitting, aim to dig silt during the autumn to take advantage of weather which will help break the soil down to a sowable tilth. Like clay, when silt gets wet and dries out again, it expands and contracts, causing the mass of soil to crack into small clods. If water then gets into these cracks and freezes, it will force them further apart, breaking the soil down even more. So by digging silt over in the autumn, you expose the maximum amount of the soil surface to the elements and work the organic material into the topsoil at the same time.

DRAINAGE

In order to improve drainage, the soil particles have to be forced apart physically, to allow free passage of air, water and plant roots. Do this by digging one or two bucketfuls of coarse grit into the soil every square meter/yard (*see page 75*) when you dig in the organic matter. Raising your ornamental beds slightly and growing vegetables on the deep-bed system will improve drainage, thus helping the soil to dry out and warm up.

ORGANIC MATTER

The structure of silt soils benefits greatly from the addition of liberal quantities of well-rotted compost or manure. Adding plenty of bulky organic matter to the soil will hold the particles apart so that roots and water can pass through more easily. If possible, keep the soil covered with a green-manure crop in order to add organic matter and remove surface water (*see page 32*).

Sand

A very light soil, sand tends to drain easily and can therefore be cultivated when other soils are lying sodden and quite unworkable. As it also warms up quickly, it is an ideal soil for raising early crops. However, sand is also hungry and very demanding. So the price of having an easy soil to work is the need to apply extra organic matter and plant food, in the form of fertilizers (*see pages 35-42*), because nutrients, as well as water, will drain away.

DIGGING

When you cultivate sand is relatively unimportant. It is not necessary to leave a sandy soil rough during the winter months for the frost and rain to break down. The large particles make it very easy to cultivate to a fine tilth anyway, so it is best to dig it in the spring a short while before you intend to sow or plant. If you never venture on the soil when it is so wet that it sticks to your boots, you will not go far wrong.

DRAINAGE

During the year, sandy soil will tend to lose water, both through surface evaporation and free-draining, and this could be detrimental to the plants. To reduce the problem, spread organic matter, or "mulch", over the beds between plants as often as you can (*see page 20*). This lowers the evaporation rate and improves the soil structure.

ORGANIC MATTER

It is very important to improve sandy soils by adding substantial amounts of bulky organic material each year. Because of the quick-draining nature of the soil, the organic matter will work down into the subsoil very quickly so, to save labor and to put it in the root zone, dig the organic matter into the top few inches or spread it over the surface.

Try to maintain a cover of vegetation over the surface more or less all the time, and certainly in the winter, when the "leaching" of nutrients is at its most rapid. In the vegetable garden, it is a good idea to grow a green-manure crop during the winter when the beds are empty and to dig it in during the spring (*see page 32*). This will not only hold many of the nutrients in the soil during the winter, but will also add quite large quantities of organic matter.

Limestone/alkaline soils

There are two big disadvantages with these soils. Firstly, they are thin, dry and "hungry". This is because the particles are very large, like those in sandy soil, so water drains through rapidly, taking plant nutrients with it. Plant nutrients, in the form of organic fertilizers, will therefore need to be added to the soil. Secondly, perhaps even worse, they are so alkaline, they are unsuitable for many plants (*see page 35*).

DIGGING

Generally there is no need to worry too much about the timing of cultivations. Like sand, these soils are normally dry enough to work, even in the depths of winter. It is not necessary to leave alkaline soils rough over the winter months for the frost and rain to break down. Instead dig it in the spring a few weeks before sowing. Because the topsoil is usually not very deep, digging should be kept shallow and, if the area is fairly small, it could be worthwhile adding a layer of topsoil to the surface.

DRAINAGE

Generally, drainage on these soils is good and the need is to retain water nutrients.

ORGANIC MATTER

On these soils – limestone and other alkaline soils of the USA, and the chalk soils of Britain – it is important to try and keep the soil covered. Grow a crop of green manure during the winter and dig it in during the spring (*see page 32*). During the growing season, it is even worth sowing a fast-growing green-manure crop between rows, just to keep the soil covered.

Mulching, or spreading organic material on top of the soil between rows, is also important during the growing season. You should use acid materials, such as peat, grass cuttings, compost or manure, in order to counteract the alkalinity of the soil.

Peat

If you are lucky enough to be growing on peaty soil, grow as intensively as you can, as it is always potentially very fertile and usually easy to work. You'll find it easy to produce bumper crops and beautiful flowers year after year. Properly managed, a peat soil is superb but, like other soils, it does have its problems. Most importantly, peat soils are liable to be acid and will therefore need generous applications of lime to restore the pH balance in the fruit and vegetable plots (*see page 36*). In the ornamental garden, provided you choose the correct plants, this should not be necessary (*see page 93*).

Furthermore, when they are drained, peat soils tend to dry out quite rapidly in hot weather. If they are allowed to dry out completely, they will shrink and may be difficult to wet again. To prevent this, some reliable irrigation or hand watering may be necessary in dry weather (*see also* Basic techniques, *pages 258-67*).

DIGGING

The timing of cultivation is not critical. It is not necessary to leave peat rough during the winter.

DRAINAGE

Peat and the more decomposed muck are often badly drained so you may need to install a drainage system (*see page 262*).

ORGANIC MATTER

A major advantage of peat is that it is not normally necessary to add any humus-making materials. Peat, unlike the other soils, is largely made up of decomposed matter. It therefore has a low mineral content but contains an excess of organic matter. However, the soil is likely to be low in nutrients to start with so you may need to add fertilizers (*see page 35*).

SOIL IMPROVEMENT

THERE ARE various cultivation techniques that you can employ to improve your particular soil; these are discussed in the previous chapter. All soil types will benefit from the addition of bulky organic matter in the form of compost or manure or some other soil conditioner. This is the key to soil fertility, and a healthy, fertile soil is the basis of the organic approach to gardening. In fact it is the basis of good gardening, whether you are wedded to organic principles or not. Organic matter will improve the drainage or increase the water-holding capacity of your soil (*see pages 17-19*). It will also, over a period of time, increase the depth of usable topsoil.

I have a perfect example of the value of organic matter in my own garden. My soil is a rich, dark brown color, fibrous and full of worms, a reliable indicator of the presence of healthy numbers of other less obvious life. Everything I plant seems to thrive, and the soil is a pleasure to work. This is because it gets the benefit of hefty doses of manure and compost every year.

Yet I need to walk only a few feet to the cornfield next door, which never sees any organic matter from one year's end to the next, to find a soil that is hard, compacted and airless. It's difficult to force a fork through the top layer of soil and, when you do, there's not a worm to be seen. Granted, there are mono-culture farmers like my neighbor who still grow very good crops of wheat, year after year, without the soil ever seeing a forkful of manure. With no cattle on their farms it would be difficult to supply the manure and, in the interests of convenience and economy, they even burn the straw after the harvest. However, they do so at the cost of enormous inputs of chemicals and of a steadily deteriorating soil.

WHAT SHOULD YOU USE TO IMPROVE YOUR SOIL?

There is no doubt at all that, if you put on sufficient well-rotted manure every year, your soil will remain fertile and your plants will prosper. But where is all the manure to come from, particularly if you live in a town? The days are long gone when you could follow the cart-horse with a shovel and bucket. And, if you live in the country, particularly if it is a

corn-growing area, the farmer's children don't even know what cows look like.

So the gardener's alternative is compost. But is that being realistic? Certainly it looks good during the early summer when you start to fill your compost container with grass cuttings. After a couple of mowings, it fills up to overflowing and you have to start another. Yet by the time it has rotted down completely, it has shrunk to no more than a few bucketfuls.

USING BOUGHT-IN MATERIAL

In fact a normal-sized garden with a productive vegetable plot will simply not produce enough compost. You will have to buy in some form of organic matter, and be constantly on the look-out for suitable composting material. Naturally, the more you can gather the better, because you will have to buy less. Even if you live in a city there are ways and means of doing this (*see page 26*).

Unfortunately it is almost impossible to garden totally organically, because virtually everything that you might use is polluted with some chemical or other. Straw has been sprayed with weedkiller, fungicide and insecticide; the cows have been force-fed with growth-promoting hormones; even the leaves swept from the pavements are polluted with lead from gasoline. So, if you are a purist – and I am – you may feel safer if you compost all imported material for at least a year in the hope that the toxins will be leached out.

FEEDING THE SOIL

Plants need certain nutrients in specific proportions to be present in the soil (*see page 39*). These nutrients will be supplied by the addition of sufficient compost or manure (*see page 20*), but you may have to use organic fertilizers as well to achieve the required balance. The techniques of feeding and the type of fertilizer you use to feed the soil will vary depending on your soil type, where you are, and how much organic matter is available to you. In addition, the degree of acidity or alkalinity, or pH, of your soil will affect the availability of some of these nutrients (*see page 35*). So, you may find that, having established the pH level and taken measures to adjust it if necessary, you release more nutrients, therefore increasing the fertility of your soil.

The four phases of soil management

I divide soil management into four phases: the first phase is testing the soil; the second involves the general soil conditioning and replacement of nutrients with organic matter; phase three involves the application of fertilizer; the fourth phase covers more specialized application of fertilizers for specific plant needs.

If you have moved into an established garden which is obviously growing good crops, or if you have decided to convert to organic methods and there are no nutrient deficiencies showing up in your garden (*see pages 38-9*), start with the second phase. However, unless you know the acidity or alkalinity, or pH value, of your soil, you should test it before you start (*see page 36*).

1 Analyzing your soil

If you are starting out, especially on virgin soil, it is a good idea to have it tested at the outset so that you know where you stand. Soils that have been uncultivated for many years are often grossly deficient in one or other of the elements necessary for healthy plant growth (*see pages 38-9*). Chemical growers would then repeat this soil test every year using sophisticated equipment to ascertain the exact requirements of the next crop. I have never believed that gardeners, however keen, need to get involved in this. Once you know what you are working with, I don't think that it is necessary; annual home pH testing is sufficient (*see page 36*).

It is best to send a sample of your soil away for professional analysis. The kits for testing nutrient levels in soil that are available to amateur gardeners are not accurate enough to be worthwhile. Used regularly, they will indicate a trend but no more than that. There are plenty of reputable companies who do soil analysis, or consult your local Cooperative Extension Service specialists. They will be able to tell you the exact chemical make-up of your soil and, if there is a deficiency, exactly how much fertilizer you need to use to correct it. Remember, though, when you send the sample, to ask them to recommend organic fertilizers.

2 Using soil conditioners

This stage deals with the general soil improvement and replacement of plant nutrients removed by previous crops. It is here that there will be variation because it depends on how much, and what type, of organic material you have available to you.

First of all, it should be understood that all organic material not actually taken for the kitchen is returned to the soil as compost, and that this should be supplemented by manure (*see page 27*) or some other bought-in soil conditioner (*see page 29*), as necessary. Organic matter should be dug in during the autumn and spread over the soil as a mulch in the growing season (*see page 20*). This will increase the water-holding capacity of light soils and open up very heavy soils, as well as supplying all the nutrients. If you can put sufficient organic matter on to the soil, there may be no need to add any concentrated fertilizers. However, it is difficult to define "sufficient" because the amount needed depends entirely on your soil, the weather, the plants you wish to grow and so on. You do need to have a great deal of compost and/or manure if you are going to avoid using concentrated fertilizers completely (*see overleaf*).

3 Adding general fertilizer

Not everyone can get sufficient supplies of manure or compost. This is, therefore, where concentrated fertilizers come in. If, for any reason, the manuring falls below the recommended levels, you will have to make up the nutrients "out of the bag". Use a general fertilizer such as blood, fish and bone meal. The application rates vary according to the soil and the plants you want to grow, so I have made recommendations in the relevant sections of the book. In fact some crops, for example peas, can generally grow quite happily without the addition of fertilizer, so there is no need to apply it. Others, such as potatoes, will need extra. Most fruit trees and bushes will need fertilizer in the spring whether or not they are mulched with manure or compost, as will the ornamental garden (*see pages 74-125*).

Where any trace element deficiencies have occurred in the past, I recommend that you give the soil a light dressing of seaweed meal at the beginning of each season to make sure it does not happen again.

4 Using specific fertilizers

Some crops always need special treatment even when the manure and fertilizer levels are sufficient to start with. If, for example, you are growing tomatoes in the greenhouse, they will benefit from extra feeding and a potash fertilizer to encourage flower and fruit formation. Leafy plants that remain in the ground for a long time, like spring cabbage, may need some extra nitrogen fertilizer towards the end of the winter. Plants such as raspberries are often prone to iron deficiencies when grown in alkaline soil; this can be corrected by spraying and liquid feeding with seaweed fertilizer. It is a good idea to apply extra phosphorus, or phosphate, before planting trees or sowing to encourage root growth. Again, all of these recommendations are discussed in more detail in the relevant chapters of the book: *The Ornamental Garden, The Vegetable Garden* and *The Fruit Garden*.

SUMMARY

Your soil management regime should be:
1 Test the soil pH and, if starting a new garden, have your soil tested. Make up deficiencies.
2 Use heavy applications of manure or compost wherever possible (*see below*).
3 If organic matter is not available in sufficient quantities, feed with a concentrated general organic fertilizer (*see pages 35-42*).
4 Give extra feeds for especially demanding plants or where specific deficiencies are noticed (*see pages 38-9*).

Applying soil conditioners

The best materials to use to condition your soil are manure and compost; they will improve drainage or water-holding capacity and provide nutrients, but you do need a great deal to maintain soil fertility levels. Well-rotted animal manure is the very best material to use but it can be difficult to obtain. Compost can be used as a substitute for manure but, if it is to be dug into the ground, it *must* be well-rotted. The alternative soil conditioners mentioned on pages 29 to 31, such as spent mushroom compost, peat and spent hops, while they are superb soil conditioners, they should not be looked upon as sources of plant nutrients.

Dig your compost or manure into the top layers of soil during the autumn and use it as a mulch during the growing season (*see below*). If it is spread over the surface of the soil between growing plants in thick layers, it acts as a weed suppressant (*see page 58*) and will eventually be worked into the soil.

The amounts of organic matter required, and the method by which it is applied – either digging in or mulching – will vary slightly depending on your soil, the time of year and the plants you want to grow. Ideally, you will need to use at least two 9-liter (2-gallon) buckets of well-rotted compost or animal manure for every square meter/yard of soil in the vegetable garden. Use one bucket per square meter/yard as a mulch around trees and shrubs, or in the ornamental borders; this should also be sufficient for fruit trees and bushes.

The quantities suggested are only a guide, if you can afford to use more, do not be afraid to do so. And you can always supplement your compost or manure with green-manure crops whenever the beds are empty for any length of time (*see page 32*). If you are unable to apply organic matter in sufficient quantities, you may have to use fertilizers as well. This is discussed in the next chapter (*see pages 35-42*).

Mulching *This involves spreading a layer of organic matter over the soil where it cannot be dug into the ground because plants cannot be disturbed. Mulching is normally carried out in spring. Make sure the soil is moist before you apply the mulch because it will absorb surface water.*

Digging in manure *The most effective way to incorporate organic material into the soil is to dig it in during autumn. Dig out a trench, taking the soil to the end of the plot. Put a layer of manure in the bottom of the trench, then half fill it with soil dug from the next trench. Add more manure, then fill the trench.*

Compost

Every garden must have a compost heap. This is the ideal way to return as much organic matter as possible to the soil, following nature's example. Decomposing vegetation provides a home for millions of soil organisms, it opens up the soil, improving drainage and easing the way for root growth, and it helps over-drained soils hold water and therefore nutrients (*see page 16*).

The plant remains that you salvage from the garden in the form of waste leaves, stems from vegetables, grass cuttings and annual flowers at the end of the season all contain a great deal in the way of plant food and should not be wasted. However, dug in immediately this material would initially do more harm than good.

The problem is that the rotting process is carried out by bacteria. Millions and millions of them begin to feed on anything that has just been removed from the soil. In order to carry on the decomposition, these bacteria need nitrogen, a very important plant food (*see page 38*). If the garden waste is dug in "green", or in an unrotted state, the bacteria will draw the nitrogen from the soil for their own use, leaving growing plants desperately short of food. If the plant material is turned into compost before it reaches the soil, it will actually add nitrogen. This is because, after the initial rotting, a species of bacteria known as *Azotobacter* is attracted by the resulting conditions. These useful micro-organisms can "fix" the nitrogen from the air – that is, they take it and convert it into a form that can be used by plants. So good compost, though not especially high in nitrogen, will at least not take any nitrogen from the soil.

The rotting, or composting, process takes time and a successful, well-planned organic garden should therefore have at least two compost heaps. That way, the contents of one heap can be left to rot down properly while the other is being filled up.

Conditions necessary for good composting

Obviously, the first requirement is something to compost. Then the heap needs air, nitrogen, lime, water, heat and bacteria.

There are a great many old wives' tales about what can and cannot be used, but the rule is, in fact, very simple: anything that is entirely organic in origin can be composted, except for a few things that common sense tells you should be left out, such as diseased material, cooked kitchen scraps and so on (*see below*).

The list of organic material that can be used is endless – you should never waste anything that will rot. Do not just throw things on to the heap, but mix different materials together to make sure that air can circulate through the heap – even if that means storing some material beside the heap until you have something else to add to it. Grass cuttings, for example, if put on the heap in thick layers, will form an airless mass and turn into slime.

AIR CIRCULATION

Air is of vital importance in the compost heap. Without it the material is worked on by a different group of micro-organisms, known as anaerobic bacteria. If allowed to develop, they turn grass cuttings and any other material into a stinking slime that is worse than useless on the garden.

So, first of all, the container itself should have plenty of air circulating through it (*see* Compost containers, *page 22*). Secondly, you must never let the compost material pack down solid. To prevent this, mix the fine material such as grass cuttings and small weeds with larger weeds, shredded newspaper or straw.

WHAT NOT TO INCLUDE IN THE COMPOST HEAP

● Any material that is diseased or infested with pests – this should always be destroyed.
● The top growth of maincrop potatoes. These should be destroyed after lifting the potatoes because they may infect the heap with potato blight spores – a completely clean crop is rare.
● Prunings from woody plants, because they take too long to rot.
● Cooked kitchen scraps; they often putrefy and will attract vermin.
● Roots of pernicious weeds such as couch grass (*Agropyron repens*), ground elder (*Aegopodium podagraria*), bindweed (*Convolvulus arvensis*) and creeping buttercup (*Ranunculus repens*). These must be destroyed immediately as they will only multiply in the compost heap (*see page 60*).
● Any weed seeds. You will often read that the heat of the compost heap will "cook" all the weed seeds rendering them unviable. This is true only if the heap reaches a very high temperature. In fact, most heaps do not get hot enough to kill the seeds. They merely remain dormant until the compost is spread and end up high enough in the soil to be able to germinate. However, weeds pulled up before they seed, or even flower, should be added to the heap.

NITROGEN

Because the bacteria in the compost heap require nitrogen as a fuel, you must add a certain amount to the heap. Ideally, use animal manure as your source. I keep hens in a movable hen house with a run which is moved around the vegetable plot whenever space becomes available. I use the cleanings from the hen house to provide the additional nitrogen for my compost heap. But I am lucky to be able to do this.

If animal manure is unavailable, you can buy organic compost fuels, or activators, in most garden shops. Alternatively, dried sewage sludge can often be obtained from the local sewage works – this is ideal not only for the compost heap but also for use as a fertilizer. Seaweed meal is excellent and dried blood, the best form of nitrogen fertilizer, makes a very good, if slightly expensive, compost activator (*see* Organic fertilizers, *pages 40-1*).

Whatever you use, you don't actually need very much – and not as much as the manufacturers would have you believe. A fine dusting every 30cm (12in) of compost is sufficient.

LIME

Adding lime will keep the compost "sweet" – that is, it will help neutralize the acidity. See page 37 for a fuller explanation of the benefits of adding lime and how it should be used.

If you have alkaline soil, you may feel that it is better to omit the lime and use very acid compost to redress the balance, and you can do this. However, the bacteria involved in rotting the compost material actually prefer conditions that are not too acid so, if you do not add lime, the rotting process takes longer. All in all it is best to use it.

COMPOSTING HARD MATERIALS

Woody material, such as prunings from shrubs and trees, should not be composted on the main heap, as it takes a long time to decompose. This is because bark contains a substance called lignin, which is difficult for bacteria to break down. The rotting of lignin is primarily carried out by fungi, rather than bacteria. These are also present in the compost heap, but their action is much slower. While the fungi do not require as much air as bacteria, they do need more light.

You can speed up the process slightly by chopping your prunings into smaller pieces which are more readily rotted by the fungi. You can buy domestic chipping machines. They are small and do take quite a long time to produce an appreciable number of chippings but, if you can afford the time and the initial outlay, they are worth the effort. The wood chippings can also be used as a mulch in ornamental flower beds to help retain moisture and to suppress weeds (*see page 59*).

You should apply a slightly heavier dusting of lime than of the nitrogen activator every 30cm (12in) (*see page 25*).

WATER

This is an essential ingredient of any compost heap. Generally, there will already be enough in the green material you put on the compost heap. Certainly this is so if you use grass cuttings. However, it is possible, in a hot summer, for the edges to dry out, in which case you may need to apply extra water. The same may be true if you have used straw in the heap. Straw makes an excellent aerating material, particularly when used with grass cuttings, and it composts well, but you do need to wet it first. I have composted straw on its own, but I found that I needed to put the lawn sprinkler on the heap for half an hour at a time to wet it sufficiently.

You may need to cover the compost heap with plastic sheeting in the winter, not only to keep the heat in, but also to prevent the compost getting too wet (*see below*).

HEAT

Although perhaps not absolutely necessary, there is no doubt that decomposition is much faster when the material is warm. In the summer you'll have usable compost in only two to three months whereas, in winter, the process slows down considerably and the compost will not be usable until the spring.

You can cover the heap with black plastic weighted at the edges; this will keep the heat in and prevent it becoming too wet, which can be a problem, particularly in winter (*see page 25*). I prefer to place a piece of old carpet over the heap; it does not need weighting down and also "breathes", allowing more air into the heap.

BACTERIA

Finally, you need the bacteria themselves. This is the easiest job of all. There are millions in just one crumb of soil, so there should be plenty in the crumbs of earth that cling to the roots of the weeds you put in the heap. Some people recommend that you add layers of soil throughout the heap. In fact, this is completely unnecessary: not only is it hard work, but it also dilutes the compost and prevents aeration.

Compost containers

Although it is not essential to make your compost in a container – you can simply pile it up in the corner of the garden – the advantage of a container is that the compost rots right up to the edges of the heap. In an open heap, the edges dry out so the whole heap has to be turned two or three times during the rotting process to push the unrotted material into the center.

The size of your compost container will depend on the size of your garden. There are plenty of containers available at garden centers, many designed with the smaller garden in mind – some even suggest that it is possible to compost by adding material to the top while shovelling out the well-rotted compost at the bottom. Frankly, this is not realistic; you need two containers, one that can be left to rot down while the other is being filled up. The most useful is a wooden box with slatted sides (*see below*). You can easily add more sections on to the side.

It is not difficult to make your own compost container. Again wooden ones are the best, they look good and they are cheap and easy to make (*see overleaf*). You can also make compost bins from brick, plastic barrels or stakes and wire (*see below*).

TYPES OF COMPOST CONTAINER

Compost containers are useful not only because they keep the compost moist right up to the edges but also because they keep it tidy. Whether you build your own bin or buy one, make sure that it enables you to get at the compost easily when it comes to putting it on the garden.

Manufactured compost containers

Wooden compost bin left
Shop-bought wooden bins normally come in kit form and you assemble them. They have slatted sides to allow sufficient air to circulate through the heap. The front panels can be lifted out so that you can remove the compost.

Plastic compost bin right
This type of bin is useful in a small garden. A small amount of air is allowed in through the bottom and a lid keeps the contents dry and the heat in.

Home-made compost containers

Wire-and-post container
This method is suitable only if you can put the compost heap somewhere it can't be seen. Hammer four stakes into the ground to make a 1m (3ft) square. Staple about 4m (12ft) of wire netting, 1m (3ft) deep, to the outside of the stakes. Tie large pieces of cardboard to the inside of the wire.

Plastic barrel container
Large plastic barrels used for fruit concentrates make ideal compost containers. Cut off the top and bottom with a sharp knife. Keep one of the cut ends and use it as a lid. Drill 2.5cm (1in) holes around the barrel – about one hole every 30 sq cm (1 sq ft).

Brick-built compost bin
This method is suitable only if you are never going to move the heap. Stagger the bricks so that air can get into the compost heap. The front should be made of wooden slats as for the home-made wooden bin overleaf. Fix battens down the inside of the walls and slide the slats in.

MAKING A WOODEN COMPOST CONTAINER

This is a very simple procedure. You do not need to buy new wood. A demolition contractor will always have suitable timber at half the price of new wood. Old floorboards are particularly good for the sides, while 7.5 × 10cm (3 × 4in) floor joists make ideal corner supports.

You need:
- 4 × 1m (3ft) lengths of 5 × 10cm (2 × 4in) wood for the uprights
- 19 × 1m (3ft) lengths of wood for the sides
- 5 × 75cm (2ft 6in) lengths of wood for the front panels (you may need to check this measurement when you have completed the main part of the bin)
- 4 × 75cm (2ft 6 in) battens
- 2 small pieces of wood
- 1cm (½in) piece of wood for a spacer
- Strong nails, about four per panel

1 Place two of the uprights on the ground so that they are lying parallel to each other and 75cm (2ft 6in) apart. Place one of the side planks across them 7.5cm (3in) from the bottom of each post and nail it into position.

2 Using a 1cm (½in) piece of wood as a spacer, nail five more pieces of wood between the two uprights. Make sure they are all at right angles to the uprights and parallel to each other. Make another wall to match.

3 Stand the two walls up parallel to each other and at right angles to a wall. Nail a piece of wood to the top of each upright to hold them in position. Working from the bottom upwards, nail six pieces of wood across the back, level with those on each side.

4 Remove the support panel. Then turn the box round so that you can make the front wall. Nail a board across the front of the uprights 7.5cm (3in) from the bottom.

5 Nail two battens on to the side edge of each upright, making sure that they are far enough apart to slide the front panels between them. Nail a small piece of wood across the bottom of the battens to prevent the front panels sliding out when you fill the bin.

6 Slide all the front panels into the bin to make sure they fit; cut down as necessary.

7 Paint the entire container, including the cut edges and the front panels, with a water-based wood preservative. Leave to dry.

8 Slide all the front panels into position. Tie a piece of string across the top of the container to prevent the sides bulging outwards when you fill it.

Managing your compost

Really good compost is supposedly brown and crumbly with the sweetest of smells, like woods in the autumn. In fact it very rarely is. If you have a really big heap and a supply of only the very best organic material to rot down, you should be able to achieve that ideal during spring and summer. If your heap is small and you're using any organic material you can find, it often won't live up to that ideal. Generally, while some material is in an advanced stage of decomposition, other material will not have rotted down nearly as much. The compost is more likely to be very variable, with a lot of semi-rotted fibrous material. But that doesn't matter. It will still improve the soil and certainly do no harm; it will just take a bit longer for it to become "humus".

Getting good quality compost takes care, and each composting material needs different treatment. For example, grass cuttings should always be mixed thoroughly with some coarser material such as larger weeds, shredded newspaper, or straw, before they are added to the heap, to prevent them turning to slime (see page 22).

Straw is a particularly good material to mix with grass cuttings and, if you have the space, it is well worth keeping a bale beside the heap just for that purpose. A word of warning though; straw is very dry, so it is very important to soak it thoroughly in a tank of water for an hour or so before adding it to the heap.

Newspaper can be difficult to rot down but it is worth persevering with, particularly when mixed with grass cuttings. As a rough guide use about 1 part newspaper to 4 parts grass cuttings. Never put it on the heap folded in thick piles because there won't be enough air in it and it won't rot. I cut it up into 2.5cm (1in) strips and keep it in a plastic bag until needed. Then, before use, I put it in a bucket of dilute seaweed (see page 41). However, I use only a small amount and I never use the paper from glossy magazines; it does not rot down well and contains a high proportion of lead. When I put kitchen scraps on the heap I make sure there is nothing cooked among them, to avoid attracting vermin. If there are any large pieces of root vegetable, I cut them into smaller pieces. I then cover the layer with grass cuttings or weeds to keep the rats and mice away. Potato peelings often cause problems because those tiny "eyes" will develop into potato plants either in the heap or when the compost is spread. But they're not difficult to pull up and provide that much more material for the next heap. Any old clothes made of natural fiber can be put on the heap as well. If you cut them into strips beforehand, they will rot down faster.

The amount of compost you can make in a year depends very much on the type of material you use but even more on the weather. From each bin you should, in a hot year, get two good binfuls in the summer – one in early summer and another in late autumn – and another in the spring if you're lucky.

BUILDING UP A COMPOST HEAP

Stand the compost container on a level surface, preferably soil. Start the heap off with a 15cm (6in) layer of coarse material, such as horse manure, straw or large weeds to make sure there is a free flow of air at the bottom. Then add more material until you have a layer 15cm (6in) deep. Sprinkle some compost activator or nitrogen fertilizer (see page 40) over this layer, or add another layer of horse manure; the nitrogen in it will act as a compost activator. Add another 15cm (6in) layer of material, then cover with a dusting of lime, and so on. When you have finished filling the bin always cover it with a piece of carpet or its lid to keep it dry. Compost rots down and shrinks quickly so that what seems like a finished heap one week, still has room for more the next week.

Lime

Grass cuttings

Horse manure, or straw then compost activator

Lime

Leaves from vegetable garden mixed with grass cuttings

Horse manure, or straw then compost activator

Grass cuttings

Horse manure

ALTERNATIVE SOURCES OF MATERIAL FOR COMPOSTING

Few gardens can produce enough waste organic material to be self-sufficient in compost. But a remarkable amount of good stuff that is thrown away can be "harvested" by the organic gardener. The local greengrocer or street market is an excellent source of greenstuff. See if you can arrange to visit the shop or market after closing time on Saturdays to take any rubbish. The local sports ground or golf-club is also worth investigating. They often have no means of disposing of massive amounts of grass-cuttings and would be delighted to have them cleared away.

If you live in the country, in an area where farmers burn straw rather than bale it, it is well worth asking if you can gather some straw before the rest is burned. One of the reasons why farmers don't plough straw back into the ground, as they should, is that the decomposing bacteria need a lot of fuel, or nitrogen, to break down the tough stalks. This causes a serious nitrogen deficiency in the soil and replacing the nitrogen with fertilizer is expensive.

The best source of free soil conditioner I have ever found was a tomato nursery which grew in peat bags. At the end of the season it was faced with an unwanted mountain of spent bags. The peat inside them was once-used and full of tomato roots but still a perfect soil conditioner, even without composting. I did, in fact, stack them for a year to ensure that any traces of chemicals had dissipated, because the nursery did not grow organically.

Building a leaf-mold container *You need four wooden stakes that are at least 1m (3ft) tall, and about 4m (12ft) of wire netting. Drive the stakes into the ground to make a 1m (3ft) square and staple the wire netting around the outside.*

water in a dry summer, otherwise, you can leave them to their own devices.

The local dump is often a good source of leaves. The leaves may be "polluted" with cigarette packets or other rubbish but these are easy to remove as you stack them. More worrying is the fact that they could contain lead from car exhaust emission, but all you can do is hope that it is reduced to an acceptable level, if not leached out entirely, by composting.

Leaf mold

Leaves are slow to rot down because they contain lignin (*see page 22*). Be prepared to wait at least a year, and possibly even two or three years, before you have a good, crumbly compost that is ready to use. When the leaves do rot down, however, they prove well worth waiting for. Leaf mold is really much too good to use for mulching or for digging in. Use it as a potting or seed-sowing compost (*see page 252*).

The decaying process is quite different from compost making. While green compost is rotted predominantly by bacteria, leaves are broken down by fungi which need more light and less air than the bacteria (*see page 22*). So build the container in a corner of the garden where it can be left undisturbed.

You will need at least two heaps because it may be two to three years before the leaf mold is ready. You do not need elaborate containers, you can make them out of stakes and wire netting (*see above*). Pile the leaves into the container as you collect them, treading down each time you add more. The leaves may need a little

Sheet composting

Making good compost takes time and trouble – time which some busy gardeners might find difficult to spare. Nonetheless, as organic matter should never be thrown away, you may find it more convenient to "sheet compost" it.

This technique simply involves spreading a thin layer of organic matter on the soil between rows of vegetables or on a vacant area, and allowing it to rot down where it lies. Naturally this method is useful only in productive parts of the garden where aesthetics are not important. Sheet compost can be particularly useful on areas where you tread regularly, like paths between rows, or it can be used as a mulch around fruit trees.

If you are using weeds, it's important to ensure that they have wilted beyond the recovery point before you spread them, or you may find them re-rooting and growing away in your carefully tended vegetable patch. As with weeds for the compost heap, you should ensure that they are not about to shed seeds. Grass cuttings are ideal for sheet composting, but you are almost certain to find annual crab grass seeds in any sample cut in late summer, so watch out for unwanted sprouting.

Whatever organic matter you use as sheet compost, it will rot down into the soil much more slowly than well-rotted garden compost. There is also a danger of its causing nitrogen deficiency in the soil (*see page 21*), so you may need to add a little nitrogen fertilizer before spreading the sheet compost.

An alternative method, which will certainly speed up the decomposition process, is to dig the sheet compost into the top few inches. If you have a power tiller, so much the better, because this will chop it up, after which earthworms will make short work of it. In this case though, extra nitrogen will definitely be necessary. As a preventive measure, before rotatilling or digging in sheet compost in this way, sprinkle a handful of dried blood over each square meter/yard of soil (*see page 40*).

Spreading sheet compost
Sprinkle dried blood over the soil – one handful per square meter/yard – then spread an even layer of the green material over the soil. Leave it to rot down.

Animal manure

Animal manures are the very best sources of organic matter you could wish for on your soil, so they are worth getting, even though they are more difficult to obtain than compost. Manure can be used on any soil, not only to improve its condition, but also to feed it with nutrients. Some, like poultry manure, have to be used with care because of their high nitrogen content.

Unfortunately, much bought-in animal manure is likely to be adulterated with hormone fatteners, herbicides, insecticides and fungicides. However, if it is stacked for at least a year, there is little evidence to show that these chemicals pollute the soil or make their way into our vegetables and fruit when they are harvested. Leaving the manure for a year does mean that some of the nutrients are lost, but this can always be made up in the soil in other ways. One day, the organic movement will be powerful enough to persuade all farmers to produce healthy, unadulterated food. In the meantime, we simply have to use what is available. There is little point in trying to beg manure from organic farmers because they need it themselves.

USING MANURE

All manure is used neat unless otherwise specified – although you should avoid putting it on young shoots because it will scorch them. General manure levels are given with each description; recommendations for specific plant needs are described in the relevant chapters.

COW MANURE

Many beef cattle are kept in the cruellest of battery conditions where they never move about or see the daylight. Their droppings are washed away through the slatted floors and disposed of as slurry. It is still sometimes possible, however, to find a farmer who grazes cattle outside some of the time and brings them into yards in the winter. So if you live in the country, cow manure can sometimes be obtained after the cows have been turned out for summer. Compared with other forms of organic material, it's very cheap and excellent as a soil conditioner and source of nutrients. But it should be stored for twelve months before use to leach out impurities and prevent scorching of roots.

On the face of it, cow manure doesn't contain a very high percentage of plant nutrients (*see below*), when compared with an inorganic fertilizer. But you will be using a far greater volume of manure than you would of an inorganic fertilizer, so the mineral concentration is less significant. Moreover, manure will hold water and maintain that high level of fertility that organic growers continually try to achieve.

NUTRIENT CONTENT			
Nitrogen	*0.6 per cent*	Potassium	*0.3-0.5 per cent*
Phosphorus	*0.2-0.3 per cent*	Trace elements	*Full range*
Coverage *9-15kg (20-30lb) per sq meter/yard*			

HORSE MANURE

An excellent source of organic matter, horse manure is often more readily available near urban areas. Large stables generally have a contract with commercial mushroom growers to remove manure. But there are plenty of smaller stables who are pleased to sell manure. You should use manure only from stables where straw or peat is used as bedding; wood-shavings may be a source of plant disease.

Fresh horse manure must not be used directly around plants since it can cause scorching of the leaves and stems. Moreover, if put on the soil in an unrotted state, much of the nutrient value will be lost and the straw mixed in with the manure will take a long time to decompose. There are two alternatives. If you have access only to small quantities of manure, they are best put on the compost heap where the high nitrogen content will assist the decomposition. Large quantities are best stacked, if possible on a concrete base, and, since there is a lot of air space in the straw, and thus a danger of it drying out, you should tread your heap down as you stack it. In winter, cover the heap with some plastic to protect it from excess rain. Horse manure will be ready for use in a couple of months unless you are concerned that any straw may be contaminated with pesticides, in which case leave it for a year before using it.

NUTRIENT CONTENT			
Nitrogen	0.6 per cent	Potassium	0.4 per cent
Phosphorus	0.6 per cent	Trace elements	Full range
Coverage 9-15kg (20-30lb) per sq meter/yard			

PIG MANURE

Somewhat colder and wetter than horse or cow manure, but certainly not to be despised on that count, pig manure has a very high nutrient content. It should be treated in the same way as horse manure but, since it is heavier, there is generally no need to tread it down.

NUTRIENT CONTENT			
Nitrogen	0.6 per cent	Potassium	0.4 per cent
Phosphorus	0.6 per cent	Trace elements	Full range
Coverage 9-15kg (20-30lb) per sq meter/yard			

SHEEP MANURE

Because sheep are not normally housed inside, you don't get a mixture of straw and muck in the way you do with cow, horse and pig manure. However, the manure itself is so high in nutrients that it is well worth going round the fields collecting it. Half a sackful will provide enough liquid manure to last the average-sized garden a whole year (*see page 42*).

NUTRIENT CONTENT			
Nitrogen	0.8 per cent	Potassium	0.4 per cent
Phosphorus	0.5 per cent	Trace elements	Full range
Use as liquid manure (see page 42)			

CHICKEN MANURE

This is very powerful manure indeed. It has an extremely high nitrogen content, and so should not be used neat. If you can find a farmer who keeps hens in an old-fashioned deep-litter house, where the hens are housed on straw, take as much manure as you can get and stack it as described for horse manure, above. If you have

CHICKENS AS SOIL IMPROVERS

If you live in the country, you may find it advantageous to keep small livestock in the vegetable garden. Half a dozen chickens, for example, require only a small amount of space and will easily keep a small family in eggs throughout the year.

To fit chickens into the vegetable-growing system, house them in a small, portable house with a movable wire-netting run to restrict them to the area. As a crop finishes, move the hens on to the space, and they will devour all the green matter there, recycling it in the form of a high-nitrogen fertilizer. They will also peck out any old seeds and soil pests that may be lurking near the surface.

your own hens, use the manure as a source of nitrogen for the compost heap.

Chicken manure from a battery-hen unit can be used to compost straw. Put a layer of straw in the bottom of a compost container, soak it with water, then cover with a sprinkling of chicken manure. Add more straw, water it, then cover with chicken manure. Continue in this way until the bin is full, ending with a layer of manure. Leave this type of compost to rot for at least a year because the manure will contain all the hormones that are fed to battery-kept chickens.

NUTRIENT CONTENT			
Fresh, wet chicken manure			
Nitrogen	1.5 per cent	Potassium	0.5 per cent
Phosphorus	1.5 per cent	Trace elements	Full range
Coverage 3.25-4.5kg (7-10lb) per sq meter/yard			
Dry			
Nitrogen	4 per cent	Potassium	1.5 per cent
Phosphorus	4 per cent	Trace elements	Full range
Coverage 20-30g (8-12oz) per sq meter/yard			

OTHER MANURES

Pigeon droppings contain even higher concentrations of nitrogen than chicken manure, so it is worth contacting local pigeon-racing enthusiasts. The manure can be used in the same way as chicken manure.

Rabbit manure is also ideal, though likely to be available in only small quantities. Use it in the same way as chicken manure.

Goat manure is similar to horse manure, but of better quality. If you can find any, or better still if you keep a goat yourself, compost the manure and use it in exactly the same way as horse manure (*see left*).

Before leaving manures, one suggestion that is not as crazy as it sounds. When the circus leaves town it is often left with a manure problem, so it could well be worth contacting it as soon as it arrives. I have actually used two trailer loads of elephant manure that the circus delivered free of charge.

Alternative soil conditioners

Apart from compost and manure, there are many other organic materials that can be dug into your soil or used as a mulch to help improve drainage or water-holding capacity depending on the soil type. These materials should be looked upon only as soil conditioners; although some contain plant nutrients, they are not present in large enough quantities.

SPENT MUSHROOM COMPOST

A mixture of horse manure, peat moss and other organic materials prepared by commercial mushroom growers. Where available, it is a very useful conditioner.

NUTRIENT CONTENT	
Nitrogen	0.71 per cent
Phosphorus	0.3 per cent
Potassium	0.26 per cent
Trace elements	Full range

WOOL SHODDY

This is waste material from the cleaning processes that a fleece goes through while being prepared for spinning and dyeing. The nutrient content can vary considerably.

NUTRIENT CONTENT	
Nitrogen	3-15 per cent
Phosphorus	0.5-10 per cent
Potassium	0.1-12 per cent
Trace elements	—

SEAWEED

An excellent soil conditioner because its alginate content helps bind soil particles together, thus improving structure. Seaweed is particularly rich in trace elements.

NUTRIENT CONTENT	
Nitrogen	0.3 per cent
Phosphorus	0.1 per cent
Potassium	1.0 per cent
Trace elements	Full range

COMPOSTED PINE BARK

This is normally sold partly composted and contains virtually no nutrients. It is best used as mulch, because it can cause a severe nitrogen deficiency in the soil if dug in.

NUTRIENT CONTENT	
Nitrogen	—
Phosphorus	—
Potassium	—
Trace elements	—

SPENT HOPS

If you have a brewery nearby, try to buy "spent" hops to use as a mulch or to dig in – they add organic matter as well as a small amount of nutrients.

NUTRIENT CONTENT	
Nitrogen	0.5 per cent
Phosphorus	1-2 per cent
Potassium	0.5 per cent
Trace elements	Full range

PEAT

Both Michigan (sedge) peat and peat moss (from sphagnum bogs) have few nutrients, but are excellent soil conditioners. Peat moss increases water retention.

NUTRIENT CONTENT	
Nitrogen	—
Phosphorus	—
Potassium	—
Trace elements	—

SPENT MUSHROOM COMPOST

The waste product of the mushroom-growing industry, this can be used instead of manure, provided its limitations are borne in mind. Mushroom compost starts as fresh horse manure that is stacked so that it heats up. It is then sown with mushrooms. Other materials such as straw or peat moss are also in the compost. After the mushrooms have been picked, the compost is thrown away or, more often than not, sold either loose at the farm gate or packed into bales and sold at garden centers. By the time it has had a crop grown in it, the compost is quite well rotted. Nonetheless, it's still worth leaving mushroom compost for at least a year before use, to leach out the chemical insecticides used by growers and to help get rid of the pests it may harbor. After a year it should have the consistency of peat.

Before using the compost, mushroom growers normally add gypsum to it; when added to soil, this helps to bind clay particles together. So, coupled with the natural "opening" effect of the organic matter, mushroom compost is ideal for use on heavy clay soils.

Mushroom compost can be put directly on to the soil in spring around emerging perennial plants and also around shrubs. Although the spent manure compost is less likely to burn plants than fresh manure, be sparing around young seedlings. Where the compost is plentiful, it is used to top-dress fine lawns. Never use it on acid-loving plants.
Coverage: 1-1.5kg (2-3lbs) per sq meter/yard

SEAWEED

If you live near the sea, the seaweed washed up on to the beach can be a valuable source of organic material for the soil. Seaweed contains a very wide range of the trace elements that plants need for growth as well as small and variable amounts of the major plant foods, in particular potassium (*see pages 38-9*). Recent research has shown that seaweed also contains growth-promoting hormones, which can be absorbed through leaves to improve plant health and growth. In the soil, seaweed has the ability to release certain nutrients otherwise unavailable to plants and its alginate content binds soil particles together, improving soil structure (*see page 16*).

Seaweed is most effective if composted for a while, although, because it will rot down very quickly, some gardeners prefer to dig it in fresh. The fronds contain alginic acid, which is very attractive to the bacteria required on the compost heap. So, apart from its soil-conditioning value, seaweed can also be used as a compost activator (*see page 22*). If you can get hold of only small quantities of seaweed, this is certainly the best use for it.
Coverage: 1-1.5kg (2-3lbs) per sq meter/yard

SPENT HOPS

The residue from the brewing industry, spent hops have a distinctive strong smell, although this soon disappears when the hops are left out in the open. They make an excellent soil conditioner and are particularly good for mulching. The problem is that spent hops are very difficult to get, but if you are fortunate and live near a brewery, then it is worth calling on the brewery and asking for a few bags. If bought direct from the brewery, spent hops will be wet and can either be dug in fresh or spread over the surface. They can be composted but it is not necessary. If you do use them fresh, keep them well away from the stems and leaves of young plants to avoid scorching them.

It is possible to buy spent hops dry but, in this form, they are really more of a fertilizer that is high in nitrogen – about 2.5-3.5 per cent.
Coverage: 1-1.5kg (2-3lbs) per sq meter/yard

WOOL SHODDY

Made up of bits of fluffy wool, this is a waste product of the clothing industry and is sometimes available in wool-processing areas. It makes an excellent soil conditioner and is best used neat and dug in wet in the autumn.
Coverage: 0.25-0.5kg (½-1lb) per sq meter/yard

COMPOSTED PINE BARK

The timber and tobacco industries strip off hundreds of tons of bark from pine logs every year. These are chipped and sometimes part-composted before being sold.

Chipped bark makes an excellent mulch for organic weed control (*see page 59*). However, it has no nutrient value, and two big disadvantages as a soil conditioner. Firstly, it is very expensive. Secondly, and perhaps more importantly, it is a very hard material in a virtually unrotted state. The lignin in bark takes a long time to break down so the bacteria use even more nitrogen in the rotting process (*see page 22*). Unless you are prepared to add large amounts of nitrogen fertilizer to your soil, it is better to use another material as a soil conditioner and bark only as a mulch.
Coverage: 5-7cm (2-3in) layer if using it as weed suppressant in ornamental borders.

PEAT

Peat can be bought in bags from horticultural suppliers. The blacker peat, known as sedge peat (the residue from sedges and grasses), is older and less stable than the younger, browner sphagnum moss peat (derived from sphagnum moss). Sedge peat decomposes rapidly and can become a soggy airless mass if allowed to get very wet. I would never use it as potting mixture and only in the garden if nothing else was available. Sphagnum peat can make an excellent, if rather expensive, soil conditioner. It is widely available and well worth its price. There is a popular misconception that the darker a peat, the more fertile it must be. Nothing could be further from the truth. In fact, peats contain no worthwhile amounts of nutrients.

On the other hand, peat has the ability to retain up to fifteen times its weight of water and it will, of course, hold plant nutrients in solution too. It opens up heavy soil and makes a fine medium for root growth. Peat is expensive, so it has to be used sparingly. Make use of it around roots when planting in heavy soils, use it to lighten the top 2.5-5cm (1-2in) of heavy soil in order to make a seed bed and certainly as a base for home-made potting and seed-sowing mixtures (see page 252).

One word of warning. Peat is very difficult to rewet once it has dried out. So, it's very important to wet it thoroughly before use and to ensure that it is never allowed to dry out. Keep the plastic bag open to rainfall before using.
Coverage: 4-5kg (10lbs) per sq meter/yard

Worm-worked compost and manure

From research carried out recently on the effects of earthworms on waste materials, it's clear that worms can be put to work by the organic gardener in the soil, compost or manure with some highly beneficial effects.

THE EFFECTS OF WORMS ON THE SOIL

Worms feed mainly on organic matter and, in the process of feeding, they break the waste down and eject it in the form of pellets. These small pellets are coated with a gel which holds them together. The resulting crumb structure helps to improve soil drainage and aeration and therefore provides a superior environment for root growth. The pellets not only change the nutrients in the organic matter into a form that is readily available to plant roots, but also convert it into a form that is released slowly, as it is required by the plants. This prevents any short-term toxicity that could otherwise develop. At the same time the water-holding capacity of soil is increased considerably – often to the level of peat (see opposite).

Equally important is the way in which worms break down the organic matter into smaller granules, enabling the soil microbes to work on a greater surface area. They also produce a range of enzymes which enable the bacteria to work more efficiently. In other words, the presence of worms in the organic matter accelerates the decomposing process.

By introducing worms into the manure or compost heap, you can dramatically speed up the rate at which it decomposes and produce an end-product that is far superior for soil conditioning and feeding.

ADDING WORMS TO THE SOIL

This is not quite as easy as it sounds and a certain amount of management is required. First of all, you will need to build a wormery to provide the environment; secondly, it is essential to use the right variety of worm. The worm you need is commonly known as a "brandling" or "tiger worm"; it is used in many parts of the world by fishermen as bait. The Latin name for it is *Eisenia foetida*. These worms do not live for long in soil, but they can be found generally in manure or compost heaps, where they multiply very quickly. If you can't find any in your heap, buy some from a fishing tackle shop or a specialist supplier (see page 283).

The worm has the convenient habit of working upwards. Once it has digested one layer of organic matter, it will move up to the next layer. You can take advantage of this when building a wormery by designing it so that you can take the worm-worked material out of the bottom of the box. This leaves the worms inside to continue working on the upper layers of material in the wormery (see overleaf).

The most useful task performed by the worms is the breaking down of compost. They work through almost anything from grass cuttings to kitchen scraps and even soaked newspapers, provided they are used in moderation. In the same way as in the compost heap, it is not a good idea to use too much of anything on its own – you should mix everything together as before – and never put more than a few inches of material on to the heap in a week (see overleaf). You can, however, put animal manure in the wormery, or hatchery, on its own.

The wormery should be placed in a sunny, sheltered part of the garden because the worms will not work if the temperature is lower than about 7°C (45°F) – in freezing weather they will die. The optimum temperature for the worms is 20-24°C (68-75°F). In cold weather, cover the wormery with a piece of old carpet to keep as much heat in as possible. In very hot weather it may be necessary to water the material. It is much better for it to be too wet than too dry.

MAKING A WORMERY

Firstly, make a wooden box that is at least 60cm (2ft) high and about 60cm (2ft) by 90cm (3ft). The important factor is that it be slightly wider and longer than your wheelbarrow. Secondly, support the box on legs so that you can wheel your barrow underneath. Staple a piece of strong mesh across the bottom of the box; the mesh should be about 5cm (2in) across. Finally, make two holes in one side of the box and slide two lengths of wood in through these holes. Fix pieces of metal or wood on the ends to make the scrapers.

When the box is complete, lay a sheet of newspaper over the mesh floor and soak it with water. Cover this with a layer of old compost, or manure if you have it, and a handful of brandling worms. Put a thin layer of uncomposted material over the top and cover it with old carpet or bubble plastic. Build the wormery up slowly, putting no more than 7cm (3in) of material into the box each week. If you have a regular supply, this may mean that you'll have to leave it beside the container until the previous layer has been worked down.

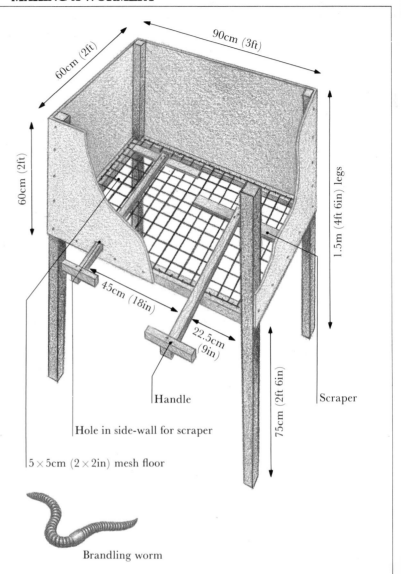

Brandling worm

USING WORM-CAST COMPOST
The resulting material is high in nutrients and micro-organisms and should be used sparingly. It makes an admirable and easily handled mulch for use around ornamental plants, fruit trees or bushes or between rows of vegetables. Sprinkle a little into your seed drill before sowing, especially if the soil is very dry. Worm-cast compost can also be raked into the top few inches of soil in a seed bed to help provide a good crumbly surface structure, and add vital nutrients to the soil.

You can also use it to make a potting mixture using equal parts of peat and worm-cast compost, or a seed mixture using one part worm-cast compost and two parts peat.

Green manure

This is a crop grown to add organic matter to beds that are empty for a period of time. It is sown with the specific intention of digging it into the soil to provide organic matter and plant food. It is perhaps of more value to the large-scale farmer than the gardener, but there are sometimes situations when a green-manure crop is useful, even in the small garden.

The biggest problem is that green manure takes up growing space. In most gardens, there's no room for the luxury of leaving an area fallow, so manure crops have to fit in with cultivated ones. However, if your soil is light or lacks organic matter, it is advisable to keep it covered with something if it is likely to be vacant for any length of time. This would generally mean sowing a winter crop in the late summer or early autumn and digging it in before planting or sowing vegetables the following spring. Some green-manure crops are fast-growing enough to allow sowing between crops in the growing season (*see below*). There may also be times when, for example, you are waiting to plant an ornamental border in the autumn and can get a summer crop in.

The most obvious value of green manure is in providing organic matter. However, the soft green material quickly rots down, leaving a small amount of stable organic matter in the soil. Nonetheless, on soils short of organic matter, anything must be a bonus. This addition of organic matter also increases the amount of biological activity in the soil and the roots serve to break it up and improve drainage.

The greater value of green manure is in its ability to make plant nutrients available. If the crop is deep rooting, it can take up minerals from the lower levels of the soil – red clover and lupins, for example, will root down over 2m (7ft) – so that when they are dug into the soil again these nutrients are nearer the surface and more readily available to the next crop of vegetables or flowers.

In addition, leguminous plants like beans and lupins have the ability to "fix" the nitrogen in the soil through bacteria living in tiny nodules in their roots. They remove nitrogen from the air and, when the plant is dug in, the nitrogen becomes available to the next crop.

On light soils in particular, the biggest loss of nutrients occurs in the winter through leaching or drainage during wet weather (*see pages 16-17*). A crop of green manure in the winter will prevent this, and is therefore very valuable indeed.

Green-manure crops also serve to suppress weeds. They generally cover the ground well, providing shade and competition for water and soil nutrients that will discourage all but the most tenacious weeds (*see page 58*). The manure crops themselves are chosen so that they will not cause a nuisance by re-growing after they have been dug or tilled in.

SOWING CROPS FOR GREEN MANURE

Choose a plant that will mature in the time available (*see overleaf*), and preferably one that is unlike either the crop you have just harvested or the one you intend to sow the following season. For example, it is unwise to sow a brassica, such as mustard, after cabbages, because of the risk of perpetuating associated pests and diseases (*see page 134*).

The soil needs to be in good condition if the crop is to be successful. If it is low in nutrients, it may be necessary to apply a fertilizer before sowing. Pre-sowing cultivation should be as thorough as for any other crop and the seed bed should be firmed by treading before sowing. Small seeds can be sown in rows about 15cm (6in) apart or scattered by hand and raked into the top few inches of soil, while large seed is sown in rows about 30cm (1ft) apart.

PLANTING AND DIGGING IN A MUSTARD CROP

Mustard is a fast- and low-growing crop. It is an ideal way to cover a piece of land that is empty for a few weeks during the growing period. As with any green-manure crop it should not be allowed to get too woody and should be cut down and worked into the soil before it flowers.

1 *Prepare the soil for sowing (see above), then scatter the seeds across the plot. Alternatively, sow thinly in seed drills about 1cm (½in) deep and 15cm (6in) apart. Most of the seeds will germinate.*

2 *When the seedlings are about 15-20cm (6-9in) tall and before they flower, they are ready for digging in. Cut plants down at the base with a spade and leave the green manure on the ground for a while to wilt.*

3 *Scrape back the green manure to expose a 30cm (12in) strip of soil at one end of the plot. Dig a shallow trench and scrape some green manure into it. Refill the trench. Continue until all the green manure is worked into the soil.*

WORKING GREEN MANURE INTO SOIL

Incorporating the green manure into the soil must be done in the right way if the maximum benefit is to be obtained.

Do not let the crop become too woody before you dig it in or the rotting process will take nitrogen from the soil. If the crop is fairly large, it may be best to cut it up finely before cultivating the soil. This can be done with a rotary mower or, with lower-growing crops like mustard, even a cylinder mower. Whichever way, allow a period of wilting before digging the

material under. Low-growing crops can simply be cut down with a spade and allowed to wilt for a few days, then dug in, while taller plants can be worked into the surface with a power tiller and then, after a few days rotatilled more deeply.

When digging in the green manure, don't bury the material deeper than about 15cm (6in). If you have allowed the crop to become hard and woody, it may be necessary to apply liquid fertilizer to assist rotting. Watering over with liquid seaweed or animal-manure would suffice.

TYPES OF GREEN-MANURE CROP

There are several types of green manure you can grow. The one you choose will depend mainly on the nature of your soil and the length of time the ground is to be fallow. The main distinction made here is between nitrogen-fixing crops and those which do not fix nitrogen.

Green-manure plants that act as nitrogen fixers

Alfalfa or Lucerne *Medicago sativa*
A deep-rooted, tall perennial, alfalfa is extremely useful in the garden as long as you have enough space to let it occupy land for a whole season. If you have, it provides plenty of green matter, is very deep rooting indeed and, being a legume, adds nitrogen. Sow at 15g ($\frac{1}{2}$oz) per sq meter/yard in spring, then dig in in autumn; in mild climates sow in late summer and dig in in spring.

Broad or fava bean *Vicia faba*
This is an excellent green-manure crop in every way. It will stand the winter in mild climates, it produces plenty of organic matter, it is a nitrogen-fixer, and the beans can be harvested and eaten. Sow in early spring in North. Space

out the seeds every 10cm (4in) in rows 30cm (12in) apart, if you wish to harvest the beans as well. In any case, it is as well to allow a row or two to produce beans because they can be used for seed for later crops of green manure.

Red clover *Trifolium pratense*
A low-growing nitrogen-fixer with an extensive root system that will supply plenty of organic matter, red clover is best sown in spring or late summer, but always before autumn. Scatter the seeds at 30g (1oz) per sq meter/yard, in rows 15cm (6in) apart and dig in when the land is needed.

Lupin *Lupinus angustifolius*
Deep-rooting tall legume that will add nitrogen and large amounts of

phosphates to the soil. Sow in spring in rows about 15cm (6in) apart, with about 7cm (3in) between each seed – 30g (1oz) of seed will sow 70m (70yd) of row. Cut down and dig in in summer. A second crop can then be sown and dug in eight weeks later.

Winter vetch or tare *Vicia villosa*
Another tall plant, this is one of the most useful crops because it grows during winter when land is vacant. Sow in rows, as for lupins, during late summer and dig them in in early spring. It can also be sown during spring and summer if land is vacant; 80g (3oz) will sow 100m (100yd) of row. Winter tare produces a large amount of green matter, has an extensive root system and fixes nitrogen.

Green-manure plants that do not fix nitrogen

Buckwheat *Fagopyrum esculentum*
Useful only where space is available for the whole summer. Sow when the weather is warm, in spring or summer, and dig in during the autumn. Sow in rows about 15cm (6in) apart, or scatter at 30g (1oz) per 7 sq meter/yard. Buckwheat is tall and has a very extensive root system. It makes copious organic matter and is a good bee plant. It also has the advantage that it attracts hoverflies, which eat aphids by the thousand (*see page 46*).

Rye *Secale cereale*
A non-legume which has an extensive root system and produces a useful amount of green material to dig in. Sow the perennial variety in late summer or autumn and dig it in during spring. Sow in rows 23cm (9in) apart or scatter at 30g (1oz) per sq meter/yard.

Rather than cutting the whole crop, leave a few plants to mature in the summer and save the seed for sowing the next crop.

Phacelia *Phacelia tanacetifolia*
This native of the American Southwest is a good bee plant but it does not fix nitrogen and has roots of only medium vigor. It is fast growing and, if dug in when still soft, will not rob the soil of nitrogen. It does not withstand cold, so sow it after the threat of frost has passed and dig it in after about eight weeks. Scatter at about 30g (1oz) per 4 sq meter/yard.

Mustard *Brassica hirta*
A quick-growing, short and shallow-rooting crop that will make plenty of organic matter for digging in and a good weed suppressor. Used widely in gardens where land cannot be spared for

long. Sow in spring and summer and dig in before flowering. It has the big disadvantage that it is a member of the cabbage family, so it could habor club-root. Scatter seeds at 30g (1oz) per 4 sq meter/yard, or in rows 15cm (6in) apart (*see page 33*).

Italian ryegrass *Lolium multiflorum*
Fast-growing and bulky, this is a good crop for sowing early in the spring. It will germinate quickly, even in cold soils, and it can be dug in before the ground has warmed up sufficiently to plant out tender vegetables. This ryegrass is suitable for many kinds of soil. The seeds are sown in the autumn in the South and other mid-climate regions. Use the annual strains not the perennial or biennial ryegrass. Scatter the seeds using about 30g (1oz) per 4 sq meter/yard.

FERTILIZERS

T HE USE OF concentrated fertilizer is probably one of the most controversial areas
in organic gardening. Opinions vary:
some gardeners claim that additional fertilizer
is unnecessary if the correct cultivation
methods are observed, whereas others employ
methods that appear to be identical to the
chemical grower except that the products used
are organic in origin.

Plants need a wide and varied range of
nutrients to be present in the soil for normal
healthy growth. All the nutrients will be added
to your soil if you follow the general soil
management techniques discussed in the
previous chapters.

Chemical growers assess the nutrient needs
of each plant every year and supply those needs
in the form of a fertilizer that is immediately
available to the plants. They simply use the
soil to hold the plant nutrients. But the result
of using fertilizer as an alternative to organic
matter is that the soil becomes an inert
medium, devoid of life, and the lost nutrients
have to be replaced every year.

The principle of organic gardening is to feed
the soil rather than the plants growing in it. If
high soil-fertility levels are maintained by
regular additions of organic matter (*see pages
16-20*), the plants can simply draw on the
material as it is required. There is no danger
of an overdose and a steady supply is ensured
by the activity of all the various organisms in
the soil (*see page 11*).

WHY USE FERTILIZERS?
For many crops, quite acceptable yields can be
obtained without the addition of fertilizers,
but you have to be realistic. Fertilizers are
normally required for several reasons. Firstly,
you may not be able to supply your soil with
all the manure or compost needed to provide
the necessary nutrients. Secondly, you may
find that your soil is grossly deficient in one or
more of the essential nutrients. To correct this
by adding bulky organic material can take
several years. It is more realistic to add concentrated organic fertilizer as well as the organic
material. Thirdly, many gardeners wish to
make much higher demands on their soil than
even the hardest-working colony of bacteria
and fungi could provide in the time.

So there are always occasions when fertilizers are required. What you must do is ensure
that they are compatible with the requirements
not only of the plants but also of the organisms
in the soil. The beauty of organic gardening
is that, provided you supply nature with the
tools of her trade, she will do the rest.

Acidity and alkalinity

Before deciding on a soil-feeding regime, you
must first discover whether the soil is acid or
alkaline. This will have a major effect not only
on your cultivation technique but also on the
plants you choose to grow.

Acidity or alkalinity of soil is determined by
its lime content. So it is obvious that you must
ascertain this before you do anything else. This
can be measured in units using a pH test. Suffice
it to say pH is measured in units on a scale of 1
to 14: neutral soil has a pH of 7; anything above
that is alkaline and anything below it, acid.
Testing the lime content of your soil is very
simple and can be done at home (*see overleaf*).

In the ornamental garden it is best to grow
plants that thrive in the soil you have, rather
than trying to change the pH level. There is a
wide range of lime-loving plants, as well as those
that prefer acid soil and many that tolerate both
(*see pages 92-3*). In the vegetable garden, however, most plants thrive in a pH of about 6.5, so
you may have to take steps to alter the lime
content (*see pages 36-7*).

It is easier to make an acid soil more alkaline
by adding lime than the other way round. Lime
has other advantages too. Adding it to heavy
clay soils, for example, will help bind the particles together (*see page 16*). However, too much
lime can chemically "lock up" some of the plant
nutrients, particularly trace elements, so that
they are unavailable to the plant roots. This
will result in nutrient deficiencies.

TESTING YOUR SOIL pH

There are several different types of kit available for testing soil pH which all work on the same principle. All are simple to use and accurate enough for home use. You should always carry out a pH test when you take over a new garden and it is a good idea to repeat the test every year, particularly if you are trying to later the pH level of the soil.

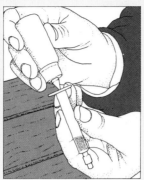

1 *Put a pH filter in the bottom of a syringe and add some soil. Pour some pH testing fluid into the syringe.*

2 *Using the syringe plunger, push the mixture through the filter and into a test tube.*

3 *Hold the test tube up against a pH color chart and match the mixture to one of the color bands to find your soil pH.*

Raising soil pH

This is not a complicated procedure; you can make an acid soil more alkaline simply by adding lime, but do not expect dramatic changes overnight. The effect is slow and, indeed, it is not a good practice to smother the land with lime as excessive quantities will scorch the plant roots. You should apply small dressings regularly. Bear in mind that, like other chemicals, lime will gradually be washed through the soil into the drainage system and the applications of manure and compost will have an acidifying effect on the soil.

WHEN TO APPLY LIME

Apply lime several weeks before sowing or planting. Ideally, dig manure into the soil in the autumn and apply lime in the spring. Never apply lime to soil that has just been manured because it will combine to form ammonia gas, which releases nitrogen into the air.

HOW MUCH LIME?

The amount of lime you use will depend to some degree on your soil type. Heavy clay soils need more than light sandy ones. As a rough guide, to increase the pH of a sandy soil by one unit, apply 1kg (2lb) lime every 100 square meter/yard. A sandy loam will need 2kg (4lb) for the same area, a medium loam about 3kg (6lb), and a heavy clay roughly 4kg (8lb). In practice, the pH level is not so critical that your plants are going to die if you do not get it exactly right. The pH levels recommended for specific plants in later chapters are intended only as a guide.

Lowering soil pH

Few garden soils are likely to be so limy that they will not grow vegetables at all. In most cases the liberal doses of compost and manure applied by organic gardeners will lower the pH sufficiently.

But, a very alkaline soil can cause problems because there may be nutrient deficiencies associated with the excess lime (*see pages 38-9*). In this case you should grow your vegetables on the deep-bed system (*see page 136*). This technique raises the growing area slightly, preventing the surrounding alkaline water from draining into it. Then, by treating beds with heavy dressings of organic matter – digging in manure or compost annually and applying regular mulches (*see page 20*) – you will make the soil more acid. The same principle applies in the ornamental garden: raise the border above the level of the lawns or paths, preferably by using lots of organic matter, when you prepare the soil for planting (*see page 75*).

TYPES OF LIME

Lime is available in several different forms. Although the most expensive, ground limestone, is the easiest to apply and lasts the longest.

Quicklime or burned lime (*calcium oxide*) This is produced by heating limestone. Although quick-acting, it is caustic and can kill plants and soil organisms.

Slaked or "hydrated" lime (*calcium hydroxide*) Very fast-acting and can often reach beyond the root zone of plants. It is also caustic and can injure plants.

Ground limestone The most commonly used source of calcium carbonate and the best to apply. It is slow-acting so remains effective for years.

Other lime sources Ground oyster shells also contain calcium carbonate and a smaller amount of phosphorus. They are slow-acting but remain effective as an alkalizer in the soil for years. Hardwood ashes are a source of lime and potash and may contain some phosphorus and magnesium.

BUILDING A RAISED BED FOR ACID-LOVING PLANTS

If your soil is particularly alkaline and you hanker after acid-loving plants such as rhododendrons, azaleas or the pieris, the only way to include them in the garden is by building a raised bed, ideally out of wooden railway ties or the smaller landscape ties. Fill it with a peaty soil mixture or with peat and sharp sand. *See page 93 for a list of suitable plants.*

Making a raised bed out of railway ties *This method is more suitable for a large raised bed because railway ties are very difficult to cut. Mark out the area for the bed and lay one row of ties on their sides along the edge. Hammer stakes into the ground at the corners, and at points where two ties meet, and nail them to the ties (see below); the wall can be one or two ties high. Fill the bed with a mixture of half acid soil and half sphagnum peat, or a mixture of three parts sphagnum peat to one part sharp sand. Plant as described for shrubs (see page 112). You can spread chipped pine bark around the bed to hide the base of the ties and provide extra interest (see right).*

Building a peat-walled raised bed

1 *Mark out the area of the bed and consolidate the base by treading the earth down firmly. Spread a layer of moist peat over the compacted soil. Thoroughly soak peat blocks and lay the first row on the bed of peat, sloping them inwards slightly. Fill in any gaps between the blocks with peat. (Peat blocks are not always available, substitutes could be heavy sod or stones.)*

2 *Fill the bed up to the top of the blocks with a mixture of equal parts sphagnum peat and acid soil or a mixture of three parts sphagnum peat to one part lime-free sharp sand.*

3 *Lay a second row of peat blocks on the first, stepped back about 2.5cm (1in) from the edge of the first row, and stagger the blocks as if building a brick wall. You can plant some acid-loving plants, such as heathers, between the blocks as you go. Fill in the bed with the soil mixture. Lay a third row of blocks, fill in the bed and plant it up in the normal way (see pages 115-7).*

The need for nutrients

All plants need oxygen, carbon and hydrogen, which they get from the air, sunlight and water. However, just as important for healthy plant growth is the presence of a range of chemical elements in the soil. These are divided into the major elements (nitrogen, phosphorus, potassium, magnesium, calcium and sulfur) and trace elements (those needed in very small amounts but nonetheless essential). Oxygen, hydrogen and carbon are needed in very large quantities (*see opposite*). By comparison, the other nutrients are needed in much smaller amounts. However, they are still needed in specific proportions, as too much of one can inactivate another. For example, too much potassium can inactivate magnesium (*see below*).

MAJOR ELEMENTS

Nitrogen (N), phosphorus (P) and potassium (K) are the major elements needed in the largest quantities. These are present in all general fertilizers, some of which also contain magnesium (Mg). Most soils have adequate levels of calcium and sulfur which can be retained by regular additions of organic matter and by using good cultivation techniques.

NITROGEN
One of the most important plant foods, this is a component of chlorophyll – the pigment that gives plants their green color – and a vital part of the structure of plant protein. It is the element in the soil responsible for the vegetative growth of the shoots and leaves of a plant.

Deficiency is not unusual because nitrogen is easily lost by leaching in open soils (*see page 13*) and can be depleted by digging in unrotted material (*see page 21*). If your soil contains insufficient nitrogen, plant leaves will become yellowed, particularly the older ones, and the plants will be stunted. Too much, on the other hand, will cause the plants to grow too quickly. There will be an abundance of "soft" leaves and these may be a darker green than normal. The softer growth will be subject to attack by insects and by frost.
Treating a nitrogen deficiency
Use a high-nitrogen fertilizer, such as dried blood (see page 40).

PHOSPHORUS
The next most important element after nitrogen, phosphorus is needed in smaller quantities (only about one-tenth of the amount). Phosphorus, or phosphate, is mainly responsible for good root growth, so a deficiency causes slight stunting of the plant. It can be diagnosed by a distinct blue color, which affects the older leaves first. Sometimes the leaves darken and develop a blue/green tinge. In addition, the plants' root system is likely to be underdeveloped.
Treating a phosphorus deficiency
Apply a dressing of bone meal fertilizer (see page 41).

POTASSIUM
Also known as potash, this is required in the same quantities as nitrogen. It affects the size and quality of flowers and fruit, and is essential for the synthesis of protein and carbohydrates. Potassium deficiency results in small, inferior flowers and fruit. The plants themselves will also be stunted. It shows up in older leaves particularly, as a yellowing around the edge of the leaves, followed by a brown scorching. Alternatively, the leaves may become bluish and eventually bronzed all over. An excess can result in plants not being able to take up magnesium (*see below*) and could cause an imbalance with other elements.
Treating a potassium deficiency
Apply a dressing of rock potash (see page 41).

MAGNESIUM
Another element needed in much larger quantities than many gardeners realize, magnesium should be present in about the same quantities as phosphorus (*see left*). It is also a constituent of chlorophyll so a deficiency causes yellowing, which starts between the veins of the leaves. The deficiency generally affects older leaves first.

A magnesium deficiency is sometimes caused by plants not being able to take up the magnesium in the soil, perhaps because there is too much potassium present. This can also happen if the soil structure is poor if there is insufficient organic matter in the soil (*see* Soil Improvement, *pages 18-34*).
Treating a magnesium deficiency
Apply a dressing of seaweed meal, liquid seaweed or liquid animal manure (see page 41).

CALCIUM
Another element required in relatively large amounts, calcium neutralizes certain acids formed in plants and helps in the manufacture of protein. Deficiency is rare in a well-managed organic garden, but plants sometimes develop an inability to distribute calcium through their systems, though no-one really knows why this occurs. The classic example is blossom-end rot in tomatoes, when the tip of the fruit blackens and rots. Lack of calcium also causes tip-burn on lettuce, black heart in celery and browning in the centers of Brussels sprouts (*see pages 146-97*). Deficiency will be most pronounced in young plant tissue.
Treating a calcium deficiency
*There is no specific cure for calcium deficiency. The only treatment is judicious use of such lime sources as ground limestone, wood ashes, hydrated lime and oyster shells, and building up a balanced nutrient level in the soil (*see Soil Improvement, *pages 18-34*).

SULFUR
This is sometimes classed as a trace element, although sulfur is in fact needed in fairly large quantities. It forms part of many plant proteins and is involved in the formation of chlorophyll. Sulfur deficiency causes stunting and yellowing of the plant. However, the problem is rare since there is generally enough sulfur in organic soils because of the regular applications of compost and manure.
Treating a sulfur deficiency
As soon as you notice a sulfur deficiency, apply a very light dusting of calcium sulfate (gypsum) over the surface of the soil.

PROPORTIONS OF ELEMENTS REQUIRED FOR HEALTHY PLANT GROWTH

Of the elements required for healthy plant growth, oxygen, carbon and hydrogen account for 96 per cent – 45 per cent oxygen, 45 per cent carbon and 6 per cent hydrogen. The nutrients described opposite and below, and some unspecified trace elements, make up the rest.

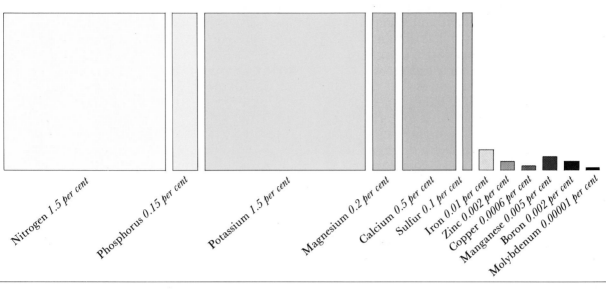

Nitrogen 1.5 per cent Phosphorus 0.15 per cent Potassium 1.5 per cent Magnesium 0.2 per cent Calcium 0.5 per cent Sulfur 0.1 per cent Iron 0.01 per cent Zinc 0.002 per cent Copper 0.0006 per cent Manganese 0.005 per cent Boron 0.002 per cent Molybdenum 0.00001 per cent

TRACE ELEMENTS

So-called because they are needed in very small quantities, these elements are nonetheless vital to plant growth. There are generally considered to be six of major importance: iron, zinc, copper, manganese, boron and molybdenum.

In a properly managed organic garden, deficiencies are extremely rare because all the trace elements are present in manure, compost and the other bulky organic matter that the organic gardener uses. However, problems can occur when the action of trace elements such as iron, manganese and boron is inhibited by alkaline, or limy, soil. This shows as a yellowing of rhododendron leaves and other acid-loving ornamental plants (*see page 92*). Raspberries too are particularly susceptible to iron deficiencies, which show up as yellowing between the veins of the leaves (*see page 228*).

It's worth stressing that the best treatment for trace-element deficiencies is to prevent them occurring in the first place. This is normally quite easily achieved in the organic garden by the continued use of bulky organic matter. Where deficiencies have occured in your garden, take the precaution of treating the soil with seaweed meal fertilizer annually.

IRON
Small quantities of iron are required in the formation of chlorophyll. Symptoms of deficiency include yellowing between the veins of the leaves, especially the younger ones. It is more likely on alkaline soils and is sometimes confused with magnesium deficiency.
Treating an iron deficiency
Spray with liquid seaweed then apply a dressing of seaweed meal and/or manure.

ZINC AND COPPER
Both zinc and copper are enzyme activators, and a deficiency of either will have the same symptoms. Younger leaves in particular are mottled yellow, and citrus trees develop a condition known as "little leaf" which is self-explanatory.
Treating a zinc and copper deficiency
Apply a dressing of seaweed meal, well-rotted manure or compost.

MANGANESE
This is necessary for the formation of chlorophyll and protein. Deficiencies are more likely to occur in alkaline soils, and will show up as a stunting of the younger leaves, and yellowing – especially between the veins.
Treating a manganese deficiency
If rapid action is needed, spray with liquid seaweed then apply seaweed meal, manure or compost.

BORON
This element is important to the growing tissue of all parts of the plant. Deficiencies are more likely to occur on alkaline soils and lead to a tissue breakdown. This causes internal "corkiness", especially in apples and many root crops, and brown heart in celery and brassicas such as cauliflower, broccoli and calabrese (*see* Pests and diseases of vegetables, *pages 198 to 201*).

Treating a boron deficiency
Boron deficiency must be prevented because, if deficiencies become apparent in a crop, it is too late to save it. Apply seaweed meal, manure or compost to ensure that the next crop will not suffer from the same problem.

MOLYBDENUM
A deficiency of this mineral, which is instrumental in the production of protein, will show up in deformed growth. It causes a condition called "whiptail" which affects the cabbage (*Cruciferae*) family, and results in their leaves becoming thin and strap-like (*see page 195*). Deficiency is generally due to acid soil conditions (*see page 35*).
Treating a molybdenum deficiency
Add lime to raise the pH of acid soil (see page 36). *Spray the plants with liquid seaweed fertilizer and apply seaweed meal and/or manure or compost to the soil.*

Organic fertilizers

The scientists will tell you that there is no evidence to suggest that yields will be significantly heavier or that fruit and vegetables will actually taste any better if the plants are fed with organic nutrients instead of inorganic ones. And of course, they are quite right.

What they do not tell you is that the reason there is no evidence is that, so far, there has been no research. I have no facilities to test scientifically for taste, but I can assure any scientist that he or she will certainly notice a difference in the taste of my early potatoes compared to the inorganically grown potatoes you will buy.

Plants will take their nutrients in the form of the same chemical elements whether they are organically or inorganically derived. Organic gardeners do not suggest that plants actually take up different chemicals if they are grown naturally. What is true is that the chemicals in organic fertilizers will not harm the soil or its many inhabitants; the inorganic ones will. Indeed, organic feeding actually benefits soil micro-organisms as well as plants.

There are several compound fertilizers that are described as "semi-organic" or "organically based". These may be more powerful than the completely inorganic equivalent but they are *not* the real thing. The main difference is generally in the potash content, which, in "semi-organic" fertilizers is sometimes supplemented with potassium sulphate. The following products will provide all that is necessary.

BLOOD, FISH AND BONE MEAL

A general compound fertilizer, this is the basis of my recommended nutrition plan. Regular dressings should maintain nutrient levels in all soils. The nitrogen contained in this fertilizer, however, is fairly quickly released so blood, fish and bone meal should not be spread more than two weeks before the crops are sown or planted.

NUTRIENT CONTENT	
Nitrogen	3.5 per cent
Phosphorus	8 per cent
Potassium	0.5 per cent
Trace elements	—

HOOF AND HORN

One of the best sources of slow-release nitrogen. The ground hooves and horns are heated to 60°C (140°F) before being packed so it is quite safe to use. It has to be broken down by bacteria before it becomes available to plant roots, so it must be applied a good two weeks before its effect is needed. Thereafter it will remain in the soil for some time.

Use hoof and horn fertilizer for a quick boost to overwintered plants, such as cabbages, in the spring or for any plants that appear to have stopped growing. Other fertilizers which are high in nitrogen include sewage sludge and cottonseed meal.

NUTRIENT CONTENT	
Nitrogen	13 per cent
Phosphorus	1.75 per cent
Potassium	—
Trace elements	—

SEAWEED MEAL

An alternative to blood, fish and bone meal but more expensive. It is, however, better balanced and its nutrients are in a slow-release form. It contains 60 to 70 different chemical elements including the complete range of trace elements. It can be raked into the soil before sowing or planting but its cost means that it is generally used as a compost activator and to supply trace elements (*see page 39*). Seaweed meal can be applied at any time, but it is best used when the soil is warm to enable the bacteria to break it down, making the nutrients available to plants.

NUTRIENT CONTENT	
Nitrogen	2.8 per cent
Phosphorus	0.2 per cent
Potassium	2.3 per cent
Trace elements	Full range

DRIED BLOOD

A very fast-acting nitrogen fertilizer. Use it where a rapid nitrogen "tonic" is required, but not later than the end of the summer or it will be washed into the subsoil. If you get frosts in your garden, do not apply dried blood later than mid-summer to avoid encouraging soft foliage that would be damaged by frost.

NUTRIENT CONTENT	
Nitrogen	12-14 per cent
Phosphorus	Small amount
Potassium	—
Trace elements	—

FISH MEAL

A useful fertilizer that contains nitrogen and phosphate (phosphorus). Some manufacturers add potash inorganically, hence it can be sold as "semi-organic".

NUTRIENT CONTENT	
Nitrogen	9 per cent
Phosphorus	2.5 per cent
Potassium	—
Trace elements	—

DRIED ANIMAL MANURES

These contain only small amounts of the major nutrients but are rich in trace elements. Mix them with peat or mushroom compost if you cannot get bulky manures.

NUTRIENT CONTENT	
Nitrogen	1 per cent
Phosphorus	1 per cent
Potassium	1.5 per cent
Trace elements	Full range

BONE MEAL

This popular phosphate fertilizer is used for activating root growth. Buy bone meal that is clearly marked "steamed". In its raw form it can carry anthrax – but it is safe if steam treated. Even so, many gardeners wear gloves when spreading it as a precaution.

NUTRIENT CONTENT	
Nitrogen	3.5 per cent
Phosphorus	22 per cent
Potassium	—
Trace elements	—

ROCK POTASH

An invaluable source of potassium – the element missing from many organic fertilizers. Rock potash is insoluble and remains in the soil for long periods, enabling plants to take it up as required.

NUTRIENT CONTENT	
Nitrogen	—
Phosphorus	—
Potassium	10.5 per cent
Trace elements	—

WOOD ASHES

A useful source of potassium and a small amount of phosphate. Put twigs and prunings, which contain useful quantities of minerals, through a shredder and use the chippings as a mulch (see page 59). Alternatively, put the ashes on the compost heap.

NUTRIENT CONTENT	
Nitrogen	Varies according to material burned
Phosphorus	
Potassium	
Trace elements	

LIQUID SEAWEED

There are a number of liquid seaweed products available. They contain nitrogen, potash and phosphate as well as the entire range of trace elements. They also contain growth hormones called cytokinins, which help increase the efficiency of photosynthesis and the production of protein. They are invaluable as a means of correcting deficiencies quickly.

Liquid seaweed is also said to help reduce attack by fungus diseases and to protect plants from frost.

NUTRIENT CONTENT	
Nitrogen	1.5 per cent
Phosphorus	Min. amount
Potassium	2.5 per cent
Trace elements	Full range

LIQUID ANIMAL MANURES

These contain all the major nutrients in small quantities, but are rich in trace elements and so very useful for treating trace element deficiencies.

NUTRIENT CONTENT	
Nitrogen	1 per cent
Phosphorus	1 per cent
Potassium	1.5 per cent
Trace elements	Full range

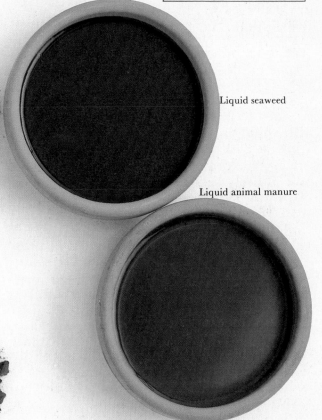

Liquid seaweed

Liquid animal manure

HOME-MADE LIQUID MANURE

It is very easy to make your own liquid manure which will be as nutritious as any you can buy. All you need is a large metal or plastic drum that holds water, a hessian sack and some animal manure.

Sheep manure is the best because it is particularly high in nutrients (*see page 28*), but cow, pig, horse or goat manure can be used. About half a sackful will give a year's supply.

Home-made liquid manure can be used neat, provided the soil has first been watered. To use it as a foliar spray, dilute the liquid with equal parts water.

1 *Fill the drum with water. Collect up half a sackful of animal droppings. Tie up the top of the sack with a double loop of string.*

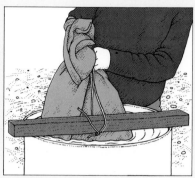

2 *Put a stout stake across the top of the drum and loop the string over it so that the sack is suspended in the water. Leave it for about a fortnight, until the water is a rich dark brown color. Remove the sack and leave the drum covered.*

Applying fertilizers

The application of organic fertilizers does not need to be quite as precise as the application of inorganic compounds. Most release their nutrients slowly so there is little chance of them scorching young plants, although you must keep granular fertilizers off the foliage.

It is impossible to give precise instructions as to how much fertilizer to apply because so much depends on your soil, the weather and the plants you wish to grow. The only way to find out is to use the "rule-of-thumb" method of simply adding general fertilizer if growth is unsatisfactory and specific fertilizers if deficiencies show up on the plants. In addition, apply an annual dressing to the ornamental garden and to the vegetables as directed in the relevant chapters (*see pages 74-125 and 132-201*).

APPLYING GRANULAR FERTILIZERS

Granular fertilizers should always be used to provide general nutrients as a supplement to compost and manure. It is usually applied in the spring or before planting. Sprinkle the fertilizer over the soil as recommended, being very careful to avoid it touching the foliage, then rake it into the soil.

The application of granular fertilizers is normally recommended in "handfuls per square meter/yard". If the recommendation is to spread the fertilizer down a row of fruit or vegetables, you will need to convert the square meter/yard measurement to a linear one. This is not difficult: if the rows are 30cm (12in) apart, spread the amount of fertilizer recommended for a square meter/yard along 3m (9ft) of the row. If they are 15cm (6in) apart, it is 6m (18ft) along the row and so on. In this way, the correct distribution of fertilizer can be maintained.

APPLYING LIQUID FERTILIZERS

These are easy to put on. Dilute the liquid according to the manufacturer's instructions and simply pour it on. But the golden rule when liquid feeding is never to do so when the soil is bone dry – you may scorch the roots. Water with clear water first and let it drain away, then add the liquid fertilizer.

If you are feeding plants growing in pots, simply fill up to the rim of the pot. If they are growing in soil, water the fertilizer on generously in a fairly wide area around the plants, until the top of the soil is saturated. For plants, such as greenhouse tomatoes, that are regularly fed in this way, it is a good idea to bury a flower pot in the soil near the plant and fill that. If you use this method, the fertilizer gets deeper into the soil and you also know exactly how much you are giving the plant every time.

The advantage of liquid feeding is that, since plants can only take up nutrients in liquid form, the nutrients are available immediately; granular fertilizer has to be dissolved first. The disadvantage is that liquid fertilizer does not remain effective for as long as granular fertilizer and is leached into the subsoil fairly quickly. Liquid feeding is used to supply short-term nutrients to hungry plants and to correct deficiencies; it should *not* be considered as an alternative to solid feeding.

FOLIAR FEEDING

This method involves spraying the leaves of the plant. It is faster acting but shorter lived than other methods so is really only of value for rapid remedial action when deficiencies are seen. Liquid seaweed sprayed on to leaves, for example, is something of a "miracle cure" for trace element deficiencies. However, it should always be supplemented by feeding the soil with seaweed meal fertilizer as well.

ORGANIC PEST AND DISEASE CONTROL

Over the last fifty years or so, gardening practices have closely followed those of the commercial grower and even the farmer. New methods of cultivation which improve yields or which reduce losses from pests and diseases have been discovered, and these have been translated into gardening terms. A great deal of research has also been directed at finding new methods of growing plants commercially. There is no doubt that much of the information that has come from this research has benefited the gardener, but it would be a mistake to fall into the trap of following the commercial grower automatically. Nowhere has the mimicry of the professional been more evident than in the field of pest and disease control. Just as soon as a new chemical has been produced for commercial use, so a slightly diluted version of the chemical appears in the garden shops and centers, accompanied by seductive claims that it has proved to be more effective than its competitors.

You have to remember that your requirements are very different. The farmer or commercial grower is constantly on the look-out for higher yielding, larger and therefore more profitable varieties of plants, while you are after fruit and vegetables with flavor, that are not contaminated with chemicals. In addition, he or she may have many acres of, for example, cabbages, that are infested with caterpillars, and so have no alternative but to spray them. If you have only one or two rows of cabbages, you do not need to cover them with chemicals. Instead, walk down the rows two or three evenings a week, pick off the offending creatures and drop them into a jar of kerosene. Likewise, a few well-direct squirts of soapy water will wash any aphids off your couple of dozen rose bushes in next to no time.

The plain fact is that, by cultivating a natural organic garden, you simply will not come across the pest and disease problems that can face the mono-culture grower. Where large acreages of one crop are grown year after year, a rapid build-up of pests and diseases can easily occur. They have a plentiful supply of food and virtually no competition. In the organic garden where there is a great diversity of planting (*see page 71*), you will attract the complete spectrum of wildlife – insects, birds and small mammals – that will create a natural balance. The result is that the hover-flies and ladybirds eat the aphids, and the birds eat the caterpillars and so on – no insect pest, fungus disease or bacterium will ever have it all its own way, so there will never be an unnatural build-up of one species. But, if you start to think that all the insects are friendly and all the fungi benign, be warned that pests and diseases will rear their heads just as surely as they will anywhere else. Prevention is the best approach and there are many physical ways of doing this. Although it would be a foolish over-reaction to think that you can do without pesticides completely, you should only resort to the few organic pesticides available when all else fails.

WHAT YOU CAN DO TO AVOID PESTS AND DISEASES

Start by growing strong, healthy plants that will have the ability to resist attacks from pests and diseases. Always plant into fertile soil and make sure the plants never go short of water and food. Rely as much as you can on physical methods of pest and disease prevention and control and constant vigilance, as outlined on the next few pages, and you will cut down the need for chemicals. Nature will do the rest for you.

Nature has worked out the most complex "balance of power" that makes modern international politics look like a nursery game. Build up as diverse a collection of plants as you can, including as many native flowers, trees and shrubs as possible, especially those that grow in your own locality, and provide a small area of water. By doing this you will build up a varied colony of useful insects and birds and thus keep problems to a minimum.

On the following pages I describe ways of preventing and controlling general garden pests and diseases. Treatment for pests or diseases that affect specific plants, such as aphids on roses, blight on potatoes or scab on fruit trees, are dealt with in the relevant chapters later in the book.

Maintaining a healthy garden

The very first rule is to adopt good cultivation practices. The organic approach to gardening – feeding the soil instead of the plant – produces much stronger growth that is, firstly, not so attractive to pests and diseases as the soft lushness of a force-fed plant and, secondly, able to cope with an attack if it does occur.

Keep the garden as clean and tidy as possible. Never leave rubbish lying around. If you've been weeding, put the waste on the compost heap straight away. If you've been thinning seedlings, this is even more important because insect pests are often attracted by the smell of the bruised stems.

Put on healthy plant waste on the compost heap. Destroy any plants that show *any* signs of disease. I very rarely compost the top growth of my maincrop potatoes after lifting, for example, because of the risk of inoculating the compost heap with spores of the potato blight; a completely clean crop is very rare (*see page 200*). Much the same rule applies to prunings from the fruit trees. They are quite likely to be infected with diseases, so are best destroyed. You can use the ash as a fertilizer (*see page 41*).

Use only pots and seed trays that have been thoroughly cleaned and, if possible, sterilized with boiling water or steam. Keep your greenhouse clean too and, if you do see a sign of a pest or a fungus on a leaf, pick it off straight away and get rid of it in the garbage can.

DAILY VIGILANCE

Make a habit, especially in the summer, when pests and diseases are most likely to appear, of walking round the garden at least once a day. Take a hoe and a plastic bag with you. Remove any errant weeds with the hoe, but above all, keep an eye open for the first signs of attack from pests and diseases. If you see signs of mildew or you find a caterpillar – pick it off immediately, put it into the plastic bag and then the garbage can. The first attack of aphids can often be removed by simply rubbing them stem of the attacked plants with your finger to squash them.

BUYING HEALTHY PLANTS

It is of vital importance to ensure that your plants are healthy when you first buy them. It is only too easy to buy in a load of trouble in the form of virus or fungus diseases or even pests or their eggs. Some plants are covered by a certificate of health from the Government. In many countries it is possible to ask for a certification number to show that the plant you are buying is free from disease. Many fruit trees and seed potatoes come within such schemes.

Check ornamental trees, shrubs, herbaceous perennials and even annuals carefully before buying them; reject anything that shows the slightest sign of disease or pest attack, or of physical damage.

Examine bulbs, corms and tubers closely. They should be firm all over and the skins should be fairly well intact. A loose skin can often mean that the bulb has become shrivelled (*see page 117*).

In some cases you should consider replacing your stock with new plants after a few years. Strawberries, for example, will lose their vigor after a while. This is often a sign that they have become infected with virus diseases and anything you propagate from them will also be infected. Potatoes too can become infected with virus diseases spread by aphids. The seed potatoes you buy are generally grown in areas where aphid attack is rare, so they are likely to be free from virus. So, unless you can be quite sure that your crop has not been attacked by aphids, it is worthwhile buying in new potato tubers every year.

Different varieties of the same plants may have varying degrees of resistance to pests and disease. Some varieties of potato, for example, are less susceptible to slug damage, while others show resistance to potato eelworm. There is quite a distinct variation in resistance to fungus diseases. I would not, for example, recommend growing Britain's favourite apple, *Cox's Orange Pippin,* or the rose variety *Frensham,* in an organic garden because both are very susceptible to mildew fungus. Mildew can be serious because, once it is established on one variety, it moves on to other plants.

Plant breeders are constantly trying to breed pest- and disease-resistant plants, so it is worthwhile checking the current position on new varieties before buying anything that is notoriously disease-prone. There are, for example, several varieties of snapdragon (*Antirrhinum* sp.) that have been bred specifically to resist rust fungus, there are eelworm-resistant *Phlox* and virus-resistant varieties of many plants including potatoes, strawberries and tomatoes.

Where it is difficult to breed-in resistance, it is sometimes possible to have the best of both worlds by grafting the required variety on to a resistant rootstock (*see page 277*).

RAISING HEALTHY PLANTS

Of course, you should also employ the same safeguards with plants you have raised yourself, though here it's much more difficult to be ruthless about weeding out the weaklings. But bear

COPING WITH CLUB ROOT

Club root is a crippling fungus disease which causes distortion and swelling of the roots of all members of the cabbage family and several ornamental plants too. Once the roots cease to function properly, the tops wilt and will not produce a satisfactory harvest. There is no cure for club root and, worse still, once it invades the soil, it is there forever whether or not you grow any host plants.

Once your soil has club root, I would not recommend growing cauliflowers, but you can get an acceptable crop of cabbages, kale and Brussels sprouts by sowing them in trays, then transferring them to pots until they establish a good root system. Even though the seedlings will still be affected by the disease when planted out, they will then be strong and healthy enough to shrug it off.

1 *Sow the seed in a seed tray (see page 271). When the seedlings are about 4cm (1½in) tall transfer each one to a 10cm (4in) pot.*

2 *Grow the plants on until the roots fill the pot – up to about 6 weeks – then plant them out. Water well after planting.*

in mind that a young plant that has been infected with a disease or attacked by a pest is at a disadvantage right from the start. Throw it away to avoid infecting other plants.

Keep your greenhouse scrupulously clean. Use plastic seed trays and pots for raising seeds and pot plants because they are easier to sterilize; wooden seed trays and clay pots are porous so can harbor pests (*see page 271*).

Time your spring sowing so that plants do not have to remain in the greenhouse getting leggy and pot-bound because the weather is too cold for them to be planted out. The real secret is to get young plants growing away and then to keep them growing steadily. In some cases, this is all you need to control even the most virulent and damaging of diseases (*see above*).

One final point to bear in mind when buying or raising plants from seed is that *F1* hybrid varieties have much more vigor than those raised from open-pollinated seed. An *F1* hybrid is the result of a first-generation cross between two selected parents. These first generations always have much more vigor, which will help to carry them over an early attack.

Companion planting

This is a technique practiced by many organic gardeners. The theory behind companion planting is that plants have specific likes and dislikes concerning their close companions in the garden and will do better if planted in close proximity to the correct plant. Similarly, by planting a particular species in the garden you can reduce the number of weeds or attract certain pest predators.

Many of the recommendations for companion planting are based on folklore and, as with many of these tales, there is some truth in them. There is a well-known theory that, because carrot-fly are attracted by smell, they can be prevented by planting carrots between rows of onions, so the smell of the carrots is disguised. I have experimented with this theory over several years in carefully controlled trials but without any success. On the other hand, the cabbage white butterfly is attracted to its host plant by smell and it can be fooled by planting the highly aromatic French marigold (*Tagetes*) between the rows of cabbages. Many

Ornamental pest control *Hover-flies, which are predators of aphids, can be attracted into the garden by planting flat, open flowers such as these French marigolds (*Tagetes*).*

scientifically controlled trials have been conducted which indicate a reduction in attack when this was done. Many gardeners have also reported similar results with eelworms, soil pests that attack potatoes in particular, where French marigolds are grown. Scientific research has confirmed that this is indeed due to a secretion from the roots of the marigolds. French marigolds are also said to help kill weeds, in particular couch grass (*Agropyron repens*), but I have not been able to test this theory in my garden.

COMPANION PLANTING TO REDUCE APHIDS

There is absolutely no doubt that marigolds (*Tagetes* and *Calendula*), planted near tomatoes or roses, for example, greatly reduce the frequency of attack by aphids – the most persistent of all garden pests. This is simply because they attract hover-flies whose larvae devour aphids by the thousand. Hover-flies are the most valuable pest predators in the garden and there are different species all over the world. Before laying her eggs, the female needs protein, which she gets from pollen. She then lays individual eggs on colonies of aphids so that the larvae have a readily available source of food when they hatch. The hover-fly has a short feeding tube so needs to feed from an open-structured flower where the pollen is easily accessible. Therefore by planting marigolds (*Tagetes* and *Calendula*), poppies (*Papaver* sp.), nasturtiums (*Tropaeolum*) or dwarf morning glory (*Convolvulus tricolor*) between plants, you minimize aphid attack.

I have grown garlic under rose bushes as a control for aphids, and savory next to beans for the same purpose – all to no avail. I have tried other combinations but, alas, I have yet to achieve success. More research is needed.

ENCOURAGING OTHER PEST PREDATORS

It is more difficult to attract some of the other predators because they do not necessarily feed on flowers. Some, such as ladybugs, lacewings and several species of wasps that feed on and lay their eggs inside aphids and other soft-bellied pests including caterpillars, can be encouraged by providing as varied a collection of plant life as possible.

It has also been found that some pests are attracted to their host plants by sight. By mixing ornamental plants and vegetables in an ornamental border, you can camouflage the host plants which deters the pests. There is also evidence that vegetable plots that are left weed-infested suffer less than clean ones. However, the yields are also lower because the weeds compete for the same light, nutrients and water.

Some of the good results reported by many organic gardeners are, I am sure, due to companion planting. By careful consideration of which plants are cultivated together, you can promote healthy growth and utilize a completely natural form of pest control.

Controlling birds and animals

The most destructive pests in gardens are the larger ones – birds, deer, rabbits, moles, mice and so on. There is no doubt that the most effective control for this type of pest is to prevent them reaching the crops by physical means.

Birds

There is no really effective bird deterrent available. Scarecrows are reasonably effective for a day or two but, after a short while, the birds get used to them and take no notice. This is even so with the more elaborate electric scarecrows that have waving arms, flashing lights and screaming sirens or blazing shot-guns. If moved around constantly, they have some effect but, in the end, they are more likely to frighten your neighbors than the birds! If a scarecrow is combined with regular shooting it will be more effective, but you will also disturb the natural balance and that is biting the hand that feeds you.

PROTECTING THE PRODUCTIVE GARDEN

The only really effective control for birds is netting and that is not nearly as expensive as it may seem. Plastic netting is relatively cheap and will last a very long time if it is used carefully.

The ideal is to build yourself a fruit cage to cover the entire productive garden. Support the netting on strong posts and wires and secure it at the edges with short wire staples.

If you do not wish to go to that kind of extreme, cover only the rows of vulnerable crops. You can place a row of small wire hoops along the beds of low plants and drape nets over the top (*see opposite*). Alternatively, with crops such as strawberries or rows of fruit bushes, you can simply drape the netting over the row. If there is a danger of plants growing through the netting, as with peas for example, it is better to support the net on stakes so that it is higher than the plants. Otherwise you will damage the plant when you remove the netting.

Unlike most of the insect pests, birds generally cause most damage during the winter, when there is little else around for them to eat. They will attack the fattening buds of fruit – particularly blackcurrants. The cabbage (*Cruciferae*) family are also greatly at risk, especially when it snows, because they are often the only edible plants visible, so will attract all the birds in the area. The answer is to drive in a few short posts along the row, put a jam-jar on the top of each post and drape the netting over the top. This can be a nuisance when you want to cut a cabbage from the middle of the row, but at least you will have some left to harvest! Ensure that the netting is firmly fixed at ground level or birds may still get under the netting and could be injured trying to get out.

PROTECTING
THE ORNAMENTAL GARDEN
This is rather more difficult because plastic netting will do nothing for the appearance of the flower borders. And some birds are particularly keen to remove buds from all kinds of plants, particularly burgeoning crocuses in the spring. It's odd that, with crocuses, they seem to go mainly for the yellow ones so they are to be avoided if birds are a problem. The rest can be protected by stringing black cotton over the top (*see below*). The birds do not see the cotton strands and, if they touch them, they will panic and fly off.

New grass seed is extremely vulnerable to attack by birds. Obviously it is impossible to rake in all the seed, so the birds are immediately attracted. Again, they can be deterred by black cotton, but this is not practical over large areas. A more effective method is to cover the seeded area with lightweight plastic or even netting. It can be removed as soon as the grass germinates. Plastic has the great advantage that it not only keeps the birds away but it also encourages germination of the grass seed by warming the soil (*see page 140*).

DETERRING BIRDS

Birds can be a tremendous asset in the garden as pest controllers and they are welcomed for their aesthetic value as well. However, they also cause a great deal of damage, so vulnerable plants must be protected. Fruit and vegetable plants are especially at risk, particularly in the winter or early spring when food is scarce. Some ornamental plants are also susceptible, especially early spring bulbs. The only really effective way to protect these plants is by physical means.

Protecting crops left
Place stakes along the rows of vegetables and put glass jars over the top of each stake to protect the netting. Leaving enough netting at the edges to reach the ground, stretch it over the stakes.

Protecting crocus buds

Protecting fruit bushes right
Birds attack the young shoots and the fruit. Low-growing bushes can be protected by draping netting over the top. Secure the netting at one end with bricks, pull it over the bush; anchor the edges.

Obviously, it is not practical to cover the ornamental garden with netting, but some plants need protecting because they are particularly susceptible. Crocuses are often the only colorful plants in the garden in the early spring so regularly have their buds removed. To prevent this, put some small sticks into the ground around the buds and loop black cotton around them and across the middle so that it forms an invisble covering. Birds will still try to attack the crocus buds because they cannot see the cotton and will fly off when they touch it.

Protecting seedlings left
Rows of vegetable seedlings seem to be particularly at risk from bird damage and are best covered with netting supported on wire hoops. You can make the hoops by bending 12-gauge wire or use the hoops supplied with small cloches. The netting can normally be removed once the seedlings are established.

Animals

Animals such as hedgehogs, frogs and toads should be encouraged in any garden because they feed on garden pests. However, others such as deer, rabbits, moles or mice, must be kept out of the garden because they either feed on the plants or undermine them. Good fencing will deter deer and rabbits, but the only solution to mice and moles is to trap them.

DEER

If you live in the country near woodland, deer can be quite a problem because they eat most vegetation and strip bark from trees in winter.

Deer can jump a 3m (10ft) fence, so building one tall enough to keep them out is expensive. An alternative is to use an electric fence powered by a car battery or through a transformer run from your mains electricity. It is important to get an expert to install this type of fencing, so seek the advice of an agricultural merchant.

RABBITS

Rabbits are a problem in many rural gardens because they eat almost anything.

There is only one way to control them effectively. No amount of shooting, trapping or ferreting will keep their numbers down; they have to be fenced out with wire netting. It is important to use 2.5cm (1in) mesh netting and to bury it at least 15cm (6in) in the ground, with 75cm (2ft 6in) above the ground (*see below*).

MICE

Mice are not usually a serious problem, although in some regions pine mice (voles), as well as the common Field mice, can be very destructive. They eat everything from tulip and lily bulbs to carrots and rose and holly roots.

To prevent them, you can either trap them with a conventional mousetrap or buy a cat.

MOLES

These animals can be a particular problem because not only do they damage plant roots when they burrow underground – sometimes even leaving the roots suspended in mid-air – but they also eat large numbers of worms. They undermine lawns and borders as well, leaving large mounds of earth and uneven soil sinkage.

Moles are almost impossible to keep out of the garden. My own experience is that smoke drives them off only temporarily, and the trick of making the tunnels uncomfortable by filling them with holly leaves simply makes them dig another tunnel elsewhere.

If all else fails, the only reasonably effective method is to trap them, though it goes against the grain because they are very attractive creatures indeed and do destroy harmful grubs.

Barrel traps are the most effective and the moles are at least killed instantly. These are set in the main runs and covered with a small amount of loose soil to keep the light out of the run. Mark the position of the barrel traps with a stock or colored marker so that you do not forget where they are and dig them up daily.

Erecting rabbit fencing
Hammer fencing posts into the ground around the productive garden and string two pieces of wire between them, one about a third of the way up the posts, the other near the top. Fix wire netting to the strands, burying the bottom 15-20cm (6-8in) in a trench so that it curves away from the base of the fence.

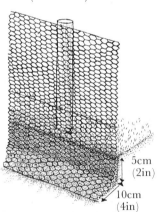
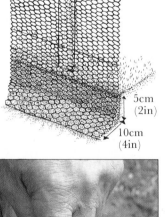

5cm (2in)

10cm (4in)

Setting mole traps
Mole traps are set in the mole runs. To find a run, follow a straight line between two mole hills and dig down into the soil. Prepare the trap and put it into the mole run. Cover it with some loose soil and mark the position with a stick. Check the traps for moles every day.

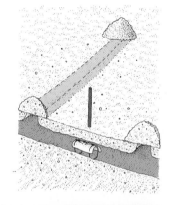

Controlling soil pests and insects

Soil pests and insects have always proved to be a great headache for organic gardeners because there is no suitable organic chemical with which to treat them. Three soil pests that cause great problems, especially on newly dug land, are wireworms, cutworms and leatherjackets, because they eat the roots of almost anything. One way of reducing all soil pests is to hoe between plants regularly (*see page 57*). This brings them to the surface, where the birds will find them.

There are, however, some very effective physical controls for some of the most troublesome, and many natural predators can be encouraged into the garden to help get rid of pests. Insects can also be controlled without resorting to chemicals. Many insects, and methods of controlling them, are specific to certain plants, so they are dealt with in the relevant chapter. Those discussed here attack a range of plants.

PHYSICAL TREATMENT FOR SOIL PESTS AND INSECTS

CATERPILLARS

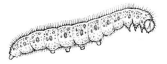

The larvae of moths and butterflies are common garden pests. Some live in the soil and feed on plant roots, others may attack plant stems or fruit, but the majority live on leaves. The most seriously affected plants are those of the cabbage (*Cruciferae*) family, and a severe attack can completely strip crops of their foliage.

What to do
If you can spot the small clusters of tiny eggs, which cabbage butterflies lay directly on the plants, simply remove them. Caterpillars themselves are usually easy to spot. Pick them off crops and drop them into a jar of kerosene.

LEATHERJACKETS

These are unmistakeable in their appearance. They are white or brown and very ugly. Leatherjackets are, in fact, the larvae of the crane fly and can be found just below the surface of the soil, nibbling away at the roots of just about anything. They sometimes come to the surface on a warm night when they may completely eat through the stem of a plant at ground level.

What to do
You will generally find leatherjackets when you are digging or hoeing. Because of their color, they are easy to see and squash, and this action is normally all that is needed to control their numbers. Ground beetles eat them so should be encouraged by growing ground-cover plants.

WIREWORMS

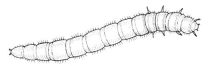

The larvae of the click beetle, these are thin, shiny worms with yellowish skins. They make very characteristic small holes in potatoes and carrots which can be mistaken for damage caused by slugs. Wireworms can attack any plant, but particularly favor those with fleshy roots, and here lies the key to their control.

What to do

In the first year or two of cultivating newly turned soil, grow a row of wheat between the crops at intervals over the plot. The wireworms will be attracted to the wheat, which can be dug up and carted to the local dump.

You can also use old potatoes or carrots to trap the wireworms. These can be spitted on a stick and buried, so that you know where the trap is and can easily remove, and destroy. Alternatively, trap them by splitting an old cabbage stalk and pushing it 5-7cm (2-3in) into the ground near the affected plants. As with the potatoes they should be lifted periodically and the worms removed and destroyed.

CUTWORMS

Perhaps even more troublesome than wireworms or leatherjackets, cutworms live just below the surface of the soil. They feed at the base of plants during the day, cutting them off at soil level.

What to do
If you find plants that have keeled over, search the soil just below the surface. Hoe an area up to about one meter/yard away from the affected plant to expose the grubs; destroy any you find, either by squashing or drowning them in kerosene. Again, attract ground beetles with ground-cover plants.

ANTS

Ants rarely do harm to growing plants directly. The major problem is that ants carry aphids from one plant to another and protect them against attack from ladybugs and hover-fly larvae. This is because the ants feed on the sticky honeydew substance excreted by the feeding aphids.

What to do
It is often enough to control the aphids (see overleaf). However, if the ants become a real nuisance, they can be killed with a mixture of equal parts icing sugar and borax. Put some down, on a piece of wood or stone, near to where there is ant activity and cover it to protect it from rain. The ants have a craving for sweet things and will devour the bait. The poison will then be carried into the ant nest and, as ants also eat their own droppings, it will not be long before the entire colony is destroyed.

PHYSICAL TREATMENT FOR SOIL PESTS AND INSECT

SLUGS

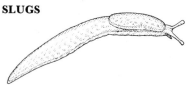

There are many different kinds of slugs, which are not insects but are soft and slimy mollusks. They hide during the day but venture forth at night to feed on soft plant growth. Slugs leave a tell-tale trail of silvery mucus on the soil. They as especially active in wet weather from spring to autumn and can be particularly destructive among lettuce plants.

What to do
The traditional methods are still some of the most effective. One involves venturing out into the garden at night when the slugs are feeding and simply picking them up and dropping them into a jar of kerosene. In this way, even the underground dwellers can be greatly reduced in number. Another trick is to surround the plants most vulnerable to attack with lime or soot. The slugs don't like crawling through either of these, so they generally avoid the plant. The addition of a thin covering of lime will not radically alter the pH of the soil, but avoid spreading it around acid-loving plants. Spreading a mulch of ornamental pine bark is also effective.

There is another very effective solution. While I would not suggest the whole garden could be protected in the early spring, seedlings or the shoots of young herbaceous plants can simply be surrounded with plastic bottles which have been cut off at the bottom. These make ideal slug deterrents (see above). Large plants can be protected by removing the top and bottom of a plastic can and placing it over them. Still another way is to sink deep saucers full of beer or ale into the soil. The slugs are attracted to the beer and quickly drown in it. If you live in porcupine country these rodents eat slugs so may help reduce their numbers. Try to attract hedgehogs as they eat hundreds of slugs.

EARWIGS

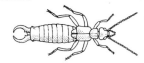

These can cause problems, particularly in the ornamental garden, but they can be trapped easily. Earwigs tend to crawl to the tip of plants just as they are coming into bud and then nibble the embryo flower; they also attack leaves. The damage is often only slight, but it is enough to distort the flower and spoil the plant. Chrysanthemums and dahlias are particularly at risk.

What to do

Put a flower pot upside down on the top of a cane near the flower heads. Fill the pot with dried grass or leaves and, because they don't like daylight, the earwigs will crawl into it during the day. About once a week, simply remove the pot and destroy the grass. If they are still a problem, smear grease on the stems just below the blooms.

APHIDS

These are amongst the most common and troublesome of garden pests, and include those species known as greenfly and blackfly. All suck the sap of plants, causing distortion and particularly attacking the young growing tips. Aphids excrete sticky honeydew on which sooty mold can grow, and transmit virus diseases.

What to do
Fortunately, there are a number of predators, such as ladybugs and hoverflies which eat aphids by the thousand. You can attract these by planting French marigolds (Tagetes), see Companion planting, page 45. You can also rub the insects off with your fingers or hose them off with a powerful spray of water. Spray badly infested plants with insecticidal soap (see page 53).

FLEA BEETLES

My favorite physical control of all is the one employed against the flea beetle. These are tiny beetles that make hundreds of small "shotholes" in the leaves of seedlings, particularly those of the cabbage (*Cruciferae*) family. Sometimes, in good growing weather, the seedlings will overcome it and suffer only a minor setback. In a bad growing year, when the weather is cold and constantly wet, the damage caused by the beetle can set them back weeks and may even kill them off completely, so it is best to control them.

What to do
These insects are called flea beetles because they jump sharply into the air when approached, just like a flea. Control them as described below.

1 *Use a piece of wood which measures about 30 × 15cm (1ft × 6in). Coat one side of it with heavy grease – old engine grease is ideal.*

2 *Holding the board grease-side down, pass it along the row of seedlings about 2.5-5cm (1-2in) above them. The beetles jump up and stick to the grease.*

WHITEFLIES

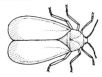

These tiny insects suck the sap of many greenhouse and outdoor plants, and those which affect brassicas are especially persistent and resilient.
What to do

Whiteflies are strongly attracted to anything yellow, so the trick is to hang up a yellow card or square of plastic, coated with thin grease, in the greenhouse. The whiteflies are attracted to the card and stick to the grease, like flies on an old-fashioned fly paper.

The cabbage whitefly can survive outdoors over winter, so you must make sure that there is no garden debris left around on which it can feed.

OTHER PESTS

Woodlice can do a lot of damage to seedlings and young plants, coming out at night to nibble on roots, stems and leaves.
Millipedes are small black insects with short legs. They usually remain beneath the soil surface, feeding on roots and aggravating damage caused by other pests, such as slugs.
Snails pose similar problems to those caused by slugs (*see opposite*), eating seedlings and all parts of mature plants.
What to do
In each of the above cases, the pests hide and breed under stones or garden debris during the day, only coming out at night to feed. The most sensible solution is therefore to keep the garden as tidy as possible. Regular and thorough cultivation of the soil will expose millipedes and woodlice to birds, hedgehogs and ground beetles. The snails can be detected by watching out for their slime trails. Pick them off the plants and drop them into a jar of kerosene, or use one of the other methods described for dealing with slugs (see opposite).

ENCOURAGING NATURAL PREDATORS

The organic garden is a far more conducive environment to all forms of wildlife than a chemically controlled one, and the natural balance ensures that there are predators which will feed on garden pests. A simple rule to follow in order to distinguish between "friend" and "foe" in the garden is that pests are generally slow-moving and predators faster and more agile. By careful observation of this pattern, we can learn to let nature take its course and plan to attract helpful creatures into the garden, often eradicating or lessening the need for other forms of pest control.

BIRDS
Although they are usually regarded as something of a garden pest in the productive garden, birds in fact do more good than harm. They eat numerous grubs, caterpillars, slugs and aphids, and can be encouraged into the garden by incorporating food tables, bird baths and nest boxes in your garden plan. Nesting requirements for different birds vary; you can obtain more information from the Cooperative Extension Service or National Audubon Society (*see page 283*).

GROUND BEETLES
Black garden beetles feed on eelworms, cutworms and leatherjackets and other larvae and insect eggs. You can encourage them in your ornamental garden by keeping the ground covered, so that they have leaf cover to hide under during the day. At night they will come out to feed on the pests. Use the closely planted deep-bed system in the vegetable garden to keep the ground covered (*see page 136*) and grow a green-manure plant between crops (*see page 32*).

CENTIPEDES
Centipedes are fast-moving predators of many small insects and slugs. They are light brown with longer legs than millipedes. Like the black beetle, centipedes need ground cover to hide under during the day. At night they will emerge in search of prey, even climbing the plants to reach it.

FROGS AND TOADS
You should definitely try and encourage frogs and toads into the garden, as they are an excellent means of slug control. They also eat woodlice and other small insects. A garden pond is perhaps the ideal environment for them, but they really only need the water for breeding purposes.

HEDGEHOGS/PORCUPINES
A family of hedgehogs is a great boon to any garden, as the creatures devour slugs, cutworms, woodlice, millipedes and wireworms. It is difficult to attract them into the garden but encourage them to stay if you have them. They will hide under piles of logs or hedges so leave a saucer of milk and water or bread soaked in milk near the suspected hiding place.

HOVER-FLIES/FLOWER FLIES
It is the larvae of these creatures, which resemble "thin wasps", that are very useful in the natural control of aphids. The adult flies lay their eggs directly in the aphid colonies and the hatched young are voracious feeders. Hover-flies can be attracted into the garden by planting certain species of flowers such as marigolds (*Tagetes* and *Calendula*) and nasturtiums (*Tropaeolum* sp.), (*see* Companion planting, *page 45*).

LACEWINGS
Again, it is the larvae who have an insatiable appetite for aphids. Adult lacewings lay their eggs on the undersides of leaves. Although they do not feed on flowers they can be encouraged into the garden by varied planting (*see* Companion planting, *page 45*).

LADYBUGS
Both the easily identifiable adult ladybug and its less-familiar, slate-gray larvae eat vast quantities of aphids. They cannot be attracted by specific plants but will be encouraged into the garden by cultivating a varied selection of plants.

Ladybugs *These insects are very attractive and eat aphids.*

General garden diseases

Many diseases only affect specific types of plant and these are dealt with in the relevant sections of the book. Other problems are more general, occurring on the whole range of plants grown in the garden, and some of the most common of these are described below.

TREATING COMMON DISEASES

BOTRYTIS (Gray mold)
This is probably the most common garden disease. It appears as brown spotting or blotching, followed by furry gray mold. Botrytis thrives in cold, damp conditions.

Treating botrytis
Careful handling of seedlings and the provision of good air circulation are essential if botrytis is to be avoided. Be sparing with fertilizers and avoid overwatering, wet mulches and planting in low, shady areas. Infected shoots should be cut off and destroyed.

POWDERY AND DOWNY MILDEWS
A mealy, pale gray coating forms on leaves, buds, flowers and young shoots of a wide range of plants, resulting in yellowing and a general loss of vigor. Downy mildew gets right inside the plant and can eventually kill it, whereas powdery mildew stays on the surface. Powdery mildew is most common on herbaceous plants and roses and is at its worst when plant roots are dry.

Treating mildew
Both diseases thrive in cool, damp and humid conditions. Downy mildew should be treated in the same way as botrytis. Mulching and hand watering will keep it at bay. Remove and burn leaves showing signs of powdery mildew. Spray with a copper fungicide (see opposite).

SOOTY MOLD
This is a superficial black fungus that grows on the sticky secretions of pests such as aphids (*see page 50*). It is not a serious problem but it restricts plant yields.

Treating sooty mold
Control the aphids (see page 50). Once they are eliminated, the mold will disappear.

FUNGUS LEAF SPOT
Leaf spotting can affect the foliage of most plants, especially in wet and high humidity. The *black spot* disease of roses is a common strain. Leaf spots may merge into large dead areas which drop out, and leaves may wither and die.

Treating fungus leaf spot
Proper crop rotation (see page 134) and the provision of adequate air circulation are important factors in the prevention of this disease. Infected plants or parts of plants should be removed and destroyed. Spray the rest of the plant with dispersible sulfur (see opposite). Hard pruning of roses in the autumn will kill off any overwintering spores; destroy all prunings immediately.

RUST
There are many different types of rust affecting a wide range of plants. Leaves and young stems develop yellow, red, brown or black raised pustules. Leaves may then wither and fall and, in severe cases, whole plants can become stunted and even die.

Treating rust
Remove and destroy leaves that have rust spots. Spray the rest of the plant with dispersible sulfur (see opposite). In the case of plants grown in the greenhouse, ensure that the humidity level is not too high and avoid wetting the foliage (see pages 252-54).

Biological control

New research into developing nature's own technique of using one organism to combat another is making significant advances in the area of pest and disease control. This involves using a parasitic insect or fungus, that is, one which lives off one particular living organism known as "the host". Though this "biological control" is, as yet, still in its infancy, it looks likely that this will be the major method of pest and disease control in the future.

The first discovery was the parasitic wasp *Encarsia formosa*, which has long been used by growers and large-scale gardeners to control whitefly in greenhouses. You simply hang a card containing several wasp pupae in the greenhouse and, when the adults emerge, they lay their eggs in the larvae of the whitefly. Control may not always be total but the whitefly are always reduced to acceptable levels.

Red spider mite in greenhouses can be very destructive indeed and are difficult to kill. But by introducing another predatory mite, *Phytoseiulus persimilis*, very effective control can be achieved. Research continues for other biological controls for indoor commercial crops.

There are also parasites which can be used on crops outside. Perhaps the most beneficial of these is a bacterium that attacks the digestive system of some caterpillars. Called *Bacillus thuringiensis*, it is sprayed on to the crop that is under attack. Within a few hours of spraying, it prevents the caterpillars feeding and they die after five days. There is no persistence, so the plants must be sprayed thoroughly so as to hit all the caterpillars directly. The spray is specific only to certain caterpillars and is harmless to other insects. A similar bacterium is available to control Japanese beetle grubs in the soil.

Research into the control of disease by using other diseases is still in its infancy but some progress has been achieved. Silver-leaf disease commonly attacks plums but is sometimes found in other tree fruit. It causes leaves to adopt a silvery sheen and, if allowed to develop, will kill an entire branch. It is caused by the fungus *Stereum purpureum* and can largely be controlled by using a parasitic fungus, *Trichoderma viride*. This has been fixed in the form of pellets which are pushed into holes drilled round the tree trunk at about 7cm (3in) intervals. If this is done before the silver-leaf fungus establishes itself, a satisfactory level of control can be achieved. Some success has been reported using the same treatment against Dutch elm disease.

Organic chemicals

There may be situations when physical pest control does not work or is not suitable, and you have to resort to chemical control. If you are intent on completely blemish-free fruit and sanitized borders then this will be the case. If a plant does have a fungus disease that is not cured by picking off the affected area in the early stages, a fungicide is the only answer.

There are several organic pesticides available that will not harm you or your "friends" in the garden provided they are used with care. The principle of organic pesticides is that they are non-persistent. Most remain active for no more than a day and nearly all are derived from plants.

Organic fungicides are a bit of a gray area. They could not really be said to be organically derived though they are certainly non-persistent. More research is needed in this area but, in the meantime, the fungicides recommended will not harm you or the beneficial wildlife in the garden. The organic chemicals recommended are safe if they come into contact with each other, can be used outside provided there is no wind, and in the greenhouse.

PERMITTED PESTICIDES AND FUNGICIDES

INSECTICIDAL SOAP
This is a potassium-salt soap and is more effective than soft soap in the control of aphids, whitefly, red spider mites, scale insects and mealy bugs. Control can only be achieved by hitting the insect, and the soap persists for only one day.

SOFT SOAP
A traditional control for all kinds of aphids and red spider mite. It can also be mixed with other sprays as a wetting agent, ensuring a better spread and more "stickability" of the insecticide. Soft soap will only kill insects it touches and is persistent for only one day.

QUASSIA
Though harmless to bees and lady-bugs quassia if effective against aphids, some caterpillars, sawfly and leaf miners. It comes from the bark of the *Picrasma quassiodes* tree.

ROTENONE (DERRIS)
A very effective insecticide for controlling pests like caterpillars. It is not, however, selective so it should be used as a last resort. It is also harmful to fish.

PYRETHRUM
Derived from the pyrethrum (*Chrysanthemum coccineum*) plant, and effective against most insects, especially aphids. Unfortunately, beneficial insects will also succumb. As it is non-persistent and acts quickly, it is possible, if you use it carefully, to spray only the pests. Pyrethrum is harmless to animals but it will not harm fish.

NICOTINE
Because nicotine is non-persistent, it is allowed as a pesticide by organic bodies. However, it is poisonous and can be fatal if taken in its concentrated form so should be avoided.

COPPER FUNGICIDE
There are several types of copper fungicide used to control mildews and blights. For example, Bordeaux mixture is a mixture of copper sulfate and slaked lime, Burgundy mixture contains copper sulfate and washing soda. Other types are avilable under various names and all are based on copper sulfate. They consist of liquids or powders that are mixed with water. They coat the leaves and stay active for several weeks, though new growth formed in that time would be uncoated and therefore vulnerable.

DISPERSIBLE SULFUR
Allowed as a fungicide, but only rarely. My own view is that it is not necessary in a well-run organic garden. It can be used against most fungi and is an effective control for rust, against which copper fungicides rarely work satisfactorily.

USING PESTICIDES AND FUNGICIDES
When handling even these "safe" pesticides and fungicides, it is as well to treat them as if they were dangerous.
- Put concentrates in a place where children or inquisitive pets cannot reach them.
- Always leave chemicals in their own bottles.
- Dilute as specified on the bottle.
- Avoid spraying beneficial insects because these chemicals are not selective.
- Use a good sprayer to apply the chemicals and wash it out thoroughly after use between sprayings. Never keep the leftover solution, pour it down the drain.
- Spray only on a windless day and always in the cool of the late evening, when all the good, respectable insects have turned in for the night.
- Never spray any open flowers, especially of fruit, for fear of harming bees.

ORGANIC WEED CONTROL

THERE IS no such thing as an organic weedkiller, and whatever may be claimed about the safety of chemical weedkillers, there is always danger in their use. If there wasn't, there would be no need for the elaborate testing and strict controls enforced by governments. Chemical manufacturers have, however, tried to persuade us that we must follow the commercial grower in soaking our plants and our soil with poisons when there are very few advantages and many dangers in doing so. The commercial grower's problem is just not the same as ours, and there is no doubt that prolonged use of chemicals has a very damaging effect on soil organisms.

It may seem attractive to use a chemical to kill everything in a new garden so that you can start clean and stay on top of the weeds. It is certainly an easier way out, but it is done at the risk of killing the beneficial inhabitants of the soil and even harming yourself. At a horticultural research station in England a few years ago, during a quite unconnected experiment on soils, it was noticed that in the soil on land that had been regularly treated with a paraquat/diquat mixture there were no earthworms. Subsequent examination revealed that most other beneficial soil organisms were either reduced in numbers or not present.

Having tested chemical weedkillers under garden conditions for many years, I am also strongly of the opinion that there is no advantage in their use in order to save labor. It is so awkward and time consuming to apply them between cultivated plants and the process often takes longer than the traditional organic methods. Of course there are some weeds that are very troublesome, such as couch grass (*Agropyron repens*) and ground elder (*Aegopodium podagraria*), but it is always possible to control them, and eventually to eradicate them, without resorting to chemicals, though in some cases it may take quite a long time. Weeds with tap roots, fleshy roots that go straight down into the soil, such as dandelions, can be a problem. As an experiment, I once nailed a big old dock root to the shed door and left it there for two years to suffer scorching sun, drying winds and frost. When I planted it again two years later it grew away as if the rest had done it good! There is only one way with these perennials and that is to dig them up, destroy them or put them in the garbage.

THE PRINCIPLES OF WEED CONTROL

Whether you are trying to clear a new garden of weeds, or deal with their habitual menace in an established one, there are many physical methods of weed control outlined on the following pages. The basic principles to remember all the time are as follows:

● All green plants must have access to sunshine to survive. There are a variety of light-deprivation measures that can be used by the organic gardener to control weeds.
● Constant vigilance is very important; remove weeds as soon as you see them. Regular hoeing will deny persistent weeds a foothold.
● Never let weeds flower or seed. Cutting them down and digging out the roots takes a moment, while coping with the hundreds of seedlings they may disperse is a time-consuming job.

Clearing uncultivated ground

If you are starting a brand new garden, taking over a weed-infested one or incorporating a new area, the first stage in weed control is to make the ground as clean as possible right from the start. First, clear the ground completely by digging it, removing weeds as you progress. Then cover the ground; sow the lawn area and plant a "cleaning crop" in the borders (*see page 56*).

DIGGING THE ENTIRE PLOT
Begin by digging over the whole site and removing as much as you possibly can. If the ground is

Controlling weeds with gravel top
*Spreading a layer of coarse gravel, at least
5cm (2in) thick, around ornamental plants
provides an effective and attractive
barrier against weed growth.*

Covering soil with plastic above
*Although black plastic is not suitable for
the ornamental garden, it is a cheap, yet
effective, way of covering soil to inhibit weed
growth in the vegetable garden.*

Mulching with bark left
*A covering of pine bark chippings controls
weeds by blocking the light. It looks
attractive and lasts for several years.*

infested with one of the more pernicious weeds, like couch grass (*Agropyron repens*) or ground elder (*Aegopodium podagraria*), you should not expect to win first time as any tiny piece of root that is left in the soil may multiply to form a massive root again.

Annual weeds can then be put on to the compost heap provided they have not been allowed to seed (*see page 21*). Roots of other perennial weeds, those that continue year after year, such as dandelions (*Taraxacum officinale*), and docks (*Rumex* sp.) should be removed and destroyed. Never put any perennial weeds on the compost heap because they will only be transplanted again when you spread the compost.

SOWING THE LAWN AREA

If you plan to lay a lawn, the area can be sown straight away after digging (*see page 79*). Even if the weeds do come through again, regular use of a mower will eventually eradicate all but the "rosetted" types like dandelions and daisies which grow close to the ground. They are easy to control afterwards by simply dropping a pinch of table salt into the center of the rosette (*see page 81*) or by digging them out of the lawn with a penknife. You may have to repeat the process a few times but they will disappear.

PLANTING A "CLEANING CROP"

Areas planned for ornamental borders or vegetable and fruit plots, in fact any bare soil, should be planted for the first year with a "cleaning crop". There is none better than potatoes, which will not only help clean the soil of weeds but will pay for themselves into the bargain. Potatoes have two great virtues as a cleaning crop. First of all their cultivation entails turning over the soil three times in the year – once when they are planted, a second time when they are earthed up and finally at harvest time. Secondly, they grow a dense canopy of leaves which excludes the light from any weeds that may be bold enough to try to compete. Together, starvation of light and not being allowed a foothold encourage most weeds to give up the ghost.

Nonetheless, some weeds still survive. Plants that climb by twining round their competitors, such as bindweed (*Convolvulus arvensis*), will not be crowded out so easily. Their climbing habit enables them to reach the sunlight even through a dense canopy of leaves, so they can always make enough food to store in their labyrinthine root system. So, in the second year, you will still have problems. But, on a small scale, they are not difficult to overcome.

PREVENTING WEEDS FROM SPREADING

There are two sources of nuisance – weed seeds flying over the fence and settling on your land, and weeds with creeping roots coming underneath the fence. The first problem is solved by asking your neighbors for permission to cut down any weeds before they seed. Accompany your request with a couple of your fresh lettuce and you may even shame them into doing it themselves. To cope with weeds that creep under the fence, you will have to install a barrier that runs deep into the soil to discourage encroaching roots. This provides effective protection for life.

1 *Close the hole between the bottom of the fence and the ground by digging out a little soil and nailing a 15×2.5cm (6×1in) board along the base of the fencing panels.*

2 *Dig a trench along the entire length of the fence. The trench must be deep enough to remove up to 15cm (6in) of subsoil.*

3 *Then put in a "wall" of heavy-gauge plastic, Nail one edge to the bottom of the wooden board so that the sheet hangs down to the bottom of the trench.*

Hoeing

The hoe is the most effective tool in your armory, and it should be used regularly, preferably during dry weather. By pulling it through the top layer of soil you can uproot any weeds that appear.

If you are waging war against persistent weeds like bindweed (*Convolvulus arvensis*), horsetail (*Equisetum arvense*), or couch grass (*Agropyron repens*), you should never allow them to reach that stage. The rule here is to hoe before you see any weeds at all on the surface. If you do that you will cut off the growing tips while they are still beneath the surface and before they have had a chance to benefit from the sun.

It is fairly easy to cope with weeds in the vegetable plot because they are easily seen, but in the borders they have a habit of hiding under foliage. So, when you take your evening walk round the garden in spring and summer, take a Dutch hoe with you and make a point of tickling between a few plants with it. Naturally, if you see so much as a glimpse of a weed, you must remove it immediately.

It must be stressed that hoeing will only kill persistent perennial weeds if you prevent them from getting above the soil surface. If you allow such weeds to do this, and you then turn them in or, even worse, chop them up with a power tiller, you will simply propagate them and make matters much worse.

DUTCH HOE

For weeding, a Dutch hoe is probably best (*see page 259*). It should be used walking backwards to avoid treading on the weeds once they are uprooted. If you walk forwards you will probably push them back into the soil and effectively transplant them, while walking backwards leaves any weeds sitting on the soil surface, a prey to drying winds and the heat of the sun.

WHEEL HOE

I would never be without a wheel hoe, particularly in the vegetable garden. This is a hand-pushed tool with a single wheel at the front and a cutting blade behind it. It may seem that there would be very little advantage in this over the conventional Dutch hoe but it is, in fact, very much quicker. Once you have hoed between the rows a couple of times to create a soft layer of soil on the top of the path, it is no trouble to push the hoe along at a slow walking pace.

If you do decide to invest in one, it is a good idea to adjust the distance between the rows when planting to suit the width of the hoe. If this makes the rows too close together so that plants are in danger of competing with one

another or too far apart so that land is being wasted, simply adjust the planting width in the row. So, if you would normally plant, say, onions with 23cm (9in) between the rows and 15cm (6in) between each onion in the row, make the rows 30cm (12in) apart to suit the hoe width and allow 7cm (3in) between the plants in the row. This will save you a lot of time.

Using a Dutch hoe *Most crops have shallow roots so keep the blade of the hoe no more than 15mm (½in) below the surface of the soil.*

Using a wheel hoe *Push the blade at the back of the hoe into the ground between two rows of vegetables, again keeping it shallow.*

Mulching

An effective way to exclude light and prevent weeds appearing is by mulching (covering the soil surface with a layer of one of several materials). Some mulching materials are not very attractive to look at, so you will want to use different materials in the vegetable and fruit garden to those used in the ornamental borders. Bear in mind, though, that the most effective and attractive method of keeping weeds out of the ornamental borders is to provide competition in the form of plants that create a canopy over the soil. Ground-cover plants are useful in this respect (see page 90).

BLACK PLASTIC

One of the most effective mulches for eradicating perennial weeds is black plastic. When the plastic is laid over the soil, no light at all can reach the leaves and the weeds will die. They will try to work their way to the sides of the mulch and appear there, so keep a special lookout at the edges of the sheeting and be ready with the hoe. The sheeting must be anchored securely or high winds will get underneath and tear it or even blow it away (see below).

Black plastic is an ideal method in the vegetable garden or between rows of fruit. Before laying the sheeting, cultivate the soil between the rows and mound it slightly in the center so that the rain will run off the sheet towards the base of the plants.

Another method is to lay a wide sheet across the entire bed and plant through it by cutting small cross slits. This is ideal for strawberries and potatoes and there is no reason why it should not be used for any other long-term crops like cabbages, cauliflowers and Brussels sprouts. This is particularly useful for potatoes because they will not need to be earthed up (see page 185).

The advantage with a wide strip is that a much bigger area can be kept weed free with no chance of weeds sprouting out between the edges of the sheeting. The disadvantage is that it is very difficult to water. The best way is to lay a seep-hose (see page 260) underneath the sheeting and leave it there for the season. This will seep water along its whole length, so all you need to do is attach a hose to it at intervals to give the soil a good soaking. There will be little water loss through surface evaporation so less water will be required than normal.

Naturally, plastic is not attractive enough to be used on its own on the borders. It can, on the other hand, be covered with gravel or even a thin layer of soil to enhance the appearance.

PAPER AND BIODEGRADABLE PLASTIC

Of the biodegrable materials available, use tough brown paper rather than the biodegradable plastic. The latter is supposed to avoid the necessity of removing the mulch when the crop has been harvested but, in fact, the plastic deteriorates into strips which blow about all over the garden. The tough brown paper is used in exactly the same way as plastic –

Weighting down plastic *It is essential to ensure that plastic sheeting is well held down with bricks. If it is not secure, wind will blow it away and this could damage plants.*

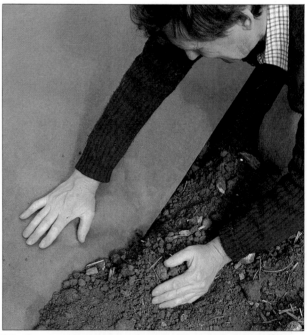

Digging in plastic or paper *The best way to secure plastic or paper is to bury the edges in shallow trenches around the edge of the bed.*

Spreading a bark mulch *Push the chippings right under the plants to cover all exposed soil in the border.*

Small electric shredders will efficiently get rid of all your woody prunings. The wood chips may look rather obtrusive in the borders, but they soon lose their stark white appearance.

Using an electric chipping machine *Put a bucket under the front of the machine to catch the chippings, then feed two or three lengths of tree prunings into the machine at a time.*

simply roll it out on to cultivated and levelled soil, anchor the edges by burying them in a shallow trench and then plant through pre-cut slits. After the crops have been harvested it is either dug or rotatilled into the soil, where it will rot down. This is ideal for use on deep beds. Paper can also be used in the ornamental garden without a covering of gravel since it is much less obtrusive than plastic (*see opposite*).

NEWSPAPER

A cheaper, but more time-consuming, alternative is to use newspaper. Lay about six sheets on top of one another, and again, anchor the edges by burying them. The paper tends to go quite hard and will certainly not rot for quite some time or until it is dug into the soil after harvesting.

PEAT AND COMPOST

A much more attractive mulch can be achieved using a 5-7cm (2-3in) layer of a loose material like peat. This is ideal because it is a fairly inert, acid medium and therefore inhospitable to weed seedlings. Although garden compost or manure should certainly be used for mulching in order to improve the soil structure and add nutrients, do not expect them to prevent weeds appearing unless the layer is very thick indeed. The weeds, of course, feel as much at home in compost or manure as do the plants you are cultivating, so they will welcome a shallow layer.

BARK MULCHES

The most effective material in the ornamental borders is either shredded or chipped bark. It is available in various grades of coarseness and it does not seem to make much difference which one is used. They should all go on at about 7cm (3in) thick and this should be sufficient to control all annual weeds and many perennials too. I have used it on a bed previously plagued with Canada thistle (*Cirsium arvense*) and not had to weed at all for two years.

The big disadvantage with bark of all types is the price. It is very expensive, although one application will last several years. A cheaper alternative is to invest in a wood chipper (*see above*) and make your own wood chips, even though it does take some time to make enough.

GRASS CUTTINGS

If they are applied thickly enough straight from the mower box, grass cuttings are effective as a mulch for weed control. However, they must be at least 15cm (6in) deep, and this can lead to problems. If the layer is too thick, no air will reach the bottom and if rotted down anaerobically (*see page 21*), they become a smelly, slimy mass and are not only unpleasant but also quite useless as a soil conditioner. Grass cuttings do not look very attractive either, so I would rather put them on the compost heap or leave them on the lawn if not too thick.

Recognizing weeds

Of course, not all weeds are to be despised and the organic gardener who gets rid of them all is wasting a valuable natural asset. Many weeds will attract insect predators, some also provide food for birds and butterflies and others, like the clovers (*Trifolium* sp.), can be used to fix nitrogen in the soil (*see page 34*). So, before making an indiscriminate onslaught on native plants, pause for thought. Indeed, I recommend growing cultivated plants in the ornamental garden that are close to their original wild species because they will attract the same insect life.

However, I am not suggesting that you allow nature to take over, as your cultivated "foreigners" will be at the mercy of some pretty tough "locals", who will give scant regard to "entente cordiale". Most weeds must be rigorously controlled, but there are a few that should be allowed to stay if you have room. I have grouped together those which have to be removed ("Bad Weeds") and those which can be beneficial ("Good Weeds").

BAD WEEDS

The underground creepers should never be allowed to flourish or they will take over in next to no time. Amongst these be particularly ruthless with ground elder (*Aegopodium podagraria*), bindweed (*Convolvulus arvensis*), couch grass (*Agropyron repens*), Canada thistle (*Cirsium arvense*), rosebay willow-herb (*Epilobium angustifolium*) and Japanese knotweed (*Polygonum cuspidatum*). The surface creepers like creeping buttercup (*Ranunculus repens*), ground ivy (*Glechoma hederacea*) and cinquefoil (*Potentilla* sp.) are slightly easier to control, but be diligent.

Weeds that spread by seed are not difficult to control, provided they are pulled out or cut down before they have a chance to seed. Keep an eye out for bull thistle (*Cirsium vulgare*) and broad-leaved willow-herb (*Epilobium montanum*).

Plants with tap roots (long, thick, fleshy roots that go straight down into the soil) like docks (*Rumex* sp.) and cow parsley (*Anthriscus sylvestris*) should be dug out.

Storage roots (tubers, corms, bulbs or rhizomes) often break off in the soil when the plant is pulled up and this can be a means of propagation. The worst of the lot is oxalis, which must be dealt with as soon as it shows even an exploratory leaf! Constant hoeing is the only answer, unless you can leave a sheet of black plastic in place for at least a year.

GOOD WEEDS

Having made sure that the real villains are banished forever, try to give room to some of the less invasive plants. As gardeners, our interest lies in the cultivation of plants for beauty and interest and for the purpose of feeding our families. How far you allow nature to take over is a matter of judgement and will depend largely on the size of your garden, and the range of wild plants you can grow will depend upon the soil, site and location. In my own garden the pretty yellow snapdragon flowers of toadflax (*Linaria vulgaris*) and the pure white clusters of white campion (*Lychnis alba*) or red campion (*Lychnis dioica*) are always allowed to remain. In the borders where these "weeds" have access to artificially fertile soil, they really thrive and produce flowers that rival any cultivated hybrid.

It has been said that if the dandelion (*Taraxacum officinale*) only grew in Tibet, we would be sending plant hunters to collect it and we would pay huge sums of money to nurserymen to propagate it. It may be common, but it is an undeniably pretty flower. Do not let it seed, however, or it will outstay its welcome.

The stinging nettle (*Urtica dioica*) is an antisocial plant, but do allow some to remain if you can because it is an extremely important food for butterflies.

The corn poppy (*Papaver rhoeas*) used to be a common sight before chemical weedkillers made it virtually extinct in cornfields. It is a favorite with finches when it seeds, so it is certainly worth growing.

Groundsel (*Senecio vulgaris*) and herb robert (*Geranium robertianum*) are valuable nectar plants for butterflies and bees, but can be a nuisance if allowed to seed.

If you have an old tree stump in the garden, you can make an attractive feature of it by covering it with ivy (*Hedera helix*). Many birds and insects use ivy as a home and a food plant.

Allow chickweed (*Stellaria media*) to grow in winter to help prevent the ground becoming waterlogged. It will rot down after digging in, supplementing compost and manure. Do not let it grow in summer as, once it gets a hold, it can be particularly troublesome.

The teasel (*Dipsacus fullonum*) is a tall, stately plant with large seed heads which attract goldfinches, who will travel far for the seeds. The flowers attract butterflies and other insects.

Another insect attractor is lamb's quarters (*Chenopodium album*), which was a favorite vegetable in the Middle Ages.

Finally, there are the leguminous plants that will fix nitrogen and release it into the soil once they are dug in. For example, the medicks (*Medicago* sp.) and clovers (*Trifolium* sp.) can be allowed to remain in winter.

WEEDS TO REMOVE FROM THE GARDEN

CREEPING BUTTERCUP right
Ranunculus repens
Found on damp soils, this weed produces long creeping stems which spread across the soil. It also spreads by seeding.

GROUND IVY above
Glechoma hederacea
A vigorous perennial which quickly becomes invasive. Its small, hairy leaves have serrated edges and a distinctive minty smell.

CINQUEFOIL above
Potentilla sp.
A persistent perennial weed with very long, creeping stems. Each leaf is made up of five leaflets.

BROAD-LEAVED WILLOW-HERB left
Epilobium montanum
This very common weed has pointed oval leaves and small purple flowers with yellow centers. Pull plants out as soon as you see them.

COW PARSLEY above
Anthriscus sylvestris
The fern-like leaves are pale green in color. The distinctive flower heads are made up of a mass of tiny white flowers.

BULL THISTLE above
Cirsium vulgare
The leaves are sharply pointed and spined. The purple flowers produce numerous seeds.

OXALIS above
Oxalis sp.
Control by hoeing, preferably before the leaves reach the surface, or by covering the ground with black plastic.

BROAD-LEAVED DOCK above
Rumex obtusifolius
Docks have a fleshy tap root and long, broad, dark-green leaves.

GROUND ELDER left
Aegopodium podagraria
The oval leaves have a strong smell if crushed. It spreads very quickly, soon taking over if allowed to remain.

COUCH GRASS below
Agropyron repens
A very invasive grass. Its roots spread quickly to form a dense underground mat. A tiny piece broken from this can produce a new plant.

ROSEBAY WILLOW-HERB below left
Epilobium angustifolium
The purple flowers produce many seeds making this a very invasive weed.

JAPANESE KNOTWEED below
Polygonum cuspidatum
This weed has oval leaves and small white flowers. Its roots are difficult to destroy.

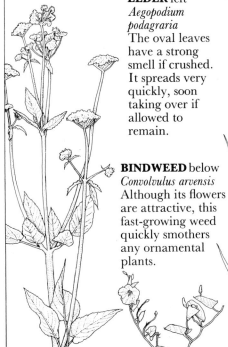

CANADA THISTLE below
Cirsium arvense
The serrated leaves are very prickly and flowers are a pale lilac color. The flower stalks do not bear thorns as most other thistles do.

BINDWEED below
Convolvulus arvensis
Although its flowers are attractive, this fast-growing weed quickly smothers any ornamental plants.

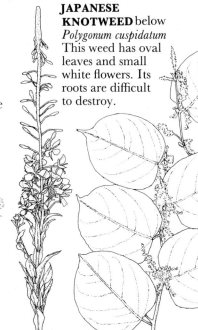

Useful weeds

Not all weeds are to be despised, and the gardener who pulls them all out regardless is wasting a valuable natural asset. Of course, weeds should not be grown where they will compete with cultivated plants but, next time, think again before you dig up the useful weeds shown here.

DANDELION below
Taraxacum officinale
Rich in minerals, young dandelion leaves blend wonderfully into salads and the roots make a caffeine-free coffee substitute. Also attracts butterflies and bullfinches.

HERB ROBERT right
Geranium robertianum
An attractive annual that seeds and colonizes quickly. It will quickly cover even the poorest soil, thus providing cover for pest predators and organic matter for the soil when it dies down.

BLACK MEDICK above
Medicago lupulina
A nitrogen-fixing plant. It also attracts butterflies, bees and hover-flies.

LAMB'S QUARTERS right
Chenopodium album
Attracts hover-flies, which eat aphids, and bees. High in iron, protein, calcium and vitamin B, and an excellent spinach substitute.

RED CAMPION right
Lychnis dioica
Attracts bees which pollinate flowers. Also butterflies and moths – drawn by a perfume released by the plant at night – which attract birds. When cultivated, the size of the flowers increases.

CHICKWEED below
Stellaria media
Good source of green manure
because it grows rapidly. Birds
like to eat the seeds of this plant.

TOADFLAX above
Linaria vulgaris
Good source of nectar;
a decorative plant
with delicate,
yellow flowers.

CLOVER above
Trifolium sp.
Nitrogen-fixing plant, taking
nitrogen from the air and
fixing it in the soil in a form
which is later accessible to
other plants.

POPPY right
Papaver rhoeas
Butterflies and
bees are attracted
by the red flowers,
and birds are drawn
to the seeds.

TEASEL left
Dipsacus fullonum
An outstanding biennial,
often cultivated in the
ornamental garden for its
striking seed heads. Birds
are attracted to the seeds
in the autumn.

NETTLE left
Urtica dioica
Important food
plant for butterflies;
the young leaves
can be boiled and
eaten as a spinach
substitute.

GROUNDSEL left
Senecio vulgaris
Good source of nectar
for butterflies and
bees, although not an
attractive plant.

IVY left
Hedera helix
Provides nesting ground and
vital cover for birds. Attracts
butterflies and bees.

PLANNING YOUR GARDEN

A SUCCESSFUL ORGANIC GARDEN depends upon growing a wide diversity of plants, including as many native plants as possible, in order to attract wildlife and useful pest predators. The result will inevitably be informal. There is, however, no reason why an informal garden should look neglected or untidy and, indeed, there is every reason why it should not. Pests and diseases go hand-in-hand with a slovenly approach to gardening; a neat and tidy garden, where regular cultivation keeps unwanted weeds at bay and where you remove rubbish before it has a chance to accumulate, is bound to be more efficient and productive.

My own belief is that a garden is essentially a personal place, and so its final design must be something that you have conceived and put into practice yourself. We all have the innate creative ability to transform that muddy patch of ground outside the back door into a beautiful, productive and, above all, enjoyable place in which to be. And bear in mind that, no matter how inexperienced you are, nature will give you a hand along the way.

WHERE DO YOU START?

First, take account of the physical characteristics of your garden – the soil type, the direction it faces and so on. Second, draw up lists of the features that you need to include in your garden such as windbreaks, or trash storage areas – and the features you would like, such as a vegetable garden, compost bins, a greenhouse or a terrace. Then, before you start any real gardening, draw up a plan of your garden and work out where you want to site things in relation to each other. These principles apply if you are starting a garden from scratch, taking over an established garden, or simply changing to organic gardening.

The physical characteristics of your garden

When contemplating the overall plan of your garden, consider its physical characteristics, such as the direction it faces, your local climate, and the type of soil you have to work with – clay, peat, silt, sand or limestone (*see pages 14-15*).

The features that are within your power to change, or improve, include drainage and the quality of your soil and the contour of the land. The techniques for improving them, however, will vary according to the soil type of your situation (*see below and pages 18-34*).

Aspect and climate

It is not possible to do anything about your garden's orientation and you can rarely remove shade, which is generally caused by the house, walls or fences. Likewise you can do nothing about the weather. Altitude, rainfall and the wind will all dictate certain features of the

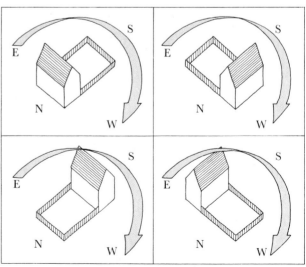

The garden's aspect *The direction your house and garden face will affect the amount of sun the garden receives. The diagrams above show the difference between north-, south-, east- and west-facing gardens: north-facing gardens can be cold and sunless, whereas a south-facing garden receives full sun all day.*

Frost pockets *Cold air tends to flow downhill so hollows in the land may trap frost. If your garden is in a frost hollow, choose late-flowering or hardier plants that can withstand the cold.*

garden, such as the amount of shade and protection you need to provide. If frosts are a regular occurrence, or you live in a frost-pocket (a low-lying area where frost accumulates), make sure that you use the correct type of hedging or fencing to minimize the problem (*see above*), and that you choose late-flowering or especially hardy plants that are not going to lose fruit and flowers every time the weather turns cold.

Soil types

There are five main soil types – clay, silt, sand, limestone and peat. Each one is made up of a mixture of minerals, the proportions of which are highly variable even within a small area. An important consideration with soil types is the degree of acidity or alkalinity, or the lime content (*see page 35*). Certain plants prefer certain types of soil and, while you can do much to improve the general fertility or drainage qualities of a poor soil (*see pages 262-65*), and even make special provisions for "unsuitable plants", it is easier, in the ornamental areas, to grow plants that are happy in the existing soil conditions. You may, though, have to take measures to alter the soil pH for your vegetable and fruit areas (*see pages 34-6*).

Steep slopes

Steep slopes are difficult to maintain. It is much better to terrace the garden to form a series of "plateaux" linked by paths or steps even though this involves a great deal of hard work initially.

It is not good enough simply to level the topsoil because that results in an extra deep layer of topsoil at the front and very little at the back. The only satisfactory way is to dig off all the topsoil from the area and level the subsoil before replacing it (*see right*).

FENCING

The easiest material to use for fencing on a slope is a wire fence, a length of plastic windbreak or even posts and rails because they can be made to follow the general fall of the land. Don't, however, try to follow every little rise and fall or the top of the fence will go up and down like a

ELIMINATING A SLOPE

The only satisfactory method of removing a slope is to dig off the topsoil and then level the subsoil before re-spreading the topsoil. The new soil level should be held back by building either retaining walls or banks.

Link the different levels of the garden with ramps or a series of stone or paved steps. Alternatively, make steps out of strong wood (old railway ties are ideal) held in position with stout stakes firmly secured in the ground. Fill in the area between the ties with soil, gravel or chipped bark. These informal steps blend in particularly well if you have planned the garden on the "cottage-garden" principle (*see page 71*). It is also possible to connect different levels of a garden with ramps if this is more convenient for you.

Levelling slopes *If you want to form a series of "stepped" borders, remove all the topsoil from the area, level the subsoil, then replace the topsoil, spreading it evenly. Build a supporting wall at the front to hold the topsoil in the bed.*

Wooden steps above
A cheap way of linking parts of your garden is with wooden steps. The steps shown here were made with railway ties. Hammer stakes into the ground behind them and nail them to the ties.

Stone steps right
Slabs of stone can be used to make attractive steps. Use stone or brick to make the step "risers".

switchback: try instead to even it out to form one overall slope.

Panel fencing is difficult to put up on a slope because the panels cannot be erected to follow the line of the slope; it would mean putting the posts in at an angle. On gently sloping ground, you can erect the panels vertically in a series of "steps". Make sure you take this into account when you buy your fencing material because you may need to order slightly more panels and longer fence posts than normal. Panel fencing is unsuitable for steeply sloping ground because you will get gaps at one end of each panel.

FENCING FOR SLOPES

If your garden slopes, putting up fencing needs a little thought. Choose a type that can be made to follow the slope and make sure that the fence posts are exactly upright.

Post-and-wire link fence

Post-and-rail fence

Fencing along a slope *These fences are ideal for slopes because they can be built to follow the line of the slope. You can plant a hedge in front of a post-and-rail fence or grow climbing plants up a wire fence.*

Fencing across a slope *If you have to build a fence across a slope, leave at least 30cm (1ft) of space between the bottom of the fence and the ground so that cold air can flow underneath and out of the garden.*

On sloping ground, fencing built across a slope can act as a barrier that prevents frost-laden air moving downhill and out of the garden, creating a frost pocket. To avoid the problem, raise the bottom of the fence slightly to allow air to flow underneath.

Improving drainage

It is easy to recognize a badly drained site, since the garden, or large parts of it, will be wet under foot and water may lie on the top, particularly in winter. Compacted topsoil or an impervious layer of compacted soil beneath the soil surface, particularly on a new garden, are common reasons for bad drainage. You can do a great deal to improve the drainage by good soil management (*see page 262*). A heavy soil such as clay, for example, can be greatly improved by digging in organic matter and coarse grit.

In very badly drained gardens, however, you may have to install a drainage system, and you will have to do this before anything else.

DRAINAGE SYSTEMS

If your soil really does drain badly, you need to install a drainage system. It is relatively easy to install the drain pipes, but not as simple to dispose of the water. If you have a ditch at the end of your garden, there is no problem. Otherwise, you should run your land drains into the storm drains that feed into the sewer system or the local authority's drainage system. Seek permission from the local authority before connecting up your garden drains in this way because it is illegal in some areas. Installing a drainage system is discussed in more detail in *Basic Techniques* (*see page 263*).

Garden boundaries

You will almost certainly need some sort of fencing or hedge around your garden for privacy. There are many different types of man-made fencing available so choose one to suit your needs and to blend with your house and style of garden.

In addition, if you live in an exposed position, fencing or hedging can go a long way to protecting your plants from high winds. Winds can be particularly damaging to all plants, especially in the winter if they are not protected by a covering of snow. If protected, your fruit and vegetables will produce heavier crops and your ornamental plants will grow and flower better too.

BARRIERS FOR WIND PROTECTION
The most effective windbreaks are those that merely slow the wind down, such as hedges, slatted wooden fences or barriers made from

Enhancing a brick wall *You can soften the effect of a brick wall by removing individual bricks, filling the gaps with soil and planting alpine plants, such as these purple aubrietas.*

Disguising a barrier *A wooden trellis serves as a practical barrier, but can also become a decorative feature when climbing plants, such as this white clematis, are grown against it.*

perforated plastic windbreak material. Solid barriers can be worse than useless as wind protection unless they are extremely high. When the wind comes up against a solid obstruction, it tends to whip over the top and swirl and eddy over the other side, increasing in speed during the process. If you are using man-made barriers, make sure that the posts are sunk deep into the ground and, if you are using a plastic windbreak material, fix it to the fence posts with battens. Do this by laying the windbreak material against the posts then nailing battens over the top.

HEDGES

Hedges make very good garden boundaries as they are far less obtrusive than man-made barriers. They also make the best windbreaks. You can choose from either formal hedges or informal ones, those that are allowed to flower (*see page 76*). Hedges do, however, take up a lot of growing room because they will compete with other plants for water and nutrients. Never, for example, choose privet (*Ligustrum ovalifolium*) unless you are prepared to sacrifice at least 1 meter/yard along either side of the length of the hedge. If your garden is small, choose a formal hedge that can be kept compact by clipping. Choose informal hedges only if your garden is large because they need at least 1-2m (3-6ft) growing room either side.

If your garden is on a slope, make sure that your hedge does not act as a barrier, preventing frost-laden air escaping (*see opposite*). Keep the area under the hedge cleaned out to allow air to pass through freely and to stop pests using the debris as winter cover.

Features to include in your garden

While you are carrying out the necessary ground work, you must think about the features you want to include in the garden and the eventual scheme you wish to achieve. Working out a plan isn't easy because there are so many possibilities. Take time over it and put your ideas on to paper first. Your budget may not allow you to complete your chosen garden design all at once but an overall plan will at least give cohesion to the finished product.

ALLOWING FOR THE ESSENTIALS

Start by making a list of the features that you simply must include in your garden – a clothes line, for example, a coal bunker or wood shed, a place to hide trash cans, or a gate to stop the children running out into the road. If you are simply changing over to organic methods, then you may already have these features; nonetheless, put them on the list in case you want to improve them, move them, or even dispense with them completely.

DESIRABLE FEATURES

In my experience, the things you would like to include in your garden always exceed the space available, so draw up a list in order of priority. If you have a family, you may decide that a large vegetable and fruit plot is most important, but that you also need an area in which the children can play, and a leisure area for yourself. After all, gardening is not all hard work!

In any organic garden, you will certainly need an ornamental area where you can grow some of the plants that attract birds and insect predators (*see pages 45 and 51*). If you have space for a greenhouse or a cold frame, make sure you include this. And don't forget to allow room for the utility area – the compost containers, the manure heap (if you are lucky enough to be able to get any) and the tool shed.

Water

From a strictly practical point of view, a water supply is absolutely essential to allow you to maintain the garden. Ideally, you should have an outside tap and a hose pipe long enough to allow you to water every part of the garden. With long gardens, you might want to install a stand-pipe at the far end. If this is your intention then make sure you lay the necessary pipes at an early stage of garden preparation.

Hard surfaces

It is important to decide the position of the hard surfaces, such as terraces and paths, before you decide anything else because they determine the level and position of many other garden features. Bear in mind right at the planning stage that areas of concrete or gravel can look stark against the background of a plant-filled

Positioning plants in containers *Large areas of paving are an integral part of many gardens, but they can look stark. Here, the problem is countered by pots of bright orange lilies.*

garden, so try to allow for softening by including raised beds or leaving space for plant-filled tubs.

TERRACES

If you decide on an area of paving for sitting out in the garden, you do not necessarily have to build it against the house, though this is certainly the most convenient place. For example, if the back of your house faces north, it will be a bleak place to sit; on the other hand, if you live in a hot sunny climate, you may prefer to sit out in the shade.

Make the area a useful shape. A narrow strip of paving or concrete running along the back of the house is almost useless, since there is simply not enough room for a table and chairs. A square or triangular area in one corner is more practical and requires no more slabs.

If you decide to butt paving up against the side of the house, take a careful look at the level of the damp-proof course on your house, or any airbricks. Paving slabs must finish no less than two courses of bricks below the level or you risk damp creeping into the house.

Use paving material that blends in with your style of garden and the house itself. Soften stark and intrusive lines by leaving a few spaces between the slabs and then include some low-growing plants such as alpines (*see pages 123-4*) that thrive in a well-drained soil and need sun.

Edging paved areas with raised flower beds allows you to bring color right up to the house; edging them with a hedge provides both privacy and a windbreak, if this is necessary. If you plan for it at the outset, it is relatively easy to build a barbecue into the paving.

PATHS

In my view, you should only use paths where they are absolutely essential because they tend to cut gardens into pieces. In a small garden, that is a disaster. If you must have a path, make it curved, so that it disappears from view here and there, giving the illusion of hidden nooks and crannies. In large gardens you can use paths extremely effectively to link one feature with another. I like to see them in either gravel or, better still, grass. Never make a dead straight path in a small, informal garden or allow a path to run either across the plot or straight down the middle.

There are some situations where a path is essential – however large or small your garden. If you have children, there is likely to be a lot of washing so you will need easy access, via a path, to a clothes line. In this case, it will probably also have to be straight, so try to site it at the edge of the garden where you can hide it with a border of flowers.

An extremely attractive way of making paths, particularly in small gardens, is to use stepping stones set in gravel. Space the stones out so that

Using bold lines *Although a path is generally considered a necessity, there is no reason why it should not be made into an attractive feature. Here, simple gray and white paving slabs provide a contrast to the colorful raised beds.*

A subtle approach *This simple gravel path is designed to act as an inconspicuous foil to the brightly colored trees and border plants. Its soft curves serve to define the shape of the central ornamental bed, without distracting attention from it.*

they deliberately slow you down, giving you the opportunity to enjoy the beauty of your garden, and plant alpines in the spaces (*see page 124*).

The lawn area

An area of grass is a highly desirable garden feature. It makes an excellent feeding place for birds, a comfortable playing surface for children, and a superb "foil" to the plants in the borders.

When planning a lawn you will also, as a result, be shaping the flower borders. Bear in mind that, if you are going to adopt traditional "cottage garden" mixed borders – with swathes of tall and short annuals and perennials, including many native plants to attract suitable wild-

life, then there is no place for formality. You should lay out the edges of the grass in long, sweeping curves to produce borders of varying widths. Long, simplified sweeps of grass make the garden look bigger and are easier to cut.

If you have the room, allow a small patch of grass to grow tall and sow some wild flowers to help attract useful insect predators (*see page 125*). The "miniature meadow" will soon become a very attractive feature. You can also include some bulbs with the wild flowers (*see page 118*).

Ponds

An area of water is particularly useful in an organic garden if you want to increase the range of wildlife you attract. If you have a small pool you will attract birds and insects, frogs and many other pest predators. You can make a pool by digging a hole and lining it with a butyl-rubber liner (*see page 122*) or simply bury plastic containers and fill them with water.

Remember, though, that any water is dangerous if you have young children. It may be worth including a bird bath until they are older.

Plan your pool with rounded edges, instead of harsh angles, to blend in with a more informal garden. And allow for very shallow water at the edges, or provide a ledge in the side of the pond, so that you can include marginal or bog-loving plants and a marshy area. If you are lucky, you will also attract frogs and that keeps your slug problem under control.

If you want moving water in the form of a waterfall or fountain, provide an underground electricity supply before laying paving or lawns.

Miniature ponds *If you do not have room for a large pond in your garden, you can still benefit from the advantages water brings. Sink tubs into the soil, fill them with water, and you can then grow aquatic plants and attract pond wildlife.*

Growing vegetables

Fresh, home-grown vegetables are part of the organic gardener's way of life, so allow as much room as possible for the vegetable plot. The idea that vegetable plants are unsightly is nonsense; a well-ordered and productive vegetable plot is a truly heartening sight. (*See also* The Vegetable Garden, *pages 132-201.*)

Plan to position the plot in a sunny part of the garden and never plant a screening hedge between the vegetables and their source of sun.

If space is limited, grow your vegetables on the deep-bed system, a method of cultivation whereby vegetables are grown in blocks rather than rows. The soil is deeply dug to form a very deep topsoil, or root zone. This encourages their roots to grow downwards, enabling them to be planted very close together (*see page 135*). It is important to note that the beds need to be about 1.2m (4ft) wide with a 30-45cm (12-18in) path between each one. If possible, leave extra room for crops such as Brussels sprouts and runner beans, which are not suited to this method of cultivation. There is no reason at all why you should not have an irregular-shaped vegetable plot if this helps it to blend in better with the rest of the garden.

If your garden is too small for even the most restricted vegetable plot, grow a few fresh salads and some of the more ornamental vegetables in among the flowers in the borders.

Decorative vegetable gardens *With an imaginative layout, the vegetable garden can be made an attractive feature – an important point in a small garden where everything can be seen.*

Growing fruit

Not so long ago, growing fruit trees in a tiny garden would have been impossible because of their size. However, you can now grow many types of fruit on special dwarfing rootstocks and, with modern pruning methods, these can be restricted so that they will grow happily in the smallest of spaces (*see* The Fruit Garden, *pages 202-35*).

If you have a sunny wall or fence, reserve it for a peach tree grown as a fan and trained close to the wall or fence so that it takes up virtually no space at all. The dwarf *North Star* cherry (a cross between a Siberian cherry and the Morello) is self-fertile and uses little space at its 1.8m (6ft) height. You can also train apples and pears up walls or fences, as either fans or espaliers (*see page 209*); east- or west-facing walls are best for these. Alternatively, you can grow them as cordons, planting the trees 60-90cm (2-3ft) apart and training them to grow parallel to each other at a 45-degree angle, to form a hedge wherever a barrier is needed. You can even train some soft fruits, such as gooseberries and redcurrants, as cordons against a wall if space is limited. More compact

still are single-tier espaliers, or stepovers, which form trees no more than 30cm (12in) high. These are ideal as a low hedge round the vegetable plot.

Birds are the biggest nuisance in the fruit garden. If you have enough space for a fruit cage, try to plan it into your scheme. In fact, if you can erect a cage to protect your vegetables as well, you will find it well worthwhile.

Growing under glass

A greenhouse is an asset to any garden, and is well worth finding space for. Obviously, it needs as sunny a place as possible. It is also best sited as near to the house as possible, since this makes the installation of electricity or gas for heating cheaper, and, above all, makes the trip to attend to it on raw winter nights less daunting.

There is a lot of controversy surrounding the question of which way to site a greenhouse, but in my view it does not really matter if it faces east-west or north-south. There are many different greenhouses to choose from. Rectangular ones are the most common, but bear in mind that, if your garden is small, a hexagonal greenhouse may be more suitable. Greenhouses are widely available with frames made of either wood or aluminium (*see page 247*).

COLD FRAME

If you plan to raise your own plants for setting out in the garden, try to find the space for a cold frame, a wood, metal or brick frame with a glass top (*see page 254*). This is essential for acclimatizing plants to outside temperatures before planting out, a process known as "hardening off". Site it as near the greenhouse as possible.

The utility area

Organic gardeners are usually do-it-yourselfers by nature, and they tend to accumulate plenty of material that other people would class as rubbish. I find it difficult to throw away a piece of wood, I keep all my old styrafoam coffee cups for use as pots, and compost bags pile up in their hundreds to make growing bags (*see page 253*) and tree ties, or for mulching between rows of vegetables for weed control. Throwing away a length of nylon string is anathema. So plenty of room is needed to store these valuable, money-saving materials.

If you have room for a garden shed, there is no problem. There is no need to hide it, since a few climbing plants will soon transform it into a thing of beauty. If you do not have room for a shed and you don't have any room in the garage, arrange some kind of cover for tools and equipment. It is possible to buy garden "chests" or "lockers" now; I have even seen an old wardrobe pressed into service as a "mini-shed".

You will also need room for the compost heaps – at least two and preferably three – perhaps a pile of manure, certainly a container for leaf-mold, and an area for storing bales of peat or bags of fertilizer (if you don't have a shed, buy them in plastic sacks and keep them outside). Set aside a general-purpose utility area for all these things and arrange to screen it from the rest of the garden. You can tuck it behind tall-growing shrubs or conceal it by planting some hedging plants in front of it. But, if space is limited, the best method of screening is to erect a trellis (or posts and wires) and plant some fast-growing climbing plants in front of it.

Choosing ornamental plants

The aim of planting in an organic garden, apart from the obvious aesthetic one, is to attract and encourage as many predators of pests as possible. The right selection of ornamental plants helps to create a natural balance of wildlife in the garden and increases the interest and pleasure you'll derive from the garden, while also reducing attacks from pests.

COTTAGE-GARDEN PLANTING

For the average gardener with just a moderately sized garden, the "cottage-garden" design offers some distinct advantages over other styles of garden. This style was developed by the old "cottagers" in England as a way of combining a productive garden with ornamental plants and later developed and romanticized by the Victorians in the nineteenth century. It is also a style that is endlessly adaptable and suits modern architecture and building materials just as well as it did old stone cottages with roses around the door and windows.

Its advantages are that, first, it allows you to grow a mixture of ornamental and vegetable plants in the same beds, so making maximum use of any available space; and that, second, the informality of the style encourages the use of native plants, which will attract useful insects and pest predators into your garden. A side-effect of the close-planting technique adopted in this style of garden is the suppression of weeds and the saving of a lot of tedious labor.

There is no need to plan all the borders at the outset. It is much better to collect all your plants slowly, learning about them first from visits to nurseries, garden centers and other gardens. Permanent plants such as trees and shrubs form the framework of the garden. Remember, though, that in ten years time, they will look very different from the small specimens that you plant, and they dislike being moved. So, before buying them, check their final spread and height to ensure that you plant them in the right place first time. Other types of plants can be moved at will, indeed, many benefit from being moved. This is discussed in more detail in *The Ornamental Garden* (*see pages 81-125*).

Varied planting *There is a vast assortment of shapes, colors and textures in this lively ornamental border, even though no fruit or vegetable plants have been planted here.*

Segregated planting *Large areas of concentrated color are created by dividing the plants in this informal garden into bold clumps of purple, yellow and white.*

Drawing up a plan

Once you have made your lists and have a good idea of your priorities, you should make a detailed plan of how you will carry the work through to completion. First, measure the boundaries of the garden, draw the area on to a piece of paper, then transfer it on to some squared paper. If your house and garden are absolutely rectangular, it is easy to measure up and transfer this to paper. If it is not, you will have to use a system of measurement known as "triangulation" (*see below*).

STARTING WORK ON THE GARDEN

Once you have finalized your plan, you can start work. Transferring your ideas from paper to the ground can be tricky, and it is a good idea to set a "datum line". This is simply a line down the middle of the garden from which you can take all your measurements. Then it is relatively easy to work out curves from the drawing and transfer them to the garden itself, marking out each step with canes.

Be prepared to be flexible when you come to dig the garden, or cut the lawn edges, for example. If, for example, the curve on a border looks wrong when it comes to cutting it out of the lawn, don't stick slavishly to the plan. There is nothing to stop you making an alteration here and there in order to perfect the final garden layout. Remember, if it looks right, it *is* right.

MEASURING YOUR GARDEN

It is rare to find a perfectly rectangular plot; most gardens are not exactly at right angles to the house. So, in order to measure accurately, you will need to master the simple skill of triangulation.

For this you need two fixed points from which to measure everything. The corners of the house are ideal. Since walls are generally at right angles to each other, you can be pretty certain that the house itself will be more or less straight. Start by measuring the house, then measure the distance to each corner of the boundary, first from one corner of the house and then from the other, and make a note of these measurements on your rough plan. Use the same method to determine the position of any features, such as trees, that you don't intend to change.

When you come to draw up your master plan, decide on a scale to use. It is best to work in units of ten – 1cm:1m, for example (or, alternatively, 1in:1ft). Start by transferring your house measurements to the paper. If you use squared paper you will find it easier to obtain accurate angles and lengths. Then, set a pair of compasses to the relevant scale distances for each feature and draw an arc from both points marking the corners of the house. The point where the arcs intersect gives the precise location of the feature in question. Draw all these details on the master plan in ink. Then fix a piece of tracing paper over the top of the squared paper. This gives you the opportunity to experiment with various designs (and make mistakes) without spoiling the master plan itself. There will inevitably be plenty of mistakes and mind-changing before the process is completely to your satisfaction. There are two plans opposite to give you an idea of how you can allocate space. The large one is based on the measurements taken for these diagrams (*see right*).

Measuring the existing features right
On a rough piece of paper mark down the distance between the corners of the house and the boundary, and the house and existing features such as trees.

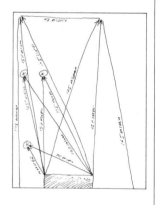

Drawing the plan below
Choose a scale to work to and draw the outline of the garden and existing features on to squared paper using compasses.

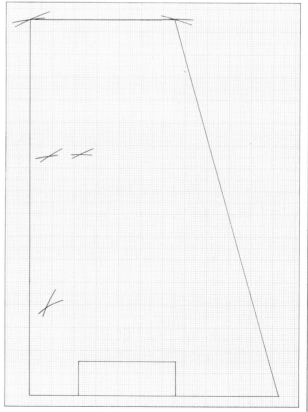

LAYING OUT A GARDEN

Below are ideas for two gardens: one for a large garden and one for a small one. Both demonstrate clearly how many different elements you can incorporate into any sized garden. The small garden is rectangular, the large garden is narrower at one end and slopes away from the house.

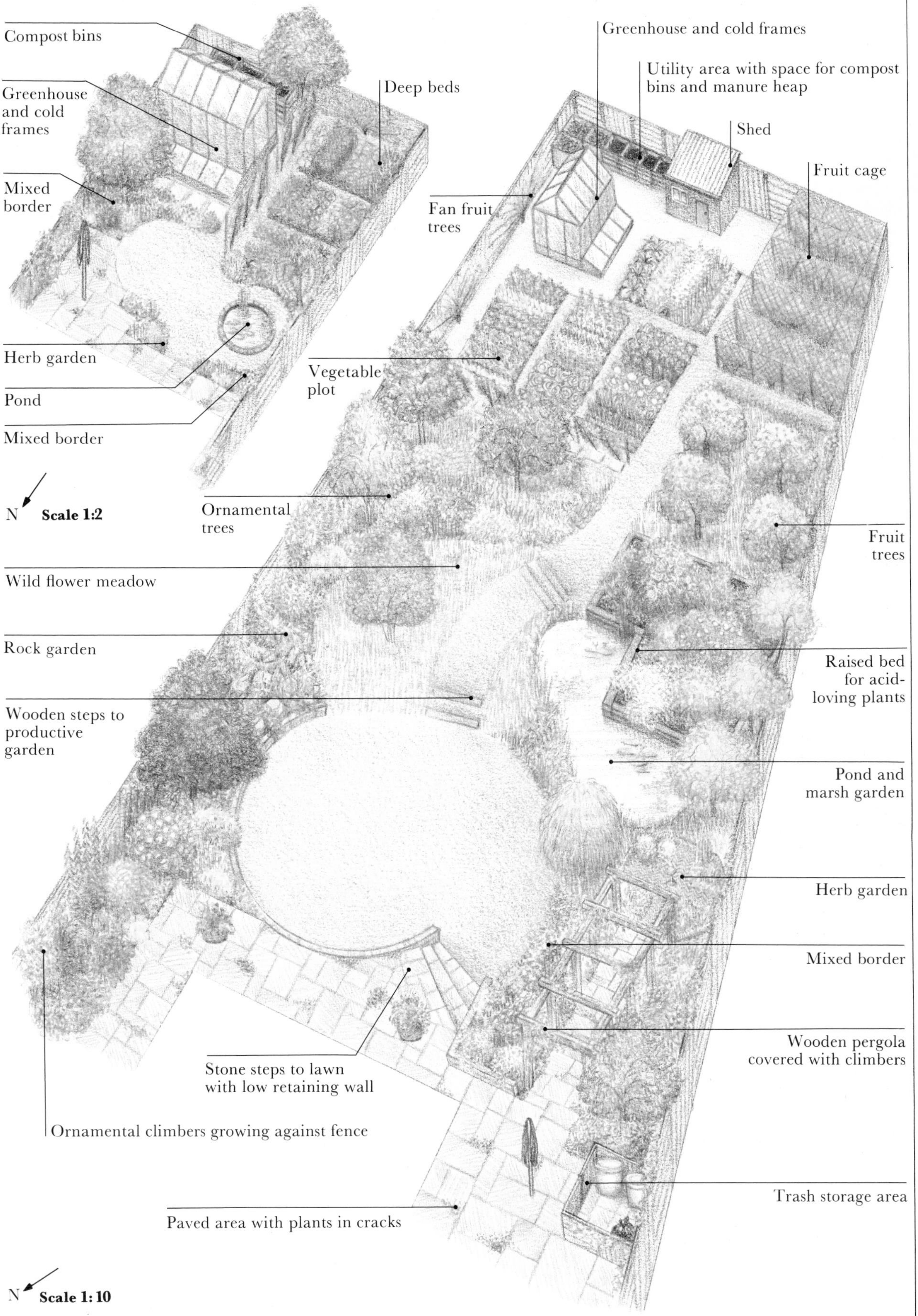

Compost bins

Greenhouse and cold frames

Mixed border

Herb garden

Pond

Mixed border

N Scale 1:2

Deep beds

Greenhouse and cold frames

Utility area with space for compost bins and manure heap

Shed

Fruit cage

Fan fruit trees

Vegetable plot

Ornamental trees

Wild flower meadow

Rock garden

Wooden steps to productive garden

Fruit trees

Raised bed for acid-loving plants

Pond and marsh garden

Herb garden

Mixed border

Wooden pergola covered with climbers

Stone steps to lawn with low retaining wall

Ornamental climbers growing against fence

Trash storage area

Paved area with plants in cracks

N Scale 1:10

THE ORNAMENTAL GARDEN

YOU MAY THINK that it is not important to manage the ornamental part of your garden organically. After all, you are never going to eat anything from the flower borders. So what does it matter if the roses are cleared of aphids with chemicals? Why shouldn't the slugs be kept at bay with toxic pellets? And what difference does it make if the weeds are killed with herbicides?

A BALANCED COMMUNITY

In fact, it matters very much. The ornamental garden is an integral part of the organic garden. One of its main functions, after the purely aesthetic one, is to attract insects, birds and, if you are lucky, small mammals, thus creating a completely balanced wild community. This balance is the one way you can ensure that no pest gets the upper hand and manages to build up a dominance that threatens not only the rest of the community but your cultivated plants too. The only way to make the system work properly is nature's way.

Creditable though they certainly are, our attempts at controlling one insect pest with a predatory insect (*see page 45*) will always have their imperfections. The problem is that, once the pests have been killed, the introduced predators die out because they have nothing left to eat. So, we have to wait for another infestation of the pests and then introduce another supply of predators to kill them. And so it goes on. By a masterly juggling trick, however, nature's system somehow manages to arrange it so that the pests are never completely wiped out and there is, therefore, always enough food for just a few predators. In other words, each is in control of the other's destiny. The predators keep the pests down to numbers which are acceptable, not only to the plants but to you as well, while the pests control the build-up of the predators by the simple process of reducing their food supply. What you must do, instead of supplying the predators, is to supply the plants that will attract them and then let nature do the rest.

Insects and birds are particularly attracted to our gardens by the colors and perfumes of flowers, the fresh green of foliage and the exotic reds and yellows of berries – all the features that make plants attractive to us too. Create a framework of trees and hedge plants and fill the ornamental borders with a glorious jumble of shrubs, herbaceous plants, wild flowers and even vegetables. Plant as many native plants as you possibly can. The choice of plants is wide, but it is very important to include the right types. It is easy, for example, to attract a whole range of butterflies by planting the ice plant (*Sedum spectabile*). It will be covered with them throughout its late summer flowering period. In order to get butterflies to breed in your garden, however, you will also need to grow those plants that provide food for their caterpillars. Without them, the life cycle cannot be completed.

CHOOSING PLANTS FOR THE ORNAMENTAL GARDEN

The range of plants to choose from varies not only with the country in which you live, but also the area within that country. There is one rule to follow: when planting, try to vary the subjects as much as possible – the wider the variety, the wider the range of wildlife you are likely to attract.

If you are lucky enough to be moving into a completely new garden, you can manage it organically right from the outset, choosing the plants and deciding on the position of the features. Start by digging over the entire garden area and preparing the soil thoroughly. Next, organize the hedging, fencing and trees to give the garden a framework and privacy, then prepare the lawn area – you could, in fact, grass over the whole garden and cut out the ornamental borders later, when time or money are more plentiful.

However, if you are moving to an established garden, it may be advisable to wait a year before putting any plans into action. This will enable you to discover exactly what the garden contains in its borders, and how much work will be necessary to create your ideal, organically managed garden. Obviously, during that time, you can start preparing certain areas, and begin the attack on any pernicious weeds.

Preparing the soil

The basic raw material of gardening is the soil and it is worth while taking time and trouble over its initial preparation. Your soil will be one of the five different types or, more probably, a mixture. Soil type varies according to where your garden is situated, and each has a slightly different management technique. This is discussed in greater detail in the second chapter, *The Soil (see pages 12-17).*

TESTING YOUR SOIL

Always begin by identifying your soil type properly *(see page 14)*, as it will affect the way you prepare the soil. If you are taking over a completely new garden, you should test the nutrient content and establish the soil's acidity or alkalinity *(see page 19)*.

In an established garden, it is not absolutely essential to test for nutrient content, because organic management will not take long to correct any nutrient deficiencies, but testing for the degree of acidity or alkalinity certainly is *(see page 36)*. This is determined by the lime content in the soil and will indicate not only whether you should add lime during cultivation, but also determine the types of plants you can grow. While it is possible to make special provision for plants that need conditions other than those prevailing in your soil, it is unwise to spend time and money trying to grow plants that find your soil entirely alien. Since, for example, one acid-loving rhododendron costs a great deal more than a kit to test your soil, it would be imprudent not to test the pH before buying the plants.

WHERE YOU SHOULD START

Prepare the soil carefully; remember, once you have planted the trees and shrubs and laid the lawn, there is no opportunity to dig organic matter into the lower levels. Since you can only do it once, you must do it well.

The first job is to get rid of all the perennial weeds *(see page 55)*. If the borders are infested with pernicious perennial weeds like couch grass (*Agropyron repens*) and ground elder (*Aegopodium podagraria*), it is a good idea to grow a "cleaning crop" like potatoes *(see page 56)* and wait a year before converting the ground into ornamental borders.

Generally such measures are not necessary. The horrifying stories of gardeners who spend their lifetimes fighting couch grass or ground elder are always due to poor soil preparation and subsequent lack of vigilance *(see page 56)*.

If you don't use a cleaning crop, begin weeding by double digging the entire garden *(see page 264)*, removing every bit of weed possible. It is hard work, but very satisfying. Take your time and do it thoroughly. Obviously, no persistent weed roots should go on the compost heap – better that they be placed in plastic bags and thrown away. Everything else can be put on the compost heap *(see page 21)*.

As the digging and weeding progresses, you are aerating the topsoil and breaking up the subsoil. Double digging also gives you the opportunity to incorporate manure, compost or one of the alternatives *(see page 30)* at the rate of 10-15kg (20-30lb) per square meter/yard.

RAISING THE BORDERS

It is a good idea, particularly if you have heavy soil, to raise the borders above the level of the lawn. Double digging and the addition of organic matter will do this. It will not only improve the drainage in the upper levels, but it will also raise the temperature by opening up the soil.

If your soil is badly drained, putting one to two bucketfuls of gravel per square meter/yard on to the soil you are digging, and working it in will help to improve drainage and raise the border even further.

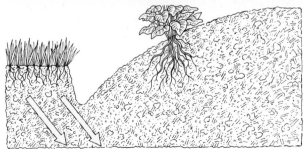

Improving drainage *If your soil is heavy and badly drained, raise the borders above the level of the lawn by digging in organic matter and grit. The borders will drain more freely and excess water on the lawn will drain straight into the subsoil.*

Hedges

All gardens, and gardeners, need a certain amount of privacy and shelter from strong wind. There are several ways of achieving this: fencing, informal or formal hedging, or even a wire fence covered with climbing plants. What you use depends largely on the space available. If your garden is tiny, you will not have the space to devote to a hedge of any kind, so a fence or wall may be more suitable. A solid barrier, however, prevents the free flow of frost-laden air and can create a frost pocket (*see page 65*).

Hedging provides the most effective windbreak because it filters the wind, slowing it down, and allows cold air to escape from the garden. If you need a windbreak and you do not have room for a hedge, a good alternative is to build a post-and-wire fence and train climbing plants up it (*see page 119*).

CHOOSING HEDGING PLANTS

There are two main types of hedging plant: those that can be neatly clipped and not allowed to flower, creating a formal hedge, and those which are allowed to grow in their natural state and flower, forming an informal hedge.

Formal hedges can be clipped back to reduce the amount of space they take up. Though the essence of the small garden is informality, a well-clipped coniferous hedge, such as the Lawson cypress (*Chamaecyparis lawsoniana*) or yew (*Taxus baccata*), or the shiny foliage of laurel (*Prunus laurocerasus*), makes a fine background to the ornamental garden. As a windbreak, the close foliage of a formal hedge is unbeatable.

Informal hedges require a lot more room, as they are allowed to grow in their natural way.

For most, you should allow for a spread of at least 1-2m (3-6ft) either side of the planting line. However, they do have the advantage of flowers, which are not cut off as they would be with a formally trimmed hedge. Almost any tall-growing flowering shrub can be used. Escallonia is useful in mild-climates; it is an evergreen with pink, red or white flowers in summer. If you are trying to keep animals out of the garden, choose one with thorns, for example, the barberry (*Berberis* sp.).

BUYING HEDGING PLANTS

Hedging plants can be bought bare-rooted, container-grown or balled. Each type has advantages and disadvantages. Bare-rooted plants are grown in the open ground and dug up for sale. They are cheaper than container-grown plants; the disadvantage is that they can only be planted when they are dormant in autumn or early spring. Generally, shrubs like privet are only available as bare-rooted plants. Container-grown plants can be planted at any time of year provided the ground is not frozen. Ensure that they have actually been grown in the container; if they pull out easily, they have just been lifted from the nursery and run a high risk of failing when planted out. Conifers are often sold balled. They are grown on a nursery and lifted for sale. The soil is left around the roots, which are wrapped in burlap. They should be planted in spring or autumn.

Whichever type of plant you decide to buy, ensure that the roots are well developed and free from disease. Bare-rooted deciduous plants should have closed leaf buds.

Formal hedging *This attractive mixture of green and copper beech (* Fagus sylvatica*) should be clipped back to control its height and spread. If you have a large garden, formal hedges make ideal screens and windbreaks.*

Informal hedging *Almost any shrub, for example, these purple and yellow brooms (* Cytisus sp.*), can be used as an informal hedge. The flowers can make a spectacular display, serving to soften the line of a boundary or the lawn.*

PLANTING A HEDGE

The essence of a good hedge is to provide effective cover quickly. It is important to prepare the soil thoroughly, to give the hedge a good start in life. The best time to plant hedging plants is in their dormant period. The plant used below is Lawson cypress (*Chamaecyparis lawsoniana*).

1 *Mark out the hedge line with string and dig a trench at least 60cm (2ft) deep and 90cm (3ft) wide along the line. Take out the topsoil to the depth of the spade and break up the sub-soil thoroughly.*

2 *Put a 7.5cm (3in) layer of well-rotted compost or manure in the trench. Cover with a layer of soil then more organic matter and refill. Cover with two handfuls of blood, fish and bone meal per meter/yard length. Allow the soil to settle for a fortnight.*

3 *If the plants are container-grown, carefully disentangle any roots that may be running around the bottom of the pot. This is especially important when planting conifers.*

4 *Plant each shrub at the recommended planting distance (see below). Use a planting board (see page 260) as a guide to ensure even planting. Water well after planting.*

RECOMMENDED PLANTING DISTANCES

When planting a hedge, there is little point in spacing the shrubs too closely. Planted at the distances recommended in the table below, they will quickly grow together, forming a close hedge at a much lower cost. The table also gives the maximum height of the shrubs.

Plant	Planting distance					Maximum height
	30cm (12in)	45cm (18in)	60cm (2ft)	75cm (2ft 6in)	90cm (3ft)	
Formal hedge shrubs						
Lawson cypress (*Chamaecyparis lawsoniana*)				●		12m (40ft)
Leyland cypress (*Cupressocyparis leylandii*)				●		14m (45ft)
Western red cedar (*Thuja plicata*)				●		16m (50ft)
Yew (*Taxus baccata*)		●				4.5m (15ft)
Hawthorn (*Crataegus monogyna*)	●					7.5-9m (25-30ft)
Common laurel (*Prunus laurocerasus*)				●		4.5-6m (15-20ft)
Holly (*Ilex aquifolium*)					●	5.5-6.5m (18-22ft)
Privet (*Ligustrum ovalifolium*)	●					3.5-4.5m (12-15ft)
Beech (*Fagus sylvatica*)		●				12m (40ft)
Informal hedge shrubs						
Barberry (*Berberis* sp.)			●			2.5-3m (8-10ft)
Escallonia (*Escallonia* sp.)			●			4.5m (15ft)
Griselinia (*Griselinia* sp.)			●			3-7.5m (10-25ft)
Pittosporum (*Pittosporum* sp.)			●			4.5m (15ft)

MAINTAINING A HEDGE

Feeding Hedges tend to get neglected, but they should be treated like any other shrub in the garden. Feed them in early spring with blood, fish and bone meal or any balanced organic fertilizer. Mulch after feeding.

Pruning Some plants, such as quick thorn (*Crataegus* sp.) or privet (*Ligustrum ovalifolium*), need to be pruned back hard immediately after planting (*see below*). This may appear to be defeating the object, but it ensures that the hedge will be bushy and well furnished at ground level.

Trim conifer hedges only when they reach the required height. The top shoots can then be cut out to limit upward growth. Prune the sides of the hedge annually in late summer. This is a good time to prune other slow-growing evergreens, but faster-growing hedges, like privet, must be pruned with shears regularly throughout the growing season too.

Clearing the hedge bottom The bottom of the hedge tends to trap all kinds of rubbish. Leaves, grass and bits of paper, for example, will blow there and remain. This will trap frost-laden air and is an ideal place for pests and diseases to overwinter. Make a habit of cleaning out the bottom of your hedge in autumn.

Pests and diseases Hedges can harbor pests and diseases on their leaves which may spread to other garden plants. Native species will attract more pests but this increase is offset by a greater attraction to the pest predators. If your garden is planted with a wide variety of species, hedge-dwelling pests should not be a problem as their natural predators will keep numbers under control (*see page 43*).

Cutting back after planting *It is recommended that some shrubs, such as privet (*Ligustrum ovalifolium*), are cut right back to within 2.5cm (1in) of the ground immediately after planting. This will encourage shoots to grow out from the base.*

Lawns

An area of grass is not essential in the organic garden, but it makes a good foreground to the ornamental borders and provides an area for children to play and you to relax in.

New lawns can be made from seed or turf. Seed is cheaper but turf is much quicker to establish. If sown in spring, it is at least three months before a seed lawn can be used, whereas a turf lawn laid in spring can be used in six weeks.

If you are buying seed, make sure you choose a mixture to suit your management regime. Very fine mixtures need regular maintenance if the lawn is to remain high quality. Coarse mixtures are hard wearing, which is worth bearing in mind if you have children.

PREPARING THE SITE

Preparation is the same whether you intend to start from seed or turf. To the organic gardener, this is the most important phase of the lawn's life because the best way to beat weed or moss problems in the lawn is to get the grass growing so well that it chokes out the unwanted plants. This requires a healthy, fertile soil (*see page 18*), with an active animal community (*see page 11*). I have never understood, for example, the chemical gardeners who kill earthworms with chlordane poison just to avoid wormcasts on their lawn. Then they have to spend hours aerating the soil with a fork, because there are no worms to do it for them. Yet it takes no more than a few minutes to brush the wormcasts over the lawn before mowing. Remember, not only do worms aerate the soil, and therefore improve drainage, but their pellets help break nutrients down into a form that is more readily available to plants (*see page 31*). Encourage earthworms and all your other allies in the soil by digging in organic matter in the form of manure, compost or one of the alternatives (*see page 30*) at the rate of at least 10kg (20lb) per square meter/yard. A layer of gravel under heavy soil will improve drainage (*see page 16*). Do this job thoroughly because it is the last chance you will get to dig below the level of the grass.

Before sowing grass seed or laying new turf check the soil's pH. Most grasses like a slightly acid soil or neutral soil. If the soil is too acid, ground limestone can be added to make it more alkaline.

Seed lawns

Sowing seed is the cheapest way to lay a new lawn, and allows you to control the different types of grasses making up the lawn. The only disadvantage of a seed lawn is that it does take three months to establish if sown in spring. If sown in autumn, it should not be used until the following spring.

MAINTAINING A NEW SEED LAWN

Watering With only a limited root system, a new lawn is very vulnerable in dry weather. Water using a lawn sprinkler to apply a fine spray at regular intervals (*see page 266*).

Mowing When the grass is about 7cm (3in) high it is ready for cutting. First, roll it with the mower with the blades right off the ground to push in any loose stones. This also bruises the grass stems, causing the buds at their base to grow out, greatly thickening up the lawn. Then, raise the mower blades as far as they will go and trim the tips of the new grass. The blades can be lowered progressively with each cut, until they are about 4cm (1½in) above the soil surface.

Any weeds growing through the new grass will be sliced off regularly. The annuals will disappear quickly and, if you missed any of the perennials during preparation, most will soon succumb. Only rosetted weeds will survive regular mowing and these can be coped with later (*see overleaf*).

Turf lawns

A turf lawn is very much an "instant lawn". It looks good straight away and is ready for use about six weeks after laying if put down in the spring. Turf must be bought from a reliable source to ensure that the grass is good quality.

MAINTAINING A NEW TURF LAWN

Watering Make sure the turves never go short of water. It takes only a little drying out to cause them to shrink, leaving ugly gaps, so use the sprinkler little and often.

Mowing You will know when the grass has rooted because it starts to look greener and stands up. It can then be cut in the way recommended for a seed lawn (*see left*).

SOWING A SEED LAWN

Grass seed should be sown in early spring or early autumn, when some wet weather can be expected. Avoid the driest months as this means constant watering. If sowing grass seed along the edge of paving, raise the level of the lawn above the paving to ensure easy mowing.

1 *Start with a stale seed bed (see page 269). Rake the area roughly level with the back of a fork to take out any local undulations before consolidating the soil.*

2 *If your soil is light or lacks organic matter, apply a 5cm (2in) layer of peat and rake it in with the fork. If the soil is heavy, use coarse grit.*

3 *Rake in about two handfuls of blood, fish and bone meal every square meter/yard, or a layer of sewage sludge. To consolidate the soil tread over the whole area with the weight on your heels.*

4 *Rake the area level. It helps to see the local undulations if you take a step back from time to time, crouch down and squint across the surface, although a completely level lawn is rarely necessary.*

5 *Sow the seed at 25-35g (1-1½oz) per square meter/yard. This is about two handfuls of seed. If you put your feet as wide apart as you can and lean forward as far as possible, you will cover about 1 square meter/yard.*

6 *Rake the seed in, barely covering with soil and, to speed up germination and protect the seed from birds, cover with burlap or perforated plastic. Remove covering when the first seed germinates.*

LAYING A TURF LAWN

Prepare the soil (*as shown on page 78*) and rake it flat, then lay the turves as described below. Always work from boards, as you should never walk on the turf you have just laid or the levelled soil. Scaffolding boards are ideal and can be lifted quite easily.

1 *Place a board along the longest straight edge of the lawn and lay the first row of turf. Lay rows of turf all the way round the edge of the proposed lawn. Tap down the strips with the back of a rake to put them into close contact with the soil.*

2 *Lay a board on the first row of turf. Standing on the board, lay a second row of turf parallel to the first and pull it into the first with the back of the rake. There's no need to bond the turves together as is sometimes recommended.*

3 *When you get to the end of a row, butt the last turf up to the edging turf by laying it on top and cutting off the excess with a penknife. When the whole lawn is down you can shape the edges with an edging knife.*

4 *When you have finished the lawn, put a sprinkler on the area. Keep the turves well watered after laying to prevent them shrinking. Once the grass has established its roots, water less frequently.*

Established lawns

If you already have a lawn in your garden, you can't dig in organic matter, but you can care for the grass to keep it in good condition.

Drainage To get the grass growing really well, proper drainage is necessary. You can improve it by incorporating grit or organic matter. If the drainage is poor, the soil will become waterlogged, preventing air getting to the roots. If the lawn drains too quickly, the grass will soon become brown and unhealthy looking.

Feeding Lawns can be fed in two ways. You can use slow-release blood, fish and bone meal once or, at most, twice a year in early spring, and again in early summer. Alternatively, if you want the instant greening results obtained by a chemical lawn fertilizer, use high-nitrogen fertilizer such as sewage sludge or cottonseed meal.

Weeding If you keep the grass growing well, and cut it regularly, you will not be troubled with a lot of weeds. But, inevitably, some rosetted weeds, like dandelions or daisies, creep in. They can be kept under control by cutting them out regularly with a knife, or by dropping ordinary table salt on the growing point.

Repairing coarse patches of lawn Sometimes patches of coarse grass appear though, if you start with good seed or cultivated turf, this

Improving drainage or water retention above
Work over the lawn with a hollow-tined fork, removing cores of soil. If your soil is heavy, brush grit into the holes to fill them. For light soil, use garden compost.

Killing rosetted weeds in lawns right
Pour table salt into the center of the weeds; this causes them to shrivel up and die overnight. Alternatively, cut them out with a penknife.

should be rare. If it does happen, it can be repaired by hatching and reseeding. Score the coarse patch in a criss-cross fashion with a pen-knife and reseed, using an equal-parts mixture of seed, moist peat and good soil.

MOWING A LAWN

Mow your lawn only during the growing season. The grass stops growing in winter and does not need cutting then. Begin by brushing any earth-worm casts around the lawn with a stiff broom, otherwise the mower flattens them, making perfect seed beds for weeds.

The lawn should be cut in opposite directions on alternate cuts (*see below*). Never shave the lawn too close as this encourages bare patches which will be colonized by moss and weeds. Always leave the grass 1cm ($\frac{1}{2}$in) long for bent grasses, but closer to 5cm (2in) for zoysia and Kentucky bluegrass varieties. Grass cuttings are also the best composting material possible, so never throw them away (*see page 21*). However, unless excessively thick after mowing, cuttings can be left in place and will quickly decompose.

One method of mowing *Cut once round the entire edge of the lawn. Then, starting in one corner, cut diagonally across the lawn. Mark your starting point so that you can work in the opposite direction next time you cut the lawn.*

Trimming the edges *When you have finished mowing the lawn, tidy the edges by trimming the bits the mower missed with long-handled shears, taking the clippers close to the edge but not shaving the grass.*

Trees

Ornamental trees serve many purposes. First they provide shade, which extends the range of plants you can grow. Second, along with the hedges and lawns, they form the framework of the garden and can be planted to act as wind-breaks, especially in the larger garden. And third, they attract wildlife to feed and breed.

Birds use them for perching and nesting and as a source of food, especially the berrying and fruiting trees such as flowering dogwood (*Cornus* sp.), mountain ash (*Sorbus* sp.) and flower-ing crab apple (*Malus* sp.). Trees with deeply furrowed or flaking bark, for example, some of the birches (*Betula* sp.) provide homes for in-sects, which are themselves food for the birds.

Flowering trees attract pollinating insects, which are important if you are growing fruit. The flowering crab apple *Malus* "Golden Hornet", for example, pollinates most varieties of apple and, as it is bred for maximum flower, there is always ample pollen.

CHOOSING TREES

When choosing trees, the first consideration should be the ultimate height and spread. Trees will compete with plants growing near them for water and nutrients and, if you plant a large tree, it will throw your whole garden into deep shade. Many gardeners have lived to regret planting the lovely weeping willow (*Salix alba* "Vitellina Pendula"), which can reach heights of up to 12m (40ft). There are many small trees which would be more suitable. For example, the Kilmarnock willow (*Salix caprea* "Pendula") would be a better choice for a small garden. It makes an attractive weeping tree which will always remain small and manageable, with a maximum height of 3m (10ft). Remember, you can always ask your local nursery if you are unsure. A selection of deciduous and coniferous trees is shown on pages 84-7.

Do not plant vigorous trees less than about 12m (40ft) from the house. Roots of trees like willows (*Salix* sp.) and poplars (*Populus* sp.) will seek out cracked drains, quickly blocking them. Worse still, they can cause soil shrinkage. When water is withdrawn from the soil by the tree, it shrinks away from underneath the foundations of the house, causing cracking and subsidence. This is particularly dangerous on clay soils.

BUYING TREES

Trees can be bought container-grown or bare-rooted and should come from a reputable nur-sery. Container-grown trees are smaller and more expensive than bare-rooted ones – their advantage is that they can be planted at any time of year when the ground is not frozen. Bare-rooted trees can only be planted in their dormant season – autumn to early winter and early spring. Plant in winter in mild climates.

PLANTING TREES

Never plant trees in holes dug in uncultivated soil. If you simply dig a hole in hard ground it acts as a sump for all the surrounding water. If the hole fills up with water in winter, the tree's roots will then be cold and deprived of air. So prepare the soil properly. Even if you are planting trees in an area of grass, you should prepare as big a hole as you can – at least 90cm (3ft) square. Break up the subsoil to improve drainage and work in plenty of organic matter – compost, manure or one of the alternatives (*see page 30*).

Add two handfuls of blood, fish and bone meal to the soil too, or use any complete (balanced) commercial organic fertilizer, such as Gardentone, which should be available in your local garden centers.

All young trees need staking when first planted. The type of stake is different for bare-rooted and container grown trees. If they are bare-rooted, the stake should be a simple post, placed as near to the trunk as possible (*see opposite*). If they are container-grown, they should be supported with a cross-bar stake (*see below*). It has been found that the movement of the trunk in the wind thickens the base and improves the root system, so the stake should anchor the base and the roots and come one-third of the way up the trunk, leaving the rest of

PLANTING CONTAINER-GROWN TREES

These can be planted at any time the ground is not frozen. Watering is important, but even more important is mutilating the root ball, which is often severely pot-bound. Do this by slicing at the ball with a knife, pulling or teasing out the roots or even banging the ball on the ground.

1 Mutilate the root ball – this drastic treatment will force new growth into the surrounding soil. Dig a hole large enough to accommodate the mutilated root ball.

2 Put the tree in the hole after "disturbing" the root ball. Check that the hole is deep enough by laying a spade across the root ball. It should touch the old soil mark on the stem.

3 If you soil is short of organic matter, add peat to the pile of soil you have dug out and supplement it with two handfuls of blood, fish and bone meal or similar organic fertilizer.

4 With a spade, mix up the soil and peat around the edge of the hole, and use this mixture to cover the root ball. Firm down gently with the ball of your foot.

5 Water retention round the root ball it vital. Use some of the dug-out soil to make a small retaining wall around the tree, so that the soil can be really soaked later.

6 Hammer two 5×5cm (2×2in) stakes inside the soil walls. They should go 45cm (1ft 6in) into the ground and come one-third of the way up the trunk. Nail a cross-bar between the stakes.

7 Tie the trunk to the cross-bar using a special tree tie with a collar to prevent chafing. Water thoroughly and make sure you check the soil regularly for drying out.

8 One month to six weeks later – when the tree should have rooted properly – level out the soil wall and mulch thickly around the trunk with well-rotted manure or compost.

the stem free to move. Secure the tree to the stake with a special tree tie or strip of plastic; never use wire or nylon twine; they cut through the trunk as the tree grows.

MAINTAINING TREES

Feeding Trees that are growing in borders will normally be fed every year when the rest of the plants receive fertilizer. In addition to two handfuls of blood, fish and bone meal every spring, try to spread a layer of manure, compost or one of the alternatives (*see page 30*) around the roots every autumn (avoiding spent mushroom compost, *see page 35*).

If trees are growing in grass, they should be fed in the same way, but just a little earlier – say mid winter – so that the fertilizer is washed down into the soil before the grass starts growing and using up nutrients.

Pruning Ornamental trees need little pruning in the first years after planting; it is generally only a case of removing branches that are dead, diseased, crossing or overcrowding during the dormant season. If you notice any branches growing towards the center of the tree, or that are beginning to grow across other branches, take them out straight away. That way you will avoid having to remove very large branches later, which spoils the shape of the tree.

Tree ties These should be checked at least every autumn. You may find that they have become too loose to hold the tree in winter storms, or that the tie is now restricting further growth. Remove and replace them as necessary.

PLANTING BARE-ROOTED TREES

This can only be done in the tree's dormant season, usually autumn or early spring, or in winter in mild climates. If the trees arrive when the ground is frozen, leave them unpacked, in a frost-free building, until better weather, or "heel in" in a V-shaped slit trench (*see page 113*).

1 *Keep the roots covered with a piece of burlap until the planting area has been prepared. This will prevent dehydration of the roots in sunny or windy weather.*

2 *Plant at the level of the old soil mark on the stem. Put the tree in the hole and lay a spade across the edge of the hole – the handle should line up with the soil mark if the tree is at the correct depth.*

3 *Take the tree out of the hole and drive a stake 45cm (18in) into the soil. It should be at least twice as thick as the stem and should come about one-third of the way up the tree.*

4 *Cover the soil you have dug out with a bucketful of organic matter. Peat can be used but, as it contains no nutrients, sprinkle on two handfuls of bone meal fertilizer.*

5 *Place the tree in the hole and put a little fine soil over the roots and then, holding the stem, jerk it up and down a few times to settle some of the soil around the roots.*

6 *Refill half the hole and tread down the soil with the ball of your foot. While the soil around the roots should be firm, it should not be over-compressed. Complete the filling and re-tread.*

7 *Tie the stem to the stake with either a proprietary tree tie or a length of thick plastic, tied in a figure-of-eight to form a collar between the tree and the stake. Nail the tie or plastic to the stake.*

8 *Mulch round the stem with a layer of well-rotted compost or manure immediately after planting, to conserve moisture and inhibit weed growth.*

Deciduous trees

These are trees which shed their leaves before the cold or dry season. Prior to this the leaves often turn orange, red or yellow. New leaves appear in spring. There are many different shapes and sizes and those shown here are just a tiny selection. When choosing a tree for your garden, check the eventual height and spread and remember that most trees will cast shade, affecting the type of plants that will grow nearby. *For details of tree planting, see pages 82-3.*

WILLOW-LEAVED PEAR
Pyrus salicifolia "Pendula"
As the name suggests, this ornamental pear tree has willow-like leaves. They are gray-green in color and covered in fine, downy hairs. This variety is best suited to smaller gardens as it has a maximum height of 4.5m (15ft) and spread of 2.4m (8ft).

WILD CHERRY
Prunus avium "Plena"
This variety is grown for its plentiful, double, white flowers which open at the same time as the leaves. They are followed in autumn by small, shiny plum-colored fruits. The leaves turn red in autumn. Height up to 12m (40ft), spread 9m (30ft).

MOUNTAIN ASH
Sorbus "Joseph Rock"
This is a small tree with leaves which turn from glossy green to deep, fiery red in autumn. In spring, clusters of cream-colored flowers appear; these develop into amber-yellow fruits by early autumn. Height up to 5.5m (18ft), spread 2.4m (8ft).

AUTUMN CHERRY
Prunus subhirtella "Autumnalis"
This ornamental cherry tree produces white, semi-double flowers intermittently from late autumn to spring. It does not fruit. In most years the leaves turn an attractive red in autumn. Height up to 9m (30ft), spread 9m (30ft).

LABURNUM
Laburnum vossii
A small tree suitable for most soils and situations. The three-lobed leaves are deep green and the tree is covered with a profusion of bright-yellow flowers in late spring and early summer. All parts are poisonous. Height up to 5.5m (18ft), spread 4m (12ft).

GUM TREE
Eucalyptus gunnii
This tree is, in fact, an ever-green, constantly shedding and replacing a few leaves at a time. Like all euca-lyptus, it should be plant-ed in a sheltered position. When they are young the leaves are round. Height up to 15m (50ft), spread 6m (20ft).

SALLOW
Salix caprea
The leaves have dark-green upper surfaces with gray undersides. Yellow catkins are borne on male plants in spring, while female plants bear silver catkins. The Kilmarnock willow (*S.c.* "Pendula") is ideal for a small garden, reaching only 3m (10ft).

BIRCH
Betula platyphylla
Birches are grown for their beautiful bark which, on some species, constantly peels to reveal the new, lighter bark beneath. The leaves turn yellow in autumn and the trees bear catkins in spring. Height up to 10m (30ft), spread 4.5-6m (15-20ft).

HONEY LOCUST
Gleditsia triacanthos
The leaflets are bright yellow in spring, turning light green in summer and back to yellow in autumn. The branches bear spines. Green flowers are pro-duced in spring and brown seed pods in autumn. Height up to 9m (30ft), spread 4.5m (15ft).

NORWAY MAPLE
Acer platanoides
Large, handsome trees grown for their leaves, which turn yellow, and sometimes red, in autumn. There are several attract-ive forms with various foliage colors including white-and-green variega-tion. Height up to 10m (35ft), spread 6m (20ft).

PAPERBARK MAPLE
Acer griseum
Grow this tree for its beauti-ful autumn coloring. The leaves turn orange-red in autumn and the peeling bark also contributes to its beauty. The brown outer bark peels away constantly to reveal the new, orange bark beneath. Height up to 6m (20ft), spread 2.4m (8ft).

Coniferous trees

Shown here is a small selection of the many coniferous trees available. Their leaves are small and waxy, in the form of scales and needles that are usually retained all year.

There is a great variety of colors, shapes and sizes – from dwarf forms for the rock garden or tubs, to large specimen and hedging varieties.

It is best to buy conifers in containers as they do not move well when bare-rooted, unless lifted with a sizeable root ball.

For details of tree planting, see pages 82-3.

WEEPING HEMLOCK
Tsuga canadensis "Pendula"
The branches of this graceful conifer rest on the ground when they are long enough. The shoots are covered with small, dark-green needles and oval-shaped cones. It is best as a free-standing specimen tree. Height up to 9m (30ft), spread 6m (20ft).

MAIDENHAIR TREE
Ginkgo biloba
An unusual conifer as its leaves resemble those of the maidenhair fern. During the summer they are dark green, becoming a beautiful transparent yellow in autumn. It is deciduous. Height up to 9m (30ft), spread 3m (9ft).

PENCIL RED CEDAR
Juniperus virginiana "Skyrocket"
This species is one of the narrowest junipers. It makes an ideal specimen for adding interest to a low planting. The foliage is made up of mid-green leaves loosely arranged on the shoots. Height up to 5m (15ft), spread 30cm (1ft).

MOUNTAIN PINE
Pinus mugo
The long narrow needles of this pine are arranged in pairs around the stems. The brown, oval cones are about 5cm (2in) long. Its prostrate habit and slow growth rate makes it an ideal subject for the rock garden. Height up to 4.5m (15ft), spread 4.5m (15ft).

DEODAR CEDAR
Cedrus deodara
Deodars look best grown as specimen trees in a large lawn. When young, the needles are light green. They darken as they become older. The branches droop as the tree matures, giving it a weeping habit. Height up to 12m (40ft), spread 3m (10ft).

LAWSON CYPRESS
Chamaecyparis lawsoniana
"Allumii"
As the tree gets older it widens at the base, making an attractive "candle-flame" shape suitable for formal planting. It can also be used for hedging. The leaves are blue-gray in color. Height up to 6m (20ft), spread 1.5m (5ft).

WESTERN RED CEDAR
Thuja plicata
This species is the fastest growing of the thujas and is a tall, conical tree when fully mature. The flattened sprays of scale-like leaves have a distinctive fruity scent. The cultivar "Atro-virens" makes an excellent hedge. Height up to 16.5m (55ft), spread 6m (20ft).

HINOKI CYPRESS
Chamaecyparis obtusa
"Nana Gracilis"
This conical bush is very slow growing, though it will eventually make a large shrub or small tree. A popular conifer for the rock garden, it will take many years to outgrow its space. Height up to 3m (10ft), spread 2m (6ft).

LEYLAND CYPRESS
Cypressocyparis leylandii
The Leyland cypress can grow very tall and is one of the fastest growing coni-fers available. It makes an excellent dense hedge growing, in good soil, 60-90cm (2-3ft) a year. Height up to 15m (50ft), spread 4.5m (15ft).

COMMON YEW
Taxus baccata
This hardy species is toler-ant of most adverse condi-tions and makes a good hedge. The narrow, waxy leaves are dark green. The red, cup-shaped berries are the only part of the tree which is not poisonous. Height up to 4.5m (15ft), spread 4.5m (15ft).

COLORADO SPRUCE
Picea pungens "Koster"
A very popular blue spruce, used widely as a specimen tree. It makes an ideal lawn planting. The needles are arranged spirally so that each shoot looks like a small bottle brush. The brown cones are 10cm (4in) long. Height up to 7.5m (25ft), spread 3m (10ft).

Planting ornamental borders

The essence of planting an organic garden is to create as wide a diversity as possible so that you will attract a balanced community of wildlife which will include pests and predators, so that no one species will build up to an unacceptable level. The "cottage-garden" style is ideal. Here each border contains a mixture of permanent plants such as trees, shrubs, perennials (soft-stemmed plants that die back in the winter every year then reappear in spring), bulbs that flower in different seasons, bedding plants in the form of annuals and biennials to provide extra color during the growing season, and even vegetables. Annuals are plants that complete their life cycle in one year; biennials are plants that are sown one year and flower the next. It is important that a number of plants native to your area, or country, are included in this type of planting. If you are not sure which are the native plants look them up in a plant directory. Unless your garden is large, there is no place for "sophisticated" planting of, perhaps, single-color borders or areas that come to a peak at one particular time and provide nothing for the rest of the year. To create a real balance you need flowers and fruits for as long a period as possible, to attract and feed insects, birds and small mammals. A selection of suitable plants is shown on pages 92-111.

Of course, you'll need to consider the type of soil in your garden, as this will govern the type of plants you can grow. If you have limy, or alkaline soil, for example, you should avoid acid-loving plants such as azaleas.

Consider the aspect of the garden too – that is, the direction it faces, and how much direct sun it gets. This will also have a bearing on the plants you can grow (*see page 64*).

Mixed planting above
Some vegetables make attractive plants to mix into the ornamental borders. This is an ideal way of growing them in very small gardens and has the advantage that the flowers will attract or encourage insect predators like hover-flies and ladybugs to control aphids, while the dense ground cover provides ideal conditions for insects such as ground beetles which prey on caterpillars.

The mature border left
This wide, mature border illustrates very well the principle of mixed, "cottage-garden" planting. All types of plants have been used together and some tall plants have been brought near the front of the border to create an attractive undulating profile.

CREATING A COLORFUL INSTANT BORDER

Permanent plants like shrubs and herbaceous perennials take some time to fill their allotted space. However, it's not difficult to create instant borders full of summer color, by interplanting the shrubs with blocks of annuals. You may occasionally need to trim back the annuals a little to ensure that they do not inhibit the growth of the more permanent subjects.

1 *Prepare the soil in the normal way, digging out any perennial weeds and working in plenty of well-rotted manure or compost through the top as well as the lower levels.*

2 *Sprinkle a light dusting of blood, fish and bone meal, at the rate of one handful per square meter/yard, over the surface of the soil before planting.*

3 *The annuals are planted in "drifts", using several plants together to create a more dramatic effect. Be sure to leave plenty of room for the permanent plants to grow. A tomato plant will not look out of place in this border.*

4 *Plants with open, flat flowers like French marigolds (*Tagetes patula*) are particularly useful for attracting hover-flies which feed on their pollen before laying their eggs amongst groups of aphids.*

The finished border *By using annuals, the border will be a blaze of color throughout the summer. By mixing the productive with the ornamental in this way, vegetable plants are camouflaged from insect pests attracted by sight and scent, the diversity of planting creates a natural balance of pest and predator.*

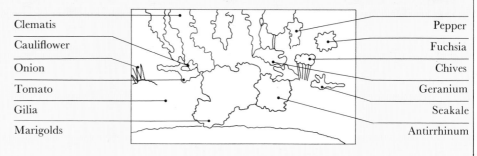

Clematis
Cauliflower
Onion
Tomato
Gilia
Marigolds

Pepper
Fuchsia
Chives
Geranium
Seakale
Antirrhinum

When you have a general idea of your plan it is worth putting it down on paper to prevent any costly mistakes (*see page 72*). You do not necessarily have to follow it religiously, but it will give you a starting point. If you have just taken over an established garden, and you are planning to change an existing border planting, leave it for one growing season to see what the border contains and start planning the new planting programme in winter or early spring of the following year.

WHAT TO PLANT FIRST

When you are planting a new border, it is best to start with the shrubs. Herbaceous plants can be slotted in later; they can easily be dug up and moved if you feel you have made a mistake – indeed they may actually benefit from being moved occasionally. Shrubs, on the other hand, need to establish themselves; they will be set back every time they are lifted.

Shrubs such as roses can also be included as a part of the border framework. This way, there is an opportunity for companion planting to help keep pests at bay (*see page 45*).

FILLING BETWEEN THE SHRUBS

Once the framework of shrubs has been planted, perennials can be intermingled with them to fill up the spaces. Bear in mind, however, that they grow quite fast so do not allow them to overcrowd and inhibit the growth of the shrubs.

For instant color, particularly in the first few years of the border, annuals and biennials can be used (*see page 89*). They are ideal for filling the spaces round young shrubs though a certain amount of care is needed. Don't plant them too close to growing shrubs or they will compete for light and inhibit the growth of the shrubs. If you find them encroaching, trim them back. Even when the borders are mature you should leave some space for annuals and biennials to brighten the garden with color, and often perfume.

Also useful in the mixed borders are bulbs (and here I include tubers, corms and rhizomes). Spring-flowering bulbs can be planted amongst shrubs and herbaceous plants to make a show when other plants are still dormant. Then, when the herbaceous plants or shrubs grow and are in full leaf, the messy, post-flowering bulb foliage is hidden from view. By choosing the kinds carefully it is possible to have bulbs in flower all the year round. If you are planting in a fairly young mixed border, put the bulbs quite near the shrubs. As you should never dig near the roots of shrubs for fear of damage, the bulbs will not be dug up accidentally when planting other herbaceous subjects in the border.

GIVING A BORDER HEIGHT

Climbing plants can be included in informal borders to add height – especially those in front of a wall or hedge that a climber can be allowed to ramble over. Climbers can also be used to cover any ugly features in the garden, such as a garage or central-heating oil tank. And some, like the less vigorous cultivars of the clematis, are invaluable scrambling over shrubs and in trees. If you choose a variety that is in flower when the tree or shrub is not, you can extend the flowering season of your border.

GENERAL MAINTENANCE OF ORNAMENTAL BORDERS

Feeding Maintain a regular supply of nutrients to the border by mulching annually with well-rotted manure or compost. Give the whole border a dressing of blood, fish and bone meal in early spring. Every three years apply a dressing of seaweed meal to ensure that the trace elements are plentiful or use green sand.

Watering Make sure the border plants get plenty of water in dry weather, and ensure they do not dry out immediately after planting. This is particularly important with container-grown shrubs. (*See* Watering plants, *page 266*.)

Pest and disease control Ornamental plants are susceptible to many of the general pests and diseases listed on pages 46-52. Constant vigilance and companion planting will help to keep problems to a minimum.

Weed control Covering any exposed soil with bark chippings or ground-covering plants suppresses weed growth, greatly reducing the workload. Bark chippings look good but are quite expensive and need to be replaced every few years. Ground-cover plants quickly cover the soil and give the borders a more complete look. There are plenty of low-growing plants available that are dense enough to suppress weeds, and the most attractive way of using them is to plant several different species to make a tapestry of colors and leaf textures under and around the taller plants. For colored leaves, plant bugle (*Ajuga reptans*) or euonymus, cinquefoil, heathers (*Erica* sp.) and periwinkles (*Vinca* sp.), all of which form flat, dense mats over the ground. Do bear in mind that some plants, such as St John's wort (*Hypericum calycinum*) and knotweed (*Polygonum* sp.), sold as ground cover, can become as invasive as the weeds if their growth is not restricted.

There are problems, however, with ground-cover plants. In the early stages, before dense cover is established, a great deal of weeding will be necessary and it can only be done by hand. Once they have spread, however, to cover the soil completely and form a dense carpet that excludes light, annual weeds will rarely be able to compete so weeding will consist only of pulling out the rare perennial weed. There are other forms of organic weed control that work on the principle of depriving any possible weeds of light (*see pages 55-9*).

Naturalizing bulbs above
In areas of rough grass, naturalize
spring-flowering bulbs such as narcissi.
They blend harmoniously with native
flowers which can be planted or sown in
the grass to provide cover for insects.

Attracting insects right
A varied insect population is vital in the
organic garden. Butterflies and hover-flies
*are attracted to the ice plant (*Sedum
spectabile*) by its brightly colored,*
nectar-filled flowers.

Covering a pergola below
If your garden is small, grow fast-
growing climbing plants, such as clematis,
over a pergola to add height to your
plantings. This is C. orientalis, *which*
produces brilliant yellow flowers
throughout summer.

Choosing suitable plants

It is important to choose plants that suit the type of soil in your garden. The charts below show a selection of plants for each soil type. The lists are divided according to the different plant types and further divided to indicate sun/shade tolerance. Bulbs, annuals and biennials are not listed because they are tolerant of most soil conditions and light levels.

On the following pages (pages 94-111) there is a photographic season-by-season guide to ornamental plants. Each plant on these pages has been given a set of symbols to explain its type, sun and soil preferences – the symbols are explained opposite.

PLANTS FOR CLAY AND SILT SOILS

Many plants grow well in heavy clay soils if drainage is reasonable and organic matter is added yearly. The following genera, and usually most – if not all – of their species and cultivars, are examples of plants that grow particularly well on these soils.

SHRUBS
Sun
Rose (*Rosa* sp.) *see page 105*
Flowering currant (*Ribes* sp.) *see page 98*
Snowberry (*Symphoricarpos* sp.)
Shade
Spotted laurel (*Aucuba japonica*)
Skimmia (*Skimmia* sp.)
Oregon grape (*Mahonia* sp.) *see page 94*
Tolerant
Witch hazel (*Hamamelis* sp.) *see page 94*
Honeysuckle (*Lonicera* sp.) *see page 96*

Hazel (*Corylus* sp.) *see page 94*
Aronia (*Aronia* sp.)

PERENNIALS
Sun
Bear's breeches (*Acanthus* sp.)
Marigold (*Tagetes* sp.)
Bugle (*Ajuga* sp.) *see page 103*
Pearl everlasting (*Anaphalis* sp.) *see page 109*
Shade
Solomon's seal (*Polygonatum* sp.) *see page 102*
Comfrey (*Symphytum* sp.)
Brunnera (*Brunnera* sp.)
Barrenwort (*Epimedium* sp.)
Tolerant
Day lily (*Hemerocallis* sp.)
Primula (*Primula* sp.) *see page 97*
Hellebore (*Helleborus* sp.) *see page 97*
Hepatica (*Hepatica* sp.) *see page 97*

CLIMBERS
Ivy (*Hedera* sp.)
Wisteria (*Wisteria* sp.)

Skimmia (*Skimmia* sp.)

Primrose (*Primula* sp.)

PLANTS FOR SANDY SOIL

A light, free-draining soil. Most plants will grow on sandy soil provided plenty of organic matter is incorporated regularly to improve water-holding capacity (*see pages 17-19*). The following genera and their species and cultivars grow well on sandy soil.

SHRUBS
Sun
Artemisia (*Artemisia* sp.)
Broom (*Cytisus* sp.) *see page 103*
Cinquefoil (*Potentilla* sp.) *see page 102*
Rock rose (*Cistus* sp.)
Shade
Shrubby germander (*Teucrium fruticans*)
Ornamental bramble (*Rubus* sp.)
Barberry (*Berberis* sp.) *see page 96*
Tolerant
Eleagnus (*Eleagnus* sp.)
St John's wort (*Hypericum* sp.)

Barberry (*Berberis* sp.) *see page 98*
Cotoneaster (*Cotoneaster* sp.) *see page 111*

PERENNIALS
Sun
Bear's breeches (*Acanthus* sp.)
Yarrow (*Achillea* sp.)
Aubrieta (*Aubrieta* sp.) *see page 96*
Campion (*Lychnis* sp.)
Shade
Bergenia (*Bergenia cordifolia*)
Liriope (*Liriope muscari*)
Pick-a-back plant (*Tolmeia menziesii*)
Cranesbill (*Geranium macrorrhizum*)
Tolerant
Cranesbill (*Geranium* sp.)
Phlomis (*Phlomis* sp.)
Euphorbia (*Euphorbia* sp.) *see page 107*
Phygelius (*Phygelius* sp.) *see page 108*

CLIMBERS
Honeysuckle (*Lonicera* sp.) *see page 96*
Rose (*Rosa* sp.) *see page 105*

Artemesia (*Artemesia* sp.)

Campion (*Lychnis* sp.)

THE PLANT SYMBOLS

The "plant type" symbols indicate whether the plant is a tree, shrub, perennial, annual, biennial, bulb or climbing plant.

The "sun preference" symbols indicate the amount of sun each plant prefers to receive. Many require full sun, full shade or partial shade at all times. Others will grow in partial shade as long as they get some full sun and are given the "sun" and "partial shade" symbols. Those that grow in a range of positions are given a "tolerant" symbol.

The "soil preference" symbols indicate whether the plant prefers an acid soil or an alkaline soil. (*See also page 35*). Some plants will tolerate a range of soil pHs and are given the "tolerant" symbol.

PLANTS FOR ALKALINE SOIL

A limy, or alkaline, soil tends to be dry as it drains quickly. It has quite a high pH and many plants won't tolerate this as it leads to certain nutrient deficiencies. The following genera and most of their species and cultivars grow well on alkaline soil.

SHRUBS
Sun
Wintersweet (*Chimonanthus* sp.) *see page 95*
Mock orange (*Philadelphus*) *see page 107*
Lilac (*Syringa* sp.) *see page 102*
Butterfly bush (*Buddleia davidii*) *see page 108*
Shade
Periwinkle (*Vinca* sp.) *see page 99*
Oregon grape (*Mahonia* sp.) *see page 94*
Tolerant
Spiraea (*Spiraea* sp.) *see page 99*

Forsythia (*Forsythia* sp.) *see page 99*
Yucca (*Yucca filamentosa*)

PERENNIALS
Sun
Peruvian lily (*Alstromeria* sp.)
Peony (*Paeonia* sp.) *see page 102*
Dutch iris (*Iris* sp.) *see page 106*
Anemone (*Anemone* sp.) *see page 99*
Shade
Dicentra (*Dicentra* sp.)
Primrose (*Primula* sp.) *see page 97*
Primrose (*Primula vulgaris*)
Plantain lily (*Hosta* sp.) *see page 110*
Tolerant
Hellebore (*Helleborus* sp.) *see page 95*
Columbine (*Aquilegia* sp.) *see page 100*
Cinquefoil (*Potentilla* sp.) *see page 102*

CLIMBERS
Honeysuckle (*Lonicera* sp.) *see page 96*
Clematis (*Clematis* sp.) *see page 97*

Yucca (*Yucca filamentosa*)

Cinquefoil (*Potentilla* sp.)

PLANTS FOR ACID SOILS

Most plants prefer a very slightly acid soil, although the ones listed below will not tolerate anything but an acid soil. Acid soils are often moisture-retentive, so incorporate plenty of organic matter to improve drainage. The following genera and their species and cultivars grow well on acid soil.

SHRUBS
Sun
Broom (*Cytisus* sp.) *see page 103*
Bearberry (*Arctostaphylos* sp.)
Rock rose (*Helianthemum* sp.)
Gorse (*Ulex* sp.)
Shade
Magnolia (*Magnolia* sp.) *see page 101*
Rhododendron (*Rhododendron* sp.) *see page 94*
Azalea (*Rhododendron* sp.)
Shadblow (*Amelanchier* sp.)

Pieris (*Pieris* sp.) *see page 98*
Tolerant
Witch hazel (*Hamamelis* sp.) *see page 94*
Heath (*Erica* sp.) *see page 95*
Dogwood (*Cornus* sp.)
Camellia (*Camellia* sp.) *see page 94*

PERENNIALS
Sun
Carex (*Carex* sp.)
Lily (*Lilium* sp.) *see page 107*
Lupin (*Lupinus* sp.) *see page 106*
Ornamental onion (*Allium* sp.)
Shade
Solomon's seal (*Polygonatum* sp.) *see page 102*
Gentian (*Gentiana* sp.) *see page 101*
Japanese primrose (*Primula* sp.)
Tolerant
Woodrush (*Luzula sylvatica*)
Campion (*Lychnis* sp.)

CLIMBERS
Trumpet vine (*Campsis radicans*)
Wisteria (*Wisteria* sp.)

Heath (*Erica* sp.)

Lily (*Lilium* sp.)

Winter plants

Even in winter the garden can be interesting. Some bulbs and tubers flower at this time of year and many shrubs have interesting leaves, flowers or catkins. Even when leafless, shrubs with colored or twisted stems are attractive.

WILLOW below
Salix sachalinensis "Sekka"

One of the many attractive willows with winter appeal. The chestnut-brown shoots are covered in furry buds in winter. Height 4.5-6m (15-20ft). *See* Shrubs, *page 112.*

GARDEN PANSY below right
Viola wittrockiana

Much valued for its long flowering period. Some hybrids flower all summer, others bloom intermittently during the winter. *See* Perennials, *page 115.*

CHINESE WITCH HAZEL below
Hamamelis mollis "Goldcrest"

This shrub bears scented flowers. Height 2.5-3m (8-10ft). *See* Shrubs, *page 112.*

RHODODENDRON below
Rhododendron "Praecox"

One of the many hybrids available in a wide range of flower colors and sizes. Height 1-1.5m (3-5ft). *See* Shrubs, *page 112.*

SKIMMIA right
Skimmia japonica "Rubella"

A small shrub with evergreen leaves and red buds. Height 1.1-5m (3-5ft). *See* Shrubs *page 112.*

IRIS below
Iris reticulata

One of the best known early flowering irises. Plant 5-7cm (2-3in) deep in well-drained soil. *See* Bulbs, *page 117.*

CYCLAMEN below
Cyclamen coum

An attractive hardy species. They dislike exposed situations. *See* Bulbs, *page 117.*

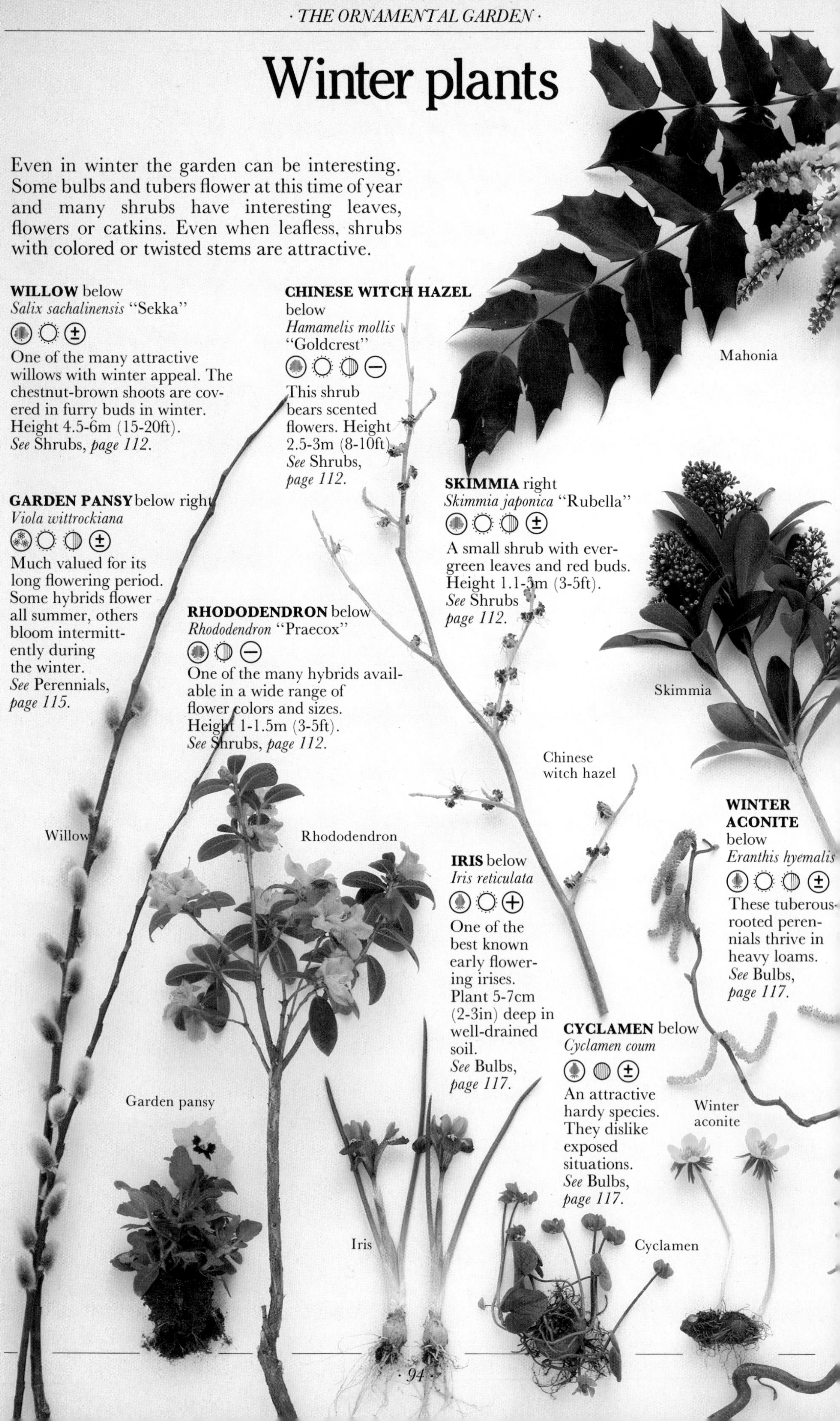

WINTER ACONITE below
Eranthis hyemalis

These tuberous-rooted perennials thrive in heavy loams. *See* Bulbs, *page 117.*

Mahonia

Skimmia

Chinese witch hazel

Willow

Rhododendron

Garden pansy

Iris

Cyclamen

Winter aconite

Plant type — Tree, Shrub, Perennial, Annual, Biennial, Bulb, Climbing plants
Sun preference — Sun, Partial shade, Shade, Tolerant
Soil preference — Acid, Alkaline, Tolerant

MAHONIA left
Mahonia "Charity"

This shrub has very frag-
rant yellow flowers. Height
1.8-3m (6-10ft).
See Shrubs, *page 112.*

Mezereon

MEZEREON
above
Daphne mezereum

A small shrub with frag-
rant, pink, purple or white
flowers. Height 1.5m (5ft).
See Shrubs, *page 112.*

HELLEBORE
below
Helleborus corsicus

A sprawling plant that
can look untidy unless
staked. Like all helle-
bores they prefer deep,
well-drained soil.
See Perennials, *page 115.*

Hellebore

WINTERSWEET
right
Chimonanthus praecox

The flowers have
a superb perfume. The
plant is best grown
against a south- or
west-facing wall.
Height 2.5-3m (8-10ft).
See Shrubs, *page 112.*

Wintersweet

SNOWDROP
below
Galanthus nivalis

One of the earliest
winter flowers.
See Bulbs, *page 117.*

**CHRISTMAS
ROSE** below
Helleborus niger

These attractive perennials
take some time to build up
large clumps but are worth
the wait.
See Perennials, *page 115.*

**CORKSCREW
HAZEL**
below left
*Corylus
avellana*
"Contorta"

A curiously
contorted
form of the
common hazel.
Height 2.5-3m
(8-10ft).
See Shrubs,
page 112.

HEPATICA below
Hepatica nobilis

There are several named
varieties in shades of blue,
white, red or purple.
See Perennials, *page 115.*

HEATH below
Erica darleyensis

This is one of the
many varieties of
heaths, available
in several colors
from white through
pink and red to
deep purple.
See Shrubs, *page 112.*

Corkscrew hazel

Snowdrop

Hepatica

Christmas
rose

Heath

Early spring plants

This is a selection of plants that are at their best in early spring. Some, such as the almond and the camellia, have been chosen because they have spectacular blooms at this time of year; others, for example, photinia, because they have particularly attractive new growth. Combined in the same border, these plants make a very impressive early spring display.

HONEYSUCKLE left
Lonicera japonica
"Aureo-reticulata"

A rampant evergreen climber. The leaves are bright green with conspicuous golden veining. Height up to 9m (30ft). *See* Climbing plants, *page 119.*

FLOWERING ALMOND right
Prunus triloba

A pink-blossomed shrub which reaches a height and spread of 3-4.5m (10-14ft). *See* Shrubs, *page 112.*

CROWN IMPERIAL left
Fritillaria imperialis

A majestic bulb that flowers freely on most soils. Available in red and yellow. *See* Bulbs, *page 117.*

HYACINTH below
Hyacinthus hybrid

One of the many hybrids in a range of colors, with an intense fragrance. It grows in most soils but likes a sunny position. *See* Bulbs, *page 117.*

AUBRIETA below
Aubrieta deltoidea

An easy-to-grow small plant for border edges, walls, or rock gardens. There are several varieties in shades of purple and pink. *See* Perennials, *page 115.*

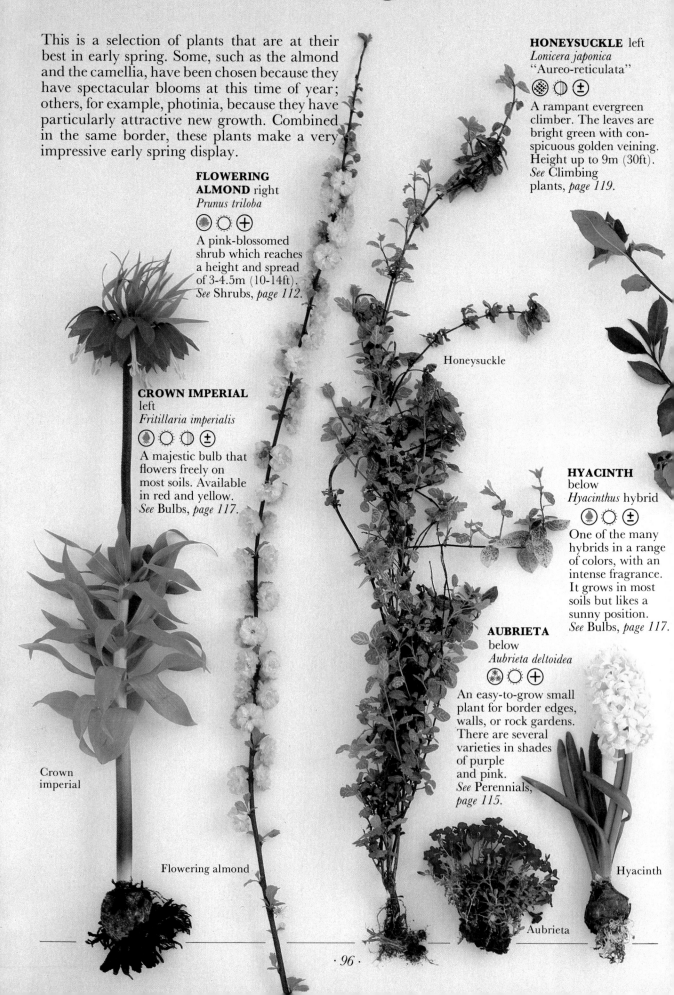

Honeysuckle

Crown imperial

Flowering almond

Aubrieta

Hyacinth

Plant type Tree Shrub Perennial Annual Biennial Bulb Climbing plants **Sun preference** Sun Partial shade Shade Tolerant **Soil preference** Acid Alkaline Tolerant

RED ROBIN below
Photinia fraseri

This evergreen shrub is grown
for its brilliant-red young growths.
Height up to 2-3m (6-10ft),
spread 1.5-2m (5-6ft).
See Shrubs, *page 112.*

Red robin

CAMELLIA left
Camellia japonica

An exotic-looking but
hardy shrub, available in
a range of colors.
Height up to 1.8m (6ft),
spread 3.5cm (11ft).
See Shrubs, *page 112.*

Camellia

DAFFODIL left **NARCISSUS** right
Narcissus sp. and cvs.

These bulbs grow in any
type of fertile soil.
See Bulbs,
page 117.

CLEMATIS right
Clematis macropetala

This plant grows
in full sun or part
shade and will
climb up a trellis or
over shrubs. Height
up to 3.5m (11ft).
See Climbing
plants,
page 119.

PRIMROSE below
Primula hybrid

A hybrid of the wild
Primula vulgaris.
Primroses are available
in many colors.
See Perennials, *page 115.*

Primrose

Clematis

Daffodil

Narcissus

Mid spring plants

As the season begins to warm up, the variety of ornamental plants in flower in the garden begins to change. By mid spring the tulips, in all their various colors and shapes, have flowered. Shrubs like forsythia will be covered in golden-yellow flowers and fresh green leaves will begin to appear. The colorful foliage of the barberry is welcome at this time of year too.

Flowering currant

FLOWERING CURRANT right
Ribes sanguineum

This relative of the black-currant bears bunches of tiny red or pink flowers. The berries produced are not edible. Height up to 2.4m (8ft), spread 1.5m (5ft).
See Shrubs, *page 112.*

BARBERRY below
Berberis thunbergii
"Atropurpurea Nana"

This shrub has deep-red foliage. Height up to 1m (3ft), spread 60cm (2
See Shrubs, *page 1*

Barberry

TULIP below
Tulipa sp. and cvs.

There are many species and hybrids of tulips that extend the flowering period for several weeks. A few have attractively marked foliage.
See Bulbs, *page 117.*

PIERIS below
Pieris formosa "Forest Flame"

The foliage of this ever-green is red when it is young, turning pink, through yellow to deep green as it matures. Height and spread up to 3m (10ft).
See Shrubs, *page 112.*

ROCK CRESS below
Arabis ferdinandi-coburgii

This plant forms mats of green leaves. It does best on well-drained soil.
See Perennials, *page 115.*

Tulipa greigii
"Good Luck"

Single early tulip
"Diana"

Pieris

Rock cress

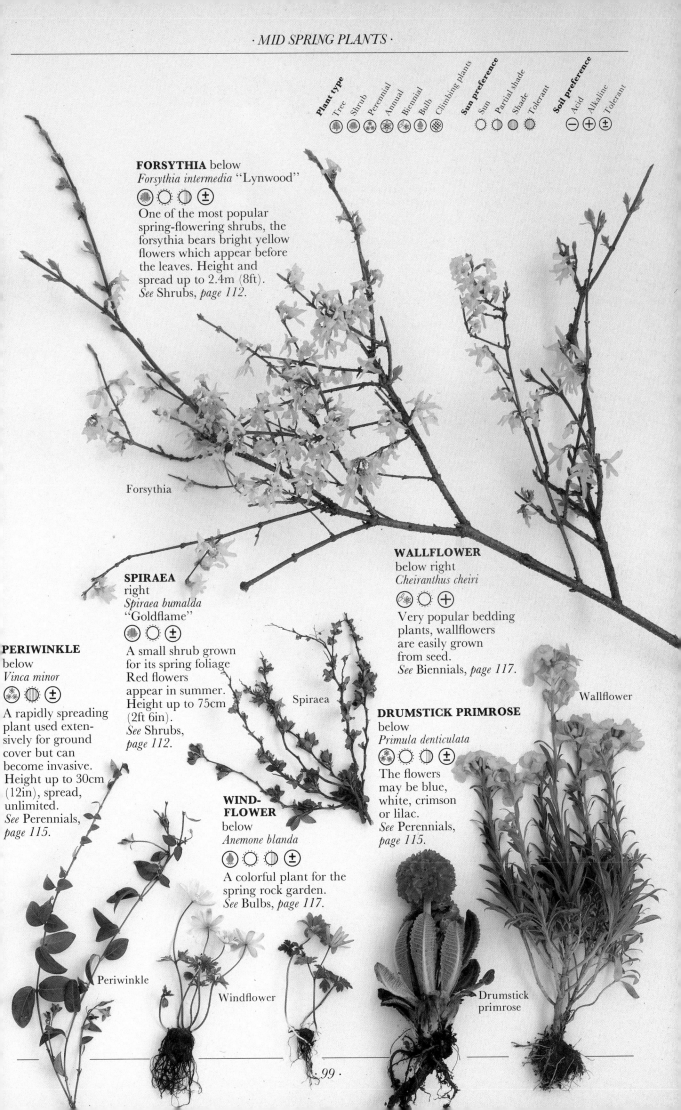

Plant type
Tree · Shrub · Perennial · Annual · Biennial · Bulb · Climbing plants

Sun preference
Sun · Partial shade · Shade · Tolerant

Soil preference
Acid · Alkaline · Tolerant

FORSYTHIA below
Forsythia intermedia "Lynwood"

One of the most popular
spring-flowering shrubs, the
forsythia bears bright yellow
flowers which appear before
the leaves. Height and
spread up to 2.4m (8ft).
See Shrubs, *page 112.*

Forsythia

WALLFLOWER
below right
Cheiranthus cheiri

Very popular bedding
plants, wallflowers
are easily grown
from seed.
See Biennials, *page 117.*

Wallflower

SPIRAEA
right
Spiraea bumalda
"Goldflame"

A small shrub grown
for its spring foliage
Red flowers
appear in summer.
Height up to 75cm
(2ft 6in).
See Shrubs,
page 112.

Spiraea

PERIWINKLE
below
Vinca minor

A rapidly spreading
plant used exten-
sively for ground
cover but can
become invasive.
Height up to 30cm
(12in), spread,
unlimited.
See Perennials,
page 115.

DRUMSTICK PRIMROSE
below
Primula denticulata

The flowers
may be blue,
white, crimson
or lilac.
See Perennials,
page 115.

**WIND-
FLOWER**
below
Anemone blanda

A colorful plant for the
spring rock garden.
See Bulbs, *page 117.*

Periwinkle

Windflower

Drumstick
primrose

Late spring plants

As the season progresses a whole new range of plants comes into flower. Trees have attractive late-spring foliage too – for example, the maple has pale orange leaves at this time of year. Combined together, this range of plants can make an interesting border.

Barberry

BARBERRY right
Berberis stenophylla

This evergreen shrub becomes covered by small yellow flowers in spring. Plant it in well-drained soil. *See* Shrubs, *page 112.*

SYCAMORE MAPLE below
Acer pseudoplatanus "Brilliantissimum"

Avoid planting in a windy site since exposed conditions will damage the foliage. *See* Trees, *page 81.*

CHERRY PLUM right
Prunus cerasifera " Nigra"

This small tree is a prolific flowerer. *See* Trees, *page 81.*

Cherry plum

Spiraea

SPIREA above
Spiraea sp.

A useful, informal hedging shrub. *See* Shrubs, *page 112.*

Maple

SYMPHYANDRA below
Symphyandra wanneri

An uncommon plant closely related to the bellflowers (*Campanula* sp.). *See* Perennials, *page 115.*

COLUMBINE right
Aquilegia vulgaris

The flowers have distinctive spurred petals. *See* Perennials, *page 115.*

Columbine

TULIP below
Tulipa tarda

These delicate tulips are best grown in light soil. *See* Bulbs, *page 117.*

FORGET-ME-NOT below
Myosotis sylvatica

A good plant for edging borders. *See* Biennials, *page 117.*

ALYSSUM below
Lobularia "Maritima"

A very popular plant for rock gardens or walls. *See* Annuals, *page 116.*

Tulip

Forget-me-not

Alyssum

Symphyandra

Plant type Tree Shrub Perennial Annual Biennial Bulb Climbing plants Sun preference Sun Partial shade Shade Tolerant Soil preference Acid Alkaline Tolerant

MAGNOLIA right
Magnolia soulangiana

Plant spring-flowering
magnolias in a sheltered
spot as their blooms can
be blemished by frost.
Height up to 6m (20ft),
spread 4.5m (15ft).
See Shrubs, *page 112.*

Magnolia

**FLOWERING
CHERRY**
right
Prunus "Kanzan"

Do not plant too
deeply as they are
shallow rooting.
Height up to 9m
(30ft), spread
4.5m (15ft).
See Trees,
page 81.

Dwarf
Russian
almond

Flowering
cherry

RHODODENDRON below
Rhododendron "Elizabeth"

Grow in a
raised bed if
your soil is
alkaline.
See Shrubs,
page 112.

Rhododendron

COWSLIP below
Primula veris

One of Britain's wild
flowers, the cowslip can
easily be grown in the
garden.
See Perennials, *page 115.*

**GRAPE
HYACINTH**
below
*Muscari
armeniacum*

An ideal edging
for a border.
They should be
grown in well-
drained soil.
See Bulbs,
page 117.

**DWARF RUSSIAN
ALMOND** above
Prunus tenella
"Fire Hill"

A small shrub that is
covered with flowers
every spring.
See Shrubs, *page 112.*

OXALIS below
Oxalis deppei

Plant in a warm, sunny spot.
See Perennials, *page 115.*

EUPHORBIA below
Euphorbia epithymoides

An attractive, dome-
shaped bush.
See Perennials,
page 115.

Cowslip

GENTIAN below right
Gentiana verna

These small plants do
well in limy soil.
See Perennials, *page 115.*

Euphorbia

Grape hyacinth

Oxalis

Gentian

Early summer plants

Summer is the most abundant time of year in the ornamental garden. The range of colors, shapes and fragrances of both flowers and foliage available in this season is immense. On the following pages, the summer plants are sub-divided by flowering period, although actual flowering times may vary with your location and the position of the plant in the garden.

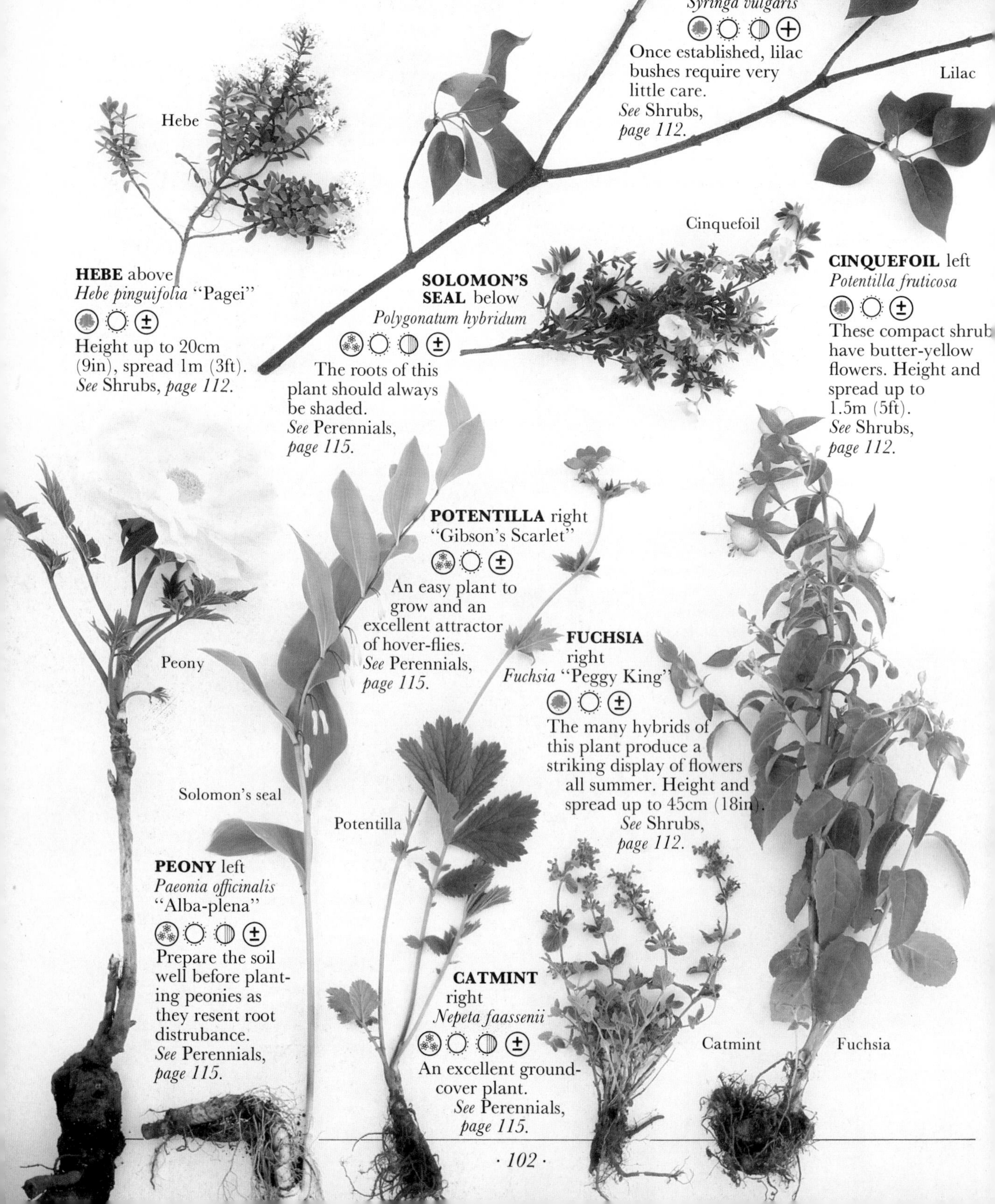

Hebe

LILAC right
Syringa vulgaris

⊛ ○ ◐ ⊕

Once established, lilac bushes require very little care.
See Shrubs, *page 112.*

Lilac

Cinquefoil

HEBE above
Hebe pinguifolia "Pagei"

⊛ ○ ⊕

Height up to 20cm (9in), spread 1m (3ft).
See Shrubs, *page 112.*

SOLOMON'S SEAL below
Polygonatum hybridum

⊛ ○ ◐ ⊕

The roots of this plant should always be shaded.
See Perennials, *page 115.*

CINQUEFOIL left
Potentilla fruticosa

⊛ ○ ⊕

These compact shrubs have butter-yellow flowers. Height and spread up to 1.5m (5ft).
See Shrubs, *page 112.*

POTENTILLA right
"Gibson's Scarlet"

⊛ ○ ⊕

An easy plant to grow and an excellent attractor of hover-flies.
See Perennials, *page 115.*

Peony

FUCHSIA right
Fuchsia "Peggy King"

⊛ ○ ⊕

The many hybrids of this plant produce a striking display of flowers all summer. Height and spread up to 45cm (18in).
See Shrubs, *page 112.*

Solomon's seal

Potentilla

PEONY left
Paeonia officinalis "Alba-plena"

⊛ ○ ◐ ⊕

Prepare the soil well before plant-ing peonies as they resent root distrubance.
See Perennials, *page 115.*

CATMINT right
Nepeta faassenii

⊛ ○ ◐ ⊕

An excellent ground-cover plant.
See Perennials, *page 115.*

Catmint

Fuchsia

Plant type							**Sun preference**				**Soil preference**		
Tree	Shrub	Perennial	Annual	Biennial	Bulb	Climbing plants	Sun	Partial shade	Shade	Tolerant	Acid	Alkaline	Tolerant

WARMINSTER BROOM *Cytisus praecox* below

The green stems become covered with a mass of creamy-yellow flowers in early summer. Height and spread up to 2m (6ft). *See* Shrubs, *page 112.*

Warminster broom

Rosemary

Clematis

ROSEMARY left
Rosemarinus officinalis

This attractive shrub is widely grown as a herb. It thrives in well-drained soil. Height and spread up to 2m (6ft). *See* Shrubs, *page 112.*

KNOTWEED left
Polygonum "Donald Lowndes"

A good ground-cover plant as it spreads rapidly. *See* Perennials, *page 115.*

Knotweed

CLEMATIS right
Clematis montana "Rubens"

A popular climbing plant. They require full sun but the roots should be shaded with a low-growing shrub. Height up to 12m (40ft), spread 6m (20ft). *See* Climbing plants, *page 119.*

Masterwort

Lily-of-the-valley

MASTERWORT left
Astrantia major "Rubra"

The flowers of astrantias have an interesting and attractive shape. They spread by underground runners. *See* Perennials, *page 115.*

Bugle

BUGLE left
Ajuga reptans "Burgundy Glow"

A useful ground-cover plant. It requires a moist soil. *See* Perennials, *page 115.*

LILY-OF-THE-VALLEY
Convallaria majalis

These plants have very fragrant flowers and should be grown in a cool, shady spot. *See* Perennials, *page 115.*

Mid summer plants

The borders will be a blaze of color at this time of year. The following four pages show just a selection of the large variety of plants which will not only look attractive in the borders but will also encourage the diversity of wildlife necessary in the organic garden.

BITTERSWEET below
Solanum dulcamara
"Variegata"

⊛ ○ ±

Not for gardens where children play as the berries are poisonous when eaten. *See* Climbers, *page 119.*

Bittersweet

FOXGLOVE
right
Digitalis purpurea

⊛ ⊛ ○ ±

Normally grown as a biennial, but can be left in year after year in peaty soil. *See* Biennials and Perennials, *pages 115 and 117.*

POTENTILLA below
Potentilla fruticosa

⊛ ○ ±

A small, compact shrub that will flower throughout summer. Height and spread up to 1.5m (5ft). *See* Shrubs, *page 112.*

Potentilla

BELL-FLOWER
below
Campanula glomerata
"Superba"

⊛ ○ ⊘ ±

If grown in fertile, well-drained soil, these perennials will spread quickly. They can become invasive. *See* Perennials, *page 115.*

YARROW left
Achillea filipendulina
"Cloth of Gold"

⊛ ○ ±

Grow yarrow in well-drained soils. It grows particularly well on limestone. *See* Perennials, *page 115.*

FREESIA below
Freesia kewensis

⊛ ○ ±

The flowers are available in a wide range of colors. *See* Bulbs, *page 117.*

DAHLIA below
Dahlia "Coltness"

⊛ ○ ±

Small bedding dahlias are raised annually from seed. The flowers attract hover-flies. *See* Annuals, *page 116.*

Freesia

Bellflower

Foxglove

Dahlia

Yarrow

Plant type
Tree Shrub Perennial Annual Biennial Bulb Climbing plants

Sun preference
Sun Partial shade Shade Tolerant

Soil preference
Acid Alkaline Tolerant

DELPHINIUM left
Delphinium "Dreaming
Spires"

The tall flower spikes need to
be supported with canes.
See Perennials, *page 115.*

Delphinium

ROSE below
Rosa "King's
Ransom"

The modern hybrid
roses are easy to
cultivate and very
soil tolerant.
See Roses *and*
Shrubs, *page 119.*

ESCALLONIA
right
Escallonia
"Slieve Donard"

Compact ever-
green shrubs
which make
good informal
hedges. Height up
to 2.5m (8ft).
See Shrubs,
pages 112-114.

Escallonia

Rose

**PLANTAIN
LILY** left
Hosta "Thomas
Hogg"

If grown on rich, damp soil
the foliage will quickly form
large, dense clumps.
See Perennials, *page 115.*

Plantain lily

DIASCIA below
Diascia barberae

Remove dead flower
heads regularly to
encourage more
flowers.
See Annuals, *page 116.*

**TUBEROUS
BEGONIA** below
Begonia tuberosa

Store the tubers in peat
over the winter.
See Bulbs, *page 117.*

Tuberous
begonia

Diascia

LUPIN below
Lupinus "New Generation"

There are many varieties of
lupin, some of which have
two-color flowers. They all
have deeply divided, dark-
green leaves and are easily
raised from seed sown outside
in spring.
See Perennials, *page 115.*

RUGOSA ROSE below
Rosa rugosa "Blanc Double de Coubert"

Rugosa roses can be grown as hedging
plants, forming a dense, wind-resistant
barrier, or as specimen shrubs. Height
up to 2m (6ft).
See Shrubs, *page 112.*

MOCK ORANGE right
Philadelphus "Virginal"

Probably the best of the double-
flowered *Philadelphus*, they have a
strong fragrance resembling that of
orange blossom. The soil must be
well drained. Height and spread
up to 3m (10ft).
See Shrubs, *page 112.*

PINK below
Dianthus allwoodii

The modern pinks
have a long flowering
period, but should
be propagated at
least every three
years to maintain the
number of flowers.
See Perennials,
page 115.

ALPINE POPPY
below
Papaver alpinum

Grow these
poppies in rock
gardens, between
paving slabs or
wherever the
drainage is good.
See Perennials,
page 115.

DUTCH IRIS below
Iris "Xiphium" hybrids

These elegant-looking
flowers are available in
many different colors.
See Bulbs, *page 117.*

Rugosa rose

Pink

Geranium

**FRENCH
MARIGOLD**
below
Tagetes patula
"Royal Crested"

The brightly col-
ored, open flowers
attract hover-flies.
See Annuals,
page 116.

Lupin

Alpine poppy

Dutch iris

French
marigold

Plant type							Sun preference				Soil preference		
Tree	Shrub	Perennial	Annual	Biennial	Bulb	Climbing plants	Sun	Partial shade	Shade	Tolerant	Acid	Alkaline	Tolerant

Mock orange

BEAUTY BUSH below
Kolkwitzia amabilis

Easy to increase by hardwood cuttings.
See Shrubs, *page 112.*

SWEET ROCKET below
Hesperis matronalis

Although a perennial, it
is best to raise new plants
from seed every few years.
See Perennials, *page 115.*

Beauty bush

Sweet rocket

LILY below
Lilium
"Pandora"

Lilies are easy
to grow in a
sheltered, well-
drained site.
See Bulbs,
page 117.

CAMPION below
Lychnis flos-jovis

These are easy to
raise from seed and
will grow in
almost any soil.
See Perennials,
page 115.

GERANIUM left
Pelargonium zonale

Flower colors range
from white through
pink, salmon-pink, red,
scarlet and magenta.
See Perennials, *page 115.*

LADY'S MANTLE left
Alchemilla mollis

Remove the seed heads
after flowering or plants
will become invasive.
See Perennials, *page 115.*

Lily

PETUNIA below
Petunia hybrida
"Peppermint Daddy"

Grow them in the borders,
hanging baskets or tubs.
See Annuals, *page 115.*

Campion

Lady's mantle

Petunia

Late summer plants

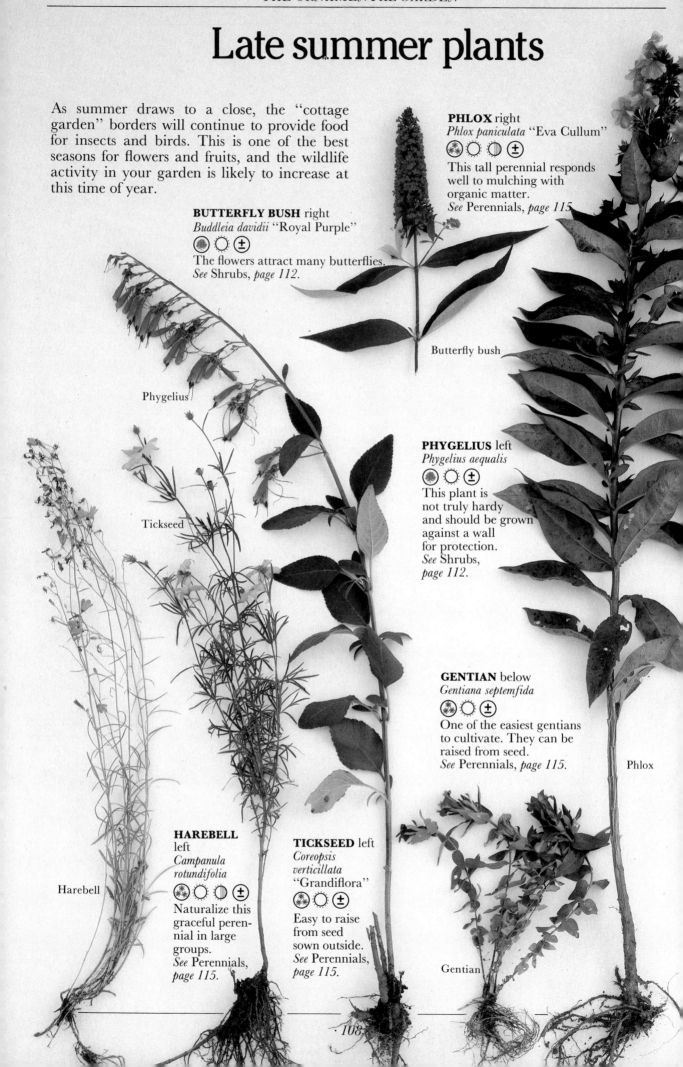

As summer draws to a close, the "cottage garden" borders will continue to provide food for insects and birds. This is one of the best seasons for flowers and fruits, and the wildlife activity in your garden is likely to increase at this time of year.

PHLOX right
Phlox paniculata "Eva Cullum"
This tall perennial responds well to mulching with organic matter.
See Perennials, *page 115*

BUTTERFLY BUSH right
Buddleia davidii "Royal Purple"
The flowers attract many butterflies.
See Shrubs, *page 112*.

Butterfly bush

Phygelius

PHYGELIUS left
Phygelius aequalis
This plant is not truly hardy and should be grown against a wall for protection.
See Shrubs, *page 112*.

Tickseed

GENTIAN below
Gentiana septemfida
One of the easiest gentians to cultivate. They can be raised from seed.
See Perennials, *page 115*.

Phlox

HAREBELL left
Campanula rotundifolia
Naturalize this graceful perennial in large groups.
See Perennials, *page 115*.

Harebell

TICKSEED left
Coreopsis verticillata "Grandiflora"
Easy to raise from seed sown outside.
See Perennials, *page 115*.

Gentian

Plant type: Tree · Shrub · Perennial · Annual · Biennial · Bulb · Climbing plants

Sun preference: Sun · Partial shade · Shade · Tolerant

Soil preference: Acid − · Alkaline + · Tolerant ±

Gladiolus

PASSION FLOWER
left
Passiflora caerulea

A very vigorous climber which should be grown on a warm south-facing wall against a trellis or wires.
See Climbers, *page 119.*

AFRICAN LILY right
Agapanthus "Bressingham Blue"

These relatives of the amaryllis for pots or tubs are not winter-hardy in the North.
See Perennials, *page 115.*

African lily

GLADIOLUS
left
Gladiolus "Peter Pears"

The flowers are borne on tall spikes. These arise from underground corms.
See Bulbs, *page 117.*

PURPLE LOOSESTRIFE right
Lythrum salicaria "Robert"

An ideal plant for growing in a damp area in the garden as it requires moist soil and tolerates light shade.
See Perennials, *page 115.*

PEARL EVERLASTING
below
Anaphalis triplinervis

Unlike other gray-leaved plants, this perennial will not tolerate drought.
See Perennials, *page 115.*

Passion flower

Purple loosestrife

Pearl everlasting

Autumn plants

At this time of year the borders are an interesting mixture of flower and foliage color. Autumn-flowering bulbs are available and can add color to the rock garden and borders. Many of the plants, like the species roses and the cotoneasters produce colorful hips and berries to brighten borders in the autumn.

SMOKE TREE right
Cotinus coggygria "Flame"

The purple foliage of this shrub turns a bright orange-red in autumn. *See* Shrubs, page 117.

PLANTAIN LILY left
Hosta fortunei "Aureo-marginata"

The large, ribbed leaves are edged in pale yellow. They are good ground-cover plants and can be left undisturbed for many years. *See* Perennials, page 115.

HYDRANGEA below
Hydrangea "Sybille"

Plant in a sheltered position to protect from frost. *See* Shrubs, page 112.

CROCUS right
Crocus scharojanii

Plant them beneath trees or near shrubs where they are less likely to be disturbed by digging. *See* Bulbs, page 117.

CARYOPTERIS right
Caryopteris clandonensis "Heavenly Blue"

This erect, compact shrub was raised in America and is one of the best deep blues available. *See* Shrubs, page 112.

MEADOW RUE below
Thalictrum dipterocarpum

These plants should be staked if grown in an exposed site as they can reach as much as 2m (6ft) high. *See* Perennials, page 115

AUTUMN CROCUS below
Colchicum byzantinum

They can be naturalized in grass or the borders. *See* Bulbs, page 117.

Smoke tree

Caryopteris

Meadow rue

Plantain lily

Hydrangea

Crocus

Autumn crocus

Plant type								**Sun preference**				**Soil preference**		
Tree	Shrub	Perennial	Annual	Biennial	Bulb	Climbing plants		Sun	Partial shade	Shade	Tolerant		Acid	Alkaline	Tolerant

ROSE left

Rosa moyesii "Geranium"

These roses have geranium-red flowers in summer and bright orange hips in autumn.
See Shrubs, *page 112.*

Rose

COTONEASTER left

Cotoneaster conspicuous "Decorus"

Cotoneasters are easy to grow and an excellent source of food for birds. This one is useful for covering banks and as ground cover. Spread up to 1m (3ft).
See Shrubs, *page 112.*

Cotoneaster

TIENTURIER GRAPE right

Vitis vinifera "Purpurea"

When they first appear the leaves are claret-red, gradually deepening to a dark purple color. Height up to 6m (20ft).
See Climbers, *page 119.*

MICHAELMAS DAISY below

Aster sp.

Asters are easy to grow if the soil is kept moist during the flowering period. Some varieties are prone to mildew.
See Perennials, *page 115.*

ICE PLANT below

Sedum spectabile "Brilliant"

The flat heads of tiny pink flowers attract many butterflies.
See Perennials, *page 115.*

GOOD-LUCK PLANT below

Oxalis deppei

Low-growing plants forming dense mats. The leaves and flowers close at night.
See Bulbs, *page 117.*

Tienturier grape

Michaelmas daisy

Sternbergia

STERNBERGIA left

Sternbergia clusiana

The bulbs can be planted in drifts which can be left undisturbed for many years.
See Bulbs, *page 117.*

Ice plant

Good-luck plant

Cultivation of border plants

The following pages give the cultivation details of the many different groups of ornamental plants which can be included in the border. You will find advice on choosing and buying, and on the method of planting each type of plant, and a section on maintenance gives general information on looking after the plants once they have been planted.

Shrubs

These form the framework of any border as well as attracting birds, butterflies and other insects. Some plants, like the beautiful butterfly bush (*Buddleia davidii*), prove irresistible to butterflies, which cluster round every nectar-filled bloom in summer.

Birds make use of shrubs for cover and food too. They particularly appreciate the berried shrubs like the snowberry (*Symphoricarpos doorenbosii*) – favorite because of its white berries and the dense cover it provides. Try to include a few native plants in the scheme because these are what will be most appreciated by wildlife.

CHOOSING SHRUBS

When choosing shrubs, cast your mind forward at least ten years, to the time when the shrubs have grown to their maximum height and spread. After checking height and spread, think about a color scheme, not forgetting to take into account the flowering season of the shrub and any others near it. It is also important to check preferences for shade or sunshine, soil type and acidity tolerance (*see pages 92-3*) before making your final selection. Remember that you can fill the spaces between small, young shrubs with annuals or other plants that have a shorter life.

BUYING SHRUBS

Like hedging plants, shrubs for borders can be bought as bare-rooted or container-grown plants. Container-grown plants tend to be smaller and more expensive – their advantage is that they can be planted at any time of the year instead of having to wait for the dormant season as you would with a bare-rooted plant.

Check all shrubs for signs of pests or disease (*see page 44*) and make sure they have a healthy root system.

PLANTING A SHRUB

Although shrubs can be planted at any time of the year from containers, there is, in my view, an advantage in buying field-grown, bare-rooted plants from a traditional nursery and planting during the autumn or early spring. A container-grown plant is more likely to suffer from the root ball drying out, so even if you do buy a plant in a container, it is still safer to wait until the autumn when the plant will not be losing so much water and the soil is more likely to remain moist.

If you plant shrubs (or trees) in an exposed spot, they dehydrate very quickly – this is especially so with conifers and other evergreens. Strong winds evaporate water from the leaf surfaces faster than the unestablished roots can take it up again so cells dry out and die. In a windy spot, it is essential, therefore, to protect newly planted specimens with a windbreak until they are established and their roots have had a chance to spread out.

1 Dig a hole large enough for the roots or root ball. Mix the dug-out soil with a bucketful of organic matter such as peat.

2 Water the plant well and remove the container. Mutilate root ball of container-grown shrubs as for trees (see page 82).

3 Plant at the level of the old soil mark on the stem. Sprinkle a little fine soil over the roots. Refill the hole and firm the soil down.

4 Mulch around the shrub with a layer of organic matter to conserve moisture and inhibit weed growth.

MAINTAINING SHRUBS

Feeding If you can provide shrubs with an annual mulch of well-rotted manure or compost, they will require little more. If not, give the whole border a dressing of blood, fish and bone meal in early spring, and a dressing of seaweed meal once every three years.

Watering Always pay particular attention to watering, especially in the first year while the shrubs are becoming established. This is particularly important with container-grown plants.

Pruning For many shrubs this should be carried out regularly. All shrubs can be shaped and, to some extent, kept smaller by regular cutting back, and many are pruned annually to produce flowering stems. Shrubs, such as the forsythia and the flowering currant (*Ribes* sp.), should be cut back hard immediately after flowering to encourage the bush to produce long shoots. The longer the shoots, the more flowers they are able to carry. Others like heaths (*Erica*) and lavender (*Lavandula*) are trimmed with shears after flowering in order to keep them compact and prevent them dying out in the center. Plants like broom (*Cytisus* hybrids) are pruned after flowering to prevent them producing seed.

Some shrubs, like the butterfly bush (*Buddleia davidii*), flower on wood made during the same season. These make long growths from buds that have been resting over winter, and they flower late in the summer. To increase the size of the blooms, all shoots made the previous year should be cut back hard in early spring.

Removing flower heads It is an advantage to remove the dead flower heads from many shrubs to increase the flower yield the following year. This is known as "dead-heading". Plants like the heaths can be trimmed with shears immediately after flowering. Other shrubs like rhododendrons, have to be dead-headed by hand (*see below left*).

Winter care If you plant in the autumn, winter frosts can lift the plants out of the ground again, so check them at regular intervals and, if they have been lifted, tread them back in.

Pests and diseases Pests like aphids and diseases such as leaf spot attack a wide variety of shrubs, so check plants regularly and treat as necessary (*see pages 49-53*).

Removing flower heads from rhododendrons
Remove the dead flowers very carefully as next year's buds are immediately beneath and could come off with the old bloom. Pinch off the flowers between finger and thumb. This tidies up the plant and promotes more flowers for the following year.

TEMPORARY PLANTING

If plants arrive when the weather is cold and the ground is frozen or if the soil is waterlogged, planting cannot go ahead. If you cannot plant immediately, it is wise to set the plants in a temporary trench, a technique known as "heeling in". Shrubs can be heeled in for several weeks and lifted and planted in the normal way when favorable conditions return.

1 *Cut a shallow, V-shaped slit trench – building the soil up on the back wall. Lay the shrubs in a single row in the trench, at an angle of 45°, so that their roots are in the trench and their tops resting on the soil you have built up. This will ensure that they do not blow about, causing root damage.*

2 *Cover the roots and lower stem with soil or peat and firm down with your boot. Cover with soil dug out of a second trench if you have a lot of shrubs to heel in.*

Roses

There are many types of rose and their classification can be confusing. Species roses are the original ancestors of modern, hybrid roses and should be grown in the same way as other shrubs. The modern, hybrid roses can be grown as bushes or standards – standard roses are simply bush roses budded on to a long stem to make a short tree. Many varieties of climbing and rambling rose are also available.

CHOOSING ROSES

With the wide variety of shapes and colors available, choosing roses can be difficult. In my view, bush standards are too formal for mixed borders in very small gardens, though "weeping standards" fit into a mixed border quite well – these are rambler roses on a long stem, with their shoots allowed to hang down instead of being trained upwards.

BUYING ROSES

Roses can be bought bare-rooted in spring or container-grown at any time of the year. Check container plants for mildew and black spot (*see page 52*) before buying them.

PLANTING ROSES

There has always been controversy among serious rose growers concerning planting depths, mainly whether the bud or graft (the bulge on the lower main stem) should be above or below ground. Today general agreement favors planting so that the bud is above ground – about 2.5cm (1in) and more in mild climates. In cold-winter regions, winter-protection is recommended to protect this bud-union area.

MAINTAINING ROSES

Feeding Feed as other shrubs, mulching annually with well-rotted manure or compost.

Watering Water well in the first year after planting. Thereafter, ensure the roots do not dry out in warm weather.

Pruning This is carried out every year on hybrid bush roses in early spring, just before the bushes start into growth, as you will be able to assess the amount of frost damage and cut it out. The principle of pruning is that the harder you cut back, the more vigorously the shoot will grow. So, get into the habit of always cutting back weak shoots further than the stronger-growing ones to balance the bush. Weak shoots should be pruned to leave one or two buds while stronger ones can have three or four. Bush standards are pruned just like the ordinary bush hybrids, while weeping standards are pruned after flowering, merely removing very old, diseased or overcrowded wood.

Suckers Rose varieties are usually grown by being grafted on to a rootstock. Occasionally the rootstock will send out a vigorous shoot, known as a sucker, which should be removed. These are easy to spot as they are light green and often more thorny than the variety.

Removing flower heads Removing the flowers of continuous-flowering varieties as they fade will ensure a supply of blooms right the way through summer and autumn and often into early winter too.

Pests and diseases Check all roses regularly for signs of pest or disease attack, particularly of mildew, black spot or aphids (*see pages 50 and 52 for treatment*).

Winter protection In cold climates consult Cooperative Extension Service for regional recommendations.

Pruning rose bushes *Cut all the shoots back to an outward- or downward-facing bud to encourage them to grow outwards, away from the center of the bush.*

Removing a rose sucker *Scrape away a little soil where the sucker arises from the root, and pull it off if you can. If not, cut it as near to the stem as possible.*

Dead-heading a rose *Remove the fading flower by breaking the stem about 1cm (½in) below the seed head with your thumb and forefinger.*

Perennials

These can be defined as plants with soft stems which generally die down every winter and produce new growth in spring, persisting for many years. As perennials number many hundreds there is a good selection for every soil type and sun preference (*see pages 92-3*).

CHOOSING PERENNIALS

Confusingly sold as "herbaceous perennials", "herbaceous plants", "hardy plants", "hardy perennials", and "hardy herbaceous perennials", they are all the same thing. Half-hardy perennials are merely perennials that need to be overwintered indoors.

BUYING PERENNIALS

Most perennials can be raised from seed or propagated by division (*see page 274*) of an existing clump. They can be bought throughout the growing season as container-grown plants or bare-rooted in spring and autumn.

The plants you choose will be governed by the soil type and aspect of your border, but do try to include as varied a selection as possible.

PLANTING PERENNIALS

Unlike shrubs, I prefer to plant perennials in the spring, just as new growth is starting. Planted in the autumn, they may suffer from cold, frozen soil or from waterlogging, which can rot the soft parts of the plant. In spring they will start to grow and make roots straight away and, provided you attend to the watering, they will never look back. If you have a large area to fill, you can plant in groups of three to five to create blocks of color.

MAINTAINING PERENNIALS

Feeding General border feeding should be sufficient to maintain perennials (*see page 90*).
Watering Perennials should be well watered when they are planted – "puddling in" is the best method (*see above right*). Afterwards they need to be watered as necessary (*see page 266*).
Supporting Many perennials require staking because their stems are often weak and floppy. Others grow tall and are likely to be bent and broken in high winds. Tall perennials, such as delphiniums, should be staked fairly early in the season, using a bamboo cane and tying the stems to the stake as they grow longer. Medium-sized perennials like hellebores can be held erect with a few twiggy sticks which also look less obtrusive than canes. Some shorter perennials like oriental poppies (*Papaver orientale*) need staking to stop them flopping, so use a special wire support or put a piece of wide-mesh wire netting over the young plants and allow them to grow up through it. The mesh will soon be hidden by

PLANTING PERENNIALS

When planting container-grown perennials it is important to ensure that the root ball does not dry out. "Puddling in" ensures that the plants get enough water when first planted.

1 *Remove the plant from its pot and dig a hole large enough to accommodate the root ball. Sprinkle a handful of a general fertilizer, such as blood, fish and bone meal, around the rim.*

2 *Once the plant is in the prepared hole, gently firm the soil down. Give the plant enough water to form a puddle on the soil surface.*

a mass of new leaves.
Propagation Most perennials should be divided and replanted every few years. Otherwise, they form large clumps which simply get tired. The young plants thrive on the outside of the clump, and the center often goes bare or dies out altogether. To rejuvenate the clump, lift and divide the whole plant every three to five years (*see page 274*).

Half-hardy perennials can be propagated by taking cuttings in late summer or early spring.
Pests and diseases Some perennials – for example, Michaelmas daisies (*Aster novi-belgii*),

Staking a delphinium *Stick a 2.5m (8ft) bamboo cane into the ground next to the plant and tie the stem with soft string. Add further ties as the plant grows.*

delphiniums and phlox are very susceptible to mildew in dry conditions. Pull out any
affected plants and increase watering around
the others, particularly if the weather is very
dry (*see page 266*). Always throw diseased plants
away; never compost them.

Annuals

These are defined as plants that grow from seed,
flower and die in the same year. Though annuals
need to be replaced each year, they provide a
very bright display of color the whole summer
through and can be very useful for covering soil
and providing flowers in a new bed until you
have planned your planting. They also attract
many beneficial insects into the garden, including bees for pollination (*see page 203*) and hover-
flies for the natural control of the many kinds of
aphids (*see page 50*).

CHOOSING ANNUALS

There are so many different varieties of annuals
that it is often difficult to choose which to grow.
Annuals are divided into those that are able to
stand a certain amount of frost and those that
are not. They are known as "hardy" and "half-
hardy" annuals respectively.

Annuals range from the sprawling sweet pea
(*Lathyrus odorata*) and the carpeting alyssum
(*Lobularia* "Maritima") to the taller cornflower
(*Centaurea*) and love-in-a-mist (*Nigella*).

BUYING ANNUALS

Annuals can be raised from seed, or bought in
trays as bedding plants, ready to plant out in
the garden. Avoid all plants with diseased or
blemished leaves. Check that the annuals you
choose are suitable for the soil type and amount
of sun that your border receives (*see pages 92-3*).

PLANTING ANNUALS

Preferably the soil for sowing or planting any
kind of annual should not be too rich. In poor

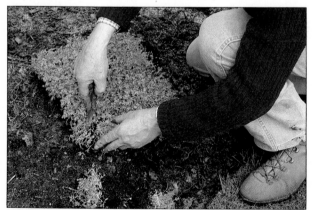

Planting hardy annuals *Sow the seeds fairly thickly in a
seed tray in early spring. When the seedlings are 2.5cm (1in)
or so tall, take the block out of the tray and cut into small
squares with a penknife. Plant out the clumps.*

soil, they will make more flower and less leaf
growth. Of course, in the small garden border
where all the plants are mixed together, it is best
to fertilize for the shrubs and perennials and let
the annuals take their chances.

Growing hardy annuals These are the easiest
annuals to grow and can be raised from seed
sown in open ground in the spring, as soon as
the soil is dry and warm enough. There is little
point in sowing until the soil temperature has
reached 7°C (45°F).

Mark out the area you wish to sow and sow
seeds in to shallow seed drills 15cm (6in) apart.
When the seedlings are large enough to handle,
carefully thin out to about 15-20cm (6-9in)
apart depending on the variety. Alternatively,
sow seeds in a seed tray. Allow them to grow
without thinning out and plant them in clumps
when they are tall enough (*see below*). This is
also a much better method if your soil is heavy
and lies wet in the early spring.

Growing half-hardy annuals These are much
more difficult to grow than hardy annuals, but
are generally worth the extra effort. They must
be sown either in a heated greenhouse, or they
can be germinated in a heated propagator in
the greenhouse, on the kitchen windowsill or
under fluorescent tubes. Most require a temperature of about 18°C (65°F) (*see page 249*).

As soon as they germinate, take them out of
the propagator or continue growing under
fluorescent lights until they have grown true
leaves. Then transfer them to another seed tray
at a wider spacing and grow on until all danger
of frost has passed for the year, then plant them
out in the garden. Before planting out, ensure
that they are "hardened off", or acclimatized
to the lower temperatures outside, by putting
them first into a closed cold frame (*see page 256*)
then increasing the ventilation gradually over a
week or so.

When you are certain that frost will not recur,
plant them out in soil that has been prepared
with manure or compost. Don't add fertilizer or
you will encourage too much leaf growth at the
expense of flowers. If frost is threatened after
planting, cover the plants with a plastic cloche
until warmer weather arrives.

MAINTAINING ANNUALS

Feeding Do not feed annuals unless they have
stopped growing completely since this encourages them to make leaf growth at the expense of
the flowers.

Watering Annuals need careful watering when
first planted, and further watering if the weather
is very dry (*see page 266*).

Pests and diseases Some annuals are prone to
fungus diseases such as botrytis in cold, damp
weather. If you see signs of disease, remove the
affected leaves immediately to prevent it
spreading (*see page 52*).

Biennials

These are defined as plants that are sown one year and flower the next, after which they die. Some, such as pansies, are really perennials, but they are best grown as biennials as they flower better in the first year.

CHOOSING BIENNIALS

If carefully chosen, biennials will give you a fine display of flowers throughout spring and summer. They grow in most soils, and include some of the true cottage-garden plants like sweet Williams (*Dianthus barbatus*) and Canterbury bells (*Campanula medium*).

BUYING BIENNIALS

Biennials can be bought as seed or small bedding plants in trays. Check specimens for diseased or blemished leaves and make sure that you can supply the right soil and sun requirements in your garden.

PLANTING BIENNIALS

They require much the same conditions as annuals. Avoid fertilizer at planting time, but incorporate well-rotted manure or compost into the soil (*see pages 18-34*).

You will need a small area set aside as a seed bed and a little more for growing on. Biennials are very easy to raise from seed sown outside in early summer (*see page 268*). When the seedlings are sturdy enough to handle without damaging them they are best transplanted about 10cm (4in) apart in rows in a corner of the garden and then transplanted again to their final positions in early autumn, after the summer-flowering annuals have finished.

Spring-flowering biennials will flower until early summer, when they can be pulled up, put on the compost heap and replaced with clumps of summer-flowering annuals.

Bulbs

I include corms, rhizomes and tubers with bulbs as they are all types of food-storage organs. After flowering, the foliage dies down and food is stored in the bulb through the dormant season. New growth appears the following season.

Bulbs are ideal for filling spaces between shrubs in the border with color. Moreover, if spring-flowering types are planted at the base of deciduous shrubs, they will be in full flower when the shrubs are dormant and then later in the season their increasingly untidy foliage will be masked by the new growth of the shrubs.

CHOOSING BULBS

Bulbs should not be considered as merely spring-flowering plants – with careful planning and planting it is possible to have a year-round display of color if you live in a region where winters are mild. They can be planted in any type of soil as long as it is well drained.

BUYING BULBS

When buying, inspect each bulb carefully. Check that the skin is intact and the bulb firm.

PLANTING BULBS

Most bulbs like to be grown in groups, which offers a convenient way of creating blocks of color. Do not mix different varieties in blocks as they all flower at slightly different times.

Bulbs can be planted in any type of soil as long as it is well drained. Because they are soft and fleshy, bulbs cannot abide bad drainage; it quickly leads to rotting. So, if your soil is heavy, make sure it is deeply dug and preferably raised above the level of the lawn or the surrounding land and plant the bulbs on a layer of grit.

Depth of planting varies, of course, with the bulb, but, as a general rule, plant twice as deep

Spreading forget-me-nots *Do not buy seed of the forget-me-not (*Myosotis sylvatica*); simply pull up a seeded plant and shake it over the border to disperse its seeds.*

Planting bulbs in heavy soil *Dig a hole about 60cm (2ft) diameter and 30cm (12in) deep. Put a bucketful of grit in the bottom, sit the bulbs on the grit, then cover with soil.*

as the depth of the bulb in light and normal soil, and the same depth as the bulb if your soil is very heavy, not forgetting to allow for the layer of grit. This is important since some bulbs will not produce flowers if they are planted too near the surface. Make sure, too, that the bulbs are the right way up – it can be difficult to tell sometimes – the "nose", or pointed end, is the top.

Some summer-flowering bulbs, such as lilies, like to have their heads in sunshine and their feet in the shade, so planting in the shade of a low-growing shrub is ideal. The bulb will grow through the shrub to expose its flower to the sun while the roots stay cool.

Spring-flowering bulbs should be planted in the late summer, and autumn- and summer-flowering types in the spring or early summer.

Bulbs can also be planted in grass – a technique known as "naturalizing". This is especially attractive in areas where the grass is cut only two or three times a year. If you want to plant bulbs on a lawn that is mown regularly, you should choose those that flower very early, otherwise cutting the grass will be delayed several weeks until the foliage has died down. Bulbs for naturalizing are best planted informally, so scatter them about haphazardly on the grass and then plant them with a bulb planter, a tool that removes a core of soil, enabling you to put the bulb in the bottom of the hole and then replace the soil and grass in one go.

MAINTAINING BULBS

Feeding It is not enough to plant bulbs and then leave them to their own devices. Bear in mind that the flower you see in the first year after planting is the result of the efforts of the grower in the previous year. To achieve as good a result the following year, you have to do what he did. After flowering, it is important to ensure that there is a plentiful supply of potash (*see page 38*); this encourages a good flower the following year. If the bulbs are in the borders, you will be applying sufficient manure or fertilizer when you feed the soil for the benefit of the shrubs and herbaceous plants. If they are planted on their own, in tubs or in beds under large trees, they will benefit from a couple of liquid feeds after flowering – seaweed or liquid manure is ideal (*see pages 41-2*). Once the foliage has died down, mulch the soil over the bulbs with well-rotted manure or compost.

Watering The soil should be moist at all times but ensure that drainage is good, otherwise the bulbs will rot (*see page 117*).

Post-flowering care It is essential, after bulbs have flowered, that you allow the foliage to remain attached so that it can build up a flower for next year. Remove the leaves only after they have turned yellow; then cut them off and compost them. If you cut them off too early or, as some gardeners do, tie them in neat little knots, the plant cannot use sunlight to make food. Consequently, the bulb gets smaller and smaller and eventually disappears. Personally, I do not object to the foliage of bulbs in the borders, provided it is fairly quickly masked by other foliage. I make sure of this by planting those bulbs with a tendency to look scruffy next to foliage plants. Daffodils (*Narcissus*), for example, can be planted next to large-leaved plantain lilies (*Hosta* sp.). When the daffodils are flowering, the lilies are dormant. Then, almost as soon as the daffodils finish, the lilies produce large leaves to cover the daffodil foliage.

Lifting and storing Some of the more tender summer-flowering bulbs like gladioli and dahlias must be lifted to prevent frost damage. Dig them up just before heavy frosts threaten. Then dry them off, clean them and store them over the winter in a cool, frost-free shed until planting time next season.

TEMPORARY STORAGE OF BULBS

Sometimes you may want to dig up bulbs after flowering to make space for annual flowers. If so, dig them up with as much root as possible and make sure the foliage remains intact. Then, in a sheltered corner of the garden, replant them in a row in a slit trench. This is known as "heeling in". They can be close together as long as the foliage is exposed to the sun. Give them a couple of liquid feeds before the foliage dies down.

1 *Dig a V-shaped slit trench, building up the soil on the back wall. Lay the bulbs in a single row against the back wall of the trench. They can be kept close together if space is at a premium in your garden.*

2 *Cover the bulbs with soil, leaving the foliage exposed to the sun. Replant the following season. If you are planting several different types of bulb, it may be worth labelling them to avoid confusion when replanting.*

Climbing plants

Whether they cover the wall of the house, hide an ugly feature, scramble through trees or shrubs, or soften the artificial look of a wooden fence, climbers are invaluable. There is no quicker way of achieving height in the garden and no better way to disguise the inevitable "man-made" look of barriers and buildings.

True climbers are plants that have some means of clinging on to a support – either tendrils, curling leaf stalks, adventitious roots or by twining. Many shrubs and some roses can, however, be trained to cover a wall or fence by regularly tying their shoots on to supports.

CHOOSING CLIMBERS
The site and function of the climber will determine the type you can grow. Some climbers, especially clematis and roses (*Rosa* sp.), can be trained to grow through trees and other shrubs to give either a contrast in flower color or to extend the season by flowering when the tree has finished. But avoid the vigorous types like *Clematis montana* and the Russian vine (*Polygonum baldschuanicum*) for this purpose, because they will swamp the tree. Other climbers, such as ivy (*Hedera* sp.), make useful ground-cover plants for weed suppression (*see page 90*). Many, like the ornamental vines (*Vitis* sp.) and Virginia creeper (*Parthenocissus quinquefolia*), are grown for their dense, colorful foliage rather than their flowers.

BUYING CLIMBERS
Climbers are normally bought as container-grown plants, at any time of year. When choosing them, look at the growth at the base of the plant rather than that at the top. It is much better to have one with short, strong shoots growing from the base than a long bare stem with shoots at the top.

PLANTING CLIMBERS
Good preparation is essential, especially if the plants are to be grown against a wall of your house. In most cases this will put them in the driest spot in the garden as they are likely to be "protected" from rain by the overhanging eaves. Yet, because they are vigorous growers, they need all the moisture and food they can get. Make sure the planting area is generously enriched with well-rotted manure, compost or one of the alternatives (*see page 30*). For each climber, try to prepare a planting site at least 1.2m (4ft) square, double dig it and work in at least a barrowload of organic matter. Supplement this with two good handfuls of blood, fish and bone meal or similar organic fertilizer.

Most climbers, like shrubs, should be planted at the level of the soil mark on the stem. The

Supporting climbers *The neatest and least obtrusive way to train climbers that do not stick to the wall or fence is with horizontal wires. These can be fixed to the wall with vine eyes driven into the mortar joints (*see page 267*). This beautiful clematis (*Clematis montana "Rubens"*) has tendrils which will twist around the wires and disguise them from view.*

exception is clematis. This is subject to a fungus disease called "clematis wilt", which causes the plant to wilt from the top – shoots suddenly collapse and die. But if you cut it back hard as soon as you see any signs of the disease, new shoots that are free from the fungus will appear from below ground. So plant clematis about 10-15cm (4-6in) deeper than it grew on the nursery to ensure plenty of new buds form underground.

After planting, cover the soil with a layer of coarse material such as pine bark to shade the roots (they like to be cool), prevent evaporation of water, help keep slugs at bay and suppress the growth of weeds.

TRAINING CLIMBERS

Climbing plants can be divided into groups according to the way they are trained. Some can support themselves, while others need to be provided with wires or a trellis. Some shrubs can be used as climbers if they are trained properly – these are known as wall shrubs.

Self-clinging climbers These are the easiest climbers to train, and include ivy (*Hedera* sp.), Virginia creeper (*Parthenocissus quinquefolia*) and climbing hydrangea (*Hydrangea petiolaris*). Simply plant them at the bottom of the wall and point them in the right direction. They will find their own way after that. They will not grow very quickly until they attach but, once they do so, they will soon make up for the delay.

Twining climbers This group of climbers needs support. Some, like honeysuckle (*Lonicera*) or wisteria, will twist themselves round any kind of support, while others, like clematis, are equipped with either tendrils or leaf stalks that are designed to twist round a support to hold up the stem. Both types will be happy climbing up wires, trellis or netting.

Supporting climbing stems *Climbers that are not self-supporting, such as honeysuckle, should have their new shoots twisted round their supports.*

Making a rose-covered pillar *Carefully wind the rose stem around the pillar and tie it in with soft string. As you are doing so, try to pull the shoots down to form a flat spiral, to increase the number of flowers produced.*

Wall shrubs Some shrubs can be trained upwards, to give the same effect as climbing plants; climbing roses are often used to decorate pergolas and arches. They are not really climbers at all, but very vigorous shrubs, sending out long shoots. These shoots need to be tied in to the support as they appear. As with climbing roses on a wall, try to pull the shoots down almost horizontally as they grow to increase flowering. It takes a little longer to cover the support this way, but the restriction of the flow of sap will ensure that many more flowers will be produced.

Other wall shrubs include cotoneaster and firethorn (*Pyracantha* "Lalandeii"). Both of these plants can be trained to cover a wall or any type of fence.

MAINTAINING CLIMBERS

Watering If the soil has been well prepared, climbers will only need watering in very dry weather. Climbers on walls need extra watering if they are protected by overhanging eaves.

Feeding If the soil has been well prepared, general border feeding should be sufficient.

Cutting back Self-clingers only need to be prevented from straying where they are unwelcome. They should be cut away from windows or they will block out the daylight quite quickly. Do this with shears or pruners whenever it is necessary. Spring is the best time.

Pruning Climbers should be pruned annually to improve flowering. They can be divided into two pruning groups – the early-flowering plants, which should be pruned and dead-headed immediately after flowering, and those that flower later in the season, which should be cut back the following spring (*see below*).

GROUPING CLIMBERS FOR PRUNING

Early-flowering climbers	Late-flowering climbers
Clematis montana	*Clematis jackmannii*
Clematis macropetala	*Clematis* "Ville de Lyon"
Clematis "Belle of Woking"	*Clematis* "Nellie Moser"
Wisteria	Trumpet vine
Summer jasmine	Russian vine
Honeysuckle (Woodbine)	Winter jasmine
Chinese gooseberry	Chilean glory flower
Akebia quinata	*Lapageria rosea*

Preventing climbers from straying *Never let a climbing plant get a firm hold on a roof. The tendrils will get beneath the tiles and could dislodge them. Cut back stems with pruners.*

Ponds and aquatic plants

The organic garden will be more attractive to wildlife if it contains a pond, because it provides drinking water for birds and small mammals, and a home for many aquatic animals. Some, like frogs and toads, should be encouraged because they eat large quantities of slugs and snails. A pond will also enable you to grow a much wider range of plants in your garden.

AQUATIC PLANTS

These can be divided into four groups – deep-water aquatics, floating plants, submerged oxygenating plants and marginal plants. Try to include plants from each group in your pond.

Deep-water aquatics are plants that root at the bottom of the pond but whose leaves float on the surface. This group includes the water lilies (*Nymphaea* sp.), which are not only very decorative but also useful in reducing the growth of algae, which turn the water green and murky. Algae live on mineral salts and sunlight, so the more leaf cover there is on the surface of the

water, the better. Attractive deep-water aquatics include the white water lily (*Nymphaea alba*) and water crowfoot (*Ranunculus aquatilis*).

Floating plants also reduce the amount of sunlight that reaches the surface of the water and include the water hyacinth (*Eichhornia crassipes*) and the water chestnut (*Trapa natans*).

Submerged oxygenating plants are not decorative but they aerate the water, and are, therefore, essential to the health of the pond. Suitable plants include spiked water milfoil (*Myriophyllum spicatum*), Canadian pondweed (*Elodea canadensis*), and curly pondweed (*Potamogeton crispus*).

Marginal plants grow in the shallowest parts of the pond and the boggy soil around the edges. There is a great range of preferences for the amount of water above the roots. They range from those which must be planted in water a few inches or so deep, like the sweet-scented rush (*Acorus calamus*), to the primulas, which should be planted in the marshy soil.

Floating plants top
*The water chestnut (*Trapa natans*),
helps to exclude light and thus algae.*

Deep-water aquatics top right
*Plant the water crowfoot (*Ranunculus
aquatilis*) in a deep part of the pond.*

Submerged oxygenators above
*The spiked milfoil (*Myriophyllum
spicatum*) will oxygenate the water.*

Marginal plants right
*Grow moisture lovers like irises around
the edge of the pond.*

CONSTRUCTING AND PLANTING A POND

There are several ways of making a pond. The simplest is to buy a ready-made fiberglass shell and dig a hole for it. Alternatively, you can dig a hole to your own specifications and line it with P.V.C. liner, although this will eventually perish. Slightly more expensive but much more durable is a butyl-rubber liner. This also enables you to choose the shape of the pond.

Dig a hole to the required size with a slope on one side. A shelf can also be cut out at the edge for the marginal plants. Line the hole with a thick layer of soft material to protect the liner from damage by sharp stones in the soil. To calculate the minimum size of liner, measure the maximum length and width of the pond. Add to these measurements twice the maximum depth.

Planting marginal plants These should be planted on the pond shelf, or in the special marsh garden.

The marsh garden A gently sloping, shallow area which provides an ideal habitat for plants which like to grow in damp soil.

Planting in pots Use heavy garden soil or rotted turf. Do not use soil rich in organic matter, it will putrefy as it rots down. A thin layer of gravel on top of the soil prevents it from floating to the surface and stops inquisitive fish disturbing it.

The marginal shelf This provides a planting area for plants which like to grow in shallow water. Make it very shallow in places as a refuge for fish fry.

Hibernation site Put rocks in the marsh garden to provide a place for frogs to hibernate.

Planting floating plants Put these into the pond in spring. You simply throw them in. Use one plant every sq yard.

Edging the pond Paving stones make the planting and maintenance of the pond easy. They also help to secure the butyl-rubber liner.

Protecting the liner Cover the soil with a special blanket, sand, old carpet or newspaper before laying the butyl-rubber liner.

Planting submerged oxygenating plants These are sold in bunches, with a small weight fixed to the stalks. To plant them, throw the bunch into the pond in spring, using one bunch per 2 sq yard of water.

Plastic containers Put plants into the pond in plastic buckets of soil.

Planting deep-water aquatics These should be planted in containers during late spring and summer. Cut off all the old leaves and lower the container to the bottom of the pond. The new leaves will soon grow up to the surface.

The pond in cross-section

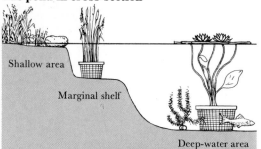

The marsh garden should consist merely of damp soil. The shallow area should be 5cm (2in) deep for those plants which like their roots covered with shallow water. The marginal shelf should be wide enough to hold containers of plants and be 7-12cm (3-5in) deep. The deep-water area should be at least 45cm (18in) deep. This will accommodate most water lilies.

PLANTING DEPTHS FOR AQUATIC PLANTS

Deep-water plants	
Water hawthorn (*Aponogeton distachyum*)	15-45cm (6-18in)
Water violet (*Hottonia palustris*)	30cm (12in)
Water lily varieties (*Nymphaea* sp.)	
N. "Alba"	30-90cm (1-3ft)
N. "Sunrise"	15-45cm (6-18in)
N. "Firecrest"	15-45cm (6-18in)
N. pygmae alba	10-20cm (4-9in)
Marginal plants	
Sweet-scented rush (*Acorus calamus*)	7-12cm (3-5in)
Flowering rush (*Butomus umbellatus*)	7-12cm (3-5in)
Bog arum (*Calla palustris*)	5-10cm (2-4in)
Marsh marigold (*Caltha palustris*)	0-7cm (0-3in)
Arrowhead (*Saggitaria japonica*)	7-12cm (3-5in)
Water forget-me-not (*Myosotis palustris*)	0-7cm (0-3in)
Primula (*Primula* sp.)	0-7cm (0-3in)
Note: *Depths refer to water above the planting soil in the pool.*	

SITING THE POND

Ideally, the pond should form a feature in the garden, rather than being tucked away out of view. Choose a site which receives plenty of sunlight for at least part of the day. Most aquatic plants prefer sunny conditions and certainly fish prefer warmer water, although they don't like very sudden changes in temperature.

Site the pond as far from deciduous trees as possible. If leaves fall into the pond they will turn the water sour as they rot anaerobically. Trees will also shade the pond.

If you have small children, even a small pond can be very dangerous. Make sure you site it where it can easily be seen from the house and, if there is any risk, it is best not to build one at all until the children are older.

MAINTAINING THE POND

Algae growth Soon after filling the pond, the water may turn pea-green in color. This is due to rapid algae growth. Pond water contains minerals and receives plenty of sunlight right at the beginning, so the algae flourish. Do not empty out the water and replace it with fresh. If you do, you are giving the algae another supply of mineral salts, which will cause them to flourish again. Leave the water in the pond as the supply of minerals is soon depleted. And, as the water plants grow larger, the other source of food – sunlight – will be excluded. Deprived of food, the algae die, and the water in the pond begins to clear.

Thinning plants You may need to thin out the oxygenating plants occasionally; this is easy to do, just pull some out by hand. Return any animal life on the plants to the pond and throw the plants on the compost heap.

Blanket weed infestation You may be unlucky enough to get an infestation of blanket weed. This is a slimy, ugly-looking green weed which floats on the top of the pond and chokes out other vegetation. Remove it as soon as you see it. Provided you do this regularly, you will prevent further infestation.

Leaves Keep leaves out of the pond, or they will turn the water sour as they rot. Try to avoid building the pond near deciduous trees; if this is impossible, cover the surface with a piece of netting in the autumn.

Keeping ornamental fish If you decide to keep fish, you should make special provision for their offspring. Fish have a habit of eating the eggs they lay, plus the tiny "fry" when they hatch out, and any frog spawn that you may be lucky enough to attract. To foil them, include a very shallow area in the pond, no more than 5cm (2in) deep, which is too shallow for the larger fish to swim in. Here, the smallest fish will gather, because it will be warmer, and you can make sure that you guide any frog spawn into the area yourself.

Alpines

Cultivated varieties of wild flowers from the high, mountainous areas of the world are amongst the most beautiful garden flowers we have. They are the "odd-men-out" in the organic garden as most have little or no value in attracting wildlife and, therefore, pest predators. Nonetheless, once you have grown a few, you will want to make room for some more. In fact, they take up very little room as the best way to grow them is in a rock garden, a scree garden or in holes in walls or between paving slabs.

CHOOSING ALPINES

The choice of plants is enormous, providing attractive flower colors and shapes and interesting foliage. Many alpines need an alkaline soil; others, including many of the gentians are lime haters and need an acid soil.

PLANTING ALPINES

Plant alpines in spring or autumn and sow alpine seeds in winter because they need a period of cold before they will germinate (*see page 270*). The one really important factor for success is good drainage. In the wild, alpines grow in cracks in rocks or in the gravel, known as scree, that has broken off and rolled down the mountain side. This is the type of environment that you need to reproduce.

One way of growing alpines that really works is in a miniature scree garden (*see below*). Alpines can also be grown in drinking troughs or old stone sinks. If you grow them in containers, make sure they have drainage material in the bottom then fill them with a free-draining soil mixture (*see page 128*).

If you grow alpines in a rock garden, make special planting pockets by arranging the rocks

A scree garden *The very formal shape of this scree garden is softened by the informal planting and the stepping stones. A wide range of alpine plants will thrive in this well-drained site. To construct the garden, dig a hole at least 60cm (2ft) deep and put in about 23cm (9in) of hardcore. Refill with equal parts of good soil, sphagnum peat and coarse grit.*

GROWING ALPINES

Alpines originate from rocky habitats, which provide them with a well-drained site. In the garden you can re-create this by growing them in a rock garden, in gaps between paving stones or in a hole in the garden wall.

A rock garden can be as large or as small as you wish and is often used as a means of growing plants on an awkward, sloping site. Walls for growing alpines can be specially constructed; build a hollow wall and fill it with soil.

Growing alpines in a wall

1 *Cut a piece of turf large enough to cover the root ball of the plant. Leave it upside down until the grass dies completely, then soak it in water.*

2 *When the turf is thoroughly wet, roll it around the root ball of the plant.*

3 *Push the turf-wrapped root ball firmly into the hole.*

Making soil pockets in a rock garden

Arrange the rocks in small horseshoe-shaped pockets and fill the area between them with a mixture of equal parts soil, peat and coarse grit (see below). Plant with a wide variety of alpines to ensure that the color and shape of the garden will change constantly. The two photographs, right, were taken two months apart: the first one was taken in late spring, the second in mid summer.

Late spring

Mid summer

into horse-shoe shapes and filling the spaces with a special soil mixture. It is possible to grow plants that need different soil types in the same rock garden provided you fill the pockets with suitable soils.

Alpines can also be grown in cracks and crevices in walls. Particularly successful are plants that do not tolerate being wet. Plant them in autumn, by wrapping the roots in old turf and pushing them into the hole (*see above*).

You can also plant them between stone slabs when making a path. Leave gaps between some of the slabs, fill with a suitable soil and plant with prostrate alpines.

MAINTAINING ALPINES

Feeding Fertilizer is rarely required. Only feed alpines if they look as though they have completely stopped growing – which should not be more often than every five or six years. Give them a light dusting of blood, fish and bone meal.

Watering Alpines need water only in very dry weather. Ensure they have good drainage.

Weeding This can be time consuming amongst alpines, especially when the plants are very small. Weeds can be kept to a minimum by covering any bare soil with coarse grit.

Protection In their natural habitat, alpines are covered with snow which protects them in winter, so many, especially those with gray woolly foliage, are not happy in the wet climate of lower areas. It is a good idea, therefore, to cover any susceptible plants with pine or other evergreen boughs, hay or other light material.

Cultivating wild flowers

Wild flowers can be grown in the borders or, in large gardens, as a wild-flower meadow. Wild or native plants that prefer or tolerate shade are ideal in woodland gardens or under individual trees. Also, some native wild flowers looked upon with scorn by gardeners can, when grown in the fertile conditions of the border, become very attractive. In my own garden I leave seedlings of red campion (*Lychnis dioica*) and white campion (*Lychnis alba*) that blow in from the nearby fields. When they grow in my manured and fertilized borders they become much bigger plants, bearing many more flowers. And, even when cultivated in this way, they are just as attractive to native insects and birds, so helping to control pests by attracting their natural predators.

CHOOSING WILD FLOWERS

There are several specialists who sell wild flower seeds and most retail seed catalogues carry a selection. Special mixtures are available, aiming to attract butterflies, bees or birds. Other seed mixtures may be selected for sun or shade, specific soil conditions and, of course, different climatic conditions.

BUYING WILD FLOWERS

Some wild flower suppliers sell rooted plants which are ready for planting; never lift plants from the wild unless you have permission, or the area is to be cleared for development. Check the soil and habitat preferences of each species before planting.

PLANTING WILD FLOWERS

Some wild flower seeds can be sown in spring, but other kinds should be sown in autumn and will germinate the following spring. Follow the directions on the packets. In general, most wild flowers for shade or woodland gardens prefer more moist and humusy soil, while the kinds for meadows and other sunny sites tolerate or need drier, less fertile soil. Few wild flowers for any conditions need fertilizers, but will require normal watering until well-established.

Underplanting with wild flowers above
Bluebells will suppress weed growth around these colorful azaleas in spring as well as providing extra color.

A summer meadow right
White daisies and bright red poppies attract butterflies and other insects. Later, the seed heads will attract a wide variety of birds.

SOWING A WILD-FLOWER MEADOW

A wild-flower meadow is suitable for larger gardens, as one of the advantages of this method is the ease of maintenance; in a large garden this could be a boon. The flower population will change a little as conditions generally favor one species or another, but there always needs to be a varied selection so as to attract the insects and birds that help control pests.

If possible, choose a patch of land with low fertility. Prepare and sow it as you would for a lawn (*see page 79*), using a mixture of grasses and flowers suitable for your soil type.

The meadow only needs cutting twice a year, once in early spring just as growth starts, and again after the wild flowers have set seed in late summer. Use the seed for next year's meadow.

THE CONTAINER GARDEN

JUST AS HOUSEPLANTS on the windowsill immediately transform a room into a "living room", so the harder man-made surfaces outside can be softened with plants in containers. By using plants in pots, tubs or window boxes, you can integrate these otherwise barren areas with the rest of the garden.

Every gardener needs those hard areas of paving or concrete as paths or patios, steps or driveways, but they always stand out a little uneasily in a plant-filled organic garden. A little softening makes all the difference. Try hanging a flowering basket either side of the front door, for example, or position a stone trough filled with alpines over an unsightly drain cover.

You can fill containers with permanent plants or you can use them for seasonal displays or a combination. Fill tubs or boxes, for example, with small shrubs surrounded by suitable annuals and biennials for winter and summer color.

Types of container

Good garden centers stock a wide range of containers made from different materials and they will also have a choice of styles – from simple wire baskets to plastic and "Greek" urns, wooden barrels and concrete vases. Provided the containers have adequate drainage, or you can drill suitable holes through the bottom, plants will grow in all of them quite happily.

PLASTIC
Containers made of plastic are certainly the cheapest and some can be quite attractive. Since most are made without drainage holes, make sure you drill holes in the bottom before planting; an ordinary wood drill will do for this. It is better to overdrain the pot, so make 1cm ($\frac{1}{2}$in) holes about 15cm (6in) apart.

Some plastic drums used for cooking oil or orange juice can make attractive containers when you cut the top off, and bear in mind that they will very soon be at least partially masked with plants. Again, you must drill drainage holes in the bottom.

If the container does not have a plinth to lift the base clear of the ground, raise it slightly on a few pieces of slate or brick so that the drainage holes are not in contact with the ground.

CLAY, STONEWARE AND CONCRETE
Clay pots in terracotta color blend in particularly well in the organic cottage garden. They do have one disadvantage, however: most are not frost-proof and will crack or flake in really cold weather. Again, drainage is vital.

Stoneware containers cost a little more but they stand up to even hard frosts so they are worth the extra investment. There is also a wide range of pots and tubs available made from reconstituted stone or concrete, but they, too, are generally expensive. This type of pot is very heavy when full of soil, so put it in its permanent position before filling and planting.

Old stone drinking troughs or wash basins look extremely effective filled with plants and covered with moss and algae on the outside. However, they can be difficult to find.

WOOD
Wooden containers are available in various designs and a range of prices. Softwoods used to make containers, with the exception of cedar, must be pressure-treated with copper-based preservative at the manufacturing stage. Hardwoods, such as iroko and teak, will last for many years without treatment.

Half-barrels make excellent containers if you can find them, but they are becoming scarce and, therefore, expensive. Most are made of oak, so you do not have to treat them, but the metal hoops will need painting from time to time. Of course, avoid buying barrels that have contained any poisonous substances.

Herbs in containers left
*A convenient and attractive
way to grow herbs such as
mint and thyme.*

Traditional urn far left
*This is made from cheaper
reconstituted stone and filled
with bedding plants.*

Wooden tubs below
*Tubs filled with annuals and
biennials brighten the terrace.*

WINDOW BOXES

These are readily available in
either wood or plastic; alternatively you can make one yourself from hardwood or softwood
treated with a copper-based
preservative. Whichever type
you use, it is very important to
secure the window box to the
windowsill or wall properly.

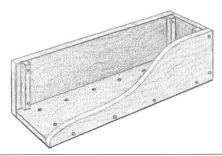

Making a wooden window box
*Make the box from 20 × 3.5cm (9 ×
1½in) wood cut to a suitable length.
Secure the corners with 2.5 × 2.5cm
(1 × 1in) blocks of wood fixed in place
with brass or galvanized screws. If your
window box is more than 1m (3ft)
long, include a cross support in the
middle. Drill 1cm (½in) holes in the
base – one hole every 15cm (6in).*

Planting containers

Though containers can be filled with permanent
plants, there is no doubt that the most colorful and eye-catching display will come from
seasonal plantings, using mainly annuals and
tender perennials. In temperate regions, you
normally plant in spring for a late spring and
summer display and in autumn for an early
spring show. You can make up an extremely
effective winter display using hardy plants, such
as winter-flowering heaths (*Erica carnea*), pansies (*Viola wittrockiana*), and euonymus (*Euonymus fortunei*) varieties.

You can use any of the plants suggested for
seasonal plantings in containers on their own.

Tubs of daffodils, for example, followed by perhaps fuchsias or geraniums look fine. I am
especially fond of the continental geranium
called "Mini Cascade", which you can obtain in
bright red or pink. See also *The Ornamental
Garden* for a season-by-season collection of
plants (*see pages 94-111*).

Whatever type of container or planting program you use, it is very important that you use
the correct growing medium (*see overleaf*).

LATE SPRING AND SUMMER COLOR

Do not think about setting out tender plants
until all danger of frost has passed. Then, start

planting at the middle of the container, using a central plant to give height. This could be a geranium (*Pelargonium zonale*) or a hybrid fuchsia (*Fuchsia blumeii*), perhaps a flame nettle (*Coleus*) or a taller-growing begonia (*Begonia tuberosa*). Around this, position slightly shorter subjects, such as petunias (*Petunia hybrida*), salvias (*Salvia splendens*), nemesia (*Nemesia strumosa*), patience plants (*Impatiens walleriana*) or slipper flowers (*Calceolaria integrifolia*). At the edges of the container, plant low-growing compact plants such as ageratum (*Ageratum houstonianum*), lobelia (*Lobelia erinus*) or sweet alyssum (*Lobularia maritima*), interspersed with trailing plants. You could use trailing geraniums or fuschias, trailing lobelia, thunbergia (*Thunbergia alata*) or ground ivy (*Glechoma hederacea*). While planting sow a few seeds of the trailing nasturtium (*Tropaeolum majus*) to flower a little later to brighten up the container when it may otherwise be beginning to look tired.

REPLANTING FOR EARLY SPRING
In the early autumn remove the summer display and freshen up the compost (*see below*) by taking out the top 23cm (9in) and mixing in some well-rotted garden compost or manure. Then refill and plant with your spring plants, again using a taller central plant surrounded by lower-growing and trailing ones. Here you could use pansies (*Viola wittrockiana*), polyanthus (*Primula polyantha*), primroses, forget-me-nots (*Myosotis alpestris*), dwarf daisies (*Bellis perennis*) and, of course, spring bulbs.

Spring bulbs

Nearly all the spring bulbs are suitable for containers but it is best to avoid tall varieties, especially if your container is in an exposed position. They will simply be broken down by heavy rain and wind. Of the shorter-growing daffodils, for example, perhaps the best for container planting are the *Narcissus cyclamineus*, *N. triandrus* and wild jonquil (*N. jonquilla*) hybrids. Of the tulips, I would recommend *Tulipa tarda*, water-lily tulip (*T. kaufmanniana*), *T. greigii* and *T. praestans*. All the hyacinths are short enough to survive and, of course, the early crocus and iris species and the anemones are especially useful.

Permanent plants

Containers planted with shrubs or herbaceous perennials require less maintenance than those that are regularly replanted, but they don't give the same flamboyant display of color over such a long period. If, however, you cannot devote much time to maintaining your containers, then you should seriously consider some of these easy-to-care-for plants.

CONIFERS
Dwarf conifers make good tub plants but you must make sure that they really are dwarf. The taller-growing species will flourish for a year or two but they will soon begin to show their displeasure at being confined. You will then have to find room for them in the garden.

One of the best real dwarfs is the Noah's ark juniper (*Juniperus communis* "Compressa"), which forms a perfect upright spire of green. Alberta white spruce (*Picea glauca* "Albertiana Conica") will last for many years in a tub, but unfortunately it is plagued by red spider mite, which can cause defoliation (*see page 257*).

Lawson cypress (*Chamaecyparis lawsoniana* "Minima Glauca") is slow growing and forms a rounded bush of sea green, while its near relative, *C. l.* "Minima Aurea" is bright golden yellow. There are other cultivars of Lawson cypress that are suitable for a few years: *C. l.* "Ellwoodii" forms a dense blue-green spire, while *C. l.* "Ellwoods Gold" is slower growing and, of course, yellow in color.

SOIL MIXES FOR CONTAINERS

In containers that are to stand outside, never use a peat-based mixture because it dries out very quickly and is very difficult to rewet. You cannot rely on rain water to water the containers because there is rarely enough. Instead, fill them with a soil-based mixture using high-quality topsoil from a garden center or fibrous loam made from stacked turf. See page 252 for details of how to "grow" your own loam.

Making soil-based mixture
Mix 7 parts loam, 3 parts sphagnum peat and 2 parts coarse grit. To each 9-liter (2-gallon) bucketful, add 30g (1oz) of garden lime and 150g (5oz) of blood, fish and bone meal.

You can replace the peat with very well rotted compost or manure or, even better, with worm-worked material or leaf mold.

Making acid mixture
If you are including acid-loving plants in a container, make up the mixture as above but use an acid soil and omit the lime. If you cannot buy acid soil, use a mixture of two-thirds peat, one-third sharp sand and add fertilizer as above.

Filling containers with the soil mixture
When you fill the containers, start by covering the holes with crocks – broken pots – laid concave-side down. Cover these with a little gravel and then either a piece of turf or some old sacking. This will prevent the mixture clogging the drainage holes. If the tub is deep enough – say, about 30cm (12in) – put in a layer of well-rotted manure or compost on top of the drainage material before topping up the container. The potting mixture will settle a little but always allow at least 3.5cm (1½in) at the top for watering.

There are several varieties of small and prostrate junipers like *Juniperus horizontalis* "Alpina" or *J. h.* "Plumosa", and a couple of thujas that you can use such as *Thuja occidentalis* "Rheingold" and *T. o.* "Midget".

SHRUBS

Certain shrubs last a long time in containers, and the root constraint tends to force them into regular and prolific flowering. One of my favorites is the evergreen pieris (*Pieris* "Forest Flame"). Its leaves pass from red in the early spring, through pink to creamy white and then green, and it has the bonus of creamy-white flowers resembling lily-of-the-valley. This plant needs to be planted in an acid mixture (*see left*). Use the same mixture to grow dwarf rhododendrons and azaleas (*Rhododendron* sp.), lithospermums (*Lithospermum diffusum*), pernettyas (*Pernettya mucronata*), heaths (*Erica* sp.), camellias (*Camellia japonica*) and other acid-loving shrubs. Bear in mind that you will have to water these containers with rain water, since most tap water contains lime. The dwarf lilac (*Syringa velutina*), on the other hand, is excellent for limy mixtures, as are any of the variegated euonymus (*Euonymus fortunei*) species.

PERENNIALS

Planted in conjunction with shrubs, ivies (*Hedera* sp.) look excellent in containers. They will trail over the sides and break up any hard lines. Most low-growing perennials are suitable but many of them die down in winter.

FOLIAGE PLANTS

Ferns and grasses make an attractive change from the more usual choices you see in containers, particularly when combined with other plants. A tub of plantain lilies (*Hosta*) mixed with ferns and one or two colored grasses makes a fine foliage tub for any shady area.

HERBS

Herbs are an obvious choice for containers when space in the garden is limited. They are all good-looking plants and you will have the advantage of a source of fresh herbs conveniently close to the kitchen door. Stick to the shorter-growing types, such as thyme (*Thymus vulgaris*), sage (*Salvia officinalis*), chives (*Allium schoenoprasum*), rosemary (*Rosmarinus officinalis*) and parsley (*Petroselinum crispum*).

ALPINES

These low-growing plants make interesting and eye-catching troughs and they are especially useful for shallow containers. Almost any alpine plant will grow happily in a trough provided that there is good drainage. This means making sure there are plenty of drainage holes in the bottom of the container and using a free-draining mixture made from equal parts of loam (made from stacked turf – *see page 252*), peat and coarse grit. There is no need to add fertilizer for alpines but include 30g (1oz) of lime per 9-liter (2-gallon) bucketful. When you have mixed it, you may think that the mixture looks much too coarse and well drained, but remember that these plants live naturally in the most inhospitable conditions, such as cracks in rocks or amongst the broken stones at the bottom of mountains. They should thrive in this type of soil mix without any feeding (*see* Maintaining alpines, *page 124*).

TENDER PLANTS

In colder areas containers can be used to grow a whole range of exotic plants, such as agaves (*Agave* sp.), yuccas (*Yucca filamentosa*), manukas (*Leptospermum scoparium*) varieties and several ornamental flaxes (*Phormium* sp.) that would otherwise be impossible to grow. You can put them outside in summer and bring them into a warm, light place in the winter.

Fruit and vegetables

If you only have limited space, there is no reason at all why you should not grow fruit and vegetables in containers. I have seen them growing happily on balconies where no other form of gardening is possible.

Apples, pears and plums do well grown this way but do remember that they must be budded on to a dwarfing rootstock (*see pages 203-4*). Standard gooseberries and redcurrant bushes make splendid tub plants, while strawberries do exceptionally well.

CONTAINER-GROWING STRAWBERRIES

The best way to grow strawberries is in shallow containers. You can also grow them in traditional strawberry pots, barrel-shaped containers with "cups" in the sides, but you may encounter mixed results. The top plants tend to do well but those growing out of the holes farther down are not at all satisfactory because

Growing in traditional strawberry barrels *It can be difficult to ensure water reaches the plants at the bottom of strawberry pots. So, put two stones into the bottom of the pot and rest a length of drainpipe on them. Surround the pipe with small stones, or similar drainage material, as you fill the pot with soil mix.*

they don't receive enough water. One method I have found reasonably successful is to put a short length of drainpipe into the barrel before filling it with soil. This way, by watering the top and filling the pipe, you will manage to get some water down to the lower plants.

MIXING VEGETABLES AND FLOWERS

Most shorter-growing vegetables do well in containers. Mix them with a few flowers, not just to improve their looks but to attract useful insects, too. A tub of, say, lettuce, onions, carrots and a few marigolds makes a fine show and they will all grow well together, while bush tomatoes on their own look every bit as good as flowers.

Maintaining container plants

Feeding Plants in containers need regular feeding because nutrients will be continually washed through the soil mix. Feed weekly with liquid seaweed or animal manure during the growing season. No feeding is necessary in the winter.

Watering Only very heavy rain will provide enough water for a container, so regular watering is necessary. In summer you may need to water the containers daily. Water in winter only when the weather is very dry.

Removing flower heads Dead-head plants as the blooms die back to extend flowering season.

Hanging baskets

You can brighten up walls considerably in summer and winter by adding a few flowering hanging baskets. They do, however, require quite a commitment to keep them well maintained. You will need to water them and feed them regularly and remove the dead flowers to extend the flowering season.

The secret of success with hanging baskets is to plant them so that they create a complete ball of flowers. This means that you need deep baskets that can be planted on top and through the sides. The shallow plastic types sold widely will not hold enough plants and they cannot be planted through the sides. The best types to choose are those made of coated wire or plastic mesh, or you can make your own (*see opposite*). Hang the basket on a special bracket; choose one long enough for the basket to hang clear of the wall. As with window boxes, it is absolutely essential to fix brackets firmly, since a planted basket can be very heavy and therefore dangerous if it should fall.

Seasonal trailing baskets *The summer basket, left, is planted with geraniums and other pendulous plants. The autumn basket, right, holds winter-flowering heaths, pansies and ivies.*

FILLING AND PLANTING WIRE HANGING BASKETS

You will need to line all wire or mesh baskets before filling them. In my view, the best method of lining is the old-fashioned way with moss. If you live in or near woodland areas, you might be tempted to find your own, but bear in mind that you will be destroying a wildlife habitat. It is better to buy moss from a florist or garden center. You can also use a piece of plastic or a special fiber lining obtainable from most garden centers.

1 *Support the basket on a flower pot. Line the sides with old-fashioned florist's moss then put a saucer or piece of plastic in the bottom – it should not come too far up the sides or it will prevent planting through them.*

2 *Half fill the basket with the soil-based mixture. Position the central plant and some slightly smaller plants around it. Then fill the basket with some more mixture.*

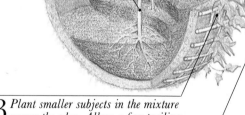

3 *Plant smaller subjects in the mixture nearer the edge. Allow a few trailing plants to hang over the edge.*

4 *Take a few trailing plants, squeeze their root balls together, and push them through the moss between the mesh of the sides of the basket and into the soil mix. Finally, top up the basket with mixture, leaving space for watering.*

PLANTS FOR HANGING BASKETS

It is quite possible to have hanging baskets for spring, summer or winter color. Use any of the plants recommended for tubs and other containers (*see pages 128-29*). A selection of flowering plants for different seasons is also shown in *The Ornamental Garden* (*see pages 94-111*).

For a summer basket, begin by planting a central "bushy" plant – geraniums or fuchsias are ideal. Surround this with several smaller potted plants such as petunias and include plants such as French marigolds (*Tagetes patula*), alyssum (*Lobularia maritima*) and patience plants (*Impatiens*) near the edges of the basket. You can then add trailing varieties of lobelia (*Lobelia erinus* "Pendula"), geranium and ground ivy *Glechoma hederacea*) at the edge of the basket or in the sides of the mesh so that grow and form a flower "ball".

The tomato variety *Basket King* fits in hanging baskets, and they are ideal, if fairly temporary, quarters for herbs. Again, as with other containers, choose the low-growing ones such as sage (*Salvia officinalis*), parsley (*Petroselinum crispum*) and thyme (*Thymus vulgaris*).

In the autumn, when baskets start to look tired, discard their contents on to the compost heap and throw the old soil and lining material away. Reline the basket, fill it with fresh soil and replant for a winter show. In all but the warmest areas, you will need to use frost-hardy plants. If there is any chance of a frost, use young shrubs such as the variegated pieris (*Pieris japonica* "Variegata") or the deep pink-flowered *P. j.* "Christmas Cheer". Surround this plant with winter-flowering or foliage heaths (*Erica carnea*) and, to trail over the sides, use ivies (*Hedera* sp.) or small plants of the evergreen honeysuckle (*Lonicera japonica* "Aureo-reticulata"). Alternatively, use the variegated euonymus (*Euonymus fortunei* "Emerald 'n Gold" or *E. f.* "Emerald Gaiety"). You can raise any of these plants from cuttings so, once you have bought your first basketful, you will not have to replace them even though the original plants will, after the first year, have outgrown their quarters (*see* Taking cuttings, *pages 274-5*).

There is no reason why you should not put a few spring bulbs into a winter hanging basket, or even plant up an early spring basket with bulbs such as crocus and low-growing varieties of some of the tulip species.

In the very coldest regions, where winters are even too severe to grow broadleaf evergreens at all, rely on cut branches of conifers.

MAINTAINING HANGING BASKETS

Feeding Spring and summer hanging baskets will need feeding once a week with a liquid seaweed or animal-manure fertilizer.

Plants in winter hanging baskets will hardly be growing at all so need no feeding.

Watering Spring and summer hanging baskets need to be watered regularly. In summer they should be watered at least daily and, if they are in a particularly warm, sunny position, they may need watering twice a day.

In winter the weather is much wetter so they may not need watering but, if the weather is unusually dry, keep an eye on the soil mix; water only when the top feels dry.

MAKING A WOODEN HANGING BASKET

You can make your own wooden baskets. Indeed, I have made them from pieces of packing case obtained free from a local factory.

You need:
● *18 × lengths 3.5 × 2.5cm (1½ × 1in) wood 40cm (15in) long with two 5mm (¼in) holes in 16 of them, 3.5cm (1½in) from either end. Use more pieces of wood if you want a deeper basket.*
● *4 × 1m (1yd) lengths of nylon string. Tie a knot in one end of each piece of string. Heat the other end with a match and roll it between your fingers to make sure it does not fray.*
● *4 short nails.*

1 *Lay the first two struts on the work surface so that they are parallel to each other. Nail the two struts without holes across them at right angles to form the base. Thread a piece of string through each hole. Start threading more pieces of wood on to the string for the sides.*

2 *Continue working on alternate sides until all the sides are complete. Tie the strings together at the top, making sure that the basket hangs straight as you do so.*

3 *Line the basket with strips of plastic. You can cut up an old compost bag or anything similar.*

4 *Fill the basket with soil mix and plant up in the usual way leaving space for watering. Hang the basket on a well-secured wall bracket.*

THE VEGETABLE GARDEN

THE ORGANIC GARDEN must always be treated as a complete entity. While the fruit and vegetable gardens produce the edible crops, the ornamental section attracts the useful wildlife that helps ensure they are free from pests and diseases. In return, the vegetable and fruit gardens provide material for the compost heap. Herbs also play an important part in attracting predators, and insects to pollinate the fruit garden.

In the ornamental garden, it is usual to choose plants which are suited to your particular soil type. But, in the vegetable garden, you will want to grow a wide range of crops with differing soil requirements. It is therefore necessary to adjust the amount of organic matter and the soil pH to specific levels which will ensure optimum growth and quality (*see pages 18-37*).

It is, however, the vegetable plot which really emphasizes the advantages of non-chemical gardening. For it is here that the transition to natural growing techniques will have a really positive effect on the health and general well-being of you and your family.

Cultivating your own vegetables is often cheaper than relying on shop-bought produce, but of far more consequence are the benefits in freshness, improved taste and, above all, freedom from pollution.

If your garden is small, adopt the "cottage-garden" approach and combine vegetables and flowers in mixed borders (*see pages 71 and 88*). You can also use the deep bed system, which encourages roots to grow downwards rather than spreading outwards, so crops can be planted closer together, giving far heavier yields.

There would be little point in growing your own food if you grew the same varieties, and used the same fertilizers and pesticides as the commercial grower. You may save a little money, but you would end up with comparatively tasteless vegetables which contain residues of often highly toxic chemicals. By combining the best of both traditional and modern gardening methods, you can have higher yields of better-tasting vegetables that you know are doing you nothing but good.

Crop rotation

All vegetables have specific soil and mineral requirements. By grouping together crops which have similar needs, and planting them in a different place each year, you will be able to make much better use of your resources and allow the soil to replenish lost minerals. This practice is known as crop rotation. If you divide your vegetable plot into three, for example, you need only manure a third of it each year and grow on it those vegetables that will most appreciate it. The slightly less demanding crops can move to that plot the following year and those that are happy in poorer soil go there in the third year. You will also make the most efficient use of fertilizer and lime in this way. Because most vegetables are cultivated as annuals, there is no difficulty in growing them in a new plot each season. Those that dislike being moved must be kept in a permanent place.

Devising a viable rotation plan is not, however, as easy as it may at first seem. For example, following peas and beans with brassicas is fine in theory, but it's likely that the brassicas will need considerably more room than the peas and beans. Or you may find that putting the pole beans anywhere but at the same end of the plot each year would prevent the sunlight from reaching the rest of the crops. That might have a more damaging effect than an attack of aphids or a mild case of mildew. So, do not be too rigid in your application of the system – serious problems are unlikely to occur if you have to deviate slightly from a strict rotation for some reason.

Though the rotation plan I have suggested provides for only one plot to be manured, it is a good idea to treat the whole vegetable patch if you can get enough manure. The idea that root vegetables will fork and split in manured soil is a

Growing vegetables in a mixed border above
If your garden is very small, and you wish it to be both decorative and productive, you can combine flowers, fruit and vegetables in a mixed border. Here, crops such as sweetcorn, tomatoes and ruby chard are growing alongside a small apple tree and an assortment of flowers.

Tending plants in a deep bed left
Plants can be spaced very close together if they are grown in deep beds of loose, organically enriched soil (see page 135). To avoid treading on and compacting the soil, the crops are tended from paths which run beside the narrow beds.

myth; provided you always use well-rotted manure, you will achieve far better results in soil that has been made water- and nutrient-retentive in this way. If you are using the deep bed system (*see opposite*), you should, in any case, manure all the plots every year. Dig the manure in during the autumn and lime in the spring just prior to sowing or planting.

PEST AND DISEASE CONTROL

Crop rotation will help guard against attacks from pests and diseases by promoting generally healthier and more robust plants. However, while moving the crops each year allows the mineral balance of the vegetable plot to be maintained, it is not always an effective means of actually deterring pests and diseases altogether. For example, whereas growing brassicas in the same bed in consecutive years certainly encourages a build-up of club root spores in the soil (*see page 45*), millions of these spores can be transported from one part of the garden to another in just the few crumbs of soil that cling to your boots or spade. Similarly, many pests are capable of flying considerable distances, so simply moving susceptible plants in no way guarantees freedom from attack. However, there is no doubt that annual crop rotation, as described below, does significantly delay the build-up of disease spores in the soil.

THE THREE-YEAR CROP ROTATION PLAN

This three-year rotation scheme is suitable for most gardens. Divide your vegetable garden into three plots and the crops you wish to grow into three groups, as detailed below. Every year, prepare the plots as described and move each group to the next plot, so that two years elapse before any crop returns to its original site. This period allows the mineral balance of the soil to be maintained, reduces the risk of disease and makes best use of organic matter.

PLOT A
Cultivation: Double digging (*see page 264*), incorporating manure in upper and lower levels, plus two handfuls of blood, fish and bone meal per square meter/yard. Some crops in the group may need extra feeding.
Suitable crops: Potatoes, carrots, beets, parsnips, onions, shallots, leeks, garlic, tomatoes, zucchini and other squash, pumpkins, celery, Florence fennel, eggplants, peppers, cucumbers, melons, celeriac, Hamburg parsley, salsify, scorzonera.

PLOT B
Cultivation: Single digging (*see page 264*) and application of blood, fish and bone meal at the rate of two handfuls per square meter/yard, over the whole plot, two or three weeks before sowing the first crops of the season.
Suitable crops: Peas, bush beans, pole beans, broad beans, Lima beans, soy beans, peanuts, sweetcorn, okra, spinach, spinach beets, New Zealand spinach, Swiss chard, lettuce, chicory, endive, cresses, globe artichokes.

PLOT C
Cultivation: Single digging (*see page 264*) and application of blood, fish and bone meal (as on plot B) and lime to bring the pH level up to 6.5-7.0. Some crops may need extra feeding during the season – refer to specific entries in this chapter.
Suitable crops: Cabbages, Chinese cabbages, Brussels sprouts, cauliflowers, mustards, broccoli, kale, swedes, turnips, radishes, kohl-rabi.

PLOT D
Space must also be left for the permanent crops, which occupy a plot of their own and do not come within the rotation plan. These are: rhubarb, globe artichokes, Jerusalem artichokes, asparagus, seakale, some herbs. (The globe artichokes are included in both plots because they can be grown as perennials or annuals – *see page 150*).

In a small garden it is sensible to grow some of the permanent crops in the ornamental border (*see page 71*).

Year 1

A	B	C	D

Year 2

B	C	A	D

Year 3

C	A	B	D

Ensuring a continuous supply of vegetables

Making sure that you always have fresh vegetables in the garden is not as straightforward as it may seem. Successional sowing plans are all very well, but there is no accounting for the variations in weather conditions that can make crops late. Although strict timetabling is out of the question it is a good idea to keep a diary which can act as a rough guide. In the first year, note down when you should be sowing or planting to provide a succession of cropping. Then record when you actually got around to doing the job and also the reason you were either delayed or early. Note too when you harvested each crop. Eventually, after two or three years, a fairly accurate pattern will emerge.

Many modern vegetable varieties are bred to remain in the ground, without deteriorating, for some time after maturing, so there is a fair amount of leeway. Others, such as maincrop onions, can be stored throughout the winter and will last almost until the next crop is ready to harvest. Ensuring continuity is easy, therefore, and you can fill in with a very early-maturing set-grown variety, a Japanese variety, or shallots. I have indicated in the individual vegetable entries where it is possible to achieve a continuous supply by successional sowing and planting.

Stick to your original rotation plan and, when it's time to sow a particular vegetable, use whatever space is available in the correct plot. If you find that there will be an area of vacant soil for more than about a month in the main season, sow a quick-maturing green-manure crop like mustard (*see page 34*). It is also worth growing a green-manure crop in winter, particularly if your soil is light (*see page 32*). If you have sufficient space, plan a four-year rotation and devote one plot each year to growing a crop which can be dug in to enrich the soil.

Preparing vegetable beds

The best way to ensure good-quality vegetables is to grow them in the best soil possible. Soil types vary widely (*see pages 13-14*) but, even if you start off with a poor-quality soil, it is not difficult to make substantial improvements by working in plenty of organic matter (*see page 20*). The techniques involved in preparing and maintaining a vegetable plot are explained fully in *Soil Improvement* and *Fertilizers* (*pages 18-42*). Refer to the individual vegetable entries for specific soil preferences and preparations. If you choose not to use the crop-rotation plan, you should still prepare the soil in the way recommended for the vegetables in each group.

The deep bed system

The deep bed method of growing vegetables has been practiced around the world for centuries. The system is basically very simple: instead of the vegetables being grown in long rows, with an access path between each row, the crops are grown in beds 1.25m (4ft) wide, with all the work being done from narrow paths at the sides.

By cutting out the unproductive paths, it's possible to double the amount of land available for crops. This is an important consideration, especially if you have a small garden.

HOW THE SYSTEM WORKS
By digging deeply, breaking up the subsoil and incorporating plenty of bulky organic matter, a deep root zone is produced which allows plants to draw nutrients from a much greater depth. Because their roots are encouraged to grow downwards, crops can be planted closer together than would otherwise be possible. Deep beds dug in heavy soils drain more easily if they are raised and the water retention of light soils is improved by working extra bulky organic matter into the top few inches.

Most crops can be grown successfully using the deep bed system. The exceptions are pole beans, which are not manageable in such short rows (*see page 159*), and Brussels sprouts – because they still need to be spaced about 45cm (18in) apart if you are to get good-sized sprouts.

CULTIVATION
Before sowing, rake into the top few inches of soil about two handfuls of blood, fish and bone meal per square meter/yard, and cover the soil with about 5cm (2in) of well-rotted garden compost. If the bed was dug and manured in the winter, the manure will have probably worked down a little way, leaving the top layer of soil liable to dry out quickly. The additional compost will help retain the necessary moisture.

Crops which have been overwintering, in mild climates, such as cabbages, will need an extra boost in the spring. A little dried blood sprinkled round the base of each plant should be sufficient. Vegetables that use a lot of nutrients – known as gross feeders – include tomatoes, various squashes and peppers, and these benefit from a fortnightly feed of liquid seaweed during the growing season.

Weeding deep beds is comparatively easy once the plants have matured. The close spacing means that they cover the surface of the soil and effectively smother any weeds. In the early stages, though, weeding can be time-consuming, as it often has to be done by hand. Always start with a stale seed bed (*see page 269*) and cover the soil with a thick layer of well-rotted manure or compost (*see page 20*). It is also possible to plant through sheets of paper or polyethylene; this is very effective as it completely eliminates weeds and the need for weeding (*see page 58*).

SOWING AND PLANTING IN DEEP BEDS

Most vegetables can be sown so that they just touch their neighbor when the plants reach maturity. I have indicated the relevant planting distances under each separate entry.

Crops should be planted in blocks, rather than rows, with the plants set out in a series of staggered lines. Some seeds, such as those of the radish and early turnip, can be sown in a wide band. Make the drill with a draw hoe, using the whole width of the hoe, and scatter the seeds thinly within it (*see page 269*). You need not thin the seedlings, but harvest them selectively, starting when the roots are quite small and allowing the rest to develop fully.

The increased drainage can make the top few inches of the soil drier than usual, so water the drill before sowing in dry weather, and then cover the seeds with dry soil.

Sometimes, vegetables that are sown at a wide spacing can be "intercropped" with a fast-maturing crop. If you sow a few rows of broad beans, which must be sown early, radishes can be sown in between them. You will be able to harvest them long before the beans are big enough to rob them of sunlight.

Deep beds are ideal for growing crops under cloches (*see page 140*). You may not be able to buy the cloches so popular in England and Europe but it is not difficult to make your own.

Spacing out plants *In order to make the best possible use of the available space, sow seeds or seedlings in blocks, or staggered rows, forming a triangular pattern where each plant is the same distance from those surrounding it.*

To achieve optimum results with a deep bed, it is essential that the soil be loose and dug deeply and enriched with plenty of organic matter so that the roots can penetrate to the required depth.

You should never tread on the bed once it has been dug as this compacts the soil. If you find it too awkward to work from the access paths, use a wooden board to spread your weight evenly over as large an area as possible.

A conventional bed *The comparatively shallow and compacted layer of topsoil means that roots cannot penetrate deeply and have to be planted further apart. Root crops may be distorted and smaller than those grown in deep beds of loose soil.*

A deep bed *A deep layer of loose, organically enriched soil encourages roots to penetrate downwards, rather than spreading sideways. This means that crops can be planted much closer together, resulting in dramatically increased yields.*

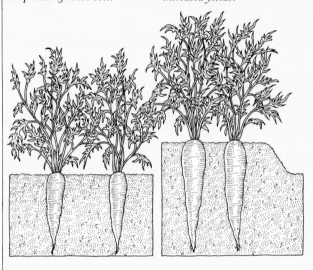

Deep bed dimensions *The usual width of a deep bed is about 1.25m (4ft). The beds can be as long as is convenient. A 3 × 1.5m (10 × 4ft) bed gives a 4.5 sq meter (40 sq ft) planting area which should produce up to four times the yield of a conventional bed of the same size.*

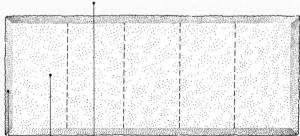

Leave a narrow access path between beds.

Divide the beds into 60cm (2ft) sections to prepare the soil.

The most convenient width of the beds is 1.25m (4ft).

DIGGING A DEEP BED

1 Mark one edge of the bed with a planting line. Measure 1.25m (4ft) across using the planting board and set up another planting line parallel to the first.

2 Using canes, mark a trench 60cm (2ft) wide. Dig out the trench one spade deep, put the soil in a wheelbarrow and take it to the other end of the bed; it is used to fill the last trench.

3 Break up the exposed subsoil in the bottom of the trench with a fork. This enables the vegetable roots to penetrate more deeply.

4 Put a 5-8cm (2-3in) layer of well-rotted manure into the bottom of the trench. This enriches the soil and improves its texture.

5 Leaving a cane in the corner of the first trench, measure the second 60cm (2ft) section with the other cane. Making all the trenches the same size ensures that they contain the same amount of soil.

6 Start digging the soil from the second trench and transfer it into the first trench, spreading it out to cover the layer of manure.

7 Put another 5-8cm (2-3in) layer of manure into the first trench. Because of the bulk of the added manure, the bed will be raised as you work.

8 Continue to dig out the soil from the second trench and cover the new layer of manure. This leaves a deep bed of loose, organically enriched soil in the first trench.

9 Scrape all the soil from the bottom of the second trench and break up the exposed soil. Repeat steps 4-8 and use the soil taken to the end of the plot to cover the manure in the final trench.

Sowing

The vegetable-growing season begins with seed sowing, either directly into the ground outside or in pots indoors from which the developed seedlings are transplanted after a period of "hardening off" (*see page 254*). You can save seeds from some plants but it is safer to buy them from mail order sources or a garden center. Remember to avoid the "dressed" seeds, those which have been treated with fungicide. Seeds must be watched and tended carefully, and the seedlings spaced and thinned as required. Some crops can be multiple sown to make the best possible use of available space (*see below*). Plants which may be slow or difficult to germinate can sometimes be pre-germinated to encourage swift growth when they are planted out, and others may benefit from some form of protection from the cold. The techniques suitable for each crop are described in the individual entries. A good harvest of vegetables at the end of the season largely depends on how well the seeds are sown initially.

Multiple sowing

In order to make the best use of the available land, aim to get the maximum yield per square meter/yard and to extend the harvesting period as much as possible. Deep beds will increase the yields, and planting under cloches means you can start earlier and continue later at the other end of the growing season (*see page 140*).

The very earliest crops, however, are best started inside, either in a heated greenhouse or on a windowsill. Even better than the one-sided light of a window is the light from fluorescent tubes left on 15-16 hours daily. In the interests of economy, you will want to keep heating costs down, so the less space these early vegetables take up, the better. The best way of achieving this economy of space is by multiple sowing. This involves sowing up to six or eight seeds together in cells, rather than individually. Leave them to grow as a clump and do not thin them out. When the seedlings are planted out, the vegetables simply push and jostle for space. Onions, for example, actually push each other so far over that some of the bulbs grow horizontally instead of vertically (*see opposite*). Multiple sowing therefore enables you to save space in the ground as well as on the propagating bench windowsill, or under fluorescent lights.

Commercial growers have been using this method successfully for many years, using individual blocks made from a special type of peat compost. The seedlings are sown in the blocks and planted out before the roots outgrow them. However, none of the composts used in this way are organic, as far as I know, and it is difficult to make your own from peat and organic fertilizer, because the special type of peat is needed if the blocks are not to fall to pieces. Also, the blocks tend to become hard and airless.

A better method is to buy trays of small styrafoam cells. These are ideal because they are sturdy and they hold heat very well – encouraging early growth. Fill them with a good open compost like peat and worm casts, or one of the proprietary animal-manure composts. The plants are easily removed at planting-out time (*see opposite*). If you cannot find anything like them, you can either divide a seed tray with cardboard strips, to make squares about 4cm (1½in) across or use peat or plastic pots.

Pre-germinating seeds

Sometimes it is beneficial to pre-germinate seeds before sowing. Really slow germinators, like parsnips for example, will just sit in the ground doing nothing or may even rot if they are sown in cold and wet soil conditions. But, if they are pre-germinated in optimum conditions, and sown when the soil is slightly warmer, they'll grow straight away and easily catch up on a normal season.

Other seeds can be inhibited, or fail to germinate, because the soil temperature is too high. For example, if lettuces are sown in a soil warmer than 19°C (68°F), they will not germinate. This is nature's way of preventing them from starting into growth during the dry season. But if they are pre-germinated in slightly cooler conditions, they can be sown and will grow normally, provided they have sufficient water.

The seeds are germinated by spreading them out on a piece of damp paper. It is possible to buy a special kit which includes a germinating dish and absorbent filter paper, but a cheaper alternative is to put a few sheets of kitchen tissue into the bottom of a plastic sandwich box. Cover them with water and drain off the excess.

Germinate the seeds in the airing cupboard or in a kitchen cupboard, depending on the temperature required, and check on them daily. In ideal conditions, they will sprout a small root much quicker than they would in the soil outside. As soon as a few roots are about 3mm (⅛in) long, they are ready to sow.

If, for some reason, it is impossible to sow them straight away, put the seeds in the refrigerator (but not in the freezing compartment);

HOW TO MULTIPLE SOW

Multiple sowing is one way to speed production of some crops. Sow groups of seeds in trays of styrafoam or plastic cells. Place the trays in a greenhouse or under fluorescent tubes. Use a sterile growing medium, such as one of the peat-based mixes. Keep seedlings cool until they are big enough to plant outdoors under cloches or plastic protection (*see overleaf*).

Styrafoam or plastic cells for multiple sowing *You can buy all sorts of blocks of styrafoam or plastic cells, often with plastic covers to conserve moisture. The cells here have holes matching pegs in a special tray.*

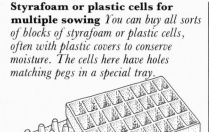

Vegetables suitable for multiple sowing
Not all vegetables are suitable for multiple sowing and there is no advantage with others. The crops listed below are some of those I have tried successfully.

LEEKS (*see page 170*)
Sow and plant out exactly as for onions. There is no need to plant them in a trench, since they will blanch each other by growing so closely together. Recommended varieties are *Broad London* and *Titan*.

CARROTS (*see page 181*)
It's essential to use the round varieties of carrots like *Short 'n Sweet* or *Little Finger*. The longer varieties tend to wind around each other underground, making them useless for the kitchen. Sow six or seven seeds per cell in late winter and plant out 23cm (9in) apart in mid spring.

BEETS (*see page 184*)
Use a round variety like *Red Ace* or *Detroit Dark Red*. Sow two beet seed clusters per cell. Harden off and transplant exactly as described for onions (*see below*).

TURNIPS (*see page 183*)
Use an early variety like *Early Purple Top Milan* and sow six per block in late winter. Plant out after hardening off, 30cm (12in) apart in early spring.

SALAD ONIONS (*see page 171*)
The best varieties are *White Lisbon* or *Evergreen Long White Bunching*. Sow six seeds per cell in late winter and plant out 15cm (6in) apart, after hardening off in early spring.

ONIONS (*see page 171*)
Sow six or seven seeds per cell in late winter, at a temperature of 15°C (60°F). After germination, the temperature can be lowered to 10°C (50°F). Harden off in a cold frame (*see page 254*) in early spring and plant out 30cm (12in) square in mid spring.

Most varieties will do, but the best for me has been *Burpees Yellow Globe Hybrid*.

1 *Fill the cells with moist peat-based medium and make a small depression in each. Place your seeds – in this case carrots – on a piece of card and, with the back edge of a penknife blade, carefully scrape six or seven seeds into each cell.*

2 *Cover the seeds with a layer of medium or sand. Water thoroughly cover with opaque plastic. Place in greenhouse or under fluorescent lights. Once germinated, remove plastic, keep seedlings cool and close to light source.*

3 *When the plants are about 2.5cm (1in) high, they are ready for planting out. Take them outside, and water the plants thoroughly with a watering can. Then press the block of cells down on to the peg tray to push the compost and plants out of the cells.*

4 *Plant the clumps in staggered rows to save space. Using a planting board to measure accurately, plant a row of carrots so that the clumps are 23cm (9in) apart. Plant a second row 23cm (9in) from the first, staggering the clumps by 23cm (9in), and water them.*

Multiple-sown onions *The bulbs are forced to grow outwards as they compete for space.*

they will keep in the refrigerator for three or four days without harm.

Of course, the difficulty lies in transferring the germinated seeds to the soil without breaking the tiny roots. They are at their most delicate stage and will not survive damage of any kind. Large seeds, like peas and beans, present no problem as they can be handled with ease. Even the medium-sized ones, like parsnips, can be carefully picked up with tweezers if you have infinite patience. But the smaller seeds, like lettuce, are impossible to sow in this way.

The answer is "fluid sowing" where the seeds are suspended in a "jelly". Special kits are available which include an alginate gel which is mixed with water, heated up and allowed to cool before use. Equally effective is ordinary wallpaper paste, mixed to a stiff consistency. This does not need to be heated. Make sure you buy a paste that doesn't contain a fungicide.

FLUID SOWING WITH WALLPAPER PASTE

This method of sowing fragile pre-germinated seeds can be used for a number of vegetables including parsnips, as shown here. If you are fluid sowing in the summer, water the newly sown seeds straightaway or you may find that the wallpaper paste hardens and traps the seeds inside. Gentle stirring enables the seeds to be distributed evenly through the paste. They can then be sown evenly, so only minimal thinning is needed when the seeds germinate.

1 *Pre-germinate the seeds in a warm place, using moist kitchen tissue (see page 139). As soon as they are ready to sow, carefully wash the seeds off the paper into a flour sieve with cold running water.*

2 *Make up the wallpaper paste mixture in a jar and put the seeds into the paste, making sure you do not damage the shoots. Stir the seeds around gently and then pour the mixture into a plastic bag and tie a knot in it.*

3 *Before sowing, rake the soil to a fine tilth. Then draw the seed drills using the edge of a draw hoe (see page 259) and water them with a liquid seaweed or animal manure fertilizer (see page 41).*

4 *Cut off the corner of the bag and squeeze the gel and the seeds down the row. Cover normally and gently consolidate the soil by tapping with the back of a rake. Water regularly and ensure that the seeds never dry out.*

Protecting crops against cold

In temperate climates, the earliest crops have to be sown in a heated greenhouse (*see pages 246-257*) or indoors underlights, but the sowing dates of many vegetables can be brought forward by at least a month by using cloches – plastic or glass covers – outside, with no heating.

After raising an early crop, cloches can be used to cover tender vegetables like squashes, beans and tomatoes. Since you will harvest these well before outside-sown crops are ready, you'll be eating them while shop prices are still high. Then, at the end of the season, the cloches can be used again to grow late vegetables when those in the outside garden are finished. Once you have used cloches, you will not want to be without them – they will certainly pay for themselves easily in the first season.

Using cloches

Cloches are most useful for early planting out of multiple-sown seedlings or early sowings. I have included sowing times for each vegetable under the separate entry (*starting on page 146*).

If your soil is heavy, start by incorporating well-rotted compost or peat into the top few inches (*see pages 15-16*). This will help to aerate the soil and warm it up. Later, it helps retain moisture. If you are using peat, rake in blood, fish and bone meal at about two handfuls per square meter/yard.

Position the cloche over the ground to be used about a month before sowing and planting, which should start in late winter. Be sure to

TYPES OF CLOCHE

Cloches can be made from glass or plastic, but glass is now so expensive that it is no longer feasible to use it for commercial cloche making. However, if you have some old glass panes, you can make a simple cloche using special cloche clips.

Fortunately, as the cost of glass has risen, the price of polyethylene and other plastics has fallen. This is ideal cloche material. Discarded plastic jugs can serve as small cloches.

There are three main types of cloche: tunnel cloches, traditional rigid tent or barn cloches, and floating cloches.

Tunnel cloches

You can buy tunnel cloche kits which simply consist of a series of wire hoops over which polyethylene sheeting is draped. Make sure there is an adequate way of tying the sheeting down and tightening it up over the top, otherwise the plastic may flap about, damaging the plants as well as itself. The sides of a tunnel cloche can be pulled up to allow easy access for watering and harvesting. They are often very long – up to 30m (100ft) – but you can always divide them up into smaller sections. It is also very simple to make your own (*see overleaf*).

Tunnel cloches for deep beds are harder to find and naturally more expensive. They need to be 1.5m (5ft) wide to allow a margin for growth at each side. There are a few available and these too are good value but, again, it's cheaper and quite easy to make your own. Polythene greenhouses are made in much the same way.

Rigid cloches

Many different designs of rigid glass or plastic cloches are available. Ensure that the ones you buy are tall enough and wide enough for the crops you intend to grow, and that there is a satisfactory means of anchoring them to the ground. Plastic cloches are light and can easily blow away if not properly anchored.

Plastic barn cloche

Glass tent cloche

Floating cloches

Cheapest of all are "floating cloches" – sheets of plastic material which cover the crop from when it is sown or planted to a short time before harvesting. Sheet polyethylene perforated with holes at about 2.5cm (1in) intervals is available, but it won't protect against frost. Much more efficient is woven polypropylene, also available at garden centers, which will protect the plants from a few degrees of frost. It can be used on all types of bed and is easy to fit and remove. Simply cover the bed with a large sheet and weight the edges down with bricks. The polypropylene "floats" up as the crops grow. When they are ready to harvest, remove the bricks and roll back the sheeting. For deep beds, buy sheets at least 2m (6ft) wide.

measure the soil temperature – which should be 7°C (45°F) before sowing or planting anything.

The soil under the cloche will dry out faster than the open ground because the structure keeps the rain out, so make sure you water by hand when necessary. If you can, install a length of seep, or perforated, hose (*see page 260*) along the length of cloche so that you only have to fit the end to the garden hose and leave it to "water itself". Remember that a polyethylene covering will exclude any pollinating insects so, if you grow a vegetable fruit or seed like eggplants or peas, which are pollinated by insects, open the cloche during the flowering period, at least during the day.

You will only need small amounts of very early pickings, so either grow several different vegetables in the same row – if you have room for a full-length cloche – or split the cloche in several lengths for adjacent rows.

MAKING YOUR OWN TUNNEL CLOCHE

A tunnel cloche is perhaps the best way of protecting crops planted outside, especially if you have a fairly large area to cover. It is quick and easy to make your own, using inexpensive and readily available materials. The technique described here can be adapted to make a cloche of any size; the measurements below will give you a cloche 45cm (18in) wide. Although they are fixed securely in the ground, tunnel cloches allow easy access to the crops they protect.

1 *Fix bolts 15cm (6in) from one end of a 1.35m (54in) long piece of wood, and 30cm (12in) from the other. Cut a piece of stout wire the same length as the wood.*

2 *Starting at the shorter end, hold the wire at the end of the wood and wind it around the nearest bolt to leave a loop and a 15cm (6in) "leg" at one end.*

3 *Pull the wire taut and wrap it round the other bolt, making a second loop and another 15cm (6in) leg. Cut more pieces of wire and repeat the process.*

4 *Peg two parallel planting lines 45cm (18in) apart. Bend the lengths of wire into hoops and push them into the soil at 60cm (2ft) intervals, using the lines as a guide.*

5 *Remove the planting lines and cover the hoops with a sheet of polyethylene. Dig a small hole and bury one end under the soil.*

6 *Pull the plastic tight over all the hoops and bury the other end in the same way. This prevents the wind lifting the plastic.*

7 *Tie a length of nylon twine through one of the wire loops. Pull it tightly over the cloche and secure it to the opposite loop.*

8 *Repeat this process with the other loops to hold the whole cloche down securely. Slide the material up when the crops need watering.*

Start by sowing seeds in a greenhouse, on a windowsill or under lights, in late winter (*see page 270*). Sow lettuce, early cabbage and cauliflower in seed trays. Carrots, spring onions, spinach, early turnips and beets should be multiple sown in blocks or cells (*see pages 138-139*), and early peas sown in guttering (*see page 157*). All these can be planted out under the cloches in early spring.

In warm climates, you can sow direct into the soil in late winter, depending on the soil temperature. Sow lettuces, for maturing later than the inside-sown ones, radishes, spinach, carrots, turnips, peas, broad beans, spring onions and potatoes. Hopefully (it's never possible to be absolutely precise), these crops can be harvested by late spring, in time to use the same beds for eggplants, peppers, various kinds of squashes, tomatoes, bush beans and cucumbers.

In mid to late summer, another sowing can be made of the early varieties of the crops you sowed in early spring. These are sown uncovered and the cloches are put on in early autumn to hasten maturity. Plastic can also be used to ripen vegetable fruits, like tomatoes, which may still be green at the end of summer.

Organic methods of increasing soil fertility are even more important under cloches. Every time you change crops, dig over the soil and work in as much well-rotted manure or compost as you can spare, to increase the water-holding capacity of the soil.

The hoops are also useful as supports for netting, which provides protection against birds.

Choosing what to grow

On the following pages are listed over 50 different vegetables – obviously too many for the normal-sized garden to accommodate at the same time. You will have to resign yourself to the fact that you cannot grow everything, so you have to make choices – and that can be difficult.

The first step is to resolve to grow only what is needed by you and your family. If you grow more of a particular crop than you can use reasonably quickly, there is also the danger of plants "running to seed". This is where they are left in the ground too long before harvesting, so that they "bolt" and flower, then produce seed.

Sow short rows of fast-maturing varieties at frequent intervals for successional harvesting of peak-condition vegetables. And try to fit some of them in between wider spaced, long-term crops like Brussels sprouts and cauliflowers.

You should also eliminate those vegetables that are easy to obtain organically grown and will cost no more to buy. Maincrop potatoes, for example, take up a lot of room and an organic farmer can grow them more cheaply than you. On the other hand, I plant a few early potatoes each year because they taste so much better when they're freshly dug.

If you choose vegetables that deteriorate rapidly after harvesting, you will get the full benefit of improved flavor. Sweetcorn, for example, starts to turn its sugar into starch the very instant it is picked so, the sooner it is eaten, the better. Cobs that have been in the shops a day or two will not be worth buying. Leaf crops are not nearly as crisp and fresh, and tomatoes, which need sun to increase their sugar content, are often picked nearly green to ensure they have not become over-ripe by the time they reach the shops. There is no time for them to develop the characteristic sweetness associated with home-grown vegetables.

Finally, make your choice on cost and availability. The so-called "gourmet" vegetables – like asparagus, celeriac, seakale, globe artichokes and scorzonera – are ludicrously expensive, especially slightly out of season, so it is well worth growing them. I doubt too whether you will find most of those grown organically, so you may well *have* to grow your own.

BUYING SEEDS

In most countries, the quality of vegetable seeds is controlled by legislation, so it is unlikely that you will find one grower's products better or worse than those of another. However, seeds are expensive, so it is worth shopping around.

Some seeds, like peas and beans, are easy to save yourself – nearly all those you buy will be just as good sown the second year after buying as they were the first, provided they are properly stored. Start by buying seeds that have been foil-packed. Then open the packet in as dry an atmosphere as possible and take out what you need, then re-seal the packet immediately and put it into an airtight container. I find the small plastic containers used to pack photographic films are ideal. Label the container and store it in a cool, but frost-free, dry place.

There are many F1 vegetable hybrids available now (*see page 44*) and all are much more expensive than the open-pollinated types. Before you consider buying these, remember that most have been bred with commercial growers in mind and that their requirements are often the reverse of yours. They need the entire crop to mature at the same time and to be of uniform size. You are looking for continuity of maturity and a range of sizes so you can choose a bigger cabbage when you have guests, for example.

The advantage of the F1 varieties is that they are often more vigorous, nearly always heavier cropping, and are sometimes bred for resistance to disease and pest attack, too. If they have these specific attributes and have not, as a result, had all their flavor bred out of them, they are an excellent proposition. Otherwise, try to stick with the older, open-pollinated varieties.

In the pages that follow, I have recommended the varieties of each vegetable that I have found superior, but you may want to try others. Make a point also of growing at least one new variety, or even one entirely new vegetable, each year. If you simply keep planting the varieties you have used in the past, you may miss out on something much better.

PREPARING THE SOIL

Even if you decide not to use the three-year rotation plan, it pays to try and keep plants with the same requirements close together. You must also prepare the soil for each vegetable in much the same way, so refer to the rotation plan which will give a general idea of how to condition the soil before sowing or planting each crop. If any extra conditioning is needed, I have included recommendations in the relevant entry.

THE VEGETABLES

The vegetables are divided into groups according to basic characteristics, so each section deals with salad, leaf or root vegetables, for example. Information regarding greenhouse cultivation is given where applicable and treatment for the pests and diseases that affect each group is discussed at the end of the chapter.

Salad vegetables

Growing your own salad vegetables is particularly beneficial, as their quality and flavor depend upon freshness. They take up comparatively little space and some can be grown all year round if some protection against freezing is given. Salad crops are fast-growing and are not usually troubled by many pests and diseases. They all require a moisture-retentive soil.

CHICORY right
Cichorium intybus
The example shown here is a "chicon" dug up and blanched in deep, moist peat. These and the unforced green leaves are used in winter salads.
For cultivation details, see page 147.

MUSTARD AND CRESS above
Brassica hirta and *Lepidium sativum*
Mustard and cress seedlings are quick and easy to grow, and can be eaten fresh all year. The seeds can be germinated on moist kitchen paper indoors.
For cultivation details, see page 146.

WATERCRESS above
Nasturtium officinale
Because it grows wild in fast-flowing streams, watercress needs shade, a moisture-retentive soil and frequent watering.
For cultivation details, see page 146.

COS LETTUCE below
Lactuca sativa
A particularly crisp and refreshing salad vegetable, the cos lettuce has erect bright-green leaves with a prominent central vein.
For cultivation details, see page 147.

RED-LEAVED LETTUCE left
Lactuca sativa
This distinctive form of lettuce has crinkle-edged leaves which are tinged with red. Like the other lettuces, it is a suitable crop for growing in the greenhouse.
For cultivation details, see page 147.

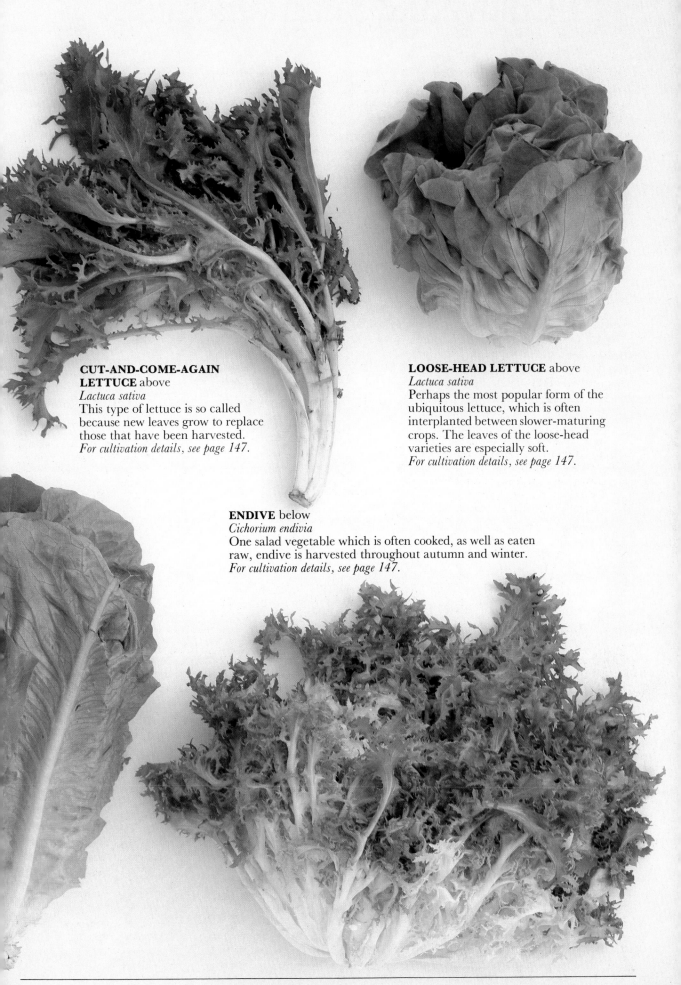

**CUT-AND-COME-AGAIN
LETTUCE** above
Lactuca sativa
This type of lettuce is so called
because new leaves grow to replace
those that have been harvested.
For cultivation details, see page 147.

LOOSE-HEAD LETTUCE above
Lactuca sativa
Perhaps the most popular form of the
ubiquitous lettuce, which is often
interplanted between slower-maturing
crops. The leaves of the loose-head
varieties are especially soft.
For cultivation details, see page 147.

ENDIVE below
Cichorium endivia
One salad vegetable which is often cooked, as well as eaten
raw, endive is harvested throughout autumn and winter.
For cultivation details, see page 147.

Cultivating salad vegetables

Mustard and cress

Mustard greens and curly cress are easy to grow – either indoors during winter, or outdoors in spring and autumn. In the seedling stage they are snipped into salads or used as a garnish. Mature mustard greens are also grown like spinach.

VARIETIES

There are several varieties of mustard, such as *Tendergreen* or *Savanna*.

SOIL AND SITE

Mustard and curly cress are fast-growing and, indoors, can be grown in shallow trays. Mustard when grown outdoors as greens, prefers a rich moist soil in sun. Both crops do best in cool weather.

SOWING

In the winter, put a little moist soil or a damp tissue into a sandwich box and scatter the seed fairly thickly on it. Cover with a sheet of newspaper and put it in a warm spot. Sow the mustard, which germinates and grows faster, four days after sowing the cress. When the seed germinates, remove the paper and place the box in full sunlight.

In the summer, sow in the same way in a corner of the plot outside, or in a pot or tub. Sow fortnightly for a succession.

Sowing mustard and cress indoors
Dampen the kitchen paper thoroughly but ensure any excess water is drained away. If the paper is too wet, the seedlings rot; if it is too dry, the crop won't mature.

MAINTENANCE

No further attention is needed during growth.

HARVESTING

The shoots will be ready for harvesting in 10 to 20 days. Cut them with scissors.

PESTS AND DISEASES

Mustard and cress are generally trouble free. See pages 46-53 for general pests and diseases.

PLANTING AND HARVESTING TIMES

	Sow inside	Plant out	Sow outside	Harvest
Early spring	•		•	•
Mid spring	•		•	•
Late spring	•		•	•
Early summer				
Mid summer				
Late summer			•	•
Early autumn			•	•
Mid autumn				•
Late autumn	•			•
Early winter	•			•
Mid winter	•			
Late winter	•			

Watercress

This highly nutritious vegetable is an ingredient of salads, sauces and soups. It grows wild in fast-flowing streams, but can be cultivated in soil without the aid of running water. Upland cress is similar in appearance and flavor and will grow in drier sites.

VARIETIES

There are no individual varieties.

SOIL AND SITE

A moisture-retentive soil is essential. Choose a shady part of the garden, dig a trench 30cm (12in) deep and half fill it with well-rotted manure or compost. Mix some more organic matter with the soil you have dug out and refill the trench.

SOWING AND PLANTING

Sow indoors in seed trays in mid spring at a temperature of about 12°C (55°F), or outside in shallow drills. Transfer the seedlings to wider spacing in another seed tray when they are big enough to handle (*see page 272*). Plant out in late spring or early summer, setting the plants 10cm (4in) apart each way. An easier way is to buy a bunch of watercress, select those shoots that have a few embryo roots showing and plant in the same way.

MAINTENANCE

The moist conditions of the watercress bed are likely to encourage annual weeds, so hoe regularly to keep them at bay, and water copiously. No feeding will be necessary. As they grow, pinch out the leading shoots and remove flowers as soon as they are seen.

HARVESTING

Cut shoots as required. This will encourage the production of more shoots, so harvesting can continue throughout the summer and autumn.

PESTS AND DISEASES

Watercress is generally trouble free. See pages 46-53 for general pests and diseases.

PLANTING AND HARVESTING TIMES

	Sow inside	Plant out	Sow outside	Harvest
Early spring	•			
Mid spring	•		•	
Late spring		•		
Early summer		•		•
Mid summer				•
Late summer				•
Early autumn				•
Mid autumn				•
Late autumn				•
Early winter				
Mid winter				
Late winter				

Chicory

There are two basic types of chicory. One is a white-blanched shoot – or "chicon" – grown for eating in the winter. In my view it is the finest winter salad vegetable. The other type needs no blanching; it can be harvested in the autumn and eaten like lettuce.

VARIETIES

The best variety to grow for producing blanched chicons is *Witloof*. For growing as unblanched, use *Sugarhat*.

SOIL AND SITE

Chicory likes a sunny position and does best in soil that is rich and moisture retentive, with a pH of 6.5. Apply two handfuls of blood, fish and bone meal per square meter/yard, preferably two to three weeks before you start sowing.

● If you are using the three-year rotation plan (*see page 134*), grow it in Plot B.

SOWING

Do not sow until early summer or the plants may run to seed. Sow in shallow drills 30cm (12in) apart and thin the seedlings to 23cm (9in).

Deep beds Sow the blanching varieties in rows 20cm (8in) apart and thin to 20cm (8in) apart in the rows. Sow non-blanching varieties in rows 25cm (10in) apart and thin to 25cm (10in). (*See page 135.*)

MAINTENANCE

Weed and water non-blanching varieties when necessary. Dig up the chicon varieties in autumn for blanching (*see right*).

HARVESTING

If the chicon varieties are kept in a frost-free shed, they can be forced as required to ensure a supply of chicory throughout the winter (*see right*). The unblanched varieties are simply cut as soon as the hearts have filled out. They will last well into the early winter.

PESTS AND DISEASES

Chicory is generally trouble-free but may be affected by some of the general garden pests and diseases. See *Organic Pest Control*, pages 46-53 for general pests and diseases.

BLANCHING CHICORY

Lift chicon varieties in autumn, trim the leaves to within 1cm (½in) of the root and lay them in a box of moist peat. Every three to four weeks, plunge some roots into a container full of peat. Use a deep box or pot, so you can pack the peat tightly around the roots. This restricts the spread of the leaves and results in firm chicons.

1 *Plunge the roots upright into a box one-third full of peat and cover them with another 23cm (9in) layer. Make sure the peat is packed down. Put the box in a warm place.*

2 *After 4-5 weeks, the chicons will have grown to 15-20cm (6-8in) long. Remove them from the box and cut them away from the roots.*

PLANTING AND HARVESTING TIMES

	Sow inside	Plant out	Sow outside	Harvest
Early spring				
Mid spring				
Late spring				
Early summer			●	
Mid summer				
Late summer				
Early autumn				
Mid autumn				
Late autumn				
Early winter				●
Mid winter				●
Late winter				●

Lettuce

As the prime summer salad vegetable, lettuce is considered a "must" for the vegetable garden. In mild climates it can be grown almost all the year round outside and, by using cloches (*see page 140*) and other plastic protection, cold frame or a greenhouse, you can harvest all-year round.

VARIETIES

For the earliest sowings choose a quick-maturing variety like *Tom Thumb* or *Buttercrunch*. For successional sowing outside, *Great Lakes* or *Minilake* are recommended, or the cos varieties *Paris White* or *Valmaine Cos*. If you prefer a loose-head lettuce, try *Salad Bowl* or the red-leaved *Red Sails*. For cut-and-come-again lettuce and summer heat tolerant varieties, rely on *Salad Bowl*, *Green Ice* and *Ruby*.

SOIL AND SITE

Lettuce prefers a water-retentive soil with a pH of about 6.5. Grow it in the soil that was manured for a previous crop as freshly manured soil is too rich and likely to cause rotting off at the base. All varieties require a relatively cool spot so, if your garden is likely to become very hot in summer, sow them in semi-shade. They need no extra feeding.

Of course, lettuce is often interplanted between other slower-maturing crops, such as tomatoes or peppers in which case the soil case the soil preparation should always be for the main crop and you should leave the lettuce to take its chances.

● If you are using the three-year rotation plan (*see page 134*), grow them in Plot B.

SOWING AND PLANTING

Make the first sowing in a heated greenhouse or indoors under lights in late winter. Start the seeds in a tray of sowing mixture (*see page 252*) at a temperature of between 15 and 18°C (60-65°F). Transfer them to a larger tray, about 5cm (2in) apart, as soon as they are large enough to handle and grow them on at about 10°C (50°F). When the seedlings are about 5cm (2in) tall, plant them out under cloches, normally in early spring, 15cm (6in) apart in rows 15cm (6in) apart.

At the same time, sow a row of seed under the cloche to follow them, using one of the larger, later varieties. Leave some to grow on under the cloche and transplant the others into the open ground 23cm (9in) apart, with 30cm (12in) between rows, as soon as they are large enough to handle. Continue sowing outside about every two weeks until early summer, thinning the sown row so that the lettuces are about 23cm (9in) apart, and use the thinnings to plant out another row or two.

Make the final sowing in mid summer. Plant out as before and cover with cloches in early autumn to mature them.

Sow cut-and-come-again lettuce in a wide band, scattering the seed thinly. Make the first sowing outside in early spring.
Deep beds Sow as described above, but set the plants out in a block rather than rows (*see page 136*). Space the seeds 15cm (6in) apart for the earliest sowings and 23cm (9in) apart for later, successional sowings.

MAINTENANCE
Weed regularly between plants and water if necessary.

HARVESTING
When the heart of the lettuce feels full and hard, pull out the whole plant, cut off the root and put it on the compost heap. Leave cut-and-come-again lettuces in the ground. Cut the leaves near the base of the plant and more leaves will grow.

PESTS AND DISEASES
Millipedes, cutworms, slugs, aphids, botrytis and downy mildew fungus can affect lettuce (*see pages 46-53*). See page 257 for greenhouse pests and diseases.

PLANTING AND HARVESTING TIMES

	Sow inside	Plant out	Sow outside	Harvest
Early spring	•	•	•	
Mid spring	•	•	•	•
Late spring	•		•	•
Early summer				•
Mid summer				•
Late summer	•		•	
Early autumn	•		•	
Mid autumn	•			•
Late autumn	•			•
Early winter				•
Mid winter	•			
Late winter	•	•	•	

CULTIVATING LETTUCE IN THE GREENHOUSE
Early lettuce can be raised in the way described for growing under cloches (*see page 140*), or sown directly in the greenhouse borders. Raise the beds to improve drainage (*see page 75*) and dig in plenty of well-rotted compost. Rake in a handful of blood, fish and bone meal per square meter/yard, and sow seeds in groups of three, 23cm (9in) apart each way. When they germinate, thin each group to one plant. Alternatively, sow in flats and transplant (*see page 272*) 23cm (9in) apart when the seedlings are 4cm (1½in) high. Plant at the same depth as the seedlings are growing in the flat to prevent rotting at the base. This is especially important with overwintered crops.

Using the varieties *Red Sails* or *Slo Bolt*, start sowing in the heated greenhouse in late summer and continue through to mid winter. In the cold greenhouse, sow in late summer for cutting in late autumn and again in late winter for harvesting from mid spring onwards.

Endive

Endive is a good salad vegetable for late summer, autumn and winter in mild regions, although it tends to be slightly tough if not properly cultivated. Like chicory, it has a bitter flavor.

VARIETIES
Green Curled or *Salad King* are varieties with heavily fringed leaves for late summer and autumn cropping. For later harvesting, *Batavian Full Heart Escarole* is best.

SOIL AND SITE
Endives need semi-shade as they may become bitter and run to seed in hot sunshine. They prefer a soil that is rich and moisture retentive, with a pH of about 6.5. Apply two handfuls of blood, fish and bone meal per square meter/yard, preferably two to three weeks before sowing.
● If you are using the three-year rotation plan (*see page 134*), grow them in Plot B.

SOWING
Sow the earlier croppers in early summer and the winter types in late summer, in shallow drills 30cm (12in) apart, in a place where they can be cloched. It's not a good idea to transplant endives, which may then run to seed, so thin the rows to 30cm (12in) apart.
Deep beds Sow in shallow drills 23cm (9in) apart and thin to 23cm (9in). (*See page 135.*)

MAINTENANCE
Weed and water if necessary. Cover the latest-sown rows with cloches in late autumn. About three months after sowing, blanch the plants by covering them with a flower-pot with the hole blocked with a lump of clay, or, provided the leaves are dry when you do it, cover the row with black plastic. Alternatively, lift the plants, tie the leaves together to exclude light from the hearts and replant them in a box of moist soil in a cool but frost-free place.

HARVESTING
About three weeks after blanching (*see left*), the hearts become creamy in color and lose their bitter taste. They are then ready to harvest.

PESTS AND DISEASES
Endive is generally trouble free. See pages 46-53 for general pests and diseases.

PLANTING AND HARVESTING TIMES

	Sow inside	Plant out	Sow outside	Harvest
Early spring				
Mid spring				
Late spring				
Early summer			•	
Mid summer			•	
Late summer			•	
Early autumn				•
Mid autumn				•
Late autumn				•
Early winter				•
Mid winter				
Late winter				

Shoot vegetables

This diverse group of vegetables, grown for their succulent stems, provides an assortment of flavors and forms. Several are highly prized as "gourmet" delicacies and they certainly demand more careful attention during cultivation than most other crops. All the shoot vegetables require plenty of water.

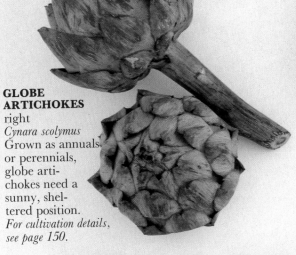

GLOBE ARTICHOKES right
Cynara scolymus
Grown as annuals or perennials, globe artichokes need a sunny, sheltered position.
For cultivation details, see page 150.

FLORENCE FENNEL above
Foeniculum vulgare dulce
Grown for its aniseed flavor, Florence fennel needs moist conditions to prevent it running to seed.
For cultivation details, see page 151.

ASPARAGUS above
Asparagus officinalis
A well-drained bed, sunshine and a lot of water are needed to grow asparagus.
For cultivation details, see page 151.

CELERY right
Apium graveolens
There are two types of celery: self-blanching and blanched, which is more demanding. Both need a moisture-retentive soil.
For cultivation details, see page 152.

RHUBARB above
Rheum rhabarbarum
Although eaten as a dessert, this hardy perennial is technically a vegetable, as we eat the stem, not the fruit. Rhubarb tolerates a wide range of conditions.
For cultivation details, see page 153.

Cultivating shoot vegetables

Globe artichokes

Globe artichokes are a real "gourmet" vegetable, but they are tender perennials and not for regions with cold winters. They can be tried as annuals and are decorative enough to grow in your flower borders if you have no room for them in the vegetable plot.

VARIETIES
New varieties appear and disappear again from time to time, but, in my opinion, *Green Globe* has yet to be bettered.

SOIL AND SITE
Choose a sunny but sheltered part of the garden. Work in plenty of organic matter to improve the drainage quality of heavy soils (*see pages 21-30*). Growing in deep beds will assist drainage too (*see page 136*). If necessary, add lime to the soil to achieve a pH of 6.5.
● If you are growing artichokes as annuals, put them with the brassicas on plot C in the three-year crop rotation plan (*see page 134*), but manure the area they will occupy. Otherwise, grow them in a plot of their own with the other perennials.

SOWING AND PLANTING
The traditional way is to buy "suckers" – shoots which arise from the roots of mature plants – and to plant them 1m (3ft) square in mid spring. Alternatively, you can grow globe artichokes from seed. Sow in late winter in 7.5cm (3in) pots in a temperature of about 18°C (65°F). When the seedlings appear, put them in full sun in a temperature of 13°C (55°F). To grow them as perennials, plant them out 1m (3ft) square in mid spring, or at the back of the ornamental border.
Deep beds The best way, in my opinion, is to grow globe artichokes as annuals in deep beds, planting them out 45cm (18in) apart in mid spring. That way, you will get the same number of heads per plant, quadrupling

Planting in a mixed border above
Globe artichokes are decorative enough to mix with plants in the ornamental border.

Harvesting selectively right
Each plant will produce 2-4 heads. Cut the biggest to encourage the others to grow.

the yield per square meter/yard. (*See page 136*).

MAINTENANCE
Artichokes need plenty of water, so mulch with well-rotted compost or manure (*see page 20*), and water them in dry weather.

HARVESTING
Cut the heads while they are still fairly tightly closed. Once they start to open they become tough. Removing the side shoots makes the individual heads bigger but reduces the yield.

After harvesting, cut the stems to within 30cm (12in) of the ground. New shoots will appear and, when they are about 60cm (2ft) long, tie them together and earth them up like celery (*see page 150*) to blanch them. After a few weeks, the stems can be cooked and eaten.

PESTS AND DISEASES
These plants are affected by slugs (*see page 50*). See also page 198 for pests and diseases that affect shoot vegetables.

PLANTING AND HARVESTING TIMES			
	Sow inside	Plant out	Sow outside	Harvest
Early spring				
Mid spring		●	●	
Late spring				
Early summer				
Mid summer				
Late summer				●
Early autumn				●
Mid autumn				
Late autumn				
Early winter				
Mid winter	●			
Late winter	●			

Asparagus

Asparagus is a perennial crop, much improved by organic husbandry. It takes up a lot of space for the amount harvested, and will not produce a full harvest of spears for three years, but the unique flavor of asparagus is well worth the time and space it demands.

VARIETIES

The American variety *Mary Washington* is strong-growing and reliable, producing thick shoots. It is also resistant to rust disease. New European varieties like *Lucullus* have the distinction of producing only male plants, so there is no reduction in yield brought about by producing seed.

SOIL AND SITE

Good drainage and lots of sunshine are essential. If your soil is light, work in plenty of well-rotted manure or compost or one of the alternatives (*see pages 21-8*) and grow the plants "on the flat" rather than in raised beds. If you have heavy soil, raise the beds by working plenty of organic matter into the soil in the same way you would make a deep bed (*see page 136*). Before planting, spread two handfuls of blood, fish and bone meal per square meter/yard, and lime if necessary to raise the soil pH above 6.5 (*see page 36*).

SOWING AND PLANTING

You can raise asparagus from seed but the range of available varieties is limited. Sow 2.5cm (1in) deep in a seed bed (*see page 269*) in mid spring and thin to 7.5cm (3in) apart when the seeds germinate. Transplant to the permanent position, 30cm (12in) apart, the following spring. Alternatively, buy in one-year-old roots ("crowns"). Dig a trench 15cm (6in) deep and 30cm (12in) wide, with the bottom slightly raised in the center. As soon as you get the crowns, soak them in water for an hour and then plant them 30cm (12in) apart, spreading out their roots before covering them.

MAINTENANCE

Make sure the plants never go short of water, especially in the first year. In early spring each year, repeat the dressing of

Cutting down asparagus tops *In autumn, cut back the yellowing stems and mulch around the plants.*

fertilizer and, in the autumn, spread well-rotted compost or manure around the plants. After about seven or eight years, start another bed and, when that is in full production, discontinue the first one.

HARVESTING

Start light cutting in the second year, when the plants have begun to get established. You can take nearly a full crop in the third and subsequent years. Cut the shoots when they are about 10cm (4in) above ground and the tip is still tightly closed. Cut just below ground or snap off each shoot. Always leave some shoots and continue cutting for no more than four weeks in the third year and six weeks in following years.

PESTS AND DISEASES

Asparagus is affected by slugs, asparagus rust and asparagus beetles (*see pages 46-53 and 198*).

Florence fennel

Florence fennel is not an easy plant to grow, but worth persevering with for its unique aniseed flavor. The swollen, bulb-like stems can be eaten either raw or cooked.

VARIETIES

The variety *Perfection* is very good, but the vegetable is normally sold just as *Florence fennel* or *Finocchio*.

SOIL AND SITE

Florence fennel requires plenty of sunshine and a moisture-retentive soil rich in organic matter, with a pH of above 6.5.
● If you are using the three-year crop rotation plan (*see page 134*), grow Florence fennel in Plot A.

SOWING

Sow in shallow drills 45cm (18in) apart from mid spring to late summer. Later, thin to 20cm (8in) apart. Sow little and often to avoid harvesting all at once.

MAINTENANCE

Ensure the plants do not dry out or they will run to seed (*see page 143*). When the bases begin to swell to form bulbs about the size of golfballs, earth up around them (*see page 186*) to keep them sweet and tender.

HARVESTING

Cut the heads two or three weeks after earthing up.

PESTS AND DISEASES

Fennel can be attacked by slugs (*see page 50*) and the pests and diseases that affect shoot vegetables (*see page 198*).

PLANTING AND HARVESTING TIMES	Sow inside	Plant out	Sow outside	Harvest
Early spring				
Mid spring	●	●	●	
Late spring			●	
Early summer			●	
Mid summer				
Late summer				
Early autumn				
Mid autumn				
Late autumn				
Early winter				
Mid winter				
Late winter				

PLANTING AND HARVESTING TIMES	Sow inside	Plant out	Sow outside	Harvest
Early spring				
Mid spring				
Late spring			●	
Early summer			●	
Mid summer				
Late summer				●
Early autumn				●
Mid autumn				●
Late autumn				
Early winter				
Mid winter				
Late winter				

Celery

If you opt for the self-blanching varieties, celery is not difficult to grow. What may be difficult for the organic gardener is finding seed that has not been "dressed", or treated with a fungicide.

VARIETIES

The blanching types are grown in trenches as described below. Varieties include *Tendercrisp, Fordhook, Improved Utah, Summit* and *Ventura*.

Self-blanching types are grown in flat ground and are much easier. They produce very light green shoots. Recommended varieties of this type of celery include *Golden Self-Blanching*.

SOIL AND SITE

A moisture-retentive soil is imperative, so dig in plenty of organic matter (*see pages 21-8*). Celery likes a soil pH of 6.5, so add lime if necessary. Trenches for blanched types must be dug out as described below.

To grow self-blanching celery, simply dig in plenty of well-rotted organic matter, and lime to a pH of 6.5.

● If you are using the three-year crop rotation plan (*see page 134*), grow celery in Plot A.

SOWING AND PLANTING

Sow both types in late winter at a temperature of 18°C (65°F). Sow on the surface of the potting mixture in a seed tray and do not cover the seeds, as they need light to germinate. When they germinate, transfer them to a wider spacing in a seed tray and grow them on at about 13°C (55°F) until late spring. Harden them off in a cold frame (*see page 254*) and plant out in early summer.

Plant rows of blanched celery in trenches (*see below*) with 30cm (12in) between plants.

Plant out self-blanching varieties in blocks with 23cm (9in) between plants. This will help the plants to shade each other, which keeps the stems whiter.

MAINTENANCE

The self-blanching types require only weeding and watering in dry weather. The blanched varieties need more attention.

They are prodigious feeders so give them a feed of animal-manure liquid fertilizer in mid summer and again a month later. Blanch the stems as described below and cover the rows with tunnel cloches in late autumn (*see page 141*).

Deep beds Self-blanching celery can be grown in deep beds at the same distances (*see page 136*). Blanched celery is too awkward to manage from the edge of the bed, so is best grown separately.

HARVESTING

Lift self-blanching celery before the first frost at the end of autumn. Blanched types can be used from then onwards, digging out a plant at a time and re-covering the rest.

PESTS AND DISEASES

These plants are affected by slugs, celery fly and celery leaf spot (*see pages 50 and 198*).

PLANTING AND HARVESTING TIMES	Sow inside	Plant out	Sow outside	Harvest
Early spring				
Mid spring				
Late spring	●			
Early summer		●		
Mid summer				
Late summer				●
Early autumn				●
Mid autumn				●
Late autumn				●
Early winter				
Mid winter	●			
Late winter	●			

BLANCHING CELERY

Certain varieties of celery must be blanched by keeping them out of direct sunlight. This is done by covering the stems with soil, but careful preparation is needed to prevent rotting.

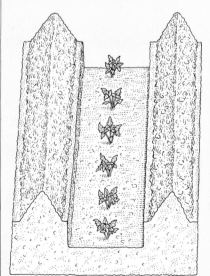

1 *Dig a trench one spade deep and 45cm (18in) wide, heaping the soil either side. Put 5cm (2in) of well-rotted compost or manure in the bottom, and cover this with 2.5cm (1in) of soil. Plant out the seedlings 30cm (12in) apart.*

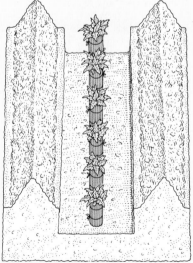

2 *In mid summer, remove any suckers from near the base and wrap the bunches of stalks with corrugated cardboard, brown paper or several layers of newspaper. This prevents soil getting between the stalks.*

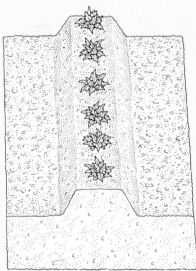

3 *Fill the trench with soil to the bottom of the leaves. As the celery grows, repeat this process twice more at three-week intervals, sloping the soil to drain off rain and prevent rotting.*

Rhubarb

I have included rhubarb among the vegetables because we eat its stems rather than its fruit. It is easy to grow and can be harvested from late winter through to mid summer.

VARIETIES

Recommended varieties are *MacDonald*, *Victoria*, *Valentine*, and *Canada Red*.

SOIL AND SITE

Rhubarb likes a soil pH of 7.0, so add lime if necessary to attain this level. It also prefers a well-drained soil with plenty of well-rotted compost or manure dug in (*see pages 21-8*). Apart from this, rhubarb is fairly tolerant and is very hardy. Plant it in a bed reserved for perennials.

PLANTING

Mature roots ("crowns") are generally planted in early spring, although you can also buy plants in pots for spring-to-autumn planting. Most people will not require more than two or three plants but, if you wish to grow more, set the plants 75cm (2ft 6in) apart with 90cm (3ft) between rows. Cover the crowns with 2.5cm (1in) of soil.

MAINTENANCE

Weed and water as necessary. Mulch with well-rotted compost or manure every year after the leaves have died down.

Mulching rhubarb *It is not practical to dig in organic matter around the plants, so mulch each autumn instead.*

HARVESTING

Leave the plants to grow on during the first year. In subsequent years, pull the thickest sticks when they are long enough, but never strip the plant. Remove any flower spikes and put the leaves on the compost heap.

PESTS AND DISEASES

Rhubarb is susceptible to aphid attack (*see page 50*), and virus disease (*see page 52*).

PLANTING AND HARVESTING TIMES			
	Sow inside	Plant out	Sow outside	Harvest
Early spring		•		
Mid spring		•	•	
Late spring		•	•	
Early summer			•	
Mid summer				
Late summer				
Early autumn		•		
Mid autumn				
Late autumn			•	
Early winter			•	
Mid winter			•	
Late winter			•	•

Seakale

Seakale is a permanent plant, not at all difficult to grow. You can grow it outside for eating in spring or bring it inside and force it for a superb winter delicacy.

VARIETIES

Lily White is a little whiter than the common type and has a slightly better flavor.

SOIL AND SITE

Seakale requires plenty of sun and a soil rich in organic matter, so dig in lots of well-rotted compost or manure (*see pages 21-8*). If necessary add lime to the soil to achieve a pH of above 6.5 (*see page 36*).

SOWING AND PLANTING

Unfortunately – for its tender shoots after being forced are considered to be most flavorsome by British and European gardeners – seakale (*Cramba Maritima*) is barely known to Americans. Its seed should be sown in spring (*see page 283* for supplier). A quicker start comes from root cuttings, unavailable in the USA.

MAINTENANCE

Hoe to keep beds weed free (*see page 57*) and water as required.

HARVESTING

Leave the plants to grow for the first and ideally the second year. If you cannot wait you can actually begin forcing a few plants in the second year (*see below*). Allow the plants to regrow, and repeat the process for three more years. Then dig up the roots, take some root cuttings and start again. Alternatively, you can then force a crop in the greenhouse or even

Forcing seakale *In late winter, place black plastic pots over a few plants, covering any drainage holes with black plastic. Harvest the shoots in spring.*

on a windowsill. Lift the plants after the first frost and pot them into large pots of moist peat. Cover with another pot, excluding all light, and keep the temperature between 10 and 15°C (50°-60°F). After forcing, the plants should be discarded.

PESTS AND DISEASES

Seakale is susceptible to attack by slugs and the pests and diseases that affect shoot vegetables (*see pages 50 and 198*).

PLANTING AND HARVESTING TIMES			
	Sow inside	Plant out	Sow outside	Harvest
Early spring		•	•	
Mid spring		•	•	
Late spring			•	
Early summer				
Mid summer				
Late summer				
Early autumn				
Mid autumn				
Late autumn				
Early winter				•
Mid winter				•
Late winter				•

Pod and seed vegetables

The vegetables in this group, with the exception of okra and sweetcorn, are all members of the *Leguminosae* family, and are an excellent source of protein and fiber. The nitrogen-fixing qualities of the peas and beans are another good reason why you should devote as much space as possible to growing them. When you have picked the vegetables, save some seeds for sowing the next year; the rest of the plants can be dug into the soil or lifted to release their nitrogen on the compost heap (*see pages 32-4*). Pod and seed vegetables are therefore doubly valuable.

OKRA above
*Abelmoschus (*syn. *Hibiscus) esculenta*
In areas where the average temperature is at least 21°C (70°F), two crops of this fast-maturing vegetable can be harvested in a single year. It is also known as "gumbo" or "lady's fingers".
For cultivation details, see page 156.

SWEETCORN right
Zea mays
Home-grown sweetcorn has an especially sweet flavor if it can be eaten as soon as it is picked, before most of the sugar has turned into starch. The crop needs lots of sun and is wind-pollinated – so grow it in blocks, rather than rows, to aid pollination.
For cultivation details, see page 156.

MANGETOUT above
Pisum sativum
These vegetables, also known as "snow peas" or "snap peas", are becoming increasingly popular. The whole pod is cooked and eaten with the tiny peas inside.
For cultivation details, see page 157.

PEAS right
Pisum sativum
Like sweetcorn, peas taste better when eaten soon after picking, before the sugar changes into starch. Sow early and maincrop varieties for successional harvesting.
For cultivation details, see page 157.

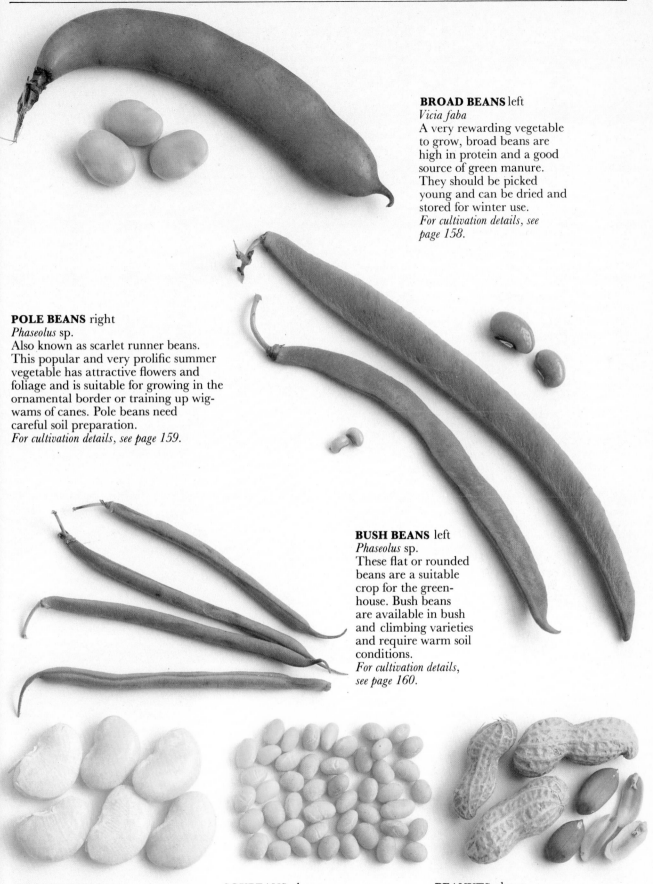

BROAD BEANS left
Vicia faba
A very rewarding vegetable
to grow, broad beans are
high in protein and a good
source of green manure.
They should be picked
young and can be dried and
stored for winter use.
*For cultivation details, see
page 158.*

POLE BEANS right
Phaseolus sp.
Also known as scarlet runner beans.
This popular and very prolific summer
vegetable has attractive flowers and
foliage and is suitable for growing in the
ornamental border or training up wigwams of canes. Pole beans need
careful soil preparation.
For cultivation details, see page 159.

BUSH BEANS left
Phaseolus sp.
These flat or rounded
beans are a suitable
crop for the green-
house. Bush beans
are available in bush
and climbing varieties
and require warm soil
conditions.
*For cultivation details,
see page 160.*

LIMA BEANS above
Phaseolus lunatus
Also commonly known as "butter
beans", these highly nutritious seeds
need particularly warm soil conditions to germinate, and can only be
grown successfully in warm climates.
They can be dried for winter use.
For cultivation details, see page 161.

SOYBEANS above
Glycine max
Rich in protein and calcium, these
highly versatile beans are considered
the most important crop in many
countries. However, they are only
successful in warm climates and are
comparatively low-yielding.
For cultivation details, see page 161.

PEANUTS above
Arachis hypogaea
Suitable only for warm areas, peanuts need to be protected against
frosts and require a light, sandy soil.
This is because the plants sow their
seeds into the soil where the nuts
develop inside protective shells.
For cultivation details, see page 161.

Cultivating pod and seed vegetables

Okra

Sometimes known as "lady's fingers" or "gumbo", this crop is only suitable for warm climates. The yield decreases dramatically when average temperatures are below 21°C (70°F). The pods are eaten whole or shelled and eaten like peas.

VARIETIES
Dwarf Green Longpod is a popular variety which matures quickly. *Clemson Spineless* is fast and very heavy yielding with pointed, spineless pods.

SOIL AND SITE
A sunny position and a well-drained, fertile soil are essential. Dig in plenty of organic matter and, if the soil is badly drained, grow the plants on a raised deep bed (*see page 136*).
● If you are using the three-year crop rotation plan (*see page 134*), grow okra in Plot B.

SOWING AND PLANTING
It is quite possible to produce two crops of this vegetable in a single growing season, sowing the first when all danger of frost has passed in the spring and the second, for autumn harvesting, in early or mid summer. Sow in shallow drills 90cm (3ft) apart and, when the plants are large enough to handle, thin them to 45cm (18in) apart. They can also be raised in the greenhouse or on a windowsill but, since they resent root disturbance, this should be done in 8cm (3in) pots. Plant out the seedlings at the same distances in late spring or early summer, when all danger of frost has passed.

MAINTENANCE
Keep the plants weed free and slightly on the dry side to prevent rotting. Apply two handfuls of blood, fish and bone meal per square meter/yard about a month after sowing, then mulch between the plants with well-rotted compost (*see page 20*).
Some people suffer an allergic reaction when working with okra, so avoid handling it when the crop is wet and, if you do get problems, wear gloves.

HARVESTING
Pick every two or three days when the pods are small. If you want to keep the pods for more than two days, put them in a cool place and cover them with a damp cloth.

PESTS AND DISEASES
Okra is susceptible to aphids and the pests and diseases that affect pod and seed vegetables (*see pages 50 and 198*).

PLANTING AND HARVESTING TIMES

	Sow inside	Plant out	Sow outside	Harvest
Early spring	●			
Mid spring	●		●	
Late spring		●	●	
Early summer		●	●	
Mid summer				●
Late summer				●
Early autumn				●
Mid autumn				
Late autumn				
Early winter				
Mid winter				
Late winter				

Sweetcorn

As soon as an ear of sweetcorn is picked from the plant, the sugar in it starts to turn to starch. Growing your own enables you to eat it freshly picked, when the cobs taste sweetest and are at their most nutritious.

VARIETIES
Modern, fast-maturing varieties are easy to grow in most climates. The sweetest are the new hybrids like *Early Xtra Sweet*, but they must be grown away from other varieties since cross-pollination will reduce the sugar content.

SOIL AND SITE
Sweetcorn likes plenty of sun and a soil pH of about 6.5.
● If you are using the three-year crop rotation plan (*see page 134*), grow sweetcorn in Plot B.

SOWING AND PLANTING
In very cold climates, start seeds in a greenhouse or under lights. Sow pairs of seeds in mid spring in 8cm (3in) pots at a temperature of 18°C (65°F), and thin to leave the strongest seedling if both germinate. Harden off in a cold frame in late spring (*see page 254*) and plant out in early summer in blocks, with 30cm (12in) between plants.
Usually, seeds are sown outside in mid spring, in furrows 60cm (2ft) apart and about 15-22cm (6-9in) deep. Sow groups of two or three seeds every 60cm (2ft) in the bottom of the furrows and cover with 2.5cm (1in) of soil. Then cover with a sheet of plastic to protect against frost. When the seedlings reach the sheeting in late spring, cut slits and help them through. When the plants come into flower, cut

Planting in blocks to encourage pollination *Plant out seedlings in a series of short, staggered rows to give the plants the best chance of wind pollination.*

the sheeting away. However, this is unnecessary in all but the coolest climates where late spring frosts are usual. To increase yields, sow more sweetcorn in the early summer.

MAINTENANCE

Keep the rows weed free and mulch with compost, manure or paper (*see page 58*). When the plants flower, they will benefit from extra watering.

HARVESTING

When the tassels at the top of the cobs turn brown and then black, the cobs are ready for harvesting.

Harvesting sweetcorn *Break off ripe sweetcorn by pulling the cob downwards with one hand while supporting the rest of the plant with the other.*

PESTS AND DISEASES

Sweetcorn is generally trouble free. See pages 46-53 for general pests and diseases and page 198 for pests and diseases that affect pod and seed vegetables.

PLANTING AND HARVESTING TIMES

	Sow inside	Plant out	Sow outside	Harvest
Early spring				
Mid spring	●		●	
Late spring		●	●	
Early summer			●	
Mid summer				●
Late summer				●
Early autumn				●
Mid autumn				
Late autumn				
Early winter				
Mid winter				
Late winter				

Peas

Despite what the processors of frozen peas may tell you about their freshness, there is no doubt that peas taste much better when they are grown organically and eaten minutes after picking.

VARIETIES

Two varieties are necessary – an early one and a maincrop type. Recommended for an early sowing are *Freezonian* and *Grenadier* while *Hurst Green Shaft* and *Onward* are fine maincrop varieties.

I also suggest that you try one of the mangetout varieties – where the pods are eaten as well as the seeds. These have improved greatly over the past ten years, and are now very succulent, with no stringiness. Try *Oregon Sugar Pod* and *Sugar Bon*.

SOIL AND SITE

Peas, like all the other legumes, make their own nitrogen and require little extra feeding. Too rich a soil leads to a great deal of foliage but a small crop of vegetables. Peas like a soil pH of 6.5, so add lime to attain this level if necessary (*see page 36*).

● If you are using the three-year crop rotation plan (*see page 134*), grow peas in Plot B.

SOWING

The earliest peas can be sown in autumn and overwintered. However, this is somewhat risky and, in a hard winter, the crop will be small. Alternatively, an early sowing can be made in plastic guttering (*see below*).

Next, make a sowing in the open ground, in early spring, about mid-March in most of the North. Peas are best sown in a wide trench dug with a spade. Make the drill about 5cm (2in) deep and scatter the seeds in it so that they are roughly 5cm (2in) apart, cover and firm down with the back of a rake.

If you have the space, make successive sowings until about mid May in most of the North. Peas languish in hot weather. In mild climates, sow seeds in autumn for winter harvest.

Deep beds Most peas are difficult to support in deep beds so here I would recommend a semi-leafless variety like *Novella*. This is a relatively new breeding breakthrough, producing plants with

SOWING PEAS IN GUTTERING

A useful way of raising an early pea crop without risking frost damage is to sow seeds in a length of plastic guttering in the greenhouse in late winter. Plant out the seedlings under cloches until they become established (*see page 140*).

1 *Fill a length of plastic guttering with soil and sow peas at 5cm (2in) intervals. Make two staggered rows 2.5cm (1in) apart and cover with soil. Leave the seedlings in the greenhouse until they are about 8cm (3in) tall.*

2 *Using a planting board as a guide, make a straight seed drill with a draw hoe. Slide the entire contents of the guttering into the prepared furrow, firm in well and water.*

few leaves but masses of tendrils. Sow the peas in a block with the rows 15cm (6in) apart and the seeds about 5cm (2in) apart in the rows (*see page 136*), and they will grow into each other and form a completely self-supporting block of plants.

MAINTENANCE

Apart from leafless varieties grown in the way described above, all types need to be supported with pea and bean netting or with sticks (*see below*). Or stretch chicken wire along rows. Mulch between the rows with well-rotted compost or manure.

Supporting peas with sticks *If you can find several twiggy sticks, cut them to a length of 1.2m (4ft) and push one into the ground beside each plant.*

HARVESTING

It is generally better to pick the pods just a little on the young side, because they are at their sweetest, but try to pick just before they are cooked, to retain the sugar. When all the peas have been harvested, cut the foliage off and leave the roots in the ground to release their nitrogen.

PESTS AND DISEASES

Peas may be affected by birds, mice, mildew, pea moths and pea and bean weevils (*see pages 46-53 and 198*).

PLANTING AND HARVESTING TIMES

	Sow inside	Plant out	Sow outside	Harvest
Early spring	●	●		
Mid spring		●		
Late spring			●	
Early summer			●	
Mid summer		●	●	
Late summer			●	
Early autumn			●	
Mid autumn			●	
Late autumn			●	
Early winter				
Mid winter				
Late winter				

Broad beans

Wonderful value in the vegetable plot, broad, or fava, beans produce an early vegetable of unique flavor and just about the best green manure possible (*see page 32*).

VARIETIES

Broad Windsor Long Lord is the primary variety in the USA. *Toto* is a dwarf variety that bears in about 63 days. Other varieties of European origin are available from firms that import seeds (*see Useful Addresses, page 283*).

SOIL AND SITE

Broad beans, like all the other legumes, make their own nitrogen and require little extra feeding. They like a soil pH of 6.5, so add lime to attain this level if necessary (*see page 36*).
● If you are using the three-year crop rotation plan (*see page 134*), grow broad beans in Plot B.

SOWING AND PLANTING

Sow the large seeds in early spring, about the time you sow your first peas, in double rows 30cm (12in) apart and 5cm (2in) deep with about 10cm (4in) between seeds. If you grow more than one double row, allow 1m/yd between them. In mild climates, sow seeds in autumn for winter harvest.
Deep beds Sow in staggered rows with 15cm (6in) between each seed (*see page 136*).

MAINTENANCE

Provide support in exposed gardens and for all winter-sown crops. A single string tied to posts either side of the plants should suffice (*see opposite*). If plants are cloched, remove the cloches

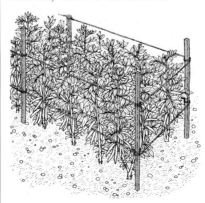

Supporting broad beans *Tie nylon twine between wooden posts either side of the plants, at the end of each row.*

when the plants touch the tops. Water if necessary and mulch between rows with well-rotted manure or compost.

HARVESTING

Pull the beans before the pods become tough and leathery. They are much more tasty when small and the plants will be encouraged to produce more. In cool climates, cut the plants back and allow them to regrow to give a second crop (*see below left*). Dry beans in the sun and store in airtight bottles for winter use in soups and stews.

Cutting down broad beans *If you garden in a cool climate, cut plants down to 5cm (2in) after harvesting. They will regrow to provide a second crop.*

PESTS AND DISEASES

Broad beans may be affected by aphids, pea and bean weevils and chocolate spot (*see pages 50 and 198*).

PLANTING AND HARVESTING TIMES

	Sow inside	Plant out	Sow outside	Harvest
Early spring			●	
Mid spring				
Late spring				●
Early summer				●
Mid summer				●
Late summer				
Early autumn				
Mid autumn				
Late autumn			●	
Early winter				
Mid winter			●	
Late winter			●	

Pole beans

Pole, or runner beans, are the climbing form of bush (snap) beans. Some have colored flowers so can be grown in a border up a wigwam of canes. The plants climb around poles or strings.

VARIETIES

Painted Lady is the one for the borders, since the flowers are an attractive red and white. *Romano* has a very distinctive flavor and the beans are fleshy and juicy. *Kentucky Wonder* in various improved varieties remains popular because of its yield and quality. Recommended heirloom varieties that can hold their own against newer hybrids include *Champagne* and the vigorous *Case Knife.*

SOIL AND SITE

Thorough soil preparation is needed to prevent pole beans drying out at the roots, since this discourages growth and could be responsible for failure of the flowers to set (*see page 198*). Dig a trench one spade deep and at least 60cm (2ft) wide and break up the bottom. Half fill it with compost, manure or even old newspapers screwed up and soaked in water or, better still, liquid manure. Then replace the soil and allow it to settle before planting. The soil pH should be about 6.5.

● If you are using the three-year crop rotation plan (*see page 134*), grow runner beans in Plot B.

SOWING AND PLANTING

Start the plants off in your greenhouse or under lights in mid spring, sowing one seed per 8cm (3in) pot. Plant out in late spring after hardening off (*see page 254*). Alternatively, sow against canes set at 30cm (12in) intervals in a double row with 60cm (2ft) between the rows. The best time for this is about a fortnight before you expect the last frost. Another way is to make a wigwam of between four and six canes spaced at about 45-60cm (18in-2ft) and tied at the top (*see below*). This is a more attractive method for the borders but is not so productive, because the plants lack light and air when they reach the top of the canes. Encourage the plants to twist around the canes.

Deep beds Pole beans are not a suitable crop for deep beds.

MAINTENANCE

Protect the young plants from slugs straight away by mulching with coarse pine bark (*see page 51*). This also helps retain water and suppresses weeds. Pinch out the growing tips when the plants reach the top of their support.

Pinching out *When the plants reach the top of their canes, pinch out the tips to encourage side-shoots to grow.*

TRAINING CLIMBING VEGETABLES

Climbing varieties of crops such as tomatoes, cucumbers, peas and beans need to be supported as they grow. Peas are usually trained up plastic netting or twiggy sticks (*see opposite*), but other vegetables require different forms of support.

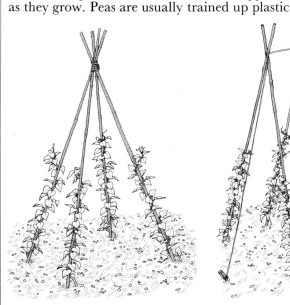

Making wigwams of canes *A wigwam of canes provides an attractive support for beans and cucumbers (see also page 175). Sow four or five seeds in a circle and train the plants up poles which are tied together at the top.*

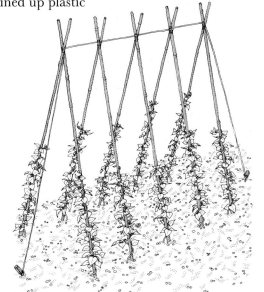

Using rows of stakes *Runner beans can be trained to grow up tall stakes. If you grow two rows, cross each pair of poles, tie them together then run nylon twine through all the supports and peg it into the ground at either end.*

Training plants up strings *Bean and tomato plants will grow up lengths of nylon twine. Tie these to a pole or a nail fixed to a wall, and plant seedlings so that the root ball anchors the string in place.*

There is a popular misconception that spraying the open flowers with water will assist pollination, but there seems to be no evidence that this is so. However, supplying plenty of water to the plant's roots at flowering time does seem to help pollination.

HARVESTING

Pick the pods when they are young and have not developed stringiness. This also encourages further production.

Harvesting bush beans *These varieties need no support and some can be harvested very early. Pick the beans when they are young and tender.*

PESTS AND DISEASES

Runner beans are liable to be affected by slugs, aphids, halo blight and failure to set (*see pages 50 and 198*).

PLANTING AND HARVESTING TIMES

	Sow inside	Plant out	Sow outside	Harvest
Early spring	●			
Mid spring	●			
Late spring		●	●	
Early summer			●	
Mid summer				●
Late summer				●
Early autumn				●
Mid autumn				●
Late autumn				
Early winter				
Mid winter				
Late winter				

Bush beans

Bush, or snap beans – also known as French beans – are just like pole or runner, beans (*see page 159*) except for their lower heights of 30cm (12in) to 60cm (2ft). They are grown the same way but do not need support.

VARIETIES

Some bush beans produce rather flat pods, examples being the outstanding *Jumbo* and *Roma*. Round or pencil-podded varieties include *Greensleeves*, *Provider* and *Royal Burgundy* with purple pods. Among yellow-podded or wax bush beans are *Pencil Pod Wax*, *Keygold*, and *Beurre de Rocquencourt*.

SOIL AND SITE

Bush beans, like all the other legumes, make their own nitrogen and require little extra feeding. They like a soil pH of 6.5, so add lime if necessary.
● If you are using the three-year crop rotation plan (*see page 134*), grow bush beans in Plot B.

SOWING

Because bush beans need a warm soil, start the first ones off in a greenhouse in early spring. Plant out under cloches in mid spring (*see page 140*), setting the plants in rows 30cm (12in) apart with 20cm (8in) between plants. The next crop can be sown under the cloches in early spring putting two seeds every 20cm (8in), again in rows about 30cm (12in) apart and about 5cm (2in) deep. Outside sowings can start in mid spring at the same distances.

The usual safe time to sow bush beans outdoors is about a week after last freeze.

MAINTENANCE

Keep beds weed free (*see page 57*) and mulch between plants with compost, bark, black plastic or paper. Water if necessary in dry weather.

HARVESTING

Pick the pods regularly when they are young, before they become stringy. If some pods are left on the plants to dry, they can be shelled and stored in airtight jars for winter use. After harvesting, cut the plants off but leave the roots in the ground to release nitrogen into the soil.

PESTS AND DISEASES

Slugs, aphids and halo blight may attack bush beans (*see pages 50 and 198*). See page 257 for pests and diseases of greenhouse plants.

PLANTING AND HARVESTING TIMES

	Sow inside	Plant out	Sow outside	Harvest
Early spring	●			
Mid spring	●	●	●	
Late spring	●	●	●	
Early summer	●		●	●
Mid summer				●
Late summer				●
Early autumn				●
Mid autumn				●
Late autumn				
Early winter				
Mid winter				
Late winter				

CULTIVATING SNAP BEANS IN THE GREENHOUSE

Climbing varieties are preferable as they make the best use of the available space. *Romano* is fleshy and stringless, while *Northeaster* is slightly earlier and very tasty.

Sow two seeds in 8cm (3in) pots of potting compost, in early spring, at a temperature of 18-21°C (65-70°F). If both seeds germinate, thin to leave the strongest when they reach the first true leaf stage.

Plant in the borders in late spring, setting the plants 30cm (12in) apart and supporting them with a string (*see page 159*).

The plants will twist round the strings of their own accord. Feed with liquid seaweed at weekly intervals throughout the growing season and pinch out the tips when they reach the tops of the string supports.

Once the first crop has been stripped, remove all the lower leaves and drop the plants to the ground carefully, coiling the stems on the ground and allowing the new growth at the top to climb up the string again. This will encourage further growth and another full crop.

Lima beans

Lima, or butter, beans are nutritious and delicious, but they can only be grown in warm climates.

VARIETIES
Burpee Improved Bush and *Burpee Fordhook* are both recommended. Climbing varieties like *Prizetaker* and *King of the Garden* crop later and are more difficult to grow.

SOIL AND SITE
The beans need sunshine and a deep rich soil with plenty of organic matter (*see pages 21-8*).
● If you are using the three-year crop rotation plan (*see page 134*), grow them in Plot B.

SOWING
Sow in late spring, or when the soil temperature reaches 18°C (65°F). Alternatively, start them off in pots inside at 21°C (70°F), to ensure rapid germination.

Sow outside 2.5cm (1in) deep in drills 60cm (2ft) apart, with 10cm (4in) between seeds. Sow climbing varieties against 2.5m (8ft) poles set in a tripod, with 90cm (3ft) between the base of each pole. Sow four to six seeds per pole and thin to three.

MAINTENANCE
Mulch around plants with well-rotted compost or manure (*see page 20*) to help retain moisture.

HARVESTING
Pick young pods regularly to encourage further production.

PESTS AND DISEASES
Lima beans may be attacked by aphids and pea and bean weevils (*see pages 50 and 198*).

Soybeans

Extremely high in protein and calcium, soybeans are only suitable for warmer climates.

VARIETIES
Frostbeater is one of the hardiest varieties and will mature even in more temperate areas. *Prize* takes a little longer to mature but has a fine flavor.

SOIL AND SITE
Soybeans prefer a well-drained soil, so dig in plenty of organic matter if your soil is heavy (*see pages 21-8*). If necessary, add lime to raise the soil pH above 6.5.
● If you are using the three-year crop rotation plan (*see page 134*), grow soybeans in Plot B.

SOWING
In late spring to early summer, sow seeds 2.5cm (1in) deep in drills 75cm (2ft 6in) apart, with 5cm (2in) between seeds.

MAINTENANCE
Use a thick mulch of compost or manure to inhibit weeds and prevent water loss (*see page 58*). Do not hoe as this would damage the shallow root system.

HARVESTING
Harvest when the beans are about 10cm (4in) long and are plump and full. The yields are generally low in relation to the space taken up by the plants.

PESTS AND DISEASES
Soybeans are generally trouble free. See pages 46-53 for general pests and diseases and page 198 for pests and diseases that affect pod and seed vegetables.

Peanuts

Although capable of withstanding a slight frost, peanuts are only really suitable for cultivation in warm climates.

VARIETIES
Jumbo Virginia produces high yields of rich-flavored nuts. *Early Spanish* is dwarf and early.

SOIL AND SITE
Peanuts need a light soil, preferably well-enriched with organic matter (*see pages 21-8*).
● If you are using the three-year crop rotation plan (*see page 134*), grow peanuts in Plot B.

SOWING
In cold areas, start the plants off in pots inside, one month before the last frost is due. Alternatively, wait until after the last frost and sow outside – 5cm (2in) deep in drills 90cm (3ft) apart – setting the seeds 15cm (6in) apart. Thin the plants to 30cm (12in) apart.

MAINTENANCE
Earth up the plants when they are 15cm (6in) tall (*see page 186*). Then mulch with a deep layer of compost, manure or grass cuttings (*see page 58*). Stop watering when the plants begin to flower.

HARVESTING
Five months after sowing, dig up the whole plant, dry the roots in the sun and remove the peanuts.

PESTS AND DISEASES
Peanuts are generally trouble free. See pages 46-53 for general pests and diseases and page 198 for pests and diseases that affect pod and seed vegetables.

PLANTING AND HARVESTING TIMES

	Sow inside	Plant out	Sow outside	Harvest
Early spring				
Mid spring	●			
Late spring		●	●	
Early summer			●	
Mid summer				
Late summer				●
Early autumn				●
Mid autumn				
Late autumn				
Early winter				
Mid winter				
Late winter				

PLANTING AND HARVESTING TIMES

	Sow inside	Plant out	Sow outside	Harvest
Early spring				
Mid spring				
Late spring			●	
Early summer			●	
Mid summer				
Late summer				●
Early autumn				●
Mid autumn				
Late autumn				
Early winter				
Mid winter				
Late winter				

PLANTING AND HARVESTING TIMES

	Sow inside	Plant out	Sow outside	Harvest
Early spring	●			
Mid spring		●	●	
Late spring		●	●	
Early summer				
Mid summer				
Late summer				●
Early autumn				●
Mid autumn				●
Late autumn				
Early winter				
Mid winter				
Late winter	●			

Fruiting vegetables

Although these crops are technically fruits – the seeds of the plant encased by a fleshy pulp – they are usually classified as vegetables because we eat them as such. They are not frost hardy, and must therefore be started off under glass or grown to maturity in the greenhouse – where their brightly colored forms are extremely decorative. Although perennial in their native tropics, they are grown as annuals in temperate climates and need a rich, moist soil and plenty of sunshine. The fruiting vegetables are all rich in Vitamin C.

Beefsteak tomato

Plum tomato

Cherry tomato

Yellow tomato

Salad tomato

TOMATOES above
Lycopersicon sp.
A very versatile vegetable, tomatoes are usually considered the most important greenhouse crop. Bush and upright types, which require support, are available. The various forms include elongated plum, large beefsteak, cherry and yellow tomatoes. *For cultivation details, see page 164.*

EGGPLANTS below left
Solanum sp.
Eggplants are treated as annuals in temperate climates, and must have a sunny, sheltered position if grown outside. They require weekly feeding at the height of the growing season. *For cultivation details, see page 166.*

Yellow pepper

Green pepper

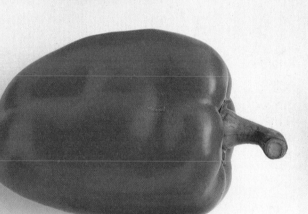

Red pepper

Hot peppers

SWEET PEPPERS above
Capsicum annuum
These attractive vegetables are available in an assortment of bright colors. The red peppers are merely green peppers left to ripen on the plant longer. This gives them a slightly more sweet taste although, as a rule, color is not a reliable guide to flavor.
For cultivation details, see page 167.

HOT PEPPERS left
Capsicum annuum
Hot or "chili" peppers vary in size, shape and hotness from sweet peppers. They are heavy-yielding plants, so only a small number is needed to provide an adequate crop. Peppers are raised in the greenhouse and then planted outside, but they often need cloche protection in all but the warmest areas.
For cultivation details, see page 167.

Cultivating fruiting vegetables

Tomatoes

Tomatoes are a popular greenhouse crop (*see opposite*) but are usually grown outside in most climates. If you live in a cold area choose early varieties or those bred for the far North.

VARIETIES

Tomatoes are available as bush (determinate) types or upright (indeterminate) types. *Basket pak* is one of the best bush varieties, giving very early crops of small tasty fruits. *Celebrity* is an excellent disease-resistant bush variety which bears fairly large fruits.

Of the upright varieties, *Gemini* is the best I have found for cooler areas, while *Lemon Boy*, a yellow variety, is recommended for flavor in warmer climates.

SOIL AND SITE

Like all the vegetable fruits, tomatoes need sun and a well-manured soil that will retain moisture and plant nutrients. They like a pH of about 6.0.
● If you are using the three-year crop rotation plan (*see page 134*), grow tomatoes in Plot A.

SOWING AND PLANTING

Sow seeds indoors about 6 weeks before last average frost in individual peat pots. Sow two seeds in each pot, pinching off the weaker after germination. The roots will grow through the

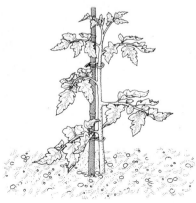

Supporting upright tomatoes *Use soft string to tie upright plants to 1.2m (4ft) canes as soon as they are planted.*

Covering bush tomatoes *Protecting plants with a cloche at the end of the growing season extends the harvesting period by helping to ripen the green fruit.*

peat pot walls and no further transplanting should be needed. Put them in the cold frame to harden off in mid spring (*see page 254*) and plant out after the frosts have ceased. Set the plants 60cm (2ft) square and plant the upright types against canes.
Deep beds Tomatoes are ideal subjects for the deep beds; plant them 50cm (20in) apart. (*See page 136.*)

MAINTENANCE

Tie the upright types to their canes regularly. Pinch out the tops when they have made three clusters of fruit – or four in warm climates. Remove the side-shoots arising from each leaf joint when they are still small. Bush varieties need no staking or side-shooting, but cover the soil underneath them with straw or bark to raise the fruit off the ground. Feed with a liquid seaweed or animal-manure fertilizer at fortnightly intervals from mid summer to early autumn.

HARVESTING

Pick as soon as the fruits are ripe to get the sweetest flavor and

encourage the production of more fruits at the end of the season. Lay upright varieties flat on straw and cover with cloches (*see page 140*).

PESTS AND DISEASES

Tomatoes may be affected by whitefly, aphids, leaf mold, red spider mites, potato blight and virus (*see pages 46-53 and 199*). See page 257 for the pests and diseases that affect plants grown in the greenhouse.

PLANTING AND HARVESTING TIMES			
	Sow inside	Plant out	Sow outside	Harvest
Early spring	●			
Mid spring		●		
Late spring		●		
Early summer		●		●
Mid summer				●
Late summer				●
Early autumn				●
Mid autumn				●
Late autumn				
Early winter				
Mid winter				
Late winter				

CULTIVATING TOMATOES IN THE GREENHOUSE

Suitable varieties for the greenhouse are *Herald* and *Sonato* which are both early and well flavored, while the cherry-fruited *Gardener's Delight* and *Sweet 100*, though they crop later and are not resistant to disease, have a superb flavor.

Sow from mid winter onwards, depending on the amount of heat you can give the plants. For cold greenhouse planting, sow in late winter at a temperature of 21°C (70°F). Transplant to individual 8cm (3in) pots as soon as the seedlings are big enough to handle. Grow them on at a temperature of 10-12°C (50-55°F), spacing them progressively so that they are not crowded, to produce short, bushy plants. Plant out in the border soil or in growing bags 30cm (12in) apart in mid spring in the cold greenhouse. If planting in the border, use a variety resistant to root-rot, such as *Floramerica* or *Celebrity* and flood the border with water about two weeks before planting to flush out excess mineral salts from the soil. Then dig in compost or manure and apply one handful of blood, fish and bone meal per plant before planting.

Water the plants in initially and then leave them to search for water, thereby encouraging extensive root growth. Water again after about a week and from then on give each plant an average of about 1 liter (2pts) per day. The smaller cherry tomatoes *Gardener's Delight* and *Sweet 100*, however, need about 1.5 liters (3 pts) per week if they are to retain their sweetness. When the plants flower, spray them with water once a day to provide the humid conditions that favor good pollination.

After about eight weeks, start feeding with a liquid seaweed or animal-manure fertilizer every time you water.

Remove the side-shoots from each leaf joint as they grow, and take off the bottom leaves when they turn yellow. Do not remove leaves above the fruit cluster that is ripening. Damp down daily (*see page 255*) and shake the supporting wires to move the pollen about. When the plants reach the top of the greenhouse, pinch out the growing points.

Training tomatoes above
Climbing tomato plants can be trained to grow up vertical strings. Tie one end of a long piece of string to the top of the greenhouse, above where each seedling will be planted. Dig out a hole and flood it with water, then remove the young plant from its pot and loop the string around the root ball.

Holding the strings in place left
Plant the young tomato plant in the prepared hole and firm it in well. The root ball anchors the string as the plant grows.

Side-shooting *Remove the side-shoots that develop from the angle between the leaf stems and the main stem of the plant.*

Eggplant

This is a good crop to grow out-side warm climates, where it can be cultivated as a perennial. In colder conditions it must be treated as a tender annual, like its relative the tomato. Young plants can be purchased or the seeds can be sown indoors.

VARIETIES

The early varieties are preferable as they give a longer period of cropping. *Black Beauty* is very early and heavy yielding. *Early Beauty* is another quick-maturing and heavy-yielding variety with excellent flavor and quality.

SOIL AND SITE

Eggplants need plenty of sun and a sheltered location, and like soil that has been well manured. They prefer a pH of about 6.5, so add lime if necessary (*see page 36*). In cold conditions, warm the soil by covering with plastic well before planting time (*see page 140*).
● If you are using the three-year crop rotation plan (*see page 134*), grow eggplants in Plot A.

SOWING AND PLANTING

Raise the plants in a greenhouse or under fluorescent tubes. Pot on if necessary and move to the cold frame in mid spring for hardening off (*see page 254*). Plant out under cloches in late spring (*see page 140*), setting the plants 60cm (2ft) apart. Stake them firmly and tie in the main stem. In warm climates, the cloches will not be necessary, so plant out in the open ground.

MAINTENANCE

Plants should branch naturally but, if they don't, pinch out the growing point when they are 23cm (9in) high. Allow no more than five fruits per plant; remove extra flowers when five have set and are swelling. Feed with a liquid animal-manure fertilizer at weekly intervals from mid summer until harvesting.
Deep beds Plant out 45cm (18in) apart in staggered rows, and protect with cloches in cold climates. (*See page 136.*)

CARING FOR EGGPLANT PLANTS

Like the other fruiting vege-tables, eggplants benefit from constant attention to their needs, whether you grow them outside or in the greenhouse.

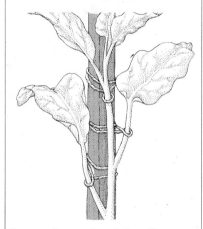

Supporting and training *Grow eggplants up canes and tie in side-shoots as they develop.*

Feeding *Bury a pot in the soil between plants, and pour liquid fertili-zer into it. This enables the roots to get the maximum benefit from the feed.*

HARVESTING

Start harvesting eggplants in late summer. Cut the fruits off before they lose their shine, or they will taste bitter.

Harvesting eggplants *Pick the fruits when they are glossy; when the skin becomes dull the fruits are too mature.*

PESTS AND DISEASES

Whitefly and aphids may affect eggplants (*see pages 46-53*). See page 199 for pests and diseases that affect fruiting vegetables and page 257 for those that affect greenhouse plants.

PLANTING AND HARVESTING TIMES

	Sow inside	Plant out	Sow outside	Harvest
Early spring	●			
Mid spring		●		
Late spring		●		
Early summer				
Mid summer				
Late summer				●
Early autumn				●
Mid autumn				
Late autumn				
Early winter				
Mid winter				
Late winter	●			

CULTIVATING EGGPLANTS IN THE GREENHOUSE

I have tried many varieties and never found one better than *Black Beauty*. Sow in early spring, in styrafoam cells or a seed tray (*see page 271*), at a temperature of 18-21°C (65-70°F). Transfer to 8cm (3in) pots as soon as the seed leaves are large enough to handle comfortably.

In the cold greenhouse, plant out in mid spring, setting the plants 60-75cm (2ft-2ft 6in) apart in the borders. Alternatively, grow them three to a deep planter, or put them into 20cm (8in) pots of worm-worked potting compost (*see page 81*). Support the plants with short canes and feed at every watering as shown above. Pinch out the top of the plant when it is about 30cm (12in) tall, and the tips of the side-shoots when the fruits have formed on them. Allow no more than about six fruits to develop on each plant. Harvest them when their flesh is shiny.

Peppers

Peppers are slightly easier to grow than eggplants in cold climates, though it is still worthwhile providing cloche protection (*see page 140*). Red peppers are the same varieties as green, but are left to ripen longer. Hot peppers, or "chili peppers" are smaller and considerably hotter than the sweet varieties. They are very prolific so you will not need to grow many plants.

VARIETIES

Of the sweet varieties, *Gypsy* produces very high yields. The fruits are a little yellow for some tastes but this does not affect their flavor. *New Ace* is a good outdoor variety because it is earlier than most. It also does well in an unheated greenhouse or under plastic cloches in temperate climates.

Chili Serrano is a very hot pepper suitable for cultivation in warm climates. *Big Jim* is milder and can be grown under cloches in cooler climates.

SOIL AND SITE

Peppers need plenty of sunshine and a sheltered location and like soil that has been well manured. They prefer a pH of about 6.0 or 6.5. In cold conditions, warm the soil by covering it with plastic well before planting time (*see page 140*).

● If you are using the three-year crop rotation plan (*see page 134*), grow peppers in Plot A.

SOWING AND PLANTING

Sow in the greenhouse or under fluorescent lights. Harden them off in a cold frame (*see page 254*) from mid spring and plant out under cloches or, in warm climates, outside in late spring with 60cm (2ft) between plants.
Deep beds Plant out seedlings in staggered rows with 45cm (18in)

Harvesting peppers *Pick the fruits when they are green or wait until they have turned red, when the flavor will be slightly more spicy.*

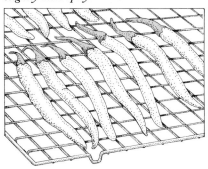

Drying chili peppers *Hot varieties can be dried outside on a raised wire frame then stored in airtight jars.*

between plants, during late spring. (*See page 136*.)

MAINTENANCE

Pinch out the growing point when the plants are 15cm (6in) high and tie them to a cane. Tie in the side-shoots as they grow. Water regularly and feed with a liquid seaweed or animal-manure fertilizer every week.

HARVESTING

Harvest once the fruits have swollen (*see left*). Hot peppers can be dried in the sun and stored for use in the winter (*see left*).

PESTS AND DISEASES

Slugs, whitefly, aphids and red spider mites may affect peppers (*see pages 46-53 and 199*). See page 257 for pests and diseases that affect greenhouse plants.

PLANTING AND HARVESTING TIMES			
	Sow inside	Plant out	Sow outside	Harvest
Early spring	●			
Mid spring		●		
Late spring		●		
Early summer				
Mid summer				●
Late summer				●
Early autumn				●
Mid autumn				●
Late autumn				
Early winter				
Mid winter				
Late winter	●			

CULTIVATING PEPPERS IN THE GREENHOUSE

Both sweet and hot peppers are suitable for greenhouse cultivation. *Bell-Boy* is one of the most reliable sweet varieties. *Long Red Cayenne* is a prolific hot pepper, while *Chili Serrano* fruits are smaller but very hot indeed.

Peppers need a temperature of 18-21°C (65-70°F). Sow in mid winter, if you can supply heat. Growing under fluorescent tubes supplies both heat and light. Peppers have a small root system, so prefer not to have too much cold mixture around their roots. As soon as the seed leaves are big enough to handle comfortably, transplant to 8cm (3in) pots and pot on progressively into the next size up as the roots fill the pot.

Again, space the plants early to give them plenty of light and air.

Plant out in mid spring, either in the borders about 35cm (15in) apart or in growing bags. I have had my best results from peppers transplanted to 20cm (8in) pots of worm-worked potting mixture. They seem to fruit better when the roots are restricted.

Peppers do not require any stopping and there is no need to remove side-shoots. Simply stake them with a short cane and tie the plants in as they grow. Water the plants regularly and feed with liquid fertilizer at every watering. Harvest when the peppers are green or wait until they turn red, for a spicier flavor.

Using a growing bag *Greenhouse peppers can be planted out in growing bags, which you can make yourself (see page 253).*

Bulb vegetables

The edible bulbs of the onion family are in fact compacted layers of swollen leaf bases in which the plant stores food. They prefer a rich soil so are particularly suited to organic cultivation. The bulbs are among the easiest of all vegetables to grow and most of them store well, so it is not difficult to maintain a year-round supply.

GARLIC below
Allium sativum
Sometimes classified as a herb, garlic is one of the easiest vegetables to grow, needing only a warm, sunny position. It is sown from cloves – the individual segments of the bulb – and can be dried and stored for year-round use. *For cultivation details, see page 170.*

ONIONS right
Allium cepa
One of the most useful vegetables in the kitchen, onions store well and can be used all year round if a combination of main-crop and Japanese varieties is planted. *For cultivation details, see page 171.*

LEEK right
Allium porrum
Hardy, easy to grow and requiring little mainten-ance, this valuable winter vegetable can be left in the ground until needed, in all but the very coldest condi-tions. It may run to seed if planted too early. *For cultivation details, see page 170.*

SALAD ONIONS right
Allium cepa
Salad or spring onions are picked before the mature bulb forms. They have a milder flavor than the larger types. *For cultivation details, see page 171.*

SHALLOTS below
Allium ascalonicum
Earlier to mature and with a milder
flavor than maincrop onions,
shallots require similar growing conditions. They are easy to grow from
"sets", rarely troubled by diseases
and store well for winter use.
For cultivation details, see page 171.

Cultivating bulb vegetables

Garlic

Garlic is one of the easiest of all vegetables to grow, provided you have a suitably sunny site.

VARIETIES

Garlic is grown from cloves – the individual segments of the bulb. These are widely available and specific varieties are not usually mentioned. However, if you can get it, *Marshall's Long Keeper* is excellent.

SOIL AND SITE

See Soil preparation for bulb vegetables, *right*.

PLANTING

Separate the cloves and plant them, pointed end up, in holes 2.5cm (1in) deep and 15cm (6in) apart. Do this in late winter to early spring in the North and in the autumn in South and other mid regions of the country.

SOIL PREPARATION FOR BULB VEGETABLES

All the bulb vegetables prefer sunshine and a soil rich in organic matter, so dig in plenty of well-rotted compost or manure. If necessary, add lime to raise the soil pH above 6.5 (*see page 36*).
● If you are using the three-year crop rotation plan (*see page 134*), grow the bulb vegetables in Plot A.

MAINTENANCE

Keep the rows weed free and, if the site is exposed, support the long stems to stop them breaking off in the wind.

HARVESTING

Dig up the bulbs in summer, clean them and dry them in the sun before stringing or storing in nets in a frost-free place.

PESTS AND DISEASES

Garlic is generally trouble free. See pages 46-53 for general pests and diseases and page 199 for specific pests and diseases that affect bulbs.

PLANTING AND HARVESTING TIMES

	Sow inside	Plant out	Sow outside	Harvest
Early spring		●		
Mid spring				
Late spring				
Early summer				
Mid summer				●
Late summer				●
Early autumn		●		●
Mid autumn				
Late autumn				
Early winter				
Mid winter				
Late winter		●		

Leeks

A superb winter vegetable that is hardy in all but the very coldest climates, leeks are easy to grow, undemanding and a valuable source of fresh greens in winter.

VARIETIES

Musselburgh is a popular variety, very hardy and with thick stems. *Titan* has a very long stem and a good blanched base. *Alaska* has as excellent flavor and is also very hardy.

SOIL AND SITE

See Soil preparation for bulb vegetables, *above*.

SOWING AND PLANTING

Leeks can be multiple sown (*see page 139*) or grown in seed boxes started in the greenhouse in mid spring, at a temperature of about 15°C (60°F). Alternatively, sow them in a seed bed outside, in a shallow drill, 15cm (6in) apart. Transplant the young leeks in a deep furrow so they can be blanched as described right.

Starting in early summer, make holes with a dibber (*see page 260*), about 15-20cm (6-8in) deep and 15cm (6in) apart, with 30cm (12in) between rows. Trim the roots of the leeks by about two-thirds and the tops by about half, and drop a plant into each hole. Do not refill the holes, but pour a little water into each to wash some soil over the roots.
Deep beds Plant in the same way, setting the plants in a block of staggered rows with 15cm (6in) between plants each way. Alternatively, multiple sow them as described on page 139 and plant them 30cm (12in) apart each way. (*See page 136*.)

MAINTENANCE

Hoe to keep the rows weed free (*see page 57*) and, as the leeks grow, pull a little soil around the base of each stem to blanch them, taking care to prevent soil getting between the leaves.

HARVESTING

Leeks are quite hardy, and can usually be left in the ground until required. But, if there is a danger of very cold weather making the soil too hard to dig, lift a few plants and put them in a box of moist peat until required.

PESTS AND DISEASES

Leeks are generally trouble free. See pages 46-53 for general pests and diseases and page 199 for specific pests and diseases that affect bulb vegetables.

PLANTING AND HARVESTING TIMES

	Sow inside	Plant out	Sow outside	Harvest
Early spring	●		●	●
Mid spring	●		●	
Late spring		●		
Early summer		●		
Mid summer				
Late summer				
Early autumn				
Mid autumn				●
Late autumn				●
Early winter				●
Mid winter				●
Late winter	●			●

Onions

Onions store well so you can eat them all year round.

VARIETIES

For continuity, grow a main crop and a Japanese variety, which will harvest much earlier. Choose maincrop varieties that store well, like *Sweet Sandwich, Southport Red Globe* or *Copra*. One of the best Japanese varieties is *Express Yellow*, which is ready to harvest in early summer.

SOIL AND SITE

See Soil preparation for bulb vegetables, *opposite*.

SOWING AND PLANTING

Onions can be multiple sown (*see page 139*) in mid winter in a heated greenhouse or sown outside in shallow drills 30cm (12in) apart in early spring. Use a stale seed bed (*see page 269*) so the tiny seedlings are not swamped by weeds, and thin to 5cm (2in) apart. Sow Japanese varieties in late summer and spread a handful of dried blood per square meter/yard in spring.

If your soil is heavy and wet, buy onion sets – tiny onion bulbs that have been specially treated to produce good-sized bulbs. Cut off any long growths of old foliage at the tips, to prevent birds pulling the sets out of the ground, and plant bulbs at the same distances, so the tips are just below soil level. Do not push the sets into the ground as they may push themselves out again when they grow roots.

Deep beds Sow or plant 5cm (2in) apart in staggered rows.

MAINTENANCE

Keep onions weed free and water in dry weather.

HARVESTING

In late summer, the onion foliage turns brown and withers. Lift the roots and leave the bulbs to dry in the sun. Then remove the tops and store the onions in nets in a frost-free shed. Alternatively, leave the leaves on, tie bunches of onions together with string.

PESTS AND DISEASES

Onions may be affected by many of the general garden pests and diseases as well as onion fly, onion eelworm, neck rot, white rot and storage rot (*see pages 46-53 and 199*).

PLANTING AND HARVESTING TIMES

	Sow inside	Plant out	Sow outside	Harvest
Early spring	•	•		
Mid spring	•	•	•	
Late spring				•
Early summer				•
Mid summer				•
Late summer			•	•
Early autumn				•
Mid autumn				•
Late autumn				
Early winter				
Mid winter				
Late winter	•			

SALAD ONIONS

The small salad or "spring" onions have a milder flavor than other types and do not store well. *White Lisbon* and *Ishikuro* are recommended varieties. Sow them under cloches (*see page 140*) in late winter, and in the open at three-week intervals from early spring. They will not need to be thinned. If you are using deep beds, scatter seeds in a wide drill (*see page 136*).

Shallots

These mild-flavored bulbs are much smaller than maincrop onions and can be harvested earlier, in summer. They are easy to grow from sets (*see above*).

VARIETIES

Dutch Yellow and *Dutch Red* are the two most popular varieties, producing heavy yields of size-able bulbs. The exhibition variety *Hative de Niort* produces bigger bulbs which do not keep as well.

SOIL AND SITE

See Soil preparation for bulb vegetables, *opposite*.

SOWING AND PLANTING

Remove any dead foliage and plant the sets in drills in early spring, putting them 15cm (6in) apart in rows 30cm (12in) apart. Ensure that the tip of the bulb is just below soil level and do not press the sets into the ground or they will push themselves out again when they grow roots.

Deep beds Plant in staggered rows with 15cm (6in) between sets. (*See page 136.*)

MAINTENANCE

Weed and water as required. In early summer, draw the soil away from the bulbs to assist ripening.

Drying shallots *Put harvested bulbs on a piece of chicken wire raised off the ground, so air can circulate around them.*

HARVESTING

Lift when the foliage dies down in summer, clean the bulbs and store in nets in a frost-free place.

PESTS AND DISEASES

Shallots are generally trouble free. See pages 46-53 for general pests and diseases and page 199 for specific pests and diseases that affect bulb vegetables.

PLANTING AND HARVESTING TIMES

	Sow inside	Plant out	Sow outside	Harvest
Early spring		•		
Mid spring				
Late spring				
Early summer				•
Mid summer				•
Late summer				•
Early autumn				
Mid autumn				
Late autumn				
Early winter				
Mid winter				
Late winter		•		

Squash vegetables

These crops are members of the *Cucurbitae* family, half-hardy annuals which can be grown outside in warm conditions. They require well-manured, slightly acid soil and plenty of water. Most summer squash form large-leaved, bushy plants, while most autumn squash, and cucumbers and melons trail.

SQUASH ZUCCHINI below left
Cucurbita pepo
These large, fast-maturing vegetables require a soil enriched with a much organic matter as possible. Other summer squash types include crookneck, straightback and patty-pan. Pick the fruits before they get too large.
For cultivation details, see page 174.

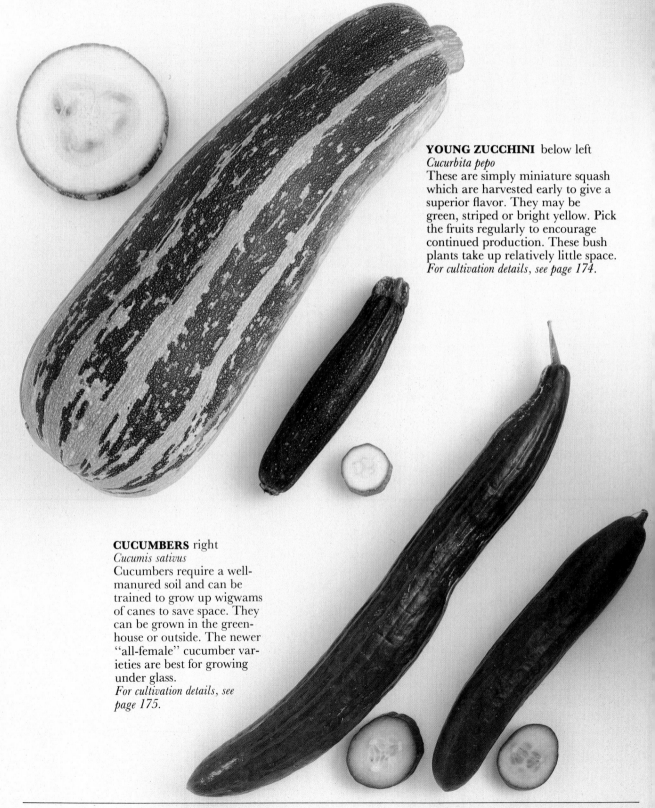

YOUNG ZUCCHINI below left
Cucurbita pepo
These are simply miniature squash which are harvested early to give a superior flavor. They may be green, striped or bright yellow. Pick the fruits regularly to encourage continued production. These bush plants take up relatively little space.
For cultivation details, see page 174.

CUCUMBERS right
Cucumis sativus
Cucumbers require a well-manured soil and can be trained to grow up wigwams of canes to save space. They can be grown in the greenhouse or outside. The newer "all-female" cucumber varieties are best for growing under glass.
For cultivation details, see page 175.

Honeydew melon

Cantaloupe melon

MELONS right
Cucumis melo
New faster-maturing
varieties are grown under
cloches or in the open in
warm areas. The heavy
fruits, which are juicy and
sweet-flavored, can be
supported by nets as they
mature. They require
plenty of water and must
be eaten fresh, as they do
not store.
*For cultivation details, see
page 176.*

PUMPKINS above
Cucurbita maxima and *C. moschata*
Because they take a long time to mature, true pumpkins
are best grown in warm areas, but there are many
related squashes that will do well in cooler climates.
They are used in both sweet and savory dishes. All
pumpkins and fall squash can be stored for winter use.
For cultivation details, see page 177.

Cultivating squash vegetables

Squash·zucchini

America's squash, including summer's zucchini and the long-keeping fall kinds, bear abundantly and are very nutritious. In Europe they are known as marrows and courgettes and, of course, all are grown the same way. Leave a few zucchini on the plants to grow into squashes for the winter.

VARIETIES

There are many varieties of all kinds. Popular among the bush summer varieties are *Golden Zucchini*, *Aristocrat* and *Burpee's Butterstick*. Among autumn squash are *Butterbush* and *Bush Acorn Table King*. For winter squash, see page 177.

SOIL AND SITE

Dig in plenty of compost or manure (*see pages 21-8*). All squashes prefer a pH of about 6.0.
● If you are using the three-year crop rotation plan (*see page 134*), grow your plants in Plot A.

SOWING

Sow the seeds outdoors when the soil has warmed or earlier under cloches or plastic protection. Sow seeds about 15cm (6in) apart in rows about 90cm (3ft) apart, finally thinning the seedlings to 45cm (18in) apart. Or start seeds indoors in peat pots.

MAINTENANCE

If space is restricted, you can grow squash up a tripod of canes in the same way as cucumbers (*see opposite*).

Mulching young squash *Surrounding plants with a layer of ornamental pine bark (*see page 58*) helps control weeds and deter slugs.*

Harvesting zucchini *Cut through the stem with a sharp knife.*

Keeping the plants in check *If you grow trailing varieties of squash flat on the ground, trim them regularly with a spade.*

Pinch out the tops when the plants reach the top of the canes. Feed at fortnightly intervals with a liquid seaweed or animal-manure fertilizer from mid summer until harvesting.

HARVESTING AND STORING
Cut when they are no more than 15cm (6in) long, to encourage further production. The vegetable spaghetti is a novelty summer vining squash. You can ripen them at the end of the season and keep them for a short time in a frost-free place.

Ripening squash *Put bricks under autumn and winter squashes to raise them off the ground and prevent rotting.*

PESTS AND DISEASES
See pages 46-53 for slugs, aphids and mildew, and page 199 for cucumber mosaic virus.

PLANTING AND HARVESTING TIMES

	Sow inside	Plant out	Sow outside	Harvest
Early spring				
Mid spring	●			
Late spring		●	●	
Early summer		●	●	●
Mid summer				●
Late summer				●
Early autumn				●
Mid autumn				●
Late autumn				
Early winter				
Mid winter				
Late winter				

Cucumbers

New varieties of cucumbers make them well worth growing outside. These are now so good that I only use the greenhouse to grow the very earliest varieties.

VARIETIES
Sweet Success produces long, almost seedless fruits and *Burpless Tasty Green* is said to be easier to digest than most varieties.

SOIL AND SITE
Cucumbers prefer a pH of about 6.0 and a well-manured soil, so dig in plenty of compost or manure (*see pages 21-8*).
● If you are using the three-year crop rotation plan (*see page 134*), grow cucumbers in Plot A.

SOWING AND PLANTING
Sow inside at a temperature of about 18°C (65°F) in mid spring, putting two seeds in each 8cm (3in) pot. When they germinate, thin to leave the strongest seedling if necessary. Plant out in late spring, setting the plants 60cm (2ft) apart. Alternatively, sow pairs of seeds outside in late spring, at the same spacings. Cover the sowing site with a cut-off plastic bottle or a cloche (*see page 140*) to protect them from cold wind and slugs.

The most space-saving way to grow cucumbers is up a wig-wam of canes (*see below*). This also keeps the fruits off the ground and out of reach of slugs, and looks attractive enough for the flower borders. If you do decide to grow them flat on the ground, space them 90cm (3ft) apart.
Deep beds Cucumbers are suitable for deep beds. They should be grown up canes at 60cm (2ft) spacings. (*See page 136.*)

MAINTENANCE
If you grow plants up canes, tie them in frequently and trim the side-shoots back to two leaves regularly to encourage compact, bushy growth. Pinch out tops when the plants reach the top of the canes. Feed with liquid

Training cucumbers up a wigwam of canes *Space four 2.5cm (8ft) canes 60cm (2ft) apart and tie them together at the top. Plant young plants at the base of each cane and tie them in with soft string as they grow.*

animal-manure fertilizer at fortnightly intervals from mid summer until harvesting. Do not remove the male flowers.

HARVESTING
Cut the fruits when they are still young and have a bloom on them. Regular cutting encourages the plants to produce more fruits.

PESTS AND DISEASES
See pages 46-53 for slugs, aphids and mildew, page 199 for cucumber mosaic virus and page 257 for pests and diseases that affect greenhouse plants.

PLANTING AND HARVESTING TIMES

	Sow inside	Plant out	Sow outside	Harvest
Early spring	●			
Mid spring	●			
Late spring		●	●	
Early summer		●		
Mid summer				●
Late summer				●
Early autumn				●
Mid autumn				●
Late autumn				
Early winter				
Mid winter	●			
Late winter	●			

CULTIVATING CUCUMBERS IN THE GREENHOUSE

New cucumber varieties are sweet-tasting, vigorous and resistant to diseases. *Fembaby* produces small fruit of superb flavor, while *Uniflora D* is very heavy cropping indded. *Superstar* is ideal for cooler conditions. All these grow perfectly well in the same temperature and humidity regime as tomatoes (*see page 165*), so they can share the house.

Sow from mid winter if the greenhouse can be heated to about 10°C (50°F) during the early part of the growing year, and in mid spring for growing in a cold house. Sow individually in 8cm (3in) pots of potting mixture, and put them in a propagator at a temperature of 24-27°C (75-80°F). When they germinate, move them to a light, airy position at 15-18°C (60-65°F).

Prepare the border soil and plant out in the borders or growing bags as for tomatoes (*see page 165*). Support the plants in the same way as tomatoes (*see right and page 165*), but handle the plants carefully when twisting them round the strings as they are delicate and can easily break.

Cucumbers like plenty of water and should never be allowed to dry out. They like a humid atmosphere, so damp down the paths and plants at least twice a day in the morning and early afternoon (*see page 255*). Ventilate to keep the temperature around 18-24°C (65-75°F) during the day and keep the vents shut at night at least until the early summer. After about eight weeks, start feeding with liquid seaweed or animal-manure fertilizer at every watering.

Trim the side-shoots regularly to leave two leaves. The newer varieties recommended here fruit mainly from the main stem. Other, older varieties may produce fruit mainly on the side-shoots, in which case remove any on the main stem.

Training greenhouse cucumbers
Guide the main stem so it twines around a string (see also page 165).

Melons

New, quick-maturing varieties are ideal for cloche culture in cool climates (*see page 140*) or growing outside in warmer areas.

VARIETIES
Varieties like *Sweetheart* water melon and *Bush Star* musk melon ripen quickly and are ideal.

SOIL AND SITE
Melons need a well-manured soil, so dig in plenty of compost or manure (*see pages 21-8*). They prefer a pH of about 6.0.
● If you are using the three-year crop rotation plan (*see page 134*), grow melons in Plot A.

SOWING AND PLANTING
Sow inside at 18°C (65°F) in mid spring, putting two seeds in each 8cm (3in) pot and thinning to one if necessary. Plant out under cloches in late spring with 90cm (3ft) between plants.

MAINTENANCE
It is important to water regularly. When the plants have made three leaves, pinch out the growing point. It will then make side-shoots which should again be stopped after three leaves. When the fruits form, pinch back to two leaves beyond the fruit.

HARVESTING
Cut the fruits as soon as they feel soft when you press the ends.

PESTS AND DISEASES
See pages 46-53 for slugs, aphids and mildew, page 199 for cucumber mosaic virus and page 257 for pests and diseases that affect greenhouse plants.

PLANTING AND HARVESTING TIMES

	Sow inside	Plant out	Sow outside	Harvest
Early spring	●			
Mid spring	●		●	
Late spring		●	●	
Early summer				
Mid summer				
Late summer				●
Early autumn				●
Mid autumn				
Late autumn				
Early winter				
Mid winter				
Late winter	●			

CULTIVATING MELONS IN THE GREENHOUSE

Because they can be grown without heat during the summer, needing only a little at the propagation stage, the modern cantaloupe and F1 hybrid varieties have replaced the old-fashioned musk or sweet melons. In warm climates, these newer varieties are quite at home outside (*see left*). As well as those mentioned above, I recommend *Burpee Hybrid* for the greenhouse.

Sow individually in 8cm (3in) pots in early spring at a temperature of 21-24°C (70-75°F). Plant out about 30-45cm (12-18in) apart in a well-manured border or, ideally, a hot bed (*see page 253*). Alternatively, grow them in growing bags or even in pots, but they will need more careful watering. In the cold house, plant out in mid spring.

Pinch out the growing point to keep only two true leaves, a week after planting. Two side-shoots will grow from this point and they are allowed to grow on the ground or can be trained up wires. Stop

Supporting greenhouse melons *Place nets around the maturing fruits and attach them to an overhead wire.*

these shoots after they have made between seven and ten leaves. Secondary shoots and flowers will then appear. When the embryo fruits appear, stop two leaves past the fruit. Only allow about five fruits to develop on each plant. Allow insects access to the greenhouse in order to pollinate the plants. Spray over the leaves and damp down the paths and borders each morning (*see page 255*). except when the fruit is ripening – then leave the atmosphere dry and ventilate freely. Feed the plants with liquid fertilizer at each watering.

Pumpkins

True pumpkins are best suited to warm climates, as they take four months to reach maturity. However, there are plenty of related squashes that can be grown for winter use, even in cooler climates, so some of these are included here.

VARIETIES

The largest pumpkins are impractical for eating unless your family is very large or you want to use them to make pies, in which case *Big May* or *Triple Threat* are suitable varieties. The smaller *Small Sugar* is one of the best for general use. Among autumn and winter squash, *Butterbush* or *Bush Buttermint* and *Bush Acorn* and *Table King* are good winter keepers. The apple squash *Gourmet Globe* is another small squash for cool or warm climates.

SOIL AND SITE

All squashes need a well-manured soil, so dig in plenty of compost or manure (*see pages 21-8*). They prefer a pH of about 6.0.

● If you are using the three-year crop rotation plan (*see page 134*), grow pumpkins in Plot A.

SOWING AND PLANTING

Sow inside at a temperature of about 18°C (65°F) in mid spring, putting two seeds in each 8cm (3in) pot and thinning to leave the strongest seedling if necessary. Most winter squashes are trailing varieties and require a lot of room, so plant them out at least 90cm (3ft) apart when all danger of frost has passed in late spring. If sowing outside, do so about a fortnight earlier than that.

MAINTENANCE

Feed with a liquid animal-manure fertilizer at fortnightly intervals from mid summer to early autumn. There is no need to remove the male flowers. Pinch back the trailing stems regularly to keep the plants in check.

HARVESTING AND STORING

Leave winter squashes on the plant as long as possible, while there is plenty of sunshine. At the end of the season, raise the fruits off the ground by putting them on a piece of wood or brick to avoid rotting. When they start to fade, cut off the fruit but leave them in the sun to continue ripening if possible. The harder the skins at the end of the season, the better they will keep. Store them in a frost-free place and eat in autumn to mid winter.

PESTS AND DISEASES

See pages 46-53 for slugs, aphids and mildew, and page 199 for cucumber mosaic virus.

PLANTING AND HARVESTING TIMES

	Sow inside	Plant out	Sow outside	Harvest
Early spring				
Mid spring	●			
Late spring	●	●	●	
Early summer			●	
Mid summer				
Late summer				●
Early autumn				●
Mid autumn				●
Late autumn				
Early winter				
Mid winter				
Late winter				

Root vegetables

Most of the root vegetables are biennials; they store food in the swollen roots for use in the second year of the growth cycle, when the plants would normally flower and produce seed. By harvesting at the end of the first year, we benefit from this reserve of nourishment.

SALSIFY AND SCORZONERA below
Tragopogon porrifolius and *Scorzonera hispanica*
Also known as black salsify and oyster plant. They are a good source of iron and are not difficult to grow.
For cultivation details, see page 181.

RADISHES right
Raphanus sativus
These roots are fast-maturing and very easy.
For cultivation details, see page 180.

CARROTS right
Daucus carota sativus
Carrots are rich in vitamins and dietary fiber.
For cultivation details, see page 181.

KOHL-RABI right
Brassica oleracea gongylodes
The swollen stem of this unusual vegetable is the part that is eaten.
For cultivation details, see page 180.

CELERIAC right
Apium graveolens
This is actually a swollen stem that grows just above the ground.
For cultivation details, see page 182.

JERUSALEM ARTICHOKES right
Helianthus tuberosus
An excellent winter alternative to potatoes, these large plants are easy to grow and can become invasive if not carefully controlled.
For cultivation details, see page 182.

Salsify   Scorzonera

TURNIPS below
Brassica rapa rapa
Turnips can be harvested from spring to autumn and stored in a frost-free place for winter use. They need plenty of water.
For cultivation details, see page 183.

PARSNIPS AND HAMBURG PARSLEY below
Pastinaca sativa and *Petroselinum crispum* var. *tuberosum*
These vegetables require similar growing conditions.
For cultivation details, see page 187.

BEET below
Beta vulgaris
This summer vegetable can also be stored for winter use. Its delicate roots will "bleed" when cut.
For cultivation details, see page 184.

SWEDE or RUTABAGA above
Brassica napus napobrassica
This member of the *Brassica* group is easy to grow and can be stored for the whole winter in moist peat or vermiculite.
For cultivation details, see page 183.

Hamburg parsley

POTATOES above
Solanum tuberosum
Always grow a few early potato varieties for their delicious flavor.
For cultivation details, see page 185.

SWEET POTATOES above
Ipomoea batatas
Sweet potatoes are only suitable for cultivation in warm climates.
For cultivation details, see page 187.

Parsnip

Cultivating root vegetables

Radishes

Grow radishes as a catch-crop between rows of slower-maturing vegetables (*see page 136*). They will put up with a wide range of soils and conditions, so long as the weather is cool. They sulk during the hot summer months in the North, so are best sown in spring and autumn. In the South, grow in winter.

VARIETIES

French Breakfast is the best variety, with long, mildly-flavored, crisp roots. *Cherry Belle* is round and red and a good fast developer.

SOIL AND SITE

Radishes will produce a reasonable crop in any soil, but they grow faster in land that is enriched with well-rotted compost or manure (*see pages 21-8*).
● If you are using the three-year crop rotation plan (*see page 134*), grow radishes in Plot C.

SOWING

Sow the first crop in very early spring (*see page 140*), scattering seeds thinly in rows 15cm (6in)

apart. Thinning is not normally necessary. After that, sow small amounts every week until warm weather arrives.
Deep beds Sow in wide, shallow bands, scattering the seeds thinly across the band. (*See page 136*).

Harvesting multiple-sown radishes
*To improve yields, multiple sow early crops indoors and plant out under cloches (*see page 139*).

MAINTENANCE

Water if the soil is dry and keep the beds weed free by hoeing (*see page 57*).

HARVESTING

Pull regularly to avoid the roots becoming hot and woody.

PESTS AND DISEASES

Radishes are susceptible to flea beetles and the pests and diseases that affect root vegetables (*see pages 50 and 200*).

PLANTING AND HARVESTING TIMES	Sow inside	Plant out	Sow outside	Harvest
Early spring		●		
Mid spring		●	●	
Late spring		●	●	
Early summer			●	
Mid summer				
Late summer		●		
Early autumn		●	●	
Mid autumn		●	●	
Late autumn			●	
Early winter				
Mid winter				
Late winter		●		

Kohl-rabi

This strange-looking vegetable is a member of the cabbage family. The swollen stem is the part that is eaten, rather than the leaves. New varieties are a great improvement on the old for flavor, and can even be eaten raw.

VARIETIES

White Vienna and *Purple Vienna* are both excellent, with a sweet flavor. But keep a look out for *Rowel* which is crisper, sweeter and juicier.

SOIL AND SITE

If your soil is heavy, use beds raised by digging in plenty of well-rotted compost or manure to improve the drainage (*see pages 21-8*). Add lime to the soil to achieve a pH over 6.5.
● If you are using the three-year

crop rotation plan (*see page 134*), grow kohl-rabi in Plot C.

SOWING AND PLANTING

Sow in a seed bed, making successional sowings from mid spring to mid summer. Transplant to rows 30cm (12in) apart with 23cm (9in) between plants.
Deep beds Transplant in staggered rows with 23cm (9in) between plants (*see page 136*).

MAINTENANCE

Hoe to keep the beds weed free (*see page 57*).

HARVESTING

Pull the roots during the summer before they get too big – about 5cm (2in) in diameter is ideal. Later, the whole crop can be lifted and stored for a short time in boxes of moist peat in a frost-free place.

PESTS AND DISEASES

Kohl-rabi is generally trouble free. See pages 46-53 for general pests and diseases and page 200 for specific pests and diseases that affect root vegetables.

PLANTING AND HARVESTING TIMES	Sow inside	Plant out	Sow outside	Harvest
Early spring				
Mid spring		●		
Late spring		●		
Early summer		●	●	
Mid summer		●	●	
Late summer			●	
Early autumn			●	
Mid autumn			●	
Late autumn				
Early winter				
Mid winter				
Late winter				

Carrots

Carrots are not hard to grow on good soil and it is possible to get a succession throughout the year. They are an excellent source of vitamins and dietary fiber.

VARIETIES

For multiple sowing (*see page 139*), use round types like *Kundulus* or *Planet*. Early outdoor sowings should be the fast-maturing varieties like *Minecor* or one of the *Nantes* strains, but choose a larger variety, like *Tondo* or *Chantenay Red Cored*, for maincrop sowing.

SOIL AND SITE

Carrots do best on light soil with plenty of well-rotted organic matter. They will not fork provided the compost or manure is well-rotted. If your soil is heavy, grow them in raised deep beds (*see page 136*). Add lime to the soil to bring the pH over 6.5.
● If you are using the three-year crop rotation plan (*see page 134*), grow carrots in Plot A.

SOWING

Earliest crops are multiple sowings planted out under cloches in mid to late winter. Sow outside in the open in early spring: sow round varieties in wide bands and long ones in drills 23cm (9in) apart. Thin long varieties when they are just big enough to eat. Sow every three weeks in drills 30cm (12in) apart, thinning to 8cm (3in) apart.
Deep beds Plant out multiple-sown carrots in staggered rows 15cm (6in) apart. Alternatively, make sowings of round varieties as above and successional sowings of long varieties in drills 15cm (6in) apart and thin to 8cm (3in) apart.

MAINTENANCE

Hoe to keep the rows weed free and, as the carrots swell, pull a little soil up to them to prevent the "shoulders" going green and to deter carrot fly (*see page 200*).

HARVESTING

Pull early and successional sowings when they are still young and crisp. In mid or late autumn lift the final sowing and store in moist peat or vermiculite. Do not leave them in the ground for a long time or some may split, attracting slugs.

PESTS AND DISEASES

Carrots are affected by carrot fly and storage rot (*see page 200*). See pages 46-53 for general pests and diseases.

PLANTING AND HARVESTING TIMES

	Sow inside	Plant out	Sow outside	Harvest
Early spring		●	●	
Mid spring			●	
Late spring			●	
Early summer			●	●
Mid summer				●
Late summer				●
Early autumn				●
Mid autumn				
Late autumn				
Early winter				
Mid winter	●		●	
Late winter	●	●	●	

Salsify and scorzonera

These two gourmet vegetables are much alike in flavor and can be grown in the same way. Salsify has a white root while scorzonera is black skinned but pure white beneath. I prefer the taste of scorzonera, but you may disagree, so try both. Both are an excellent source of iron and are not difficult to grow. As well as the roots, you can eat the stems and leaves of both crops.

VARIETIES

I find *Mammoth* and *Sandwich Island Mammoth* quite indistinguishable, and both are good varieties of salsify, while *Habil* is the best scorzonera.

SOIL AND SITE

Both scorzonera and salsify like a very deep, well-manured soil but ensure that the manure is well-rotted or the roots will fork. Scorzonera is a particularly deep-rooting vegetable.
● If you are using the three-year crop rotation plan (*see page 134*), grow your plants in Plot A.

SOWING

Sow outside in mid spring in drills about 2.5cm (1in) deep and 30cm (12in) apart. Thin the seedlings to 15cm (6in) apart.

MAINTENANCE

Hoe to keep the beds weed free (*see page 57*) or, better still, mulch with well-rotted compost in autumn to safeguard against damage to the roots.

HARVESTING AND STORING

In late autumn, lift and store in moist peat in a frost-free shed. Alternatively, the leaves and stems can be used. Leave some roots in the ground and cover them with soil to blanch them (*see below*). Then harvest them in spring and use raw in salads or leave them unblanched and cook them like spinach.

PESTS AND DISEASES

Salsify and scorzonera are both generally trouble free. See pages 46-53 for treatment of general pests and diseases and page 200 for specific pests and diseases that affect root vegetables.

Blanching salsify or scorzonera
After harvesting the roots you need, cover a few plants with soil to provide blanched leaves which can be used in salads.

PLANTING AND HARVESTING TIMES

	Sow inside	Plant out	Sow outside	Harvest
Early spring			●	
Mid spring			●	
Late spring				
Early summer				
Mid summer				
Late summer				
Early autumn				
Mid autumn				●
Late autumn				●
Early winter				●
Mid winter				
Late winter				

Jerusalem artichokes

This superb winter vegetable has all the flavor of globe artichokes, but is much easier to grow. Indeed, the plants are very invasive if not kept in check. They can attain a height of 3m (9ft), so they make a useful windbreak.

VARIETIES
They are generally just sold as Jerusalem artichokes. You can buy tubers from most mailorder catalogues for planting in early spring or autumn.

SOIL AND SITE
Although they will grow practically anywhere, you can ensure bigger, smoother tubers by reserving a permanent, well prepared site for them. Dig a trench about 60cm (2ft) wide and one spade deep. Break up the bottom and refill, working in as much well-rotted compost, manure, or one of the alternatives, as you can spare (see pages 21-8). Jerusalem artichokes like an acid soil, so keep the pH down below 6.5.

PLANTING
Plant as early in the year as the soil conditions will allow, usually late winter or early spring. Set the tubers 15cm (6in) deep and 30cm (12in) apart. You will

Using Jerusalem artichokes as a windbreak *You can position these tall vegetables to protect other plants from wind.*

Planting tubers *Make a deep drill for the tubers or some may force their way to the surface and turn green. Plant to avoid casting shade over other crops.*

generally only need one row but, if you want more, make the rows at least 1.5m (5ft) apart.

MAINTENANCE
Weed and water as required. Mulch annually in early spring with well-rotted compost or

manure (see pages 21-8), and spread a handful of blood, fish and bone meal per meter/yard of row. In exposed areas you may need to support plants with a length of nylon string tied between two posts (see page 159).

HARVESTING AND STORING
Cut down the stems in mid autumn to leave 30cm (12in), and dig up the tubers as required. Leave some in the ground to replace the crop for next season.

PESTS AND DISEASES
Jerusalem artichokes are generally trouble free. See pages 46-53 for general pests and diseases and page 200 for those that affect root vegetables.

PLANTING AND HARVESTING TIMES

	Sow inside	Plant out	Sow outside	Harvest
Early spring		•		
Mid spring				
Late spring				
Early summer				
Mid summer				
Late summer				
Early autumn				
Mid autumn		•		•
Late autumn		•		•
Early winter		•		•
Mid winter				
Late winter		•		

Celeriac

This superb vegetable is really a swollen stem that grows just above the ground. It has all the flavor of celery hearts.

VARIETIES
There is little to choose between *Alabaster* and *Large Smooth Prague*.

SOIL AND SITE
Celeriac prefers plenty of sun and a water-retentive soil rich in organic matter (see pages 21-8), with a pH of about 6.0.
● If you are using the three-year crop rotation plan (see page 134), grow celeriac in Plot A.

SOWING AND PLANTING
Sow in your greenhouse or under lights at a temperature of about 18°C (65°F) in mid spring. Do not be tempted to sow earlier

or the crop will certainly run to seed. As soon as the first true leaf develops, transplant to wider spacings (see page 272). Plant out in late spring, after hardening off in the cold frame (see page 254), so that the swelling at the base of the plant is at soil level. Plant 30cm (12in) apart with 35cm (15in) between rows.
Deep beds Plant in blocks, with 30cm (12in) between plants (see page 136).

MAINTENANCE
Mulch with well-rotted manure (see page 20) and keep the plants well watered in dry weather. In early autumn, draw soil round the stems to blanch them.

HARVESTING
Lift regularly between mid and late autumn and store in boxes of moist peat in a frost-free shed.

PESTS AND DISEASES
Celeriac is generally trouble free. See pages 46-53 for general pests and diseases and page 200 for specific pests and diseases that affect root vegetables.

PLANTING AND HARVESTING TIMES

	Sow inside	Plant out	Sow outside	Harvest
Early spring				
Mid spring	•			
Late spring		•		
Early summer				
Mid summer				
Late summer				
Early autumn				
Mid autumn				•
Late autumn				•
Early winter				
Mid winter				
Late winter				

Turnips

One of the easiest root vegetables to grow, turnips can be harvested in succession from spring to autumn, when they can be dug up and stored for winter use.

VARIETIES
Early Purple Top Milan has tender white flesh and is undoutedly best for the first crops and for successional sowings. *Tokyo Cross* is a good-flavored variety that stores well, as does *Golden Ball*, which is quite hardy, with yellow flesh and an excellent flavor.

SOIL AND SITE
Grow the earliest varieties in well-manured soil for fast growth. The maincrop varieties and those for storage can be grown on the brassica plot. You may need to add lime to the soil to bring the pH above 6.5.
● If you are using the three-year crop rotation plan (*see page 134*), grow maincrop turnips in Plot C.

SOWING AND PLANTING
The earliest crop can be multiple sown (*see page 138*) in late

Harvesting multiple-sown turnips
To improve yields, multiple sow early crops indoors and plant out under cloches.

winter at a greenhouse temperature of 18°C (65°F) and planted out under cloches in early spring. Sow outside from mid spring to mid summer, in shallow drills 30cm (12in) apart. Thin to leave the plants 15cm (6in) apart in the rows.

MAINTENANCE
Keep the rows meticulously weed free by hoeing (*see page 57*) or hand-pulling, and water if necessary. Mulch between plants with well-rotted compost or manure (*see page 20*), to help retain

moisture and prevent the roots becoming tough and stringy.

HARVESTING AND STORING
Pull the first roots at golf-ball size and the biggest at tennis-ball size. In mid autumn, lift the maincrop varieties, twist off the tops and store in moist peat.

PESTS AND DISEASES
Turnips are affected by flea beetles and soft rot (*see pages 50 and 200*).

PLANTING AND HARVESTING TIMES

	Sow inside	Plant out	Sow outside	Harvest
Early spring		●		
Mid spring			●	
Late spring			●	●
Early summer			●	●
Mid summer			●	●
Late summer				●
Early autumn				●
Mid autumn				
Late autumn				
Early winter				
Mid winter				
Late winter	●			

Swedes

These are also known as rutabaga. New varieties are a great improvement on the old ones that were grown mainly for cattle feed. A member of the cabbage family, swedes are one of the most straightforward vegetables to grow.

VARIETIES
Purple Top Yellow is large and well flavored with a fine-textured orange flesh. *Marian* is of good quality and flavor, and bred for its resistance to club root and mildew.

SOIL AND SITE
Provide a well-drained soil with a pH of over 6.5, to help combat club root (*see page 201*).
● If you are using the three-year crop rotation plan (*see page 134*), grow swedes in Plot C.

SOWING
Sow swedes late in the season – late spring or early summer – as a safeguard against mildew (*see page 52*). Sow seeds in shallow

Sowing swedes *Sow seeds very thinly, as about 90 per cent will germinate. Hold a few between your thumb and finger and sprinkle them down the row.*

drills 45cm (18in) apart and thin to 30cm (12in) in the rows.

MAINTENANCE
Keep the plants free from weeds by hoeing (*see page 57*), and water if necessary. Mulch with well-rotted manure or compost (*see page 20*).

HARVESTING AND STORING
Roots can be left in the soil in milder areas, but this may encourage disease so I recommend you lift them after a frost in mid autumn, twist off the tops and store in boxes of moist peat or vermiculite.

PESTS AND DISEASES
Swedes are affected by flea beetles, mildew, soft rot and club root (*see pages 50, 52 and 201*).

PLANTING AND HARVESTING TIMES

	Sow inside	Plant out	Sow outside	Harvest
Early spring				
Mid spring				
Late spring			●	
Early summer			●	
Mid summer				
Late summer				
Early autumn				
Mid autumn				●
Late autumn				●
Early winter				
Mid winter				
Late winter				

Beets

A superb summer vegetable that can be eaten cold, hot or pickled. Autumn crops can also be stored to last well into winter.

VARIETIES

The earliest sowings should be of quick-maturing *Early Egypt* or *Early Red Ball*, which produce quite large round roots and store well – so there is really only need to buy one packet of seeds if your garden is small. For successional sowings, you could also use *Cylindra* or *Burpees Golden*.

SOIL AND SITE

Beets like a deep, rich, soil, with a pH of about 6.5. Dig in plenty of well-rotted manure or compost to improve drainage.
● If you are using the three-year crop rotation plan (*see page 134*), grow beets in Plot A.

SOWING

Start by multiple sowing (*see page 139*) in mid or late winter and plant out under cloches (*see page 140*). Make the first sowings outside under cloches in early spring. The seeds come in "clusters", so put one or two clusters every 8cm (3in) in 2.5cm (1in) deep drills 30cm (12in) apart. Before sowing, put the seeds into a flour sieve and wash them vigorously under the tap. This removes chemicals which inhibit germination, encouraging the

seedlings to germinate faster. Thin by pulling roots selectively when they are no bigger than a golf ball.

Continue sowing every three weeks until mid summer. The maincrop sowing is made then and the roots are thinned to leave one every 8cm (3in).
Deep beds Sow the earliest crop in wide bands and pull selectively. Successional sowings are made in staggered rows 8cm (3in) apart, thinning to 8cm between plants.

MAINTENANCE

Hoe regularly to remove weeds (*see page 57*), taking great care not to damage the roots; they will "bleed" if the skin is broken. Mulch between plants with rotted compost, manure or wet newspaper (*see page 58*).

HARVESTING AND STORING

Never let the roots get too big or they will become woody. Pull early sowings as "baby beet" at about golf-ball size, and main

crops at about tennis-ball size. Lift maincrop roots in mid or late autumn and store for winter use (*see below*).

PESTS AND DISEASES

Beets are susceptible to mildew (*see page 52*). See also page 200 for specific pests and diseases that affect root vegetables.

PLANTING AND HARVESTING TIMES

	Sow inside	Plant out	Sow outside	Harvest
Early spring			●	
Mid spring	●	●		
Late spring			●	
Early summer			●	●
Mid summer				●
Late summer				●
Early autumn				●
Mid autumn				●
Late autumn				●
Early winter				
Mid winter				
Late winter	●			

LIFTING BEETS FOR WINTER STORAGE

Many of the root crops, such as swedes, turnips and beets, can be harvested and stored in a similar way, ensuring a ready supply of fresh vegetables throughout the winter months. Beets will bleed if the skin is broken, so take care when harvesting and handling. Store in a cool, frost-free shed.

Preparing beet seeds *To encourage rapid germination, put the clusters of seeds into a sieve and wash them in cold running water.*

1 *Dig up the last of the plants in late autumn. Trim the roots by twisting off the tops or cutting them with a knife, but leave 2.5cm (1in) of leaf stem.*

2 *Put some moist peat or vermiculite into a wooden box. Place trimmed roots on top and cover with more peat. Repeat until the box is full.*

Potatoes

The potato really does justify organic gardening methods, but it may not be worth growing maincrop varieties in small gardens if you can find a supply of organically grown ones from a farmer or a local shop. Potatoes take up a lot of room and are relatively cheap to buy. Early varieties, however, are desirable, as the flavor is so much better when they are eaten fresh from the garden. Maincrops make a superb cleaning crop in new gardens (*see page 56*).

VARIETIES

Always buy seed potatoes that have been certified free from disease and, if possible, select small tubers with few sprouts (*see right*). This avoids undue competition producing a larger number of inferior tubers.

Seedsmen in the USA supply potato eyes rather than the whole tuber. These are sold packed in moist vermiculite and are shipped at the proper planting time for your region. Upon arrival, they should be planted at once.

Early varieties are dug and eaten straightaway. Recommended varieties are *Maris Bard*, a heavy-yielding type with a fair flavor, *Irish Peace*, which is early and has an excellent flavor, and *Arkula* – a very early and well-flavored variety. There are numerous varieties and they perform differently in different areas, so try a few tubers of a different type each year. In the USA, *White Cobbler* is an excellent early variety, and *Arran Pilot* and *Cliff's Kidney* are recommended in Australasia.

Maincrop varieties are dug in the autumn and stored for winter use. *Desirée* is a good, large European red with a fine flavor and texture, while *Drayton* is a fine white. In the USA, one of the best keepers is *Red Pontiac* while, in Australasia, *Sebago* is highly thought of.

SOIL AND SITE

Potatoes need a water-retentive soil with plenty of organic matter for the best results. If you do not have enough well-rotted compost or manure for the whole potato plot, dig the planting furrows deep and put a layer in the bottom. The tubers can be set directly on it. Do not lime the potato plot at all, as potatoes prefer an acid soil.

● If you are using the three-year crop rotation plan (*see page 134*), grow potatoes in Plot A.

PLANTING

Buy seed potatoes as early in the year as possible and put them in boxes or – if you only have a few – in egg cartons, in a light place at a temperature of about 10°C (50°F). They will then form good, short, bushy green sprouts. American growers send specific instructions for handling and growing the eyes.

The earliest crops come from tubers planted through black plastic sheeting under cloches in late winter (*see overleaf*). This is an ideal deep-bed method (*see below*). Alternatively, plant in rows 60cm (2ft) apart, setting the tubers 30cm (12in) apart and about 15cm (6in) deep at the same time. The rows must then be covered with a sheet of woven polypropylene for protection against frost.

Plant the first unprotected crop using the early varieties at the

Good sprouts

Bad sprouts

Good and bad potato sprouts *To encourage healthy green sprouts, keep seed potatoes in cool, light conditions. If they are kept in a warm, dark place, they will produce pale and weak sprouts.*

GROWING POTATOES UNDER BLACK PLASTIC

Early varieties can be planted through holes made in black plastic sheeting. This restricts weeds and protects the young plants from frost by warming the soil. Lay the sheeting over the area to be sown and bury the edges or secure them with bricks.

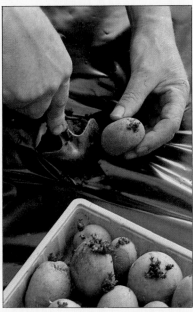

1 *Cut slits in the plastic every 30cm (12in), in staggered rows 30cm (12in) apart. Plant the potatoes 15cm (6in) deep with the sprouts uppermost.*

2 *The plastic can be lifted or cut away and the tubers harvested as normal. Lift early varieties for immediate use, leaving the rest of the crop to grow on.*

same distances in early or mid spring. Maincrop varieties are planted at the same time, but here the rows are spaced 75cm (2ft 6in) apart and the tubers spaced about 35cm (15in) apart (*see below*).

If plants are raised from eyes, plant them at the same distances in early to mid spring.

Planting tubers *Maincrop potatoes can be planted directly on to a layer of well-rotted organic matter. Mound up the row slightly after planting.*

MAINTENANCE

If shoots emerge before the danger of frost has passed, draw a little soil over them for protection.

When the shoots are 15-20cm (6-8in) tall, spread a handful of blood, fish and bone meal dressing down each meter/yard of row. Then earth up by pulling soil from between the rows up to the shoots, leaving a few inches still showing through. A second earthing up can be done later if the plants have not met in the rows in about three weeks. This is an excellent means of controlling weeds, as well as ensuring that the tubers do not push up into the light.

HARVESTING AND STORING

Lift early potatoes when they begin to flower. Take only what is needed immediately, leaving the rest to grow on.

Maincrop types are dug in mid autumn. Cut down foliage and put it on the compost heap but, if there is any sign at all of disease on the leaves, they must be burned. Dig from the sides of the ridges to avoid damaging the tubers, lift the potatoes and

throw them into a heap, leaving them for a few hours to dry out. Then store them in paper or burlap sacks in a frost-free place. Store only perfect tubers; those which are blemished must be used immediately.

PESTS AND DISEASES

Potatoes are affected by slugs, wireworms, potato cyst eelworm, potato blight, scab, potato blackleg, spraing and wart disease (*see pages 50 and 200*).

PLANTING AND HARVESTING TIMES

	Sow inside	Plant out	Sow outside	Harvest
Early spring		●		
Mid spring		●		
Late spring				
Early summer				●
Mid summer				●
Late summer				●
Early autumn				●
Mid autumn				
Late autumn				
Early winter				
Mid winter				
Late winter	●			

HARVESTING AND STORING POTATOES

Maincrop potatoes are stored in a different way from many of the other root crops (*see page 184 and opposite*). As with beets, care is needed when harvesting them, as damaged roots may rot.

1 *Cut off the potato foliage and inspect it carefully for signs of disease. If there are none, put it on the compost heap; otherwise destroy it.*

2 *Using a garden fork, dig from the side of the ridge and lift the plants. Shake off excess soil and leave the tubers to dry for a few hours. They are liable to rot if stored damp.*

3 *Store blemish-free tubers in sacks, reserving any damaged ones for immediate use. Inspect the stored crops regularly for signs of storage rot and remove any potatoes that are affected.*

Sweet potatoes

Sweet potatoes are very nutritious and tasty, but can only be grown in warm climates.

VARIETIES
Centennial produces high yields even in northern regions. *Porto Rico* has a delicious flavor and moist, reddish flesh.

SOIL AND SITE
Sweet potatoes prefer a sandy soil but can be grown on heavier land with plenty of organic matter worked in. Make deep furrows and put a layer of compost or manure in the bottom. Then ridge up the soil to make mounds about 25cm (10in) high.
● If you are using the three-year crop rotation plan (*see page 134*), grow sweet potatoes in Plot A.

PLANTING
Buy plants from the nurseryman or seedsman. Set them 30cm (1ft) apart in the rows about a month after the last frost.

MAINTENANCE
Keep the rows weeded until the plants meet in the rows to smother weeds. Sweet potatoes thrive in hot, dry weather so there is usually no need to water.

HARVESTING
Lift and store in the same way as ordinary potatoes (*see opposite*) after the first frost of autumn.

PESTS AND DISEASES
Sweet potatoes are susceptible to slugs, wireworms, cutworms, aphids (*see pages 46-53*). See page 200 for pests and diseases that affect root vegetables.

PLANTING AND HARVESTING TIMES

	Sow inside	Plant out	Sow outside	Harvest
Early spring				
Mid spring				
Late spring		●		
Early summer		●		
Mid summer				
Late summer				
Early autumn			●	
Mid autumn			●	
Late autumn				
Early winter				
Mid winter				
Late winter				

Parsnips and Hamburg parsley

The distinctive sweet taste of parsnips makes them popular winter roots. In cold climates, they can be lifted and stored for the winter but, in most areas, sow later and leave them in the ground. Hamburg parsley looks very much like parsnips and is grown in exactly the same way.

VARIETIES
Hollow Crown forms long, tapering roots of white flesh with a thick shoulder. *Harris Crown* is smaller and slimmer, and forms few side-roots. Hamburg parsley is simply sold as such by growers.

SOIL AND SITE
Parsnips and Hamburg parsley are tolerant of fairly poor conditions but will do best when plenty of well-rotted compost or manure is incorporated into the soil (*see pages 21-8*). They prefer a soil pH of about 6.5, so add lime to the soil if necessary. If you want to grow long roots in stony soil, make holes at 15cm (6in) intervals with a crowbar, about 45cm (18in) deep and 8cm (3in) in diameter. Fill these with good soil or organic matter, then sow two or three seeds in each hole and later thin to leave one.
● If you are using the three-year crop rotation plan (*see page 134*), grow these plants in Plot A.

SOWING
The seeds germinate very slowly when the soil temperature is below 12°C (45°F), so there is little point in sowing too early. In cold climates, sow in mid spring and in warmer climates in early autumn. Sow two or three seeds at 15cm (6in) intervals in shallow drills 30cm (12in) apart. Always sow in a stale seed bed (*see page 269*) and sow a few radishes in the drill to mark the rows for hoeing. Alternatively, pre-germinate the seeds and fluid sow them (*see page 140*).
Deep beds Sow in blocks 15cm (6in) apart in each direction. (*See also page 136*.)

MAINTENANCE
Keep the rows weed free and the water supply fairly constant to prevent the roots cracking.

HARVESTING AND STORING
Although they can be left in the ground, lifting and storing these vegetables avoids the risks of pests and diseases.

1 *Lift the roots after the first frosts. These will improve the flavor and kill off the top growth, so there is no need to remove the leaves by hand.*

2 *Loosely pack harvested parsnips and Hamburg parsley in boxes, between layers of moist peat or vermiculite. Store in a cool, frost-free shed.*

PESTS AND DISEASES
Both are affected by carrot root fly and parsnip canker (*see page 200*). See pages 46-53 for general pests and diseases.

PLANTING AND HARVESTING TIMES

	Sow inside	Plant out	Sow outside	Harvest
Early spring			●	
Mid spring			●	
Late spring				
Early summer				
Mid summer				
Late summer				
Early autumn			●	
Mid autumn				
Late autumn				●
Early winter				●
Mid winter				●
Late winter				●

Leaf vegetables

Many of these vegetables are members of the *Cruciferae* family and are able to store large amounts of water in their leaves, making them fleshy and succulent. Because they are biennials, they also store nutrients during the first year of growth and these are available to us if the crops are harvested before they flower and seed. Many leaf vegetables are especially rich in iron and vitamins. The brassicas are prone to a wide range of pests and diseases, but correct cultivation techniques and strict crop rotation will prevent many of these problems.

KALE left
Brassica oleracea acephala
New varieties are a great improvement on the old, making kale a valuable winter vegetable, rich in vitamins. Smooth- and curly-leaved varieties are available.
For cultivation details, see page 190.

BRUSSELS SPROUTS above
Brassica oleracea gemmifera
These vegetables are often interplanted between other crops. New varieties can stay on the plant for a long time.
For cultivation details, see page 190.

SPINACH BEET right
Beta vulgaris cicla
This is even easier to grow than spinach and, as it is a biennial, there is no danger of it running to seed. Just two sowings will ensure a succession.
For cultivation details, see page 192.

SWISS CHARD left
Beta vulgaris cicla
The stems of this broad-leaved vegetable, also known as "seakale beet", can be eaten as well as the leaves.
For cultivation details, see page 192.

SPINACH right
Spinacea oleracea
Very nutritious and easy to grow, spinach can be harvested in spring and fall. The seed should be sown in early spring or early fall.

CALABRESE AND BROCCOLI above and above right
Brassica oleracea italica
This cool season vegetable produces green or purple curds.
Calabrese or sprouting broccoli forms a looser head.
For cultivation details, see page 193.

CAULIFLOWER above
Brassica oleracea botrytis
It is the central "curds" of
the cauliflower that are
actually eaten, not its
leaves. There are three
main seasonal types, so
they can be harvested all
year round in some areas.
Cauliflowers are the most
difficult of the brassicas
to cultivate successfully.
*For cultivation details, see
page 194.*

CHINESE CABBAGE
below
Brassica rapa pekinensis
Also known as
bok-choy, this fairly demanding
cabbage needs plenty of water and a
moisture-retentive soil.
For cultivation details, see page 193.

Red cabbage

White cabbage

Spring cabbage   Savoy cabbage

CABBAGES above and right
Brassica oleracea
It is possible to harvest cabbages throughout the entire
year in some climates and if suitable varieties are sown
and transplanted at the correct time. Cabbages produce
a large weight of edible material for the amount of
space they occupy. As well as conical and round-
hearted varieties, there are savoy and red cabbages.
For cultivation details, see page 196.

Cultivating leaf vegetables

Kale

Perhaps not the most flavorsome of brassicas but hardy and useful in hard winters, kale is also known as "Borecole" – which comes from the Dutch "Boerenkool", meaning "peasants' cabbage". It is a highly nutritious plant, especially rich in vitamins. The newer varieties are a great improvement on the older ones and are well worth a try.

VARIETIES

There are curly and smooth-leaved types. *Cottagers* will stand most winters but it not as well flavored as *Dwarf Blue Curled Vales* or *Winterbor*.

SOIL AND SITE

See Soil preparation for brassicas, *opposite*.

SOWING AND PLANTING

Sow in a seed bed in mid or late spring, in shallow drills 15cm (6in) apart. Plant out with 45cm (18in) between plants each way. **Deep beds** Plant 35cm (15in) apart each way. (*See page 136*.)

MAINTENANCE

Water regularly, hoe and, if possible, mulch to keep the beds

Harvesting kale *Pull young leaves from the center of each plant. Do not completely strip the plants.*

weed free (*see pages 58-9*). The plants may need support if the site is exposed.

HARVESTING

Pull a few leaves from the center of each plant, while they are still young and tender.

Guarding against disease *After harvesting the young leaves, pull up the rest of the plant to deter the build up of club root.*

PESTS AND DISEASES

Kale can be affected by many of the general garden pests and diseases, as well as cabbage butterflies, cabbage moth, cabbage root maggot and club root (*see pages 46-53 and 201*).

PLANTING AND HARVESTING TIMES

	Sow inside	Plant out	Sow outside	Harvest
Early spring				●
Mid spring		●		
Late spring		●		
Early summer				
Mid summer				
Late summer				
Early autumn				
Mid autumn				
Late autumn			●	
Early winter			●	
Mid winter			●	
Late winter			●	

Brussels sprouts

Brussels sprouts are an invaluable winter vegetable, improved greatly by a touch of frost. Although they take up a fairly large area, fast-maturing vegetables, like lettuces and radishes, can be interplanted between rows in the early stages of development.

VARIETIES

To ensure a long harvesting period and make the most of your space, grow those types that will stand for a long period without deteriorating. The more expensive F1 varieties are far superior in this respect. You will only need to grow two seasonal crops. *Jade Cross* is an early variety ready in early autumn and holding on the plant until early winter. *Early Dwarf Danish* will then take over and go on into spring if insulated by snow.

SOIL AND SITE

See Soil preparation for brassicas, *opposite*.

SOWING AND PLANTING

Brussels sprouts need a longer growing period than most other brassicas, so start them in the seed bed in early or mid spring. Sow seeds thinly in shallow drills 15cm (6in) apart, and use netting to protect the seedlings against birds (*see page 47*).

Plant out when the seedlings are no more than 5-8cm (2-3in) tall. Space them 1m (3ft) square if you want them for eating fresh but, if you want smaller sprouts for freezing, plant them out 50cm (20in) square. Use a dibber (*see page 260*) and firm in well. Water afterwards and then leave the plants for at least a week, before watering again. **Deep beds** If your garden is committed to the system, Brussels sprouts can be grown perfectly well, planting out at the same distances, and you can plant other crops between rows. There is no need to firm the soil in the beds, but you may need to support the plants during the winter. However, because they

SOIL PREPARATION FOR BRASSICAS

Lime the soil if necessary to raise the pH to between 6.5 and 7.0, and dig in well-rotted compost or manure if you have it to spare. Add two handfuls of blood, fish and bone meal per square meter/yard.

The soil for brassicas should be well-firmed, so there is no need to dig after the last crop was lifted, except in the case of summer cabbages, which are planted in spring.

● If you are using the three-year crop rotation plan (*see page 134*), grow all brassicas in Plot C. Since brassicas generally follow the legumes in the rotation scheme, there will be a reserve of nitrogen in the soil from the bacteria in the root nodules of the peas and beans.

Never grow brassicas in the same plot in consecutive years. Strict crop rotation helps deter the build-up of club root disease (*see pages 45 and 201*).

---

require such wide spacing, the yield per square meter/yard is not increased by deep bed planting (*see page 136*).

MAINTENANCE

There is not much to do during the summer except keep the plants watered and the beds weed free. If you are not growing "catch-crops" between the plants (*see page 143*), cover the soil between the rows with compost, paper or black plastic to control weeds and reduce the need for watering. If you do grow lettuces, onions, radishes or any other fast-maturing crop, be careful not to add too much extra fertilizer or the sprouts may become "soft". This is particularly important later in the season as winter approaches. On fertile organic soil, catch-crops grown between the rows should thrive without added fertilizer.

Pick off and remove yellowing leaves in autumn and compost them. Protect the plants against birds by covering them with netting (*see page 47*).

Tall varieties may need staking in exposed areas; this can be done with a post at each end of the row and a length of nylon twine stretched either side of the plants (*see page 158*).

HARVESTING

Start in early autumn, or when the bottom sprouts are firm, and go on until early spring. Always pick from the bottom upwards, removing and composting yellowed leaves as you go to prevent fungus diseases. Once the plants have been stripped, remove them entirely and either shred them mechanically or pulverize them with a hammer (*see below*). They can then be put on the compost heap, where they will rot down.

PESTS AND DISEASES

Brussels sprouts can be affected by many of the general garden pests and diseases, as well as cabbage butterflies, cabbage moth, cabbage root maggot and club root (*see pages 46-53 and 201*).

PLANTING AND HARVESTING TIMES

	Sow inside	Plant out	Sow outside	Harvest
Early spring			●	
Mid spring		●		
Late spring		●		
Early summer				
Mid summer				
Late summer				
Early autumn				●
Mid autumn				●
Late autumn				●
Early winter				●
Mid winter				●
Late winter				●

Picking off leaves *It is important to pick off the large lower leaves as they turn yellow in autumn. They can easily be infected with fungus diseases which may spread to infect the whole crop.*

Harvesting Brussels sprouts *Pick from the bottom of the stem and work upwards, as this is the order in which the sprouts mature. Snap them off at the base.*

Pulverizing the stems *After harvesting, dig up the whole plant so the build-up of disease spores is deterred. Break up the stem with a hammer so it will rot down more quickly on the compost heap.*

Swiss chard

Sometimes also called "seakale beet", this is an excellent, easy-to-grow vegetable. It is often regarded as a "spinach substitute", but has a quite different flavor and is considered a delicacy in some parts of the world.

VARIETIES

The major varieties are *White Icing*, with celery-like stalks, and *Fordhook Giant. Ruby Chard* is also available, and this has distinctive blood-red stems. It has no advantage in flavor but looks very attractive and can be grown in flower borders.

SOIL AND SITE

A rich, moisture-retentive soil is best so, if you have some organic matter to spare, use it. Lime is generally required, so check that the soil pH is above 6.5.
● If you are using the three-year crop rotation plan (*see page 134*), grow Swiss chard in Plot B.

SOWING

Sow in shallow drills in mid spring, setting the seeds 30cm (12in) apart in groups of two or three. The rows should be 35cm (15in) apart. Later, thin the clusters to leave the strongest seedlings. One sowing should be enough as this is a cut-and-come-again plant. A late summer sowing can be made in mild climates.

Planting chard in the ornamental border *The dramatic bright-red* Ruby chard *is often grown for its decorative qualities as well as its flavor.*

Deep beds Sow at the same time, so that the thinned plants are 23cm (9in) apart each way in staggered rows. (*See page 136.*)

MAINTENANCE

There is little to do except water and weed when necessary. In very cold regions, harvesting can be prolonged by covering plants with cloches (*see page 140*).

HARVESTING

Start harvesting the leaves in mid summer. Pull them off the plant as you would rhubarb, as cutting them would cause bleeding. Take just a few leaves from the outside of the plant, leaving the remainder to grow on. The fleshy mid-ribs are considered a delicacy and are sometimes cooked separately. Because it can withstand some freezing, Swiss chard can be harvested into early winter.

PESTS AND DISEASES

See page 50 for slugs and page 201 for specific pests and diseases that affect leaf vegetables.

PLANTING AND HARVESTING TIMES

	Sow inside	Plant out	Sow outside	Harvest
Early spring				
Mid spring		●		
Late spring				
Early summer				
Mid summer				●
Late summer			●	●
Early autumn				●
Mid autumn				●
Late autumn				●
Early winter				●
Mid winter				
Late winter				

Spinach beet

This is an easier vegetable to grow than spinach (*see opposite*). Being a biennial, it will not run to seed (*see page 143*) and will withstand quite cold conditions.

VARIETIES

The beet relative is not well known in USA, but a few seed houses offer seed as perpetual, or perennial, spinach.

SOIL AND SITE

A rich, moisture-retentive soil is best so, if you have some organic matter to spare, use it. Lime is generally required, so check that the pH is above 6.5. Provide some shade if possible.
● If you are using the three-year crop rotation plan (*see page 134*), grow your plants in Plot B.

SOWING

Sow in drills about 2.5cm (1in) deep in spring for summer picking and again in summer for winter crops. Sow two seeds every 30cm (12in), with 30cm (12in) between rows. Thin to single seedlings.
Deep beds Sow in staggered rows with 23cm (9in) between seeds. (*See page 136.*)

MAINTENANCE

Water copiously in dry weather and keep the beds weed free.

HARVESTING

Pick a few outer leaves from each plant while they are still young and crisp. Never completely strip a plant, as the leaves will regrow and you can continue picking for most of the year where winters are mild.

PESTS AND DISEASES

Spinach may be attacked by slugs and birds (*see pages 46 and 50*). See also page 201 for pests and diseases that affect leaf vegetables.

PLANTING AND HARVESTING TIMES

	Sow inside	Plant out	Sow outside	Harvest
Early spring			●	
Mid spring			●	
Late spring				
Early summer				●
Mid summer			●	●
Late summer			●	●
Early autumn				●
Mid autumn				●
Late autumn				●
Early winter				●
Mid winter				
Late winter				

Spinach

No garden should be without spinach. It is highly nutritious, easy to grow, and can be harvested in spring and again in autumn. Amaranth spinach, also known as "Tampala" or "Hinn Choy", has a spinach flavor with a hint of horseradish. It is worth growing, particularly in hot areas, as it will withstand high temperatures.

VARIETIES
True spinach has a much better flavor than the spinach substitutes. *Bloomsdale* is an excellent long-standing variety with large, deep-green leaves. *Melody* is fast growing, high yielding and resistant to some diseases.

SOIL AND SITE
A rich, moisture-retentive soil is best so, if you have some organic matter to spare, use it. Lime is generally required, so check that the soil pH is above 6.5. Provide some shade, as spinach has a tendency to run to seed very quickly if it gets too warm.
● If you are using the three-year crop rotation plan (*see page 134*), grow spinach in Plot B.

SOWING AND PLANTING
Although spinach can be grown in a greenhouse or perhaps in a planter on a windowsill in late winter, most gardeners prefer to wait until early spring to make the first sowing outdoors, perhaps when peas are sown. Sow in shallow drills about 30cm (12in) apart and thin to 15cm (6in) apart in the row. Or broadcast the seeds in wide bands, then lightly rake to cover the seeds. Make successive sowings, if you have the space, from early to late spring. Except in far northern regions where summers remain cool, forget true spinach in summer. Instead, sow amaranth spinach in late spring or New Zealand spinach (*see below*). Sow

amaranth seed in shallow rows 23cm (9in) apart. Thin to 15cm (6in) apart.
Deep beds Plant out or sow in blocks with 20cm (8in) between plants each way. (*See page 136.*)

MAINTENANCE
There is little to do except water and weed as necessary.

HARVESTING
Take a few leaves from each plant, or pull the whole plant to thin rows. Pick amaranth spinach leaves regularly.

Harvesting spinach *Start picking the outer leaves 6-10 weeks after sowing.*

PESTS AND DISEASES
See pages 46-53 for aphids and downy mildew and page 201 for mosaic virus.

PLANTING AND HARVESTING TIMES	Sow inside	Plant out	Sow outside	Harvest
Early spring	●	●		
Mid spring			●	
Late spring			●	●
Early summer				●
Mid summer				
Late summer			●	
Early autumn			●	●
Mid autumn				●
Late autumn				●
Early winter				●
Mid winter				
Late winter				

NEW ZEALAND SPINACH

This is a useful spinach substitute as it thrives in the hottest weather. It does form seeds but they are no problem as leaves can be picked separately. The seeds have a tough coat so soak them first overnight or plant in early spring. They will then not germinate until the soil warms. The plants have a sprawling habit; thin to about 45-60cm (18-24in) apart in the row. Hoe to keep row weed free and harvest regularly.

Broccoli

This brassica is easy to grow and produces spears like the individual florests of cauliflower. It is a nutritious vegetable that grows best in cool weather.

VARIETIES
For summer harvest use *Green Comet*, which produces succulent heads just about 40 days after its seedlings are transplanted (actually 55 days from sowing to harvest). This is a heat resistant variety. For late summer into late autumn, *De Cicco*, which bears many side shoots, and *Green Valiant*, which is frost tolerant.

SOIL AND SITE
See Soil preparation for brassicas, *page 191.*

SOWING AND PLANTING
For summer harvest sow seeds indoors about a month and a half before setting outdoors. Grow under fluorescent lights. Harden off in a cold frame and set out in mid spring 50-75cm (20-30in) apart. Sow seeds for late crops from late summer to early summer.

MAINTENANCE
Water regularly and keep the soil weed free by mulching with

Sowing calabrese and broccoli *Always sow in a seed bed so that they can be transplanted easily. Sow in short rows with 15cm (6in) between plants.*

organic matter or, failing this black plastic (*see pages 58-9*).

HARVESTING

Cut the central shoot first, while it is still green, to encourage the production of side-shoots. If you can, try to prevent flowering, which will reduce yields. Broccoli will continue to produce side-shoots over a considerable period provided they are removed at regular intervals.

Harvesting broccoli *To maximize yields, cut the central stem first. Smaller side-shoots will then be encouraged.*

PESTS AND DISEASES

These plants can be affected by many of the general garden pests and diseases, as well as cabbage butterflies, cabbage moth, cabbage root maggot and club root (*see pages 46-53 and 201*).

PLANTING AND HARVESTING TIMES

	Sow inside	Plant out	Sow outside	Harvest
Early spring	●			
Mid spring		●		
Late spring			●	
Early summer			●	●
Mid summer				●
Late summer				
Early autumn				●
Mid autumn				●
Late autumn				●
Early winter				
Mid winter				
Late winter	●			

Cauliflowers

Although cauliflowers are the most difficult of the brassicas to cultivate, they are well worth growing if your land is free of club root disease (*see page 201*). If you follow closely the cultivation methods outlined here, the plants will be kept growing steadily and you should also avoid the problem of premature curding, where the plant flowers before it is big enough to support a decent-sized curd, resulting in a small "button" which is useless. Cauliflower varieties are divided into three types but most gardeners concentrate on autumn kinds.

VARIETIES

Summer cauliflowers *Snow King* is fast-growing and well flavored and *Snow Crown* is also recommended.
Autumn cauliflowers *All the Year Round* lives up to its name but is best from late summer to early autumn. *Earli-Light* is a superb variety which matures 58 days after planting and will go on to late autumn. *Self Blanch* matures in late autumn and is frost resistant. It has firm white heads, well protected by leaves. Alternatively, the Australian varieties *Barrier Reef*, *Canberra* and *Snowcap* are now available in many countries and they all provide a good succession of harvesting.
Winter/spring cauliflowers *Snow Pak* produces large, white heads and withstands very low temperatures. It does well in the south in winter. *Purple Cape* produces purple curds which turn green on cooking. It crops in early spring and is reliably hardy in mild winter regions. *White Countess* is a vigorous variety recommended as an autumn crop in the North and for spring in mild climates.

SOIL AND SITE

See Soil preparation for brassicas, *page 191*. Few plants in the garden will show such a marked reaction to nutrient deficiencies (*see opposite and pages 38-9*). In the well-managed organic garden, none should occur but, if you are in the process of changing to organic techniques, be on the look-out and take immediate steps to correct any deficiency. If the lime levels are correct and

the symptoms still occur, hoe in about two handfuls of seaweed meal per square meter/yard. This will ensure the necessary trace elements are replaced.

SOWING AND PLANTING

Summer cauliflowers Make your earliest sowing in a heated greenhouse or on a windowsill in mid winter. Transfer the seedlings to wider spacings in a larger seed tray when plants are large enough to handle. Plant out under cloches 50cm (20in) square in late winter (*see page 140*). Before transplanting, check each plant to make sure it has a growing point. Cauliflowers sometimes go "blind" and these plants are useless. Make sure too that the plants never stay too long in the trays. This will starve them and cause excessive root damage on planting out and may result in premature curding. Plant out when the seedlings are no more than 5cm (2in) high.

Sow the second crop in the same way in late winter and plant out in the open in early spring. Continue sowing outside

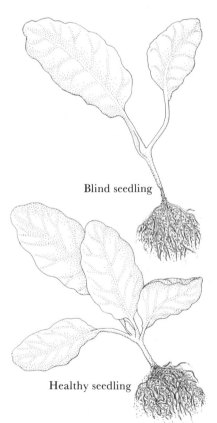

Blind seedling

Healthy seedling

Examining young cauliflower plants *When you take seedlings from the seed tray to be planted out, inspect them carefully. They should have developed a tiny central bud. Any "blind" plants, without this bud, must be discarded as they will not develop curds.*

MAINTAINING CAULIFLOWERS

Cauliflowers are generally considered to be amongst the most difficult vegetables to grow. However, while they certainly demand a lot of attention, proper soil preparation and maintenance should enable you to produce perfectly acceptable crops.

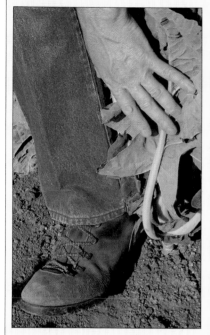

Supporting the plants *Draw a little soil around the roots of each cauliflower and press it down firmly with your heel to prevent the wind rocking the plants.*

Protecting the curds *Cauliflower curds must be kept out of direct sunlight. A simple way of doing this is to bend one of the large leaves over to cover them.*

Storing summer cauliflowers *Tie string round the stems and hang plants upside down in a cool shed. Spray regularly with water to keep them fresh.*

in a seed bed in shallow drills 15cm (6in) apart at three-week intervals from early to late spring for a succession. Transplant at the same distances before the seedlings exceed 8cm (3in) and water before lifting and after transplanting.

Autumn cauliflowers Sow in a seed bed in mid spring in shallow drills 15cm (6in) apart. Plant out in early or mid summer, setting the plants no deeper than they were in the seed bed. Space the plants 60cm (2ft) square.

Winter/spring cauliflowers Sow in a seed bed in mid or late spring. Transplant 75cm (2ft 6in) square before the seedlings reach more than 8cm (3in) high.

Deep beds Plant out summer cauliflowers in staggered rows, 45cm (18in) apart each way, and other types 60cm (2ft) apart each way, at the same time as for ordinary beds. (*See page 136.*)

MAINTENANCE

Keep all plants weed free (*see page 57*) and ensure they never go short of water. As a single day of dryness can result in the loss of an entire crop, cover the soil with a layer of organic matter or with plastic or paper to retain moisture, and water by hand if the weather is dry.

Autumn cauliflowers Provide support for the plants by firming them in the ground in late summer (*see above*).

Winter/spring cauliflowers Bend plants over to face north in late autumn, to ensure that the sun doesn't strike the curd first thing in the morning. This action prevents rapid thawing of frozen curds, which would cause discoloration and may also spoil the flavor.

HARVESTING AND STORING

Summer cauliflowers Cut curds as they develop. Remove the stumps completely and put them on the compost heap. If too many are ready at the same time, summer cauliflowers can be lifted and stored for a few weeks in a cool shed (*see right*).

Autumn and winter/spring cauliflowers Break a few leaves over the curds when they mature and cut them as required, then remove the rest of the plant. You will not need to lift and hang them, since they will have stopped growing by harvest time, and there will be no risk of them running to seed.

PESTS AND DISEASES

Cauliflowers can be affected by many of the general garden pests and diseases, as well as cabbage butterflies, cabbage moth, cabbage root maggot and club root (*see pages 46-53 and 201*).

Prompt action is especially important as an attack from any pest or disease could destroy the crop by causing premature curding (*see opposite*).

A shortage of molybdenum may result in a strange condition known as "whiptail", which makes the leaves thin and deformed. Boron deficiency causes small, bitter curds and makes the stems and leaves turn brown, while a shortage of magnesium may turn the leaves yellow, reddish or purple. Prevent these deficiencies by correct soil management.

PLANTING AND HARVESTING TIMES			
	Sow inside	Plant out	Sow outside	Harvest
Early spring	●		●	
Mid spring		●		
Late spring				
Early summer				
Mid summer				●
Late summer				
Early autumn		●	●	
Mid autumn			●	
Late autumn			●	
Early winter				
Mid winter	●			
Late winter				

Chinese cabbage

Sometimes known as "bok-choy", this vegetable is more difficult to grow than other types of cabbage. However, if you can provide favorable conditions it is well worth growing.

VARIETIES
The essence of a good variety is its resistance to bolting (*see page 143*). *Dynasty* and *Two Seasons Hybrid* are both very resistant.

SOIL AND SITE
See Soil preparation for brassicas, *page 191*. Grow in sun or light shade, alongside the other brassicas, but dig a special bed for it with plenty of well-rotted compost or manure.

SOWING
Sow in shallow drills about 30cm (12in) apart, three months before the first severe frost. Sow two seeds every 23cm (9in). Thin later to leave the strongest of each pair of seedlings.
Deep beds Sow in blocks, 23cm (9in) apart, and thin to 23cm (9in). (*See page 136.*)

MAINTENANCE
Always keep the soil moist and hoe regularly between plants (*see page 57*) to eliminate weeds.

HARVESTING
Harvest eight to twelve weeks after sowing. As they do not store, sow at two-week intervals in short rows to ensure a succession.

PESTS AND DISEASES
Flea beetles, slugs, earwigs and club root may affect these plants (*see pages 46-53 and 201*).

PLANTING AND HARVESTING TIMES	Sow inside	Plant out	Sow outside	Harvest
Early spring				
Mid spring				
Late spring			●	
Early summer			●	
Mid summer			●	
Late summer				●
Early autumn				●
Mid autumn				●
Late autumn				
Early winter				
Mid winter				
Late winter				

Cabbages

It is possible to harvest cabbages all year if you live in moist, cool yet mild winter regions, that is if you want to grow that much cabbage. Elsewhere early summer and autumn harvests are sufficient.

VARIETIES
Spring cabbages *April* is a fine, pointed cabbage with a marked resistance to running to seed. *Early Marvel* is an older variety producing good-quality, medium-sized heads.
Summer cabbages *Hispi* is probably the most popular variety in Great Britain. The pointed hearts are hard and crisp and the leaves make fine collards. *Hornspi* is much the same but even earlier. *Primax* is an improved strain of the old favorite *Golden Acre*, producing very heavy, solid heads.
Autumn/winter cabbages In order to maintain a succession you will need two varieties. For early autumn harvesting, use *Minicole* or *Custodian* – which will go on through the winter too. Other good winter varieties are the savoys like *Savoy King* or *Savoy Ace Hybrid*. Of the red cabbages, *Ruby Perfection* is outstanding for quality and flavor.

SOIL AND SITE
See Soil preparation for brassicas, *page 191*.

SOWING AND PLANTING
Spring cabbages Sow in a seed bed (*see page 269*) in mid or late summer in shallow drills 15cm (6in) apart. Bear in mind that you'll only need a very short row – no more than 45cm (18in) long – to produce between 50 and 100 plants. Plant out as described below in early or mid autumn (mild climates only).
Summer cabbages Sow the earliest crop in seed trays in late winter. Put them in the greenhouse or under lights and transplant them, when they are big enough to handle, to a wider spacing in the seed tray. Then harden them off (*see page 254*) and plant out under cloches (*see page 140*) in early spring, setting them 45cm (18in) apart each way. At the same time, plant out hardened-off plants to be harvested later. Sow seeds outside in mid spring in a seed bed and

Using brown paper *A good way of controlling weeds is to plant cabbage seedlings through slits made in bio-degradable brown paper.*

transplant 45cm (18in) apart when they are large enough, in late spring or early summer.
Autumn/winter cabbages Sow autumn/winter and red cabbages in a seed bed in mid or late spring in shallow drills about 15cm (6in) apart. Transplant the seedlings 45cm (18in) square in mid summer.
Deep beds Cabbages grown in a deep bed produce perfectly good results in the uncompacted soil. Plant out spring cabbages in blocks with the plants staggered and 15cm (6in) apart each way (*see page 136*). For summer and autumn/winter cabbages the timings are the same as for a normal bed, but they can be planted out 35cm (15in) apart. Closer planting produces smaller heads, which you may prefer if you have a small family.

MAINTENANCE
Spring cabbages Weed around the plants and provide plenty of water in the early stages. In late

Deterring birds *Cover seedlings with netting to protect against birds.*

PLANTING OUT AND HARVESTING CABBAGES

All types of cabbage are normally transplanted. It is important that the development of the seedlings is not interrupted unduly. By following a few simple rules, you can encourage the plants to become re-established as quickly as possible.

1 *The seedlings are ready to be planted out when they have grown to about 5-8cm (2-3in) high. Water the seed bed the night before you intend to dig them up. Lift clusters of seedlings with a small hand fork.*

2 *Fill a shallow trench with water and swill the roots of the young plants in it for about a minute until the roots are coated in muddy water. This ensures they do not dry out when they are planted.*

3 *Make holes with a dibber (see page 260) 15cm (6in) deep every 45cm (18in), in rows 45cm (18in) apart. Plant the seedlings and firm in with your heel before watering.*

4 *When the hearts feel firm, harvest the cabbages by cutting through the base of the stems with a sharp knife. You can store certain varieties by hanging them upside down in a cool shed.*

winter, they will benefit from a boost to get them growing again so apply one handful of dried blood per four plants.
Summer and autumn/winter cabbages Keep the beds weed free and the plants watered.

HARVESTING AND STORING
Spring cabbages Harvest the first pickings as "spring greens" or collards. Do this selectively to leave the final spacings at 30cm (12in) each way. Leave the remaining plants to heart up for later so you can harvest spring cabbages from early spring until early summer.
Summer cabbages Cut the plants when the hearts feel firm. If you cut a cross in the top of the remaining stem, a couple of new small cabbages will grow. Alternatively, dig up the root to avoid the possibility of attracting pests and diseases.
Autumn/winter cabbages Begin harvesting when the heads are firm and solid. Pull *Minicole* in late autumn and hang it upside down with stalk attached, in a cold shed, where it will keep for about two months. Savoys stand any amount of frost, so can be left in the ground until needed.

Start cutting red cabbages as soon as the heads are firm and solid. Continue until late autumn and then pull any that remain and hang them in a cool shed for use in the winter months.

PESTS AND DISEASES
Cabbages can be affected by many of the general garden pests and diseases (*see pages 46-53*), as well as cabbage butterflies, cabbage moth, cabbage root maggot and club root (*see page 201*).

PLANTING AND HARVESTING TIMES

	Sow inside	Plant out	Sow outside	Harvest
Early spring	●	●		
Mid spring	●	●		
Late spring		●		
Early summer			●	
Mid summer			●	
Late summer			●	
Early autumn			●	
Mid autumn				●
Late autumn				
Early winter				
Mid winter	●			
Late winter	●			

Vegetable pests and diseases

Most vegetables are susceptible to a range of specific pests and diseases in addition to those that may attack all garden plants (*see pages 46-53*). Correct soil management techniques and crop rotation should prevent mineral deficiencies (*see pages 38-9*), but it is important that the more serious problems are identified quickly and treated correctly.

Shoot vegetables

Mineral deficiencies can cause black heart or brown heart in celery (*see pages 38-9*).

ASPARAGUS BEETLE

Adult beetles and their grubs feed on the shoots and foliage of asparagus. A severe attack can strip the foliage completely or girdle stems, causing the death of the plant.

What to do
Dust with rotenone as soon as you see signs of an attack.

CELERY FLY

Damage is likely to be seen first in late spring, when leaves turn pale green, then brown and shrivelled.

What to do
Remove affected leaves and destroy.

ASPARAGUS RUST

Rust appears as reddish pustules on stems and foliage in summer.

What to do
As soon as the first signs are seen, remove affected shoots and spray the crop every two weeks with a copper fungicide until early autumn.

CELERY LEAF SPOT

Brown spots appear on leaves and stems, and develop into black pustules. Most celery seed is treated by the seedsmen, but the fungicide used is not organic.

What to do
Remove affected leaves and spray the rest of the crop with Bordeaux mixture every fortnight until two weeks before harvest.

Pod and seed vegetables

Birds (*see page 47*) can be a major pest with pea crops, and broad beans are sometimes attacked by black bean aphid (*see page 50*).

PEA MOTH

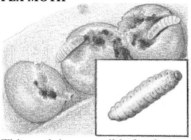

This moth is responsible for the small maggots that can make peas inedible. It lays its eggs on plants in flower throughout the summer. Pea moth is a difficult pest to control since a spray will also kill insects that are beneficial to the garden.

What to do
If attacks are severe, there is no alternative but to use rotenone (see page 53). It should only be a very short time before pheromone traps are available, since commercial growers have them in use already. These consist of a sticky pad on which is placed a capsule of pheromone – a chemical naturally secreted by the female pea moth to attract the male. The males stick to the pad, preventing them from mating with the female. The method is already available to catch codling moth adults which attack apples (see page 234) and it works very well.

PEA AND BEAN WEEVIL

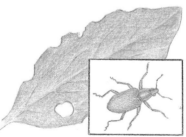

A grayish-brown beetle that attacks mainly peas and broad beans. It makes characteristic U-shaped notches in the margins of the leaves.

What to do
This is not a great problem unless young seedlings are being attacked, in which case dust them lightly with rotenone powder (see page 53).

HALO BLIGHT

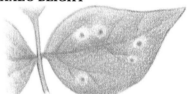

Angular spots on the leaves are surrounded by a lighter-colored halo. Later they turn reddish brown and can ooze white.

What to do
The disease is seed-borne, so buy only from a reputable seedsman and, if you have been using home-saved seed, buy in a fresh stock.

CHOCOLATE SPOT

This affects broad beans and shows as brown spots or streaks on leaves and stems. These marks may join up and stems can become completely blackened, leading to the death of the plant.

What to do
Avoid it by good cultivation methods (see page 158), especially adequate feeding and manuring, and pull up and burn affected plants. As soon as you see signs of the problem, spray the whole crop with a copper fungicide (see page 53).

FAILURE TO SET

The flowers of bush and pole beans may drop off having failed to set, usually because the roots are dry or the plants have not been pollinated by insects.

What to do
Protect the plants from cold winds to encourage pollinating insects. In very dry weather, water the plants to prevent the flowers wilting and closing, which makes it impossible for bees to reach the pollen without destroying the flower.

Fruiting vegetables

See also page 257 for greenhouse pests and diseases.

RED SPIDER MITE

This will only be a problem in very dry years. The tiny mites cannot be seen with the naked eye, but they form visible webs and the leaves take on a characteristic mottled and yellowed appearance.

What to do
The mites like dry conditions, so avoid attack by spraying with water regularly.

POTATO BLIGHT

This shows as black or brown spots or patches on the leaves.

What to do
Spray with Bordeaux mixture at two-week intervals when the symptoms appear.

LEAF MOLD

Yellow patches on the upper surface of leaves and brown patches beneath are typical symptoms.

What to do
Most modern varieties are resistant. Spray once with copper fungicide to control any outbreak that does occur.

VIRUS

This shows as a stunting of the plant, and a yellowing and mottling of the leaves.

What to do
There is no cure. The disease is carried by aphids (see page 50) so try to control them as a preventative measure.

Bulb vegetables

Although prone to a range of disorders, onions are most likely to suffer from those described here. Other bulbs are less susceptible.

ONION FLY

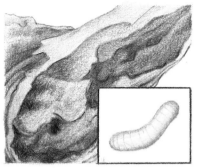

Damage is generally seen in early or mid summer, when the plants begin to yellow and die. If the soil is scraped from round the roots, white maggots can be found.

What to do
Hoe around the plants regularly to expose grubs to birds. The female fly is attracted by the scent of the onions, and this is strongest when the seedlings are thinned. Grow from sets or multi-sown blocks and you will not need to thin plants.

ONION EELWORM

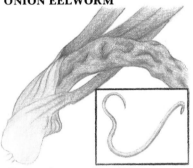

These microscopic, soil-borne creatures get inside the bulbs, causing swelling and distortion.

What to do
Dig up affected plants and use the area to grow brassicas and lettuce for two, or preferably four, years to avoid providing a host for the eelworms to feed on.

WHITE ROT

This shows as a moldy growth near the neck of stored onions which then become soft and rotten.

What to do
Remove affected bulbs as soon as you see them. Do not overfeed and only store fully ripe bulbs. Never bend the tops over to induce ripening as this may encourage the disease.

NECK ROT

This shows as a white, fluffy fungal growth on the roots. Diseased plants turn yellow and eventually die.

What to do
Treat affected plants with Bordeaux mixture immediately and do not resow onions in the same area for at least two years, to deter the build up of the disease.

STORAGE ROT

There are several different fungi that can attack bulbs in storage, causing them to go soft and slimy.

What to do
Try to ensure that the bulbs are completely ripe and that stored bulbs have plenty of air circulating around them. Inspect stored bulbs regularly and remove any that are affected straightaway.

Squash vegetables

Only one major disease affects crops grown outdoors. Greenhouse plants can also suffer from the diseases described on page 257.

CUCUMBER MOSAIC VIRUS

This disease attacks all the squash vegetables, not just cucumbers. Affected plants develop puckered leaves which turn mottled and yellow, and growth is stunted.

What to do
Guard against aphids which carry the disease (see page 50). Affected plants must be destroyed as there is no cure.

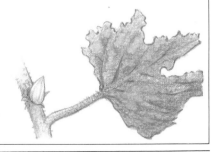

Root vegetables

The root crops include several members of the cabbage family, which are prone to the same disorders as cabbages (*see opposite*). Boron deficiency may cause corkiness in some roots (*see pages 38-9*).

CARROT FLY

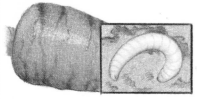

The female fly lays her eggs at the base of carrots, parsnips, parsley and celery. The grubs burrow into the root, causing characteristic brown marks and tunnels.
What to do

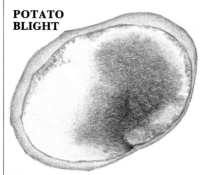

There is a very simple solution to this problem; surround the row of plants with a plastic barrier supported by short posts. The pests fly a few inches above the ground and, when they meet the barrier, they will fly upwards and miss the crop. Erect the barrier as soon as the carrots are planted out.

POTATO CYST EELWORM

A microscopic pest that causes premature death of the plants and results in undersized tubers.
What to do
Grow resistant varieties only and rotate crops annually (see page 134).

POTATO BLIGHT

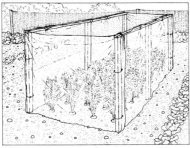

This fungus causes brown patches on leaves, especially in warm, wet weather. The patches spread and become black and the foliage dies. If left untreated, the spores can affect the tubers too, causing them to turn black inside and rot.
What to do
Spray with Bordeaux mixture in mid summer and at fortnightly intervals thereafter until harvesting.

SCAB

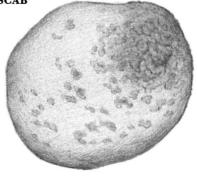

A disease which causes ugly corky marks on the outside of tubers.
What to do
Avoid trouble by incorporating plenty of organic matter into the soil and watering during dry spells. Use resistant varieties.

GANGRENE

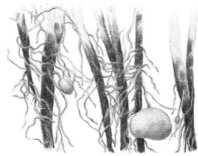

A fungus disease attacking potatoes in storage, gangrene causes the inside of the tuber to rot. Only damaged or wet potatoes are likely to be affected.
What to do
Lift and store as described on page 186. Burn infected tubers.

POTATO BLACKLEG

A bacterial disease that causes the base of the stems to blacken and die. If tubers have formed, they too can be affected. It is transmitted through diseased seed tubers, so only buy seed which has been certified disease free, from a reputable seedsman.
What to do
Remove and burn affected plants as soon as the symptoms are seen.

SPRAING

The symptoms of spraing are red-brown lesions on the tubers. If you cut one in half you'll find wavy, semi-circular marks.
What to do
There is no cure, so grow resistant varieties only.

SOFT ROT

This is a bacterial disease affecting swedes and turnips. It shows as a white or gray mushy rot and is worse on badly drained soil that is not rotated.
What to do
Avoid the disease by growing swedes and turnips on raised deep beds if your soil is heavy (see page 135).

PARSNIP CANKER

This disease causes reddish brown marks on the shoulder of the root and these often spread further into the root, causing it to rot.
What to do
Concentrate on good cultivation methods (see page 187) to produce healthy, fast growth, and use resistant varieties.

Leaf vegetables

The brassicas are especially prone to problems, but correct soil management and cultivation can avoid a lot of trouble. Boron deficiency causes brown heart in leaf crops (*see pages 38-9*).

CATERPILLARS

Several butterflies lay their eggs on leaf crops and the caterpillars make characteristic round holes in the leaves. The attacks start in mid summer and continue through until autumn. The worst offender is the cabbage-white butterfly.

What to do

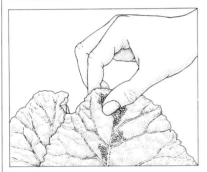

Simply pick off the caterpillars regularly and drop them into a jar of kerosene. The eggs can often be rubbed off by hand too. As a last resort, spray with the bacterium Bacillus thuringiensis (see page 52) or with rotenone (see page 53).

MEALY CABBAGE APHID

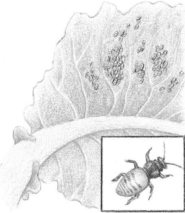

Dense colonies of this aphid sometimes gather on the undersides of leaves, where they suck sap. It is rare in organic gardens.

What to do

Hover-flies and ladybirds generally set the balance straight. See page 51 for ways of encouraging these natural predators into your garden. If the pests do build up, a spray with insecticidal soap will control them (see page 53).

CABBAGE ROOT MAGGOT

Perhaps the worst of all cabbage pests, causing complete collapse of young plants. The adult fly lays her eggs in the soil right next to the stem. When the larvae hatch out, they immediately burrow into the root and begin to feed. Symptoms are wilting and collapse of the plant, by which time it is too late to save it, so precautions must be taken at planting time.

What to do

The organic answer – and the only one, incidentally, that is completely successful – is to surround the stem at soil level with foam-rubber carpet underlay.

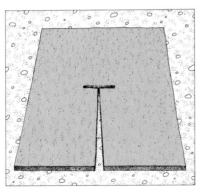

1 *Cut a piece of the underlay into 15cm (6in) squares, make a slit into the center and a small cross-slit at the end.*

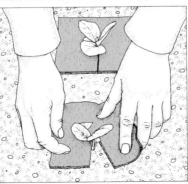

2 *Slip the piece of carpet underlay around the base of the plant, ensuring that it fits tightly.*

CLUB ROOT

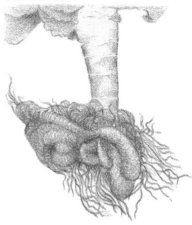

Undoubtedly the most debilitating disease of the cabbage family, club root is caused by a soil-borne fungus which distorts and thickens the root and causes stunting. Affected plants fail to develop at all. It is worse on badly drained soil and especially where acid conditions prevail, so attend to drainage and add plenty of lime whenever you grow brassicas (*see page 36*). Swedes can also be affected by club root.

What to do

There is no cure for club root and it will live in the soil indefinitely – certainly longer than the seven years often quoted. A method of overcoming it is to give plants a healthy start by raising them in pots in the greenhouse before planting them outside (see page 45). Although the seedlings will still be partially affected by the disease, you will be able to produce satisfactory crops – except for cauliflowers which must, alas, be abandoned. Rotate crops regularly.

MOSAIC VIRUS

Sometimes known as "spinach blight", this shows as a yellowing of the younger leaves and later of the older ones too.

What to do

There is no cure, but you can prevent the disease by controlling the aphids that spread it and by using resistant varieties like Melody. (See page 193.)

THE FRUIT GARDEN

AS WITH VEGETABLES, the advantages of growing fruit organically are mainly obvious. As you crunch that juicy apple, you will know that it hasn't been drenched with insecticide or coated with arsenic to improve shelf-life; your strawberry jam will taste like real strawberries, without a hint of monosodium glutamate. You may have to put up with the odd blemish from the birds which were ridding your garden of aphids, but the organically grown crop is usually large enough to withstand a few bird attacks.

The plants in the fruit garden will be productive over a longer period than those in the vegetable garden. Most vegetables are annuals, bearing fruit the same year they are planted, the plant then being discarded. Many fruit plants, however, take a few years to come into production, but will then continue to produce fruit for several seasons. The olive tree is an extreme example of longevity – it can bear fruit for 1,500 years!

Growing your own fruit frees you from having to rely on the small variety of relatively inferior fruit available in the shops. Commercial growers put flavor fairly low on their list of priorities, preferring to choose varieties that produce fruit which looks good, travels well and has a long shelf-life. Gardeners have a much wider choice and the fruits you grow in your own garden will often be far superior to any of the commercial ones.

GROWING FRUIT IN A SMALL GARDEN

Few people have room to set aside for a large fruit plot but, even if your garden is small, there is no reason why fruit should not be grown in the ornamental part. Most fruit trees are very decorative, giving a show of blossoms in the spring, followed by attractive fruit in summer and autumn. Walls or fences can be utilized for growing fan-trained fruit (*see page 206*). In some temperate regions you can grow peaches, nectarines and figs on warm, south-facing walls. Pears and apples can be grown on east- and west-facing walls and morello cherries and quinces on walls facing north. Vines also look good scrambling up walls and will give a good crop of wine berries (*see page 231*). Redcurrants and gooseberries can be grown as decorative double or triple cordons (*see page 208*) against walls or fences.

Grow strawberries, gooseberries, redcurrants and blackcurrants in the ornamental borders and you should consider using a cherry, mulberry, orange, lemon, peach, plum, apple or pear tree as a lawn specimen. If you need a hedge to divide one part of the garden from another, think about using cordon apples and pears (*see page 206*). You could even use single-tier espaliers, or stepovers (*see page 206*), only 30cm (12in) high as a decorative and productive edging to the fruit plot.

THE EFFECT OF SITE

Many local features, such as slopes, which may cause frost pockets, altitude and wind protection, will affect the fruit in your garden. There are, however, several simple measures you can take to prevent any adverse effects.

Frost is one of the main problems. If your garden is in a frost pocket (*see page 65*) you may be limited to growing only varieties that flower late and so escape spring frosts. Recommendations are given in the appropriate cultivation sections (*see pages 215-31*).

Strong winds can also be a problem, since they desiccate foliage, damage flowers and discourage the vital pollinating insects (*see opposite*). If your site is exposed, it is worth protecting fruit; initially by erecting a temporary plastic windbreak and planting a hedge nearby to take over from the plastic windbreak when it has grown high enough. To avoid creating an artificial frost pocket in your garden by cutting off the escape route of cold air (*see page 65*), raise the foot of the windbreak 30cm (12in) off the ground and keep the bottom of the hedge free of vegetation and rubbish (*see page 78*). The best site for each type of fruit is given in the cultivation details (*see pages 215-31*).

Soil preferences and optimum pH are also given for each plant in the cultivation details (*see also pages 215 and 225*). Before planting fruit, it is essential to prepare the soil well. There are some plants that have specific requirements and these are dealt with in the relevant sections but, for most, the normal organic methods of soil care will ensure healthy trees and bushes and so produce bigger yields. Details of preparing and improving the soil are given in *The Soil* (*see pages 12-17*) and *Basic Techniques* (*see pages 258-67*).

Selecting plants

Firstly, always buy your plants from a specialist grower to ensure a wider choice and better quality. If you can visit the nursery, you will have the opportunity of choosing the best-shaped trees and bushes – look for a uniform shape and a good root system.

Secondly, buy young plants; the old wives' tale that trees take seven years to come into bearing, so the older the tree you buy the better, is untrue. In fact, the reverse is the case. Young trees establish very quickly and will crop earlier than those that have been languishing in a pot or a field for four or five years.

Thirdly, I recommend buying fruit trees and bushes as bare-rooted plants and planting in the months when they are dormant. Bare-rooted plants tend to be better quality and cheaper than container-grown plants too.

There are several important points to bear in mind when choosing varieties. Pollination is the first essential. Some varieties are self-fertile, while others need to be fertilized with pollen from a plant of a different variety – if this is so you will need to grow at least two varieties in your garden (see below for details).

The ultimate size of the tree is an important consideration too. If you have a large garden, a standard or bush tree can be very attractive. However, if your garden is small, many of the larger trees can be grown on "dwarfing root-stocks" (see below for details) to keep them small.

Take into account the keeping qualities of the fruit too. Early apples, for example, though wonderful picked and eaten straight from the tree, will not keep as well as late-maturing varieties, so aim for a succession of harvesting.

Finally, bear in mind that, in most countries, fruit is covered by a Government health scheme. If the nursery can't guarantee that their stock has been certified free from disease, go elsewhere.

POLLINATION

Many fruit trees will not produce a full crop unless they are pollinated by a different variety of the same species. If you choose to grow varieties that are not self-fertile, you will have to grow at least two different ones, but do make sure you choose two that will pollinate one another. These are generally varieties that flower at the same time.

Some varieties, known as "triploids", are incapable of pollinating others, but need pollinating by another variety so, if you want to grow a triploid variety, you will have to have at least three different varieties. If you only have the space for one tree, you could grow a "family tree", which has three to five compatible varieties budded on to the same tree. Apples and pears can both be grown in this way.

Pollen is usually transferred from flower to flower, and from tree to tree by insects, who visit the flowers in search of nectar. The pollen sticks to the visiting insects and some of it is rubbed off in the next flower the insect goes to. Plants that flower very early in the year, before the pollinating insects are around, will have to be pollinated by hand. Pollen is transferred from flower to flower using a soft camel-hair brush – simply dab the centre of each flower. Plants in the greenhouse need hand-pollinating.

ROOTSTOCKS

Research into new "rootstocks", dwarf varieties of trees and pruning methods, means that fruit trees no longer have to be large, so you can grow trees in the smallest of spaces, even pots on a terrace.

A rootstock is a specially selected root system on to which is grafted the particular variety you wish to grow. The rootstock will control the growth rate and eventual size of the tree, while the grafted variety will decide the type of fruit produced. Rootstocks are generally labelled with 'M' numbers named for the East Malling station that developed them.

When planting, make sure the grafting point is at least 10cm (4in) above the soil to prevent the variety rooting into the soil – if this happens the vigor of the rootstock will be lost. Rootstocks can also confer resistance to certain diseases on the variety.

There are many rootstocks available and recommended types are listed in the appropriate cultivation details (see pages 215-31). You can buy trees ready grafted or you can prepare your own (see page 276).

The rootstock grafting point
The bump near the base of the stem is the graft between rootstock and variety.

Planting and training fruit trees and bushes

Fruit trees and bushes are generally planted in the same way as the ornamentals (*see pages 82-3 and page 112*). Bare-root trees and shrubs are planted when dormant in late autumn or early spring in northern regions or during the winter in mild climates. However, container-grown plants can be planted throughout the growing season. If bare-root fruit plants arrive too early and the ground is still frozen or too wet, heel them in temporary trenches until the ground is ready (*see page 113*).

If you are growing fruit against a wall, plant so that the base of the plant is at least 30cm (12in) away from the wall. This is likely to be the driest spot in the garden and may even be protected by overhanging eaves, so ensure the plant has plenty of water immediately after planting. Later, the roots will spread away from the wall and find their own water.

If you buy one-year-old trees, it is often not necessary to stake them unless they are container-grown, or on a very dwarfing rootstock, when they should be staked with a short stake as recommended for ornamental trees (*see page 82*). If you decide to grow trained fruit that requires a post-and-wire support, make sure you erect it first to avoid root disturbance later. (See page 266 for the different types of support.)

PLANTING A CORDON APPLE TREE

All fruit trees should be planted in well-prepared soil. When planting a cordon, erect the post-and-wire support first. This can be free-standing as shown opposite or the wires can be put up against an existing fence, as shown below. (*For pruning details see page 209.*)

1 *Fix three wires to the fence, one 60cm (2ft) from the bottom, one at the top and one in the middle and tie canes to them at an angle of 45°. The canes should be 75cm (2ft 6in) apart.*

2 *Prepare a strip of land along the fence. It should be at least 1.2m (4ft) wide. Dig deeply, breaking up the subsoil to the depth of the fork.*

3 *Incorporate plenty of well-rotted manure or compost throughout all levels of the trench.*

4 *Dig a hole at the base of each cane. Put the tree in the hole, planting it at the same angle as the cane. Cover the roots with soil.*

5 *Tie the stem of the tree to the cane at intervals, using soft string. The cane prevents the stem chafing against the wires.*

6 *Mulch around the stem of each tree with well-rotted manure or compost to conserve moisture and suppress weed growth.*

The effect of growing on a rootstock above
If a very dwarfing rootstock is used, a good crop can be produced from tiny trees grown in pots. The tree in the fore-ground shows clearly the grafting point between the rootstock and the variety.

A screen of apple blossom right
This row of cordon-grown apple trees will produce an attractive display of blossoms in spring. As the trees mature they will form a dense, productive screen along the path.

TREE SHAPES

If you have a very large garden, you can grow tall, spreading fruit trees. These standard trees, and the slightly shorter bush trees, make attractive features. But if you have a small garden, your fruit trees are better trained to one of the space-saving shapes shown below. Training details are given on the following three pages. Fan-training involves complex pruning and is recommended mainly for cherries, plums, peaches and nectarines (*see pages 217-8*).

STANDARD TREE

This type of tree is grown on a tall stem. It makes a fine specimen tree but is difficult to pick and prune without working from a ladder. It needs no special pruning other than the removal of dead, diseased or crossing branches. Height varies but ranges from 6-9m (20-30ft).

BUSH TREE

This is exactly the same as a standard tree, except that it is grown on a stem which is about 1.2m (4ft) shorter. However, it can still grow too large to pick and prune from the ground. Height varies according to variety and rootstock but can be anything from 5-8m (15-25ft).

DWARF PYRAMID

This makes an attractive free-standing tree which is grown to a pyramidal shape, with the lower branches being longer than the upper ones. It is very easy to prune and pick. Apples, pears and plums are suitable. Grow to a height of 2.5m (8ft) and a spread of 1.5m (5ft).

FAN

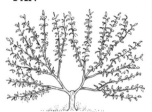

A fan is normally pruned so that two opposite shoots grow from the main stem. Shoots from these form the fan shape. Peaches, nectarines, plums and cherries can be grown as fans. Grow them to a maximum height of 2.5m (8ft) and spread of 3.5m (12ft).

CORDON

Usually a single stem, grown at an angle of about 45° to the ground and supported on a post-and-wire support to make a hedge. Soft fruits such as gooseberries and red-currants can be grown as single, double or triple cordons. Grow cordons to a maximum height of 1.8m (6ft) and a spread of 75cm (2ft 6in).

FESTOONED TREE

A relatively new idea, whereby branches are bent down and tied either to the main stem or the branch below in a series of hoops, making an attractive small tree which can carry heavy crops. Apples and pears, and plums on *Pixy* rootstocks, can be grown as festooned trees. Grow them to about 1.8m (6ft) high with a spread of 90cm (3ft).

ESPALIER

This is trained so that its branches come horizontally from the stem at 30cm (12in) intervals. It is normally trained against a wall or fence. Suitable fruits include apples and pears. Grow espaliers to a maximum height of 2.5m (8ft) and a spread of 4.5m (15ft).

STEPOVER

A foreshortened version of an espalier with only one branch on either side, so consisting of only one tier. Stepovers can be used as a productive edging round the vegetable garden or along paths. Apples and pears can be grown as step-overs and plums are possible on a *Pixy* rootstock. Grow to a maximum height of 30cm (12in).

TIPS FOR PLANTING AND TRAINING

There are several general guidelines that should be followed if you are buying and planting trees or bushes for training.
● Use one- or two-year-old trees or bushes.
● Buy and plant in early spring in the North.
● Prepare as large an area as possible. Dig deeply and incorporate plenty of well-rotted manure or compost throughout all levels.
● Once the tree is planted, mulch around the stem with well-rotted manure or compost.
By judicious pruning and thinning at the start of growth, and throughout their life, you can train trees and bushes into a variety of shapes.

Each shape has its specific methods, but there are some general pruning points to bear in mind.
● Always use a sharp pair of pruners.
● Always prune to a point just above a bud – if a stub of shoot is left it will die back and may introduce disease.
● If you cut out a branch altogether, cut back to the branch "collar", the slight bulge from the main stem.
● A bud will grow out in the direction it is facing so always cut back to an outward-facing bud to prevent branches growing into the middle of the tree or bush where they will cause congestion.

PRUNING TERMS AND TECHNIQUES

Pruning is the deliberate cutting back of plants, usually applied to trees and shrubs. It is a method of controlling size, training to shape and encouraging flower or fruit buds to form. Commonly used pruning terms are listed below.

Side-shoot A shoot arising from the main stem of the plant.

Secondary shoot A shoot arising from a side-shoot.

Fruiting spur A collection of shoots on which the fruit is produced. Made by cutting side-shoots and secondary shoots back hard.

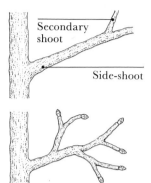

Secondary shoot

Side-shoot

Leading shoot The main stem (or stems) which extends the branch system.

Downward-facing bud Refers to the angle of the bud on the shoot. Buds can also be outward-, inward- and upward-facing. They are used to advantage when training to shape. Bear in mind that a bud grows in the direction it faces.

Making a cut A pruning cut should be angled away from the bud, and be made slightly above it. Do not leave too much stem above the bud as this "snag" will rot. Do not cut too close to the bud.

Too close   Too far away Wrong angle   Correct

TRAINING A DWARF PYRAMID

If you want to grow a free-standing tree but don't have the room for a standard or bush tree, a dwarf pyramid is an ideal alternative. Its final shape resembles that of a Christmas tree and the initial pruning establishes the conical shape. After that, all pruning is done in summer to restrict growth. If you are growing more than one, they should be planted 1.5m (5ft) apart.

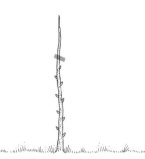

1 Immediately after planting, *cut the stem back to a bud within 60cm (2ft) of ground level.*

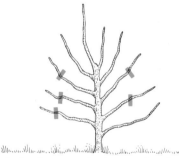

2 In the second winter, *select five or six evenly spaced lower branches that have a wide angle to the stem. Cut them back to a downward- or outward-facing bud to leave them 25cm (10in) long; if they are less than 25cm (10in) long, simply remove 2.5cm (1in) from the tip.*

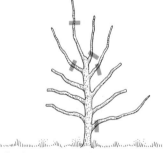

3 At the same time, *any other branches at this level should be removed completely. Any branches above this level should be cut back to 15cm (6in) to form a second tier. The tip of the main stem is cut back to leave it 30cm (12in) above the top branch.*

4 Every summer, *cut back the tip of each branch to leave 15cm (6in) of the current year's growth. Prune side-shoots to 10cm (4in) long and any secondary shoots to 5cm (2in).*

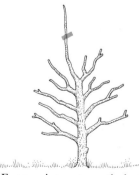

5 Every winter, *prune the leading shoot to leave 20cm (8in) of the last season's growth.*

6 Once the tree has reached the required height and width, *prune back twice as hard, so that new growth is cut back to 7cm (3in) long, side-shoots 5cm (2in) long and secondary shoots 2.5cm (1in) long.*

TRAINING A CORDON

Cordon-grown fruit takes up very little room and forms a decorative feature. The cordons should be grown against a post-and-wire support or wires strung at 60cm (2ft) intervals on an existing fence. Before planting, tie canes on to the wires to prevent the stems chafing against them. Plant the trees 75cm (2ft 6in) apart. Plant bushes so that each arm will be 30cm (12in) from the next.

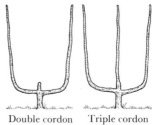

Double cordon   Triple cordon

Multiple bush cordons
Grow fruit bushes as cordons with one, two or three arms. As they grow less vigorously than tree fruit, there is no need to restrict growth by training plants at an angle.

1 Immediately after planting, *cut the leading shoot back to remove a third of the growth it made that year. Cut back any side-shoots to a downward-facing bud, leaving each shoot 7cm (3in) long.*

2 In the first summer, *prune back side-shoots coming directly from the main stem to 7cm (3in). Prune any secondary shoots to 2.5cm (1in).*

3 In the second winter, *prune the leading shoot, cutting off one-third of that year's growth.*

4 Every summer, *prune in this way until the end of the cane is reached. Make more room by lowering the cane. When the tree is as long as you want it, prune the main shoot in summer, to 7cm (3in) and side-shoots to 2.5cm (1in).*

TRAINING A FESTOONED TREE

The aim of summer pruning fruit trees is to restrict growth and encourage the trees to produce fruiting buds instead. This can also be done by restricting the flow of sap by bending the branches into severe curves; this is known as festooning. Great care is needed in bending the branches and it must be done in summer when they are young and supple. Plant trees 1.5m (5ft) apart.

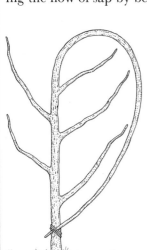

1 At the end of the first summer, *pull the main shoot downwards, bending it into a hoop. Secure it by tying the end to the base of the tree with soft string.*

2 In the second summer, *plenty of shoots will grow on top of the curve. Prune these back in summer like cordons (see above).*

3 Also in the second summer, *select more shoots and bend them down into hoops. Secure to the main stem with soft string. Prune any unwanted branches.*

4 In subsequent summers, *prune all the fruiting spurs like cordons. The tree will be permanently bent in a festooned form.*

TRAINING AN ESPALIER

As they take up very little room, espaliers are suitable for small gardens and make a decorative feature of a bare wall. Plant the trees at least 3.6m (12ft), and preferably 4.5m (15ft), apart, against a wall or fence strung with wires at 60cm (2ft) intervals. Fix wires to a wall with vine eyes.

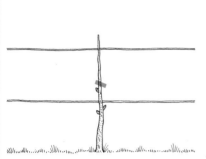

1 Immediately after planting, *prune to 5cm (2in) above the first wire. (This is 60cm (2ft) above the ground.) Make sure there are three good buds below the pruning position.*

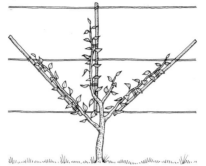

2 In spring, *train the resulting shoots on to canes fixed to the wires. Train the side-shoots at an angle of 45° from the main stem.*

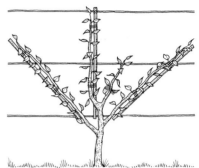

3 In the first summer, *cut back any side branches that may have formed on the main stem to 7cm (3in).*

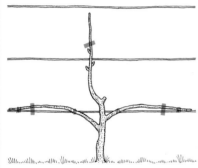

4 In the second winter, *tie the two branches that will form the first tier to the lower wire. Prune them back to remove a third of the previous season's growth. Prune the main stem to 5cm (2in) above the second wire to encourage three new buds to form the second tier.*

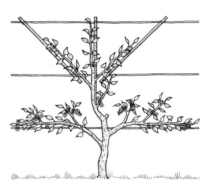

5 In the following summer, *prune the side-shoots on the lower two branches to 7cm (3in) and secondary shoots to 2.5cm (1in). Treat the second tier as you did the first, in the previous summer.*

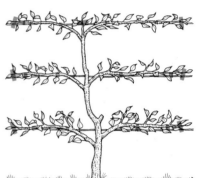

6 Every summer, *repeat the process for as many tiers as you wish. At the required height, select only two buds and train these horizontally as the final tier. Thereafter, prune each arm as for cordon training, pruning in the summer (see step 4 opposite).*

TRAINING A STEPOVER

A modern variation of the espalier, stepovers are simply single-tier espaliers, developed to take advantage of every inch of space in a small garden. They should be grown on wires strung on short posts 30cm (12in) above the ground. Plant trees between 3.5-4.5m (12-15ft) apart.

1 Immediately after planting, *prune the main stem to 5cm (2in) above the wire. Ensure that there are two buds below the cut.*

2 In the spring, *when the buds grow, train the shoots out along the wires, either side of the main stem.*

3 Thereafter, *each arm is pruned like a cordon (see cordon training, step 4). Stop growth when the arms meet those of the next plant.*

Cultivation of fruit

The detailed cultivation techniques vary somewhat and are given for each fruit (*see pages 215-31*). There are, however, some cultivation points common to all fruit.

FEEDING

The organic method of feeding is very simple. In early spring apply two handfuls of blood, fish and bone meal per square meter/yard around the plants. The feeding roots are at the tips of the plant's main root system rather than near the stem, so apply fertilizer in a wide band round it. In addition to this, mulch around the stem with well-rotted manure or compost, which, apart from inhibiting weed growth and conserving water, will supply all the necessary trace elements. In the unlikely event of trace element deficiency symptoms becoming apparent (*see page 39*), spray immediately with liquid seaweed fertilizer and apply seaweed meal to the soil. Any special feeding requirements are given in the cultivation details (*see pages 215-31*).

WATERING

Applying water at the right time can greatly increase the weight of a fruit crop. Water when the fruit is swelling for best results. Stop watering when the fruits color up or you could encourage fungus disease.

However, it is a mistake to put just a little water on the soil since this brings the roots nearer the surface where they are in more danger of drying out. It is essential to apply water through a hose and sprinkler, which must be left on for at least an hour at a time in dry weather.

Any special watering requirements are given in the cultivation details (*see pages 215-31*).

THINNING

Most people are quite happy to grow fruit that is smaller than that on sale in the shops, especially if there are children in the family. But, if you want bigger fruit, you will have to thin clusters as they develop. Trees and bushes will drop fruits naturally if they are carrying more than they can support. This normally happens in mid summer so delay thinning until then. To thin, remove the central fruit from each cluster, it will probably be badly shaped anyway. How much you want to thin depends on the variety, but bear in mind that thinning will not reduce the weight of fruit harvested – there will be fewer fruits but each one will be bigger.

ENCOURAGING GROWTH

Sometimes fruit trees of all types will fail to produce shoots along one part of the stem. For

Applying fertilizer *Feeding roots are towards the outer limits of a tree, so apply fertilizer around the tree, roughly from the furthest extent of the branches to half-way back to the trunk. Mulching with manure or compost will also supply nutrients.*

Thinning fruit *If the developing fruits are growing in a crowded cluster, thin by removing the central fruit known as the "crown" fruit. This allows the others to swell. Always thin after the tree has dropped its fruit naturally.*

Encouraging bud growth *To encourage growth of a particular bud on a barren length of shoot, divert the flow of growth-retarding hormone by taking a notch out of the bark above the bud you want to encourage.*

some reason the buds simply don't grow out. This can be corrected by manipulating nature. In order that the top of the tree grows more strongly than the rest, nature has provided a growth-retarding hormone, which is sent down the tree from the top bud to retard all the others. The transport channels are just below the bark so, to prevent the retarding hormone reaching the bud you wish to encourage into growth, simply take out a tiny notch in the bark above it. The hormone then flows round the bud without affecting it. Conversely, if you want to ensure that a bud does not grow, nick underneath it to concentrate the hormone.

WEED CONTROL

With all garden fruit, it is essential to reduce the competition from weeds. Many fruit plants are shallow-rooted so hoeing should be light. The best method of weed control is mulching with manure, compost or black plastic (see pages 58-9).

PESTS AND DISEASES

There is no doubt that the most persistent and troublesome pest of fruit of all sorts are our allies, the birds. We don't want to frighten them away because of the good work they do, but they can't be ignored. To deter mice, wrap tree trunks with special plastic protectors.

Specific pests and diseases are given for each type of fruit at the end of the chapter (see pages 232-35). Pests and diseases such as aphids, mildew and botrytis are common to all garden plants, not only fruit, and are dealt with in detail in Organic Pest and Disease Control (see pages 43-53); treatment of common fruit pests such as wasps and red spider mite are given at the end of the chapter (see pages 232-35).

PROTECTING FRUIT FROM BIRDS

Always protect your fruit from birds, whatever the size of your garden. If it is large you can grow all the fruit together and put up a fruit cage.

Otherwise, small bushes and trees can be covered with netting, or individual fruits protected with transparent, perforated polythene bags.

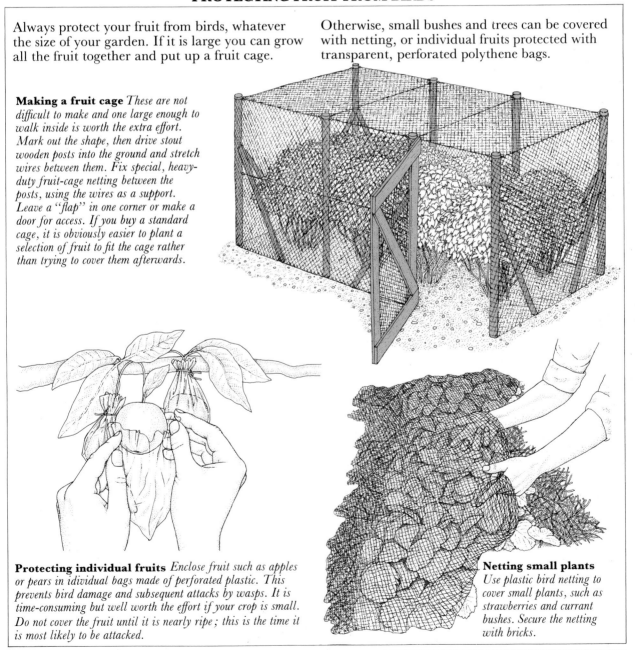

Making a fruit cage *These are not difficult to make and one large enough to walk inside is worth the extra effort. Mark out the shape, then drive stout wooden posts into the ground and stretch wires between them. Fix special, heavy-duty fruit-cage netting between the posts, using the wires as a support. Leave a "flap" in one corner or make a door for access. If you buy a standard cage, it is obviously easier to plant a selection of fruit to fit the cage rather than trying to cover them afterwards.*

Protecting individual fruits *Enclose fruit such as apples or pears in individual bags made of perforated plastic. This prevents bird damage and subsequent attacks by wasps. It is time-consuming but well worth the effort if your crop is small. Do not cover the fruit until it is nearly ripe; this is the time it is most likely to be attacked.*

Netting small plants *Use plastic bird netting to cover small plants, such as strawberries and currant bushes. Secure the netting with bricks.*

Tree fruit

No garden is too small for a fruit tree. With the increased use of special rootstocks, which limit the size of the tree, trees can be used as decorative, as well as productive, features. You can make use of walls, by training trees as fans or espaliers. If your garden is very small, fruit trees can be grown in tubs on the terrace.

CHERRIES *Prunus* sp. and cvs. above
If space is tight, grow just one 3-on-1 sweet cherry as the 3 varieties pollinate each other.
For cultivation details, see page 216.

NECTARINES *Prunus* sp. above
These are smooth-skinned peaches.
For cultivation details, see page 216.

APRICOTS *Prunus armeniaca* above
Plenty of sun is required if a crop is to be guaranteed. In temperate areas they are best grown in a protected area but hardy varieties are available.
For cultivation details, see page 218.

PEACHES *Prunus persica* above
They need well-drained soil and a sunny position. Grow the trees as fans on a south-facing wall.
For cultivation details, see page 216.

PLUMS *Prunus domestica* above
Fan-trained trees are hardy enough to be grown on north-facing walls, although they will fruit later than those on south- or west-facing walls.
For cultivation details, see page 218.

FIGS *Ficus carica* above
Figs will tolerate any type of soil as long as it is well drained yet moisture retentive.
For cultivation details, see page 219.

OLIVES *Olea europaea* above
Long-lived trees that are only suitable for warmer areas. The tree eventually develops a twisted, gnarled appearance which adds greatly to its decorative value.
For cultivation details, see page 219.

MULBERRIES *Morus* sp. below
The trees are large enough and slow growing and female and male trees are necessary for fruits. *For cultivation details, see page 220.*

QUINCES *Cydonia oblonga* above
These relative of the pear need plenty of sun; grow them against a south-facing wall in a temperate climate. *For cultivation details, see page 220.*

DESSERT APPLES *Malus* sp. and cvs. below
The most popular fruit of temperate climates, apples are easy to grow in the organic garden. They can be grown in several different tree shapes to suit even the smallest of gardens. There are many different varieties available; grow one that flowers later if your garden is in a frost pocket. However, most varieties are not self-fertile. *For cultivation details, see page 220.*

Suntan   Greensleeves   Jonared

PEARS *Pyrus communis* below
As they flower fairly early in the year, pears should not be planted in a frost pocket, so try to choose a sunny, sheltered spot in the garden. *For cultivation details, see page 221.*

COOKING APPLES *Malus* sp. and cvs. below
These are usually larger and more sour tasting than dessert apples. The branches may need supporting as the crop can be heavy. *For cultivation details, see page 220.*

William

Conference

Bramley

Citrus fruit

Only for warmer areas, these sub-tropical fruits grow on evergreen trees which need plenty of warmth and shelter. In temperate climates they can only be grown successfully in the greenhouse as they cannot endure prolonged sub-freezing temperatures. But, with the right conditions they are not difficult to grow and are very rewarding. They grow best in well-drained soils: if your soil is heavy, raise the planting area above the surrounding soil.

KUMQUATS below
Fortunella japonica
These dwarf evergreen trees produce good crops of miniature oranges. They can be grown outside provided the temperature will not drop lower than −10°C (15°F).
For cultivation details, see page 222.

ORANGES below
Citrus sinensis
Like all other citrus fruits, oranges are injured by prolonged freezes. So, unless your garden is in mild climates, they must be grown in greenhouses.
For cultivation details, see page 223.

LIMES above
Citrus aurantiifolia
Limes are cultivated in exactly the same way as their close relations, the lemons. They have a slightly more acid flavors.
For cultivation details, see page 222.

LEMONS above
Citrus limon
They grow best on slightly heavy, acid soils. If grown outside on badly drained soil, the planting area should be raised by at least 45cm (18in).
For cultivation details, see page 222.

GRAPEFRUITS above and right
Citrus paradisi
Grow grapefruits in a sunny, sheltered site, on an acid soil. Ensure that the soil is well drained.
For cultivation details, see page 223.

Cultivating tree fruit

If your garden is small, a large fruit tree will cast a lot of shade, reducing the number of plants you can grow, so it makes sense to train dwarf trees as fans or espaliers and make a decorative feature of all available wall and fence space.

All fences and walls can be utilized, whichever direction they face, but a south-facing wall is particularly valuable, especially for the more tender types, such as peaches, nectarines or citrus fruits.

TREE FRUIT

Fruit	Shape and planting distance		Site	Soil preference	Bearing age	See page
Cherry	Standard	6-9m (20-30ft)	Sour: sunny	Well-drained loam	2-7 years	216
	Bush tree	3-4.5m (10-15ft)	Sweet: sunny			
	Fan	5.5m (18ft)				
Nectarine	Bush tree	4.5m (15ft)	Sunny	Well drained. Not too rich	2-3 years	216
	Fan	3.6m (12ft)				
Apricot	Fan	4.5m (15ft)	Sunny	Well drained. Not too rich	2-3 years	218
	Dwarf pyramid	1.5m (5ft)				
Peach	Bush tree	4.5m (15ft)	Sunny	Well-drained medium loam	2-3 years	216
	Fan	3.6m (12ft)				
Plum	Standard	3m (10ft)	Tolerant	Heavy loam or clay	2-3 years	218
	Dwarf pyramid	1.8m (6ft)				
	Fan	3.5m (12ft)				
	Festoon	1.8m (6ft)				
Fig	Bush tree	3m (10ft)	Sunny	Any, well drained	3-4 years	219
	Fan	4.5m (15ft)				
Olive	Standard	7.5-12m (25-36ft)	Sunny	Any, well drained	5-6 years	219
Mulberry	Standard	9m (30ft)	Sunny	Any	10 years	220
	Bush tree	9m (30ft)				
Quince	Bush tree	6m (20ft)	Sunny	All well-drained deep soils	1-2 years	220
	Fan	4.5m (15ft)				
Apple	Standard	6m (20ft)	Sunny	All well-drained deep soils	2 years	220
	Bush tree	6m (20ft)				
	Dwarf pyramid	1.5m (5ft)				
	Fan	4.5m (15ft)				
	Espalier	4.5m (15ft)				
	Cordon	75cm (2ft 6in)				
	Stepover	4.5m (15ft)				
	Festoon	1.5m (5ft)				
Pear	Standard	9m (30ft)	Sunny	All well-drained deep soils	2-4 years	221
	Bush tree	6m (20ft)				
	Dwarf pyramid	1.5m (5ft)				
	Fan	4.5m (15ft)				
	Espalier	4.5m (15ft)				
	Cordon	75cm (2ft 6in)				
	Stepover	4.5m (15ft)				
	Festoon	1.5m (5ft)				
Kumquat	Bush tree	4.5m (15ft)	Sunny	Medium heavy	7-8 years	222
Lime	Bush tree	4.5m (15ft)	Sunny	Slightly heavy	7-8 years	222
Lemon	Bush tree	4.5m (15ft)	Sunny	Slightly heavy	7-8 years	222
Orange	Bush tree	7.5m (25ft)	Sunny	Light, sandy	7-8 years	223
Grapefruit	Bush tree	9m (30ft)	Sunny	Acid, well drained	7-8 years	223

Cherries

Sweet cherries grown as standard or bush trees grow very large. In order to avoid the problems caused by excessive shade, grow them as fans against a south-facing wall. They should only be grown as bush trees on the root-stock G.M.9. Sour (cooking) cherries are not as vigorous and can be grown fan-trained against north-facing walls.

VARIETIES

Stella is the only self-fertile sweet cherry and is suitable for small gardens. All sour cherries are self-fertile, but they will not pollinate sweet cherries. Three-in-one sweet cherry trees pollinate each other. *Windsor* is a good pollinator for *Napoleon*, *Bing*, and some other sweet cherry varieties.
Rootstocks There is no satisfactory dwarfing rootstock for sour and sweet cherries, but there are some naturally semi-dwarf and bush types, such as *North Star*, *Meteor* and *Hansen's Bush*.

TREE SHAPES

Sweet and sour cherries can be grown as standard or bush trees or fan-trained against a wall (*see page 206*).

SOIL AND SITE

Sweet and sour cherries do best on deep, well-drained loams. It is essential to prepare the soil by deep digging, and add organic matter before planting. The soil pH should be 6.0-7.0.
Both cherries should be grown in the sun, although sour cherries tolerate some shade.

PLANTING

Standard and bush trees should be planted in winter as shown on pages 82-3, at least 4.5-6m (15-20ft) apart. Fan-trained trees should be planted against a wired wall, spaced 5.5m (18ft) apart.

MAINTENANCE

Feeding An annual mulch with well-rotted manure or compost is normally sufficient. Too much lime in the soil sometimes causes magnesium deficiency (*see page 39*); this can be corrected with a dressing of seaweed meal.
Pruning Standard and bush trees are pruned very little. Allow the tree to grow naturally for a few years, then, every mid summer, remove dead, diseased, crossing or overcrowded branches, taking them right back to the main stem. Fan-trained sweet cherries are pruned in the same way as plums (*see page 218*), and fan-trained sour cherries like peaches (*see opposite*).
Protection Sweet cherry trees must be netted against birds.

HARVESTING AND STORING

Leave the cherries on the tree as long as possible, but pick them before they split. Sweet cherries should be eaten straight away. Sour cherries should be cooked and eaten no more than a few days after picking, or stored bottled or made into jam.

PESTS AND DISEASES

Cherries are affected by aphids, winter moth, bacterial canker and silver-leaf (*see page 232*).

Peaches and nectarines

Peaches and nectarines are identical in all their cultivation requirements, the only difference is their skins – peaches have furry skins, while nectarines have smooth ones. They are both ideal fruits for warmer climates, but will grow in temperate regions as fan-trained trees against a south-facing wall. Peaches are slightly more hardy than nectarines so these are a better choice for temperate regions. They can also be grown in the greenhouse (*see right*). Peaches and nectarines do not fruit until their fourth year but bear fruit for about 30 years.

VARIETIES

Peaches and nectarines are self-fertile so only one tree is needed.
Peaches Choose from *Red Haven*, *Sun Haven* and *Rochester*. In colder regions grow *Golden Jubilee* or *Reliance*.
Nectarines Grow *Maricrest* or *Nectacrest*.
Rootstocks Dwarfing rootstocks for peaches and nectarines are not essential but are available from most fruit specialists. Dwarf peaches for fan training or growing in tubs include varieties such as *Garden Gold*, *Jumbo* and *Champion White*.

TREE SHAPES

Free-standing bush trees should only be grown in warm areas where the flowers will not be damaged by frosts in early spring. In colder regions, grow them against a south-facing wall (*see page 206*).

SOIL AND SITE

Good drainage is essential so prepare the soil well. If you are

---

CULTIVATING PEACHES AND NECTARINES IN THE GREENHOUSE

Peaches and nectarines in the greenhouse are grown in the same way as those grown outside, against a wall or post-and-wire support. The only difference in cultivation may arise from the better growing conditions that make it necessary to keep growth and fruiting in check. During the winter the greenhouse should be kept as cold as possible to keep the tree dormant. In early spring mulch round the tree with well-rotted manure or compost and water well. Then allow the greenhouse temperature to reach 10°C (50°F) before ventilating.
Spray daily with clear water during the spring and summer, except at flowering time.

Hand pollination *To transfer pollen from flower to flower, dab the center of each one with a soft camel-hair brush.*

When in flower, hand pollination will be necessary as there will be few insects in the greenhouse. Feed weekly during the growing season with liquid seaweed fertilizer. Don't let too many fruits develop or they will be small. Allow 15 fruits per square meter/yard.

FAN-TRAINING PEACHES AND NECTARINES

Fan-training (similar to espalier) produces trees that grow flat against the wall. The reflected and stored heat allows otherwise tender fruits to be grown successfully in temperate climates. Grow the trees against wires fixed to a wall, 23cm (9in) apart.

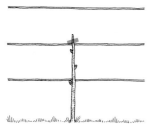

1 Immediately after planting, *cut back to a strong bud, making sure there are two buds beneath this. Leave the tree about 45cm (18in) high. The following season, three shoots will grow.*

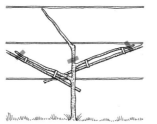

2 In the second winter, *remove the central shoot. Prune the two remaining shoots to 45cm (18in) long and tie them to canes fixed to the wires about 20° above the horizontal.*

3 In the following summer, *select four shoots from these side-branches; two from the top, one underneath and its extension. Tie them in and rub off any other buds which appear.*

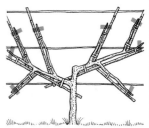

4 In the third winter, *cut back the selected shoots, leaving them 45cm (18in) long.*

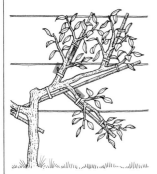

5 In the following summer, *tie in branches as they grow. Select side-shoots 10cm (4in) apart to form the fruit-bearing shoots. Rub off any unwanted buds.*

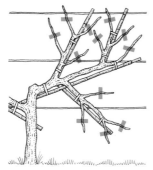

6 In the fourth winter, *reduce the growth from the main framework branches by about half. From now on, pruning is aimed at producing fruit.*

7 In the following summer, *allow the side-shoots to grow four to six leaves and form a new shoot at their base. Pinch out any other new growth.*

8 Once the fruit has been picked, *prune the fruited shoot out. Tie the replacement shoot at its base into its place. Repeat the process every year.*

growing standard or bush trees follow the general recommendations on page 210. For wall-trained plants dig out a trench 60-90cm (2-3ft) wide, 3m (10ft) long and a spade deep. Dig some old rubble or broken bricks into the bottom and cover this with a layer of well-rotted manure or compost. Refill, working more organic matter into the upper levels. Peach and nectarine trees will grow on sandy soils if plenty of organic matter is added. They prefer a soil pH of 6.5-7.0 and they need a sunny position, above all, they should not be planted in a frost pocket.

PLANTING

Plant standard or bush trees in spring as recommended on pages 82-3. For fan-training use one-year-old trees, planted in spring, against wires spaced at 23cm (9in) intervals.

MAINTENANCE

Feeding Feed as suggested on page 210 in the years before they are old enough to fruit. Once they come into bearing, an annual mulch with well-rotted manure or compost will probably be enough. If deficiency symptoms are noticed (*see pages 38-9*), reinstate the feeding program.
Pruning Prune free-standing trees in spring, removing all dead, diseased or crossing branches, and prune fan-trained trees as recommended above.
Pollination Both peaches and nectarines flower early, before the pollinating insects have appeared in some regions, so pollen may have to be transferred by hand, taking it from flower to flower with a camel-hair brush (*see left*).
Protection Protect the blossoms with woven polypropylene or fine netting (net curtains are ideal), if a late frost is forecast.

HARVESTING AND STORING

The fruit is ripe when it comes off the tree easily when gently lifted and twisted. Take great care when harvesting as it bruises very easily. Peaches and nectarines will not store for more than a few days unless refrigerated.

PESTS AND DISEASES

Aphids (*see page 50*). Peach-leaf curl and red spider mite affect fruit grown outside (*see pages 232-3*) and in the greenhouse; they are also affected by scale insects and mildew in the greenhouse (*see page 257*).

Apricots

Apricots are grown in the same way as plums, although they require plenty of sun to guarantee a crop. They can be grown in temperate climates as fans against a south-facing wall.

VARIETIES

All varieties of apricot are self-fertile so only one tree is necessary, although you may have to transfer the pollen by hand as they flower early. Choose from *Moorpark*, *Early Golden* or the super hardy *Chinese*, which requires *Moorpark* as a pollinator.

TREE SHAPES

Apricot trees can be grown as fans and as dwarf pyramids in warmer areas (*see page 206*).

SOIL AND SITE

Apricots will grow in light soils if plenty of organic matter is incorporated. The pH should be about 6.0. The site should be well drained, very sunny and sheltered from the wind.

PLANTING

Apricots need well-drained soil so, unless your soil is very light, prepare by digging an area 1m × 3m (3ft × 10ft), two spades deep, putting a layer of rubble in the bottom and refilling with soil liberally mixed with well-rotted organic matter.

MAINTENANCE

Thin the fruits if the tree becomes overburdened (*see page 210*).

HARVESTING AND STORING

Pick and eat when they are soft. To dry them, pick and split them when they are still firm.

PESTS AND DISEASES

General pests include birds and aphids (*see pages 46, 50 and 232*). Red spider mite, sawfly, rust, silver-leaf and bacterial canker (*see page 233*).

Plums

Plums are relatively easy to grow and can bear very heavy crops, although they may not be worth growing in areas which get late-spring frosts. Damsons are related to plums and are grown in exactly the same way.

VARIETIES

All the varieties given here are self-fertile. Suitable plum varieties include *Greengage, Iroquois, Yellow Egg, Stanley, Big Blue* and *Tellenberg*.

The best damson varieties are *French Damson, Shropshire* and *Blue Damson*.

Rootstocks Plum and damson trees can grow very large unless grown on one of the two dwarfing rootstocks. *St. Julien A* is a semi-dwarfing rootstock suitable for making dwarf pyramids and fans. *Pixy* is a new dwarfing rootstock, producing small trees suitable for training against a support.

FAN-TRAINING PLUMS

Fan-trained plums grow best on south- or west-facing walls. They can be grown on north-facing walls but fruit will produced later in the year.

Varieties for fan-training should be grafted on to *St. Julien A* or *Pixy* rootstocks. Sweet cherries and damsons should be fan-trained as below.

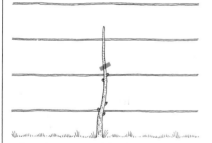

1 In winter, *attach horizontal wires to the wall at 23cm (9in) intervals and plant a one-year-old tree against the wall. In the first spring, cut it back to 45cm (18in) high.*

2 In summer, *select three strong shoots. Let these grow on, but pinch back any other shoots to two leaves.*

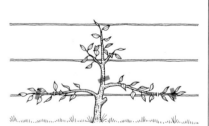

3 The following spring, *prune the two main side-branches to 45cm (18in) in length and tie them to the first horizontal wire. Remove the central stem.*

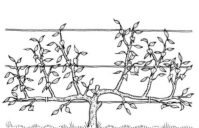

4 Every spring and summer, *tie upward-growing shoots from the side branches on to the wires, using soft string, to make a fan shape.*

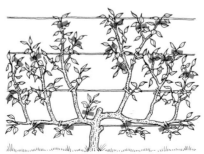

5 Later in summer, *pinch out any shoots growing into or away from the wall. Pinch out any other shoots not required to form the fan shape.*

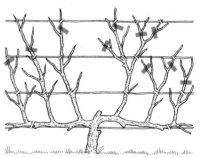

6 When the fruit has been picked, *cut out any dead wood and shorten the shoots you have pinched out by half.*

TREE SHAPES

Dwarf plums can be trained as pyramids or fan-shaped trees (*see page 206*).

SOIL AND SITE

Plum trees like deep loam or clay soils which are well-drained. Damsons are more tolerant of shallow topsoil. The soil pH should be between 6.0-6.5. Fan-trained trees should be grown on south- or west-facing walls.

PLANTING

Plant bare-rooted trees in early spring (*see page 83*). Plant standard plums about 6-7m (18-24ft) apart. Set dwarf trees about 3m (10ft) apart or follow recommendations sent by the nursery. When growing plums as fans, set them 3.5m (12ft) apart against a wall or fence.

When tying plum trees to their supports, use a proprietary tree tie with a collar to prevent chafing, as the debilitating silver-leaf disease enters through wounds.

MAINTENANCE

Feeding Feed as recommended in the general cultivation techniques (*see page 210*).
Pruning As plums and damsons are susceptible to silver-leaf disease, never prune in winter because pruning wounds will remain unhealed for a long time.
Thinning Heavy crops can lead to breakage of branches. If the crop is large, wait for the natural drop in mid summer, then thin so that the fruits are 7cm (3in) apart. Support the laden branches with a forked prop covered in burlap to prevent chafing, or tie the branch up to the main stem (*see page 221*).

HARVESTING AND STORING

The fruit is ripe when it comes off the tree easily. Pick fruit for cooking or bottling when a bloom appears on the skin. For eating fresh, fruit is best left on the tree until it is fully ripe, this is when it feels soft to the touch.

PESTS AND DISEASES

General pests that attack plums include aphids and birds (*see pages 46, 50 and 232*). Wasps can also attack the fruits (*see page 232*). Specific pests and diseases are plum sawfly, red spider mite, rust, silver-leaf and bacterial canker (*see page 233*).

Figs

The cultivation details below apply to figs grown outside and in the greenhouse.

VARIETIES

The darker-skinned *Brown Turkey* and *Brunswick* are the hardiest, *Mission*, *Celeste* and *Verdone* are recommended for warmer areas.

TREE SHAPES

Figs can be grown as bush trees or fans (*see page 206*). No pruning is needed to form the fan, simply tie the branches on to wires spaced at 23cm (9in) intervals.

SOIL AND SITE

They will grow on any soil as long as it is well drained yet moisture retentive, with a pH of 6.5-7.0. Grow against a south-facing wall as they require plenty of sun to produce fruit.

PLANTING

Plant free-standing bushes 3m (10ft) apart, and trees for fan-training 4.5m (15ft) apart. To encourage fruiting, restrict root growth by digging a hole 1m × 1.5m (3ft × 5ft) and two spades deep. Cover the base of the hole with rubble and contain the sides with corrugated iron sheets or bricks. Refill with an equal mixture of topsoil and well-rotted manure or compost. This kind of preparation may appear to be over-elaborate but, without it, trees will produce abundant growth at the expense of fruit.

MAINTENANCE

Watering Figs may need hand-watering during the first year.
Pruning Cut out old wood in winter and thin in summer to allow sunlight to ripen the fruits.
Frost protection Protect the shoots from frost by wrapping the plant in straw. Secure it in place with burlap.

HARVESTING AND STORING

Figs should be eaten straight from the tree when they change color – the dark-skinned varieties turn deep purple and the light ones yellow. They can only be stored if dried or frozen.

PESTS AND DISEASES

Pests and diseases are botrytis and birds (*see pages 46, 50 and 232*) and canker (*see page 233*).

Olives

Olives will grow in areas that can provide cool winters and hot summers, which is why they are grown so extensively in Mediter-ranean countries. African olives bear beautiful flowers but the fruit is not edible, so buy these for ornamental purposes only. European olives take five or six years to produce fruit but are extremely long-lived.

VARIETIES

The European, self-fertile varieties *Mission*, *Sevillano* and *Verdale* are recommended.

TREE SHAPES

Olives are always grown as standard trees (*see page 206*).

SOIL AND SITE

Olive trees will grow in any type of soil as long as it is well drained. Like grape vines, they are a useful crop to grow on soil that is poor or stony. The site should be in full sun.

PLANTING

Container-grown, grafted trees are available and can be planted at any time of year – however, they are best planted in autumn when wetter weather can be expected. If growing more than one tree plant them 7.5-12m (25-36ft) apart.

MAINTENANCE

Feeding They need plenty of nitrogen so they should be mulched annually with well-rotted manure or compost. If growth appears slow, apply hoof and horn or dried blood fertilizer at the rate of two handfuls per square meter/yard in spring.
Pruning Prune out overcrowded or crossing branches as olives need plenty of sunlight for maximum fruit production.

HARVESTING AND STORING

Pick olives by hand to avoid bruising. Gather in autumn when they are green and use for pickling, or leave them on the tree until winter, when they will turn black, and press for oil.

PESTS AND DISEASES

Organically grown olives have no specific pests but can be affected by the general garden pests (*see pages 46-51*).

Mulberries

These trees are very decorative although slow-growing, taking up to ten years before they bear fruit but then doing so for 40 years or more. A decided benefit from growing mulberries near cherry trees is that birds prefer mulberries saving the cherries.

VARIETIES

Plant two or more trees for cross-pollination. There are three types of mulberry – red (*Morus rubra*), white (*M. alba*) and black (*M. nigra*). The black mulberry produces the best fruit – recommended varieties are *Russian* and *Downing*.

TREE SHAPES

Mulberries are grown as bush or standard trees (*see page 206*).

SOIL AND SITE

They will grow in any soil, provided it is deep, fertile and has a pH of about 6.0-6.5. The site must be warm and sunny.

PLANTING

Because of their size – mulberry trees can reach 9m (30ft) at maturity – they require, generous spacing, so plant them about 9m (30ft) apart. Try to buy container-grown specimens as mulberries have very brittle roots which are easily damaged. Keep the area round the tree clear of grass until the tree is old enough to bear fruit.

MAINTENANCE

Pruning Prune back any over-crowded shoots to 10cm (4in) in late summer.

HARVESTING AND STORING

The fruit ripens in late summer and can be picked from the tree or shaken on to sheets laid on the grass. Mulberry juice stains skin and clothes badly, so take care when harvesting. Mulberries do not store well unless bottled.

PESTS AND DISEASES

They are affected by general garden pests (*see pages 46-51*).

Quinces

These are relatives of the pear. They flower later in the year than pears so are in little danger of frost damage.

VARIETIES

Quinces are self-fertile so only one tree is needed. Choose from *Meeches Prolific, Vranja, Champion, Fuller* or *Apple-Shaped*.

TREE SHAPES

They can be pruned to make fans (*see page 206*). In temperate climates, grow them as fans on a south-facing wall, like plums (*see page 218*).

SOIL AND SITE

Quinces prefer a soil with a pH between 6.0 and 6.5. Lime the soil only if soil tests show that the pH is below 6.0. Plant them in a sunny place.

PLANTING

The best time to plant is in early spring, using bare-rooted plants (*see page 83*).

MAINTENANCE

Feeding Follow the general details given on page 210.
Watering Follow the general details given on page 210.
Pruning Details of pruning to shape are given on page 218.

HARVESTING AND STORING

Quinces are ripe when they become yellow and give off a strong aroma. Make jelly immediately after harvesting or store the fruits on shelves or in boxes, in a cool, moist, frost-free shed for up to three months.

PESTS AND DISEASES

General pests and diseases that attack quinces include aphids and mildew (*see pages 46-51*). Specific pests and diseases are winter moth, woolly aphid, codling moth, sawfly, canker, fireblight, bitter pit, brown rot and scab (*see pages 234-5*). Wasps also damage fruit (*see page 232*).

Apples

The most popular tree fruit of temperate climates, apples can be grown on any type of soil provided it is prepared and managed properly. It is possible to grow apples in most parts of the world with relative ease. If you live in an area where late frosts may damage blossoms, choose varieties which flower later in the year.

Though much depends on variety, rootstocks and the prevailing conditions, trees on modern rootstocks should start to fruit in their second year and continue for about 30 years.

VARIETIES

For a full crop, apple trees need to be pollinated by a different variety (*see page 203*), so choose at least two trees which flower at the same time.

Early-flowering dessert apples Choose from *Yellow Transparent, McIntosh, Lodi, Idared, Criterion, Mutsu, Early Geneva, Gravenstein.*
Late-flowering dessert apples Choose from *Golden Delicious, Jonagold, Granny Smith, Spigold, Northern Spy, Liberty, Cortland, Early McIntosh.*
Early-flowering cooking apples *Red Astrachan, Twenty Ounce, New Summer Scarlet.*
Late-flowering cooking apples *Roxbury Russet, Baldwin* and most of the late-flowering dessert.
Rootstocks *M106* is the standard rootstock and this should be used for all trees except dwarf pyramids and cordons. *M9* is a dwarfing rootstock and the trees produced will always require staking. Use it for apples grown as cordons or dwarf pyramids (*see page 206*), but only if your soil is very fertile. The *M27* rootstock is very dwarfing and suitable only for trees growing in tubs. *M7* rootstock is used for semi-dwarf trees. There are also some genetically dwarf apples.

TREE SHAPES

Apple trees can be grown as standards, bush trees, dwarf pyramids, fans, espaliers, cordons, stepovers and festooned trees (*see page 206*).

SOIL AND SITE

They prefer a soil with a pH between 6.0 and 6.5. Lime the soil only if soil tests show that the pH is below 6.0. A sunny, sheltered site is preferable.

PLANTING

Plant in early spring or late autumn, using bare-rooted plants (*see pages 82-3 for details of tree planting*). Try to get the preparation done in advance and, if the soil is wet, work from boards to avoid damaging soil structure.

MAINTENANCE

Feeding Follow the general details given on page 210.
Watering Follow the general details given on page 210.
Pruning Details for the various shapes are given on pages 207-9.

HARVESTING AND STORING

Apples are fully ripe when they come easily from the tree as the fruit is lifted slightly and gently twisted. They should come off without pulling. Always pick carefully. Place the fruit in a basket lined with a soft cloth to avoid bruising; this is important if you are going to store it.

Early varieties should be picked in summer, just before they are fully ripe. If you like to eat them at the peak of their ripeness, pick them and leave them for a couple of days. Left on the tree to full ripeness, they tend to go slightly soft and mealy.

Supporting an apple-laden branch *Tie a length of string around the center of the branch, fixing the other end to the main trunk of the tree.*

Pick late varieties in autumn or early winter, when they are fully ripe. When storing, look them over very carefully and reject any that show the slightest sign of damage or disease – these will not store well and will affect the healthy fruit. Pack one variety at a time into plastic bags and seal with a twist tie. Never mix varieties in the same bag. The fruit should be able to breathe so make pinholes in the bag. Store them in as cool a place as possible, making sure it is frost

Storing apples *Put the fruit in plastic bags and seal with a tie. Prick two pinholes for each 1kg (2lb) fruit in the bag, to enable it to breathe.*

free. Check them regularly, removing any that show signs of disease or rotting.

PESTS AND DISEASES

General pests and diseases that attack apples include aphids and mildew (*see pages 46-51*). Specific pests and diseases are winter moth, woolly aphid, codling moth, apple sawfly, canker, fireblight, bitter pit, brown rot and apple scab (*see pages 234-5*). Wasps can also be a nuisance (*see page 232*).

Pears

Pears flower early and so may be subject to damaging frosts in temperate climates.

Fruiting varies according to conditions but, on average, pear trees will begin producing fruit after about two years and continue for 25-30 years.

VARIETIES

They need pollinating with a different variety, so choose trees that flower at the same time. Or choose a three-on-one dwarf tree with varieties that pollinate each other.
Early-flowering varieties
Choose from *Bartlett, Clapp's Favorite, Moonglow* (blight-resistant), *Chajuro* (self-fertile).
Late-flowering varieties
These include *Hybrid Red Anjou, Beurre d'Anjou, Seckel, Beurre Bosc.*
Rootstocks Dwarf pears are grafted on various quince selections, which vary in hardiness and degree of dwarfness, so choose carefully.

TREE SHAPES

They can be grown as standards, bush trees, cordons, espaliers, dwarf pyramids, fans, stepovers and festooned trees (*see page 206*).

SOIL AND SITE

Pear trees prefer a soil with a pH between 6.0 and 6.5. Lime the soil only if soil tests show that the pH is below 6.0. Plant them in a sheltered, sunny place.

PLANTING

The best time to plant is in early spring, using bare-rooted plants (*see page 83*). Try to get the preparation done in advance and, if the soil is wet, work from boards.

MAINTENANCE

Feeding Follow the general details given on page 210.
Watering Follow the general details given on page 210.
Pruning Details for the various shapes are given on pages 207-9.

HARVESTING AND STORING

Pears are ripe when they part

easily from the tree if gently lifted and twisted.

Early varieties should be picked before they are ripe, when still hard and green. Put them on a shelf in a cool shed and, a few days before you want to eat them, bring them indoors for final ripening. They will keep for two weeks. If kept too long, they become mushy and metallic-tasting.

Late-maturing varieties should be left on the tree longer. Pick them when they come off the tree easily and store them in the same way. If you want to keep pears longer, you will have to preserve or dry them. Do this before they become too ripe.

PESTS AND DISEASES

General pests and diseases that attack pears include aphids and mildew (*see pages 46-51*). Specific pests and diseases are winter moth, woolly aphids, codling moth, fireblight, sawfly, canker, bitter pit, brown rot and scab (*see pages 234-5*). Wasps can also be a nuisance (*see page 232*).

Kumquats

These are dwarf, evergreen citrus trees grown widely in the Far East. They are grown outdoors in warmer areas but can be grown in pots or large tubs in a heated greenhouse in temperate climates. Trees grown in tubs are always smaller than those grown outside.

VARIETIES

Two species, *Marumi* and *Nagami* kumquats, are available.

TREE SHAPES

They are always grown as bush trees (*see page 206*).

SOIL AND SITE

The ideal soil is a medium-heavy loam that drains well. Work in plenty of organic matter to improve water retention. On heavier soils, the planting site should be raised. The pH should be between 6.0 and 6.5.

They prefer an open, sunny position not overshadowed by other trees.

PLANTING

Plants are available balled or container-grown so can be planted at any time of year. Plant 4.5m (15ft) apart to avoid undue competition.

MAINTENANCE

Feeding Mulch with well-rotted manure or compost.
Watering Water well when the fruit is swelling.
Pruning Cut back the current season's growth after harvesting.

HARVESTING AND STORING

Harvest when the fruits begin to turn orange. They can be eaten raw or made into marmalade.

PESTS AND DISEASES

Gall wasp, little leaf and lemon scab (*see page 232*); red spider mite, aphids and scale insects (*see page 257*).

Lemons and limes

These are both sub-tropical fruits which will only grow outside in frost-free areas. The *Meyer* hybrid lemon, however, is slightly more hardy and will withstand temperatures as low as −9°C (15°F), provided it is grown in a sheltered spot. Limes are more acid and contain more sugar than lemons. Both can be grown in tubs in the greenhouse and the *Meyer* lemon as a houseplant.

VARIETIES

Lemon *Meyer, Lisbon, Eureka.*
Lime *Mexican, Tahitian.*

TREE SHAPES

Both lemon and lime trees are grown as bush trees (*see page 206*).

SOIL AND SITE

They grow best on slightly heavy soils. The beds should be raised at least 45cm (18in) above the surrounding land. Enrich the soil with plenty of well-rotted manure or compost. These trees prefer slightly acid conditions, with a pH of between 6.0 and 6.5.

The site must be very sunny and sheltered from winds.

PLANTING

Lemon and lime trees can be planted at any time of year as they are sold balled or container-grown. If they are being planted outside, spring or autumn are the best times. Plant so that the grafting point is about 10cm (4in) out of the ground and, if planting more than one, reduce competition, particularly for light, by planting at least 4.5m (15ft) apart.

MAINTENANCE

Feeding Young citrus roots are easily scorched by an excess of fertilizer, so restrict feeding to manure mulches. Alternatively, feed with one handful of blood, fish and bone meal per square meter/yard in early spring and repeat in summer, making sure you water the fertilizer in well.
Watering Make sure the roots have plenty of water, especially in the first few years.
Pruning Lemon trees need pruning to keep them compact; cut out any straggling or inward-pointing shoots. Prune back shoots that have borne fruit.

Lime trees need thinning and any dead, diseased or crossing wood removed.

HARVESTING AND STORING

Both fruits should be cut off the trees with pruners when they are ripe. Fruit is produced all year round in favorable climates.

Store in paper-lined boxes or wooden crates, each fruit covered with a layer of dry sand. Put the

Storing lemons *Store them in layers of dry sand in a wooden crate or paper-lined box for up to two months.*

boxes in a cool place. The fruit will keep this way for up to two months.

PESTS AND DISEASES

Gall wasp, little leaf and lemon scab (*see page 232*); red spider mite, aphids and scale insects (*see page 257*).

CULTIVATING CITRUS FRUIT IN THE GREENHOUSE

In temperate climates, grow citrus fruit in a greenhouse. Grow the varieties recommended for outdoor use in tubs, with a diameter no less than 45cm (18in). Use the soil-based potting mixture recommended on page 254 and keep the temperature in the greenhouse at a minimum of 7°C (45°F) at all times. Water well during the growing season, but allow the plants to dry out between waterings. In summer, spray the foliage with water every morning. Stop spraying when the plants are in flower. Keep the plants slightly drier in winter. Feed weekly during the growing season with liquid seaweed fertilizer.

Little pruning is required except to thin out crossing, over-crowded branches and remove dead or diseased wood and to prune out the fruited shoots after harvesting.

Oranges

As they are not frost-hardy, oranges should be grown in tubs in the greenhouse in temperate regions. In warmer climates they will produce a good crop when grown outside. The fruits are a good source of Vitamin C.

VARIETIES

Sweet oranges These are recommended for eating. Suitable varieties are: *Jaffa, Majorca, Valencia, Hamlin, Washington*.
Sour oranges For making marmalade use *Seville*.

TREE SHAPES

Orange trees are grown as bush trees (*see page 206*).

SOIL AND SITE

The soil should be light and sandy as they abhor bad drainage. To grow them on heavier soils, the planting area should be raised at least 45cm (18in) above the surrounding soil. Enrich the soil with plenty of well-rotted manure or compost. Oranges prefer slightly acid conditions, with a pH of between 6.0 and 6.5.

The site must be as sunny as possible and sheltered from wind if the trees are grown outside, so this may mean erecting or planting a windbreak.

PLANTING

Orange trees are sold balled or container-grown, so they can be planted at any time of year. If they are being planted outside, spring or autumn are the most favorable times. Plant so that the grafting point is about 10cm (4in) out of the ground and, if planting more than one, plant them at least 7.5m (25ft) from one another so that they don't compete, particularly for light.

MAINTENANCE

Feeding Young citrus roots are easily scorched by an excess of fertilizer, so restrict feeding to manure mulches – if you cannot get manure, feed with one handful of blood, fish and bone meal per square meter/yard in early spring and repeat in summer, watering the fertilizer in well.
Watering Make sure the roots have plenty of water, especially in the first few years.
Pruning Thin out by removing branches if the tree becomes overcrowded. After harvesting, prune every fruit-bearing shoot to 10cm (4in) (*see right*).

HARVESTING AND STORING

Pick oranges when they are well colored, by twisting them gently off the tree. The fruits can be left on the tree until you are ready to

Encouraging more fruiting spurs
When the fruit has been harvested, cut the fruit-bearing shoots to 10cm (4in) long.

use them – they can hang there for up to six months. They can also be stored in paper-lined boxes or wooden crates, each fruit covered with dry sand. Keep the box in a cool place. They will keep up to two months. Or keep in refrigerator.

PESTS AND DISEASES

Gall wasp, little leaf and lemon scab affect oranges grown outside (*see page 232*). Grown in the greenhouse they can be affected by red spider mite, aphids and scale insects (*see page 257*).

Grapefruits

Grapefruits originate from the West Indies and are not frost-hardy. They can be grown outside in sub-tropical and Mediterranean-type climates, but must be greenhouse-grown in temperate climates. Like all citrus trees, they are evergreen.

VARIETIES

Marsh's Seedless, Ruby and *Duncan* are recommended.

TREE SHAPES

Grapefruit trees are grown as bush trees (*see page 206*).

SOIL AND SITE

If they are to be grown outside, good drainage is essential. Deep dig the bed, incorporating plenty of well-rotted manure or compost (*see page 30*). On heavy soil, raise the bed 45cm (18in) above ground level. The soil should be

slightly acid, with a pH of between 6.0 and 6.5. The site should be sunny and sheltered.

PLANTING

Grapefruit trees are sold balled or container-grown, so they can be planted at any time of year; spring or autumn are the most favorable times if they are being planted outside. Plant so that the grafting point is about 10cm (4in) out of the ground. Avoid competition, especially for light, by planting at least 9m (30ft) from one another.

MAINTENANCE

Feeding Restrict feeding to manure mulches as young citrus roots are easily scorched by an excess of fertilizer. If you cannot get manure, feed with one handful of blood, fish and bone meal per square meter/yard in early spring and repeat in summer. Water the fertilizer in well.

Watering Make sure the roots have plenty of water, especially in the first few years.
Pruning Thin overcrowded wood and remove weak, sappy growth in early spring.

HARVESTING AND STORING

Pick grapefruits when they begin to turn yellow, by twisting them gently off the tree. They can be left on the tree until you are ready to use them and they can hang there for up to six months. They can also be stored in boxes or wooden crates, each fruit covered with dry sand and put in a cool place. Or keep them in the refrigerator.

PESTS AND DISEASES

Gall wasp, little leaf and lemon scab affect fruit grown outside (*see page 232*). Grown in the greenhouse it can be affected by red spider mite, aphids and scale insects (*see page 257*).

Soft fruit

Soft fruits grow on bushes, canes or briars and are ideal subjects for the small garden. The fruits soon deteriorate after picking, so those you grow in your garden will be of superior quality to anything you buy in the shops. Most of the fruits illustrated are relatively easy to grow and will suit a wide range of climates and conditions.

STRAWBERRIES *Fragaria × ananassa*
One of the simplest and most rewarding of the soft fruits. They prefer a well drained but moisture-retentive soil. *For cultivation details, see page 226.*

REDCURRANTS *Ribes sativum*
Easy to grow and very prolific. They can be grown in very small spaces as cordons. Whitecurrants are grown using the same cultivation techniques. *For cultivation details, see page 226.*

BLACKCURRANTS *Ribes nigrum*
A rich source of vitamin C, black-currants will produce heavy crops in a sunny position. They require plenty of minerals so prepare the soil well. *For cultivation details, see page 227.*

RASPBERRIES *Rubus idaeus*
These are easy to grow in temperate climates and respond well to organic methods of growing. They can suffer from iron deficiencies. *For cultivation details, see page 228.*

BLACKBERRIES *Rubus* sp.
These briar fruits take up a lot of room, but are worth growing if you have the space in your garden. The newer varieties taste much better. *For cultivation details, see page 229.*

GOOSEBERRIES *Ribes uva-crispa*
The earliest soft fruits of the season, gooseberries may not be suitable for very cold areas as they flower in early spring. *For cultivation details, see page 229.*

BLUEBERRIES *Vaccinium* sp.
These shrubs respond well to organic culture and, as they look decorative, they can be grown in the ornamental border. They need an acid soil. *For cultivation details, see page 230.*

LOGANBERRIES *Rubus ursinus* var.
These briar fruits need cooler climates. They need regular attention to tying in and training. *For cultivation details, see page 229.*

GRAPES *Vitis vinifera*
In temperate regions grapes grown outside are generally only suitable for wine, juice and jelly, though in a sunny year they form enough sugar

for dessert purposes. Dessert grapes should be grown outside in warmer climates or in the greenhouse in temperate climates. *For cultivation details, see page 230.*

Cultivating soft fruit

The fruits in this group range from briars and shrubs to herbaceous perennials, and the cultivation techniques vary accordingly. Cane and briar fruits need supporting, but are well worth growing if the space is available. Bush fruits are generally grown as free-standing shrubs. Strawberries are the only herbaceous perennials in the group. They take up little room and are attractive enough to grow in the borders if space is limited.

All soft fruits are very attractive to birds so it is essential to protect fruit with plastic netting.

SOFT FRUIT

Fruit	Shape and planting distance		Site	Soil preference	Bearing age	See page
Strawberry	Herbaceous plant	*60cm (2ft)*	Sunny	Any, well drained	¾-1 year	*225*
Redcurrant	Bush	*1.5m (5ft)*	Sunny	Heavy, moisture retentive	1-2 years	*226*
	Cordon	*30-90cm (1-3ft)*				
Whitecurrant	Bush	*1.5m (5ft)*	Sunny	Heavy, moisture retentive	1-2 years	*226*
	Cordon	*30-90cm (1-3ft)*				
Blackcurrant	Bush	*1.5m (5ft)*	Tolerant	Heavy, rich	2 years	*227*
Raspberry	Canes on wire support	*45cm (18in)*	Tolerant	Heavy, rich	1 year	*228*
Briar fruit	Briars on wire support	*3m (10ft)*	Tolerant	Any, well drained	1-2 years	*229*
Gooseberry	Bush	*1.5m (5ft)*	Sunny	Heavy, moisture retentive	1-2 years	*229*
	Cordon	*30-90cm (1-3ft)*				
Blueberry	Bush	*1.8m (6ft)*	Sunny	Acid, humus-rich	3-8 years	*230*
Grape	Vine on wire support	*1.5m (5ft)*	Sunny	Well drained	2 years	*230*

Strawberries

In the organic garden, strawberries can be grown with relative ease. They grow best in cool, moist climates, but can be grown in warmer climates if suitable varieties are used. Varieties for the regions are listed below.

VARIETIES

The varieties offered for sale are constantly changing as further research into this profitable commercial crop takes place. In very cold regions with little or no snow, plant *Catskill, Royalty, Senator Dunlop* and *Totem*. In the Northeast and Midwest, *Catskill, Guardian, Premier, Sparkle* and *Sunburst* are recommended. They are all self-fertile.

SOIL AND SITE

Strawberries grow best in a well-drained but moisture-retentive soil. To increase drainage, raise the growing area to form 1.2m (4ft) wide beds (*see page 135*). The site should be sunny, avoiding areas where there is little flow of air, as this will increase the risk of mildew.

PLANTING

Buy plants from a reputable grower who can guarantee freedom from disease. Plant them in late summer; planted any later they will not produce a crop the following year.

Dress the soil with two handfuls of bone meal per square meter/yard. Plant 60cm (2ft) apart with 45cm (18in) between the rows. If you are planting in 1.2m (4ft) wide raised beds, plant the first row 15cm (6in) from the edge of the bed to give three rows 45cm (18in) apart. Water thoroughly after planting.

It is important to set the crown of the plant (the point where the leaves join the roots) at soil level – if set too high the plant will not establish itself and frost may lift it out of the ground. If set too low the crown will rot.

Strawberries can also be planted through black plastic (*see below*). This helps to prevent the evaporation of water from the soil, suppresses weed growth and prevents the runners shooting into the soil.

Planting through black plastic
Cover a raised bed with a sheet of black plastic. Cut slits for planting in the plastic, spacing them 45cm (18in) apart. The raised bed will protect strawberries from soil-borne diseases; the plastic suppresses weeds.

MAINTENANCE

Feeding Little fertilizer is necessary. If there is too much nitrogen in the soil, the plants will make excess leaf growth at the expense of fruit so, after the crop has been picked, sprinkle a handful of rock potash along each meter/yard run of row.

Mulching The fruits will hang on or near the ground, where they can be splashed with mud or damaged by slugs. To protect them, mulch with straw once they start to swell. Tuck the straw right under the plants to raise the fruit off the ground. Take care, however, not to mulch too early. If the straw is put under the leaves while there is still a danger of frost, it will insulate the flowers from the rising warmth of the soil. This lowers the temperature around the developing fruit and could result in a lighter crop.

Propagating Healthy strawberry plants produce new plantlets on stems known as runners. To provide plants for forcing in the greenhouse, pin the plantlets into pots sunk into the soil beside the parent plant. Once they have rooted, they can be separated from the parent plant. Don't use them to restock your beds; you could spread virus disease.

Protection Strawberries are prone to bird damage when ripe. To protect them, cover the ripening fruit with netting. Cover autumn-fruiting strawberries with a cloche if there is a danger of a hard frost.

Protecting strawberries *Surround the developing fruits with straw to raise them off the ground. This will provide protection from slug damage and prevent them being splashed with mud.*

HARVESTING AND STORING

Pick the fruits when they are red all over, pulling off the plug, or central core, as well – leaving the plug on the plants attracts fungus diseases. Pick over the plants regularly as new fruits will ripen each day. The fruits can easily be frozen and all strawberries can be made into jam. They store only for a few days. Once the fruits have been picked, cut all the plants to within 2.5cm

Propagating from runners *Pin the plantlet, still attached to its runner, into a pot of soil buried near the parent plant. Use a piece of wire bent to a hairpin-shape to secure the plantlet.*

(1in) of the crown using shears or, if you grow a lot, a rotary grass cutter. Compost the old leaves and straw. Make sure you remove any diseased leaves first.

PESTS AND DISEASES

Strawberries are prone to attack by aphids, slugs, botrytis, mildew and virus diseases (*see pages 46-51*). They are also affected by red spider mite and birds (*see page 232*).

Redcurrants and whitecurrants

Grown against a wall or fence as cordons, they are suitable for even the smallest plot. They do best in temperate climates.

VARIETIES

Red Lake is the most popular redcurrant, while *White Imperial* is the most commonly grown whitecurrant. Currants are self-fertile so do not need to be pollinated with another variety.

BUSH SHAPES

Red- and whitecurrants can be grown as free-standing bushes or as single, double or triple cordons against a fence, wall or post-and-wire support (*see page 208*).

SOIL AND SITE

Currants do best in soils with a pH of about 6.5 and prefer a sunny position. They flower in early spring so may not be suitable for very cold areas without some protection from frost.

PLANTING

Though container-grown plants may be available for planting during the summer, currants are best planted in the late autumn. At this time the weather is likely to be wetter and there will still be enough warmth in the soil to encourage the plants to make some roots before winter.

Red- and whitecurrants are grown on a "leg"; they differ from blackcurrants in this respect, (*see opposite*), so before planting remove any suckers which may be present.

To encourage root growth, add two handfuls of bone meal per square meter/yard to the soil. Plant free-standing bushes at the level they grew in the nursery, setting the plants 1.5m (5ft) apart, with 1.8m (6ft) between each row. Cordons should be planted so that the "arms" are 30cm (1ft) apart – single cordons should be planted 30cm (1ft) apart, double cordons 60cm (2ft) apart and triple cordons 90cm (3ft) apart. After planting, tie the arms so that they are at right-angles to the wires and mulch round the bushes with a thick layer of well-rotted manure or compost as a weed inhibitor.

SUPPORTING AND TRAINING

Free-standing bushes need training to produce a strong, cup-shaped bush with an open center. In the first three winters, prune back the main branches to leave half the wood made that year. Any side-shoots should be cut back to 7cm (3in). At the same time, remove any branches that are broken, dead or diseased and any that are overcrowded or growing towards the center of the bush. After three years, prune in the summer, immediately after harvesting. Reduce all the side-shoots to five leaves and, when the main branches have grown as long as you want them, cut them back in the same way.

Train cordon-grown currants upwards, rather than at an angle. Train by pruning the main arms in winter, cutting back the leading shoot to leave two-thirds of the last season's growth. In summer, prune after harvesting by cutting any side-shoots back to 7cm (3in). Any secondary shoots should be cut back to 2.5cm (1in).

MAINTENANCE

Feeding Currants require a lot of potassium, or potash, so they need extra feeding. In early

PLANTING CURRANT BUSHES

Blackcurrants are grown as "stooled" plants, with the shoots arising from ground level. Red- and whitecurrants are grown on a "leg", with the shoots arising from a short stem.

Growing on a leg *Buy bushes with a good stem beneath the branches. Pull off any suckers arising at root level. Plant the bush at the level it grew in the nursery.*

Stooling a blackcurrant bush *Plant the bush 5cm (2in) lower than it grew in the nursery and cut all the shoots back to ground level.*

spring apply one handful of rock potash per square meter/yard. A browning of the leaf margins indicates a potash deficiency (*see page 39*). To remedy, spray the plants with liquid seaweed and feed with rock potash as recommended above.

Pruning After the initial shaping prune in summer as above.

Protection If there is a danger of hard frost when the plants are in flower, cover the bushes with woven polypropylene or fine-meshed netting.

Currants are very susceptible to bird damage. Cover the bushes with garden netting.

HARVESTING AND STORING

Pick the sprigs from the bush and remove the individual currants later with a kitchen fork. They will not store fresh, although they can be frozen or canned.

PESTS AND DISEASES

Currants can be attacked by aphids, birds and mildew (*see pages 46, 50 and 232*). More specific attacks of sawfly and leaf spot (*see page 235*) also occur. Leaf spot is part of the white pine blister rust cycle, which kills white pines. Consult County Extension Service before planting currants.

Blackcurrants

Blackcurrant bushes take up a lot of room, but are worth growing as the currants are a rich source of Vitamin C.

VARIETIES

Carter's Black Champion and *Black Naples* are two old varieties popular in some countries, and no doubt other varieties exist in the USA in regions where white pine and some other 5-needled pine species do not grow. Because blackcurrant is reputed to be especially susceptible to diseases, such as leaf spot, it is a rare fruit in America.

BUSH SHAPES

Blackcurrants are always grown as free-standing bushes and are not really suitable to grow as

cordons. They are pruned to form "stools" (*see above*) with the majority of shoots coming from ground level or below.

SOIL AND SITE

Blackcurrants will grow in part shade but produce heavier crops in a sunny position. The bushes like a rich soil as they are gross feeders, and so will repay good soil preparation. The soil pH should be maintained at 6.5.

PLANTING

The best plants are bare-rooted ones, planted in autumn or early winter. Set them 1.5m (5ft) apart, with 1.8m (6ft) between rows.

To create a stooled plant, plant it 5cm (2in) lower than it grew in the nursery and, after planting, prune all the shoots back to ground level.

SUPPORTING AND TRAINING

Blackcurrant bushes require no special support or training.

MAINTENANCE

Feeding Blackcurrants have a high nitrogen requirement so apply two handfuls of blood, fish and bone meal per square meter/yard in early spring and mulch with well-rotted manure or compost. If growth still seems poor, give the plants further fertilizer at the same rate in early summer.

Pruning Blackcurrants produce most fruit on wood made the previous year, so there will be no pruning and little fruit in the first year.

In the second and subsequent years cut all the fruited shoots to ground level to encourage further strong growth. This is usually done in late summer, but you can bring pruning forward slightly, to mid summer, and cut off the fruited shoots with the fruit still attached. As bushes get older, you may find that fewer shoots are produced from below ground level. If this is the case, prune out the fruited wood as low as possible, just above a new young shoot. At the same time, take a few of the older shoots right back to ground level, even if this means cutting out some of the new wood.

HARVESTING AND STORING
Harvest as suggested under pruning, or pick the sprigs and remove fruits with a fork. Eat blackcurrants straight away.

PESTS AND DISEASES
Blackcurrants are attacked by aphids and birds (*see pages 46, 50 and 232*), sawfly, big bud mite, leaf spot, mildew and reversion disease (*see page 235*).

If you live in white pine regions, consult County Extension Service before ordering currants or gooseberries.

Raspberries

Easy to grow in cool, temperate climates, raspberries respond well to organic methods of growing. Although they take up more room than many other fruits, they will handsomely repay the use of space since they produce very heavy crops.

VARIETIES
Raspberries are self-fertile. Recent research has produced virus-free varieties so grow these if you can. Recommended varieties are *Lathem, Bristol, Jewel, Hilton* and *Taylor*.

For autumn fruit grow *Heritage* or *Fall Red*.

BUSH SHAPES
Raspberries are grown as canes tied in to a post-and-wire support. Autumn-fruiting varieties are grown as free-standing canes.

SOIL AND SITE
Raspberries prefer a deep, well-prepared soil that holds plenty of moisture. The soil pH should be 6.0 or a little below. Above pH 7.0, iron deficiency is likely to occur (*see page 39*). They will tolerate a little shade.

PLANTING
This is best done in autumn and early winter, using bare-rooted plants. Dig a trench a spade deep and at least 60cm (2ft) wide. Break up the bottom and put in a 10cm (4in) layer of well-rotted compost or manure. Mix more organic matter with the soil as you refill. Sprinkle a dressing of bone meal on the soil at the rate of one handful per meter/yard run of trench. Set the plants a little deeper than they grew on the nursery to encourage plenty of growth from below ground and after planting, cut the canes to within 15cm (6in) of the ground. The plants should be 90cm (3ft) apart with at least 1.8m (6ft) between rows.

SUPPORTING AND TRAINING
Grow raspberry canes against a post-and-wire support erected in the same way as the support for cordon apples (*see page 204*). Tie the canes to the wires as they grow, spacing them 10cm (4in) apart. When the canes reach the top of the support, their tips should be cut off 7cm (3in) above the top wire. Everbearing varieties generally need no support, though on windy sites you may find it necessary to run nylon twine or wire down either side of the row.

MAINTENANCE
Feeding Mulch with well-rotted manure or compost in late winter. A yellowing between the veins of the leaves indicates iron deficiency (*see page 39*). To remedy this, spray with liquid seaweed and give a dressing of seaweed meal at the rate of one handful per square meter/yard. However, the dressing of manure should ensure that this deficiency does not occur.

Pruning Once the fruit has been picked, cut the old canes down to ground level and tie the new ones in their place. Pull out any suckers that are spreading towards the paths. Everbearing varieties bear fruit on one-year-old canes in early summer, which are then cut down to ground level. The new canes bear in autumn and the following summer.

Protection Cover the canes with garden netting before the fruit colors to deter birds.

HARVESTING AND STORING
Berries for cooking can be picked a little before they are fully ripe. Leave the plug, or central core of the fruit, on the canes. Unless frozen or canned, raspberries will not store.

PESTS AND DISEASES
General pests and diseases include birds, aphids, botrytis and virus diseases (*see pages 46-51 and 232*). More specific pests and diseases affecting raspberries are raspberry beetle, spur blight and cane spot (*see page 235*).

PRUNING RASPBERRY CANES
Raspberry canes will only produce fruit on one-year-old wood so fruited canes need to be cut out every year. Take the opportunity to pull out any unwanted suckers at this time of year too.

1 *When the fruit has been picked, cut all the fruited canes, and any weak ones, down to ground level.*

2 *Space the new shoots at 10cm (4in) intervals along the support. Cut out all excess canes.*

Briar fruits

These include blackberries, loganberries and hybrid berries. Their great value lies in their late harvesting period, following on from raspberries.

VARIETIES

All the varieties are self-fertile so only one kind need be grown.
Blackberry Choose from *Darrow, Ebony King, Thornfree, Ranger.*
Loganberry No special varieties generally available.
Hybrid berries Dewberry, Boysenberry, Youngberry.

BUSH SHAPES

The briars should always be trained on wire supports.

SOIL AND SITE

Briar fruits prefer a deep, well-prepared soil that holds plenty of moisture. The soil pH should be 6.0 or a little below. Above pH 7.0, iron deficiency is likely to occur (*see page 39*). They tolerate partly shady sites. Some of the hybrid berries will grow in warmer climates if the winters are suitably cool.

PLANTING

They are best planted in early autumn, after which they should be mulched with well-rotted organic matter, or in early spring. Dig a trench a spade deep and at least 60cm (2ft) wide. Break up the bottom and put in a 10cm (4in) layer of well-rotted compost or manure. Mix more organic matter with the soil as you refill. Sprinkle a dressing of bone meal on the soil at the rate of one handful per meter/yard run of trench. Allow 3m (10ft) between plants, and cut the canes down to about 15cm (6in) after planting.

SUPPORTING AND TRAINING

Support them on wires on 1.8m (6ft) posts. The wires should start 1m (3ft) from the ground and continue at 30cm (12in) intervals to the top of the posts.

It is essential to train the briars on to the wires as they grow. If you leave them sprawling on the ground for too long, they become intertwined and impossible to unravel without damage.

As they fruit on one-year-old wood, it is necessary to keep the fruiting wood and the new wood separate (*see below*).

MAINTENANCE

Feeding Mulch with well-rotted manure or compost in late winter. If plants show signs of yellowing between the veins of the leaves, it is almost certainly due to iron deficiency (*see page 39*). To remedy this problem, spray with seaweed and give a dressing of seaweed meal at the rate of one handful per square meter/yard. However, the dressing of manure should ensure that this deficiency does not occur.
Pruning After the fruit has been picked, cut all the fruited briars down to ground level.
Protection Net the bushes before harvest time to protect the berries from bird damage.

HARVESTING AND STORING

The plug should be left in, so twist them slightly when picking. Unless frozen or canned, they will not store.

PESTS AND DISEASES

Briar fruits can be attacked by aphids, botrytis, virus diseases and are very prone to bird damage (*see pages 46–51 and 232*). They are also affected by raspberry beetle, spur blight and cane spot (*see page 235*).

Gooseberries

These are the earliest soft fruits of the year. They can be grown as cordons against a wall or fence and, like this, will take up no more than about 15cm (6in) of garden room so they are suitable for even the smallest plot.

VARIETIES

One of the best varieties is *Pixwell*, which has few thorns and bears long-stemmed berries. *Welcome* and *Oregon Champion* are American varieties that are less susceptible to mildew. All varieties of gooseberry are self-fertile.

BUSH SHAPES

Gooseberries can be grown as free-standing bushes or as single, double or triple cordons against a fence or wall, or on a post-and-wire support (*see page 208*).

SOIL AND SITE

Gooseberries do best in soils with a pH of about 6.5 and prefer a sunny position. They flower in early spring so may not be suitable for very cold areas without some protection from frost.

PLANTING

Though often available in containers for planting during summer, gooseberries are best bought bare-rooted and planted in autumn or early spring.

Gooseberry bushes are grown on a "leg", a short stem below the branches (*see page 227*), so before planting remove any suckers that may be present.

Before planting add two hand-meter/yard to the soil. Plant free-standing bushes at the level they grew in the nursery, setting the on the nursery, setting the plants 1.5m (5ft) apart, with 1.8m (6ft) between each row. Cordons should be planted so that the "arms" are 30cm (12in) apart – single cordons should be planted 30cm (12in) apart, double cordons 60cm (2ft) apart and triple cordons 90cm (3ft) apart. After planting, mulch round the bushes with a thick layer of well-rotted manure or compost as a weed inhibitor – gooseberries are difficult and painful to weed!

SUPPORTING AND TRAINING

Gooseberries are supported and trained in the same way as red- and whitecurrants (*see page 227*).

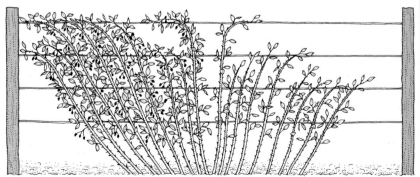

Training briar fruits *Train all the shoots in the first year to one side of the support. As the new shoots grow, train them to the other side. This will keep the one-year-old fruiting shoots away from the new wood.*

MAINTENANCE

Feeding Gooseberries need a lot of potassium, or potash, so they require extra feeding. In early spring apply one handful of rock potash per square meter/yard. A browning of the leaf margins indicates a potash deficiency (*see page 38*). To remedy this, spray the plants with liquid seaweed and apply rock potash as above.

Pruning Prune free-standing bushes immediately after harvesting. Reduce side-shoots to five leaves and, when the main branches have filled their allotted space, cut them back in exactly the same way. At the same time, completely remove any main branches that are dead, diseased or overcrowded.

Prune cordon-grown gooseberries after harvesting by cutting any side-shoots back to 7cm (3in). Any secondary shoots should be cut back to 2.5cm (1in).

Thinning If the crop of gooseberries is heavy, start picking before they are fully ripe. This allows the remaining berries to swell to their proper size. Use the unripe berries for cooking.

Frost protection If there is a danger of a hard frost, cover the bushes with woven polypropylene or fine netting.

Harvesting gooseberries *This is made easier if the bushes are grown as upright cordons.*

HARVESTING AND STORING

Pick gooseberries for cooking before they are fully ripe. Gooseberries will not store fresh but can be frozen or bottled.

PESTS AND DISEASES

Gooseberries can be attacked by aphids, birds and mildew (*see pages 46-51 and 232*). More specific pests and diseases include sawfly and leaf spot (*see pages 227-8 and 235*).

Blueberries

The best edible blueberries are highbush blueberries. They take between three and eight years to bear fruit; however, once they do, the bushes crop very heavily for many years.

VARIETIES

Highbush blueberries are not self-fertile, so two or more varieties are necessary to ensure good pollination. Recommended varieties include *Bluecrop, Darrow, Earliblue, Blue Ray* and *Berkeley*.

BUSH SHAPES

They are always grown as free-standing bushes.

SOIL AND SITE

Blueberries must have an acid soil – a pH of 5.0-5.5 is ideal. If your soil is alkaline, grow them in a raised bed (*see page 37*), in a sunny spot.

PLANTING

Plant bushes in autumn or early winter, setting them 1.8m (6ft) apart. They should be planted slightly deeper than they were grown in the nursery. Incorporate two handfuls of bone meal per square meter/yard into the soil, and mulch with a thick layer of manure, compost, wood chips or oak leaf mold.

MAINTENANCE

Feeding Mulch as recommended above every year and, in late winter, apply an organic fertilizer formulated for acid-soil plants, at rate given on package.

Pruning In the first few years the tips of the branches should be removed in autumn. As the bush gets larger, any old or weak growths should be pruned out. Ensure the free passage of light and air by pruning out any branches that are less than 15cm (6in) apart.

Protection The bushes should be netted to protect against bird damage as the fruits ripen.

HARVESTING AND STORING

Blueberries are fully ripe about ten days after they turn blue. The berries store well in the refrigerator or can be frozen.

PESTS AND DISEASES

They are prone to attack by birds (*see pages 46 and 232*).

Grapes

In temperate regions grapes grown outside are generally only suitable for wine, juice and jelly. In semi-tropical climates, vines grown outside will produce dessert quality fruit.

VARIETIES

All varieties are self-fertile. In cold-winter regions, such varieties as *Interlaken Seedless, Concord,* and *Steuben* are popular. Consult County Extension Service for advice on what to grow in your area.

SOIL AND SITE

Grape vines will thrive on poor soil provided it is well drained and contains plenty of organic matter. The soil pH should be 6.5-7.0 and the site sunny.

PLANTING

Plant in autumn or early spring, setting plants 1.5m (5ft) apart. After planting, mulch with well-rotted manure or compost.

MAINTENANCE

Feeding Feed annually with a mulch of well-rotted compost or manure. If growth seems poor, feed with blood, fish and bone meal at the rate of two handfuls per square meter/yard.

Pruning Prune out the fruited shoots as shown right.

Thinning Thin dessert grapes using nail-scissors or special grape-thinning scissors. Remove any berries that are mis-shapen or diseased, allowing the others to become pea-sized. Then begin removing berries judiciously to enable the others to swell. Thinning is unnecessary if grapes are for wine, juice or jelly.

HARVESTING AND STORING

When the stems turn brown the fruit is ready for picking. Cut off the bunches carefully using pruners. To store grapes, lay the bunches on a tray and keep in a cool, shady place. They will keep for about a month.

PESTS AND DISEASES

Grape are prone to attacks by wasps, birds, mildew and botrytis (*see pages 46-51 and 232*). In the greenhouse they may be affected by red spider mite, vine weevils and scale insects (*see page 257*).

TRAINING A GRAPE VINE OUTSIDE

Vines can be grown outside against a post-and-wire support or a south-facing wall. The method of training against a post-and-wire support is shown below. To grow against a wall, simply space out the shoots to form a decorative shape.

Making the support *Before planting vines, make a post-and-wire support by erecting a row of 1.2m (4ft) posts. Run wires between them; the top wire should be 1.2m (4ft) from the ground, the bottom one 45cm (18in) from the ground, with a wire strung in between them. Put a 1.8m (6ft) post at each planting point.*

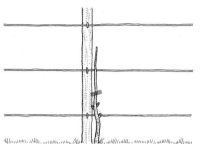

1 Immediately after planting, *cut the main shoot back to leave three strong buds.*

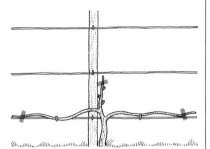

2 In the first summer, *three shoots will grow up. These should be tied on to the stake. In autumn, pinch back the growing point of the main stem.*

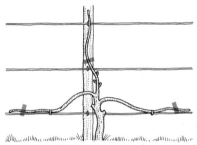

3 In the second winter, *tie the two strongest shoots to the bottom wire, one either side of the stake. Prune them back to 75cm (2ft 6in). Prune the central shoot back to leave three buds.*

4 In the second summer, *the central shoot will again produce three shoots and these should be tied to the stake. Pinch back any side-shoots,*

which may develop to three leaves. Over the summer, the shoots which have been tied in horizontally will produce side-shoots – these will bear the fruit and should be tied to the wire above. As they grow longer, tie them in to the top wire and pinch off their tips. Pinch back any secondary shoots to one leaf. In the first fruiting year only four bunches of fruit should be allowed to develop, but in subsequent years allow one bunch per shoot to grow. Cut out the fruited shoots after harvesting.

5 The following season, *tie two shoots from the central stake to the wires, cut back the middle shoot and start the process again.*

CULTIVATING GRAPES IN THE GREENHOUSE

In colder areas, dessert grapes can be grown in the greenhouse. *Muscat of Alexandria* needs some heat but *Black Hamburgh* can be grown in an unheated house.
Planting Plant in late autumn. Dig a wide, deep hole, put in a 30cm (12in) layer of gravel and cover with turf. Plant the vine on top.
Training Shoots can be trained horizontally along the wall, 1m (3ft) from the ground. Fruit-bearing shoots from these are trained upwards.

Alternatively, plant 1m (3ft) apart in the border and train the shoots up to the ridge on wires set 30cm (12in) away from the glass. After planting, remove a third of the previous year's growth. In the first year, pinch back side-shoots to five leaves.

After leaf-fall, prune the main shoot to leave half the previous year's wood. Prune all side-shoots to three buds to form fruiting spurs. In subsequent summers, allow only two shoots to grow from each spur, and stop the weakest of the two after three leaves. When an embryo bunch of grapes forms on the other shoot, allow it to make three more leaves and then pinch out the tip. Repeat the winter pruning as soon as possible after leaf-fall.
Maintenance In early winter, untie the vines and lay them on the border to prevent the top spurs growing faster than the lower ones. Put the vines back on the wires when spring growth starts. Keep the temperature at 20°C (70°F) and spray to

increase humidity. When vines flower, stop spraying and tap the wires to dislodge pollen. Water and feed weekly.

Ensuring a good crop *Remove mis-shapen or overcrowded berries. The supporting wires should be at least 30cm (12in) from the glass to prevent scorching.*

Fruit pests and diseases

Fruit is attacked by a number of general garden pests and diseases such as aphids, birds, botrytis and mildew; and also some more specialized pests which attack only certain species of fruit.

Advice on how to deal with general pests and diseases can be found in *Organic Pest and Disease Control* (*see pages 43-53*), however, any details specific to fruit are given below.

General pests and diseases

Some pests and diseases will affect any plant, whether it is in the fruit garden, vegetable garden or in an ornamental border. Many will be kept under control automatically if organic measures, such as companion planting, are employed. Control measures specific to fruit, however, are given below.

BIRDS

These are one of the most troublesome pests of the fruit garden. They are particularly fond of soft fruits, although they do peck holes in hard fruits, which are then attacked by wasps. They also eat fruit buds, greatly reducing your crop.

What to do
*The only real protection from bird attack is to use netting, since birds soon get used to any deterrent such as silver foil or scarecrows. Cover the fruit with netting, individual plastic bags or, better still, build a fruit cage (*see page 211*).*

WASPS

These insects attack fruit as it is ripening, and will damage both tree and soft fruits. As they tend to attack after there has been an initial blemish, like a bird peck, try to protect the fruit from damage in the first place (*see left*).

What to do

One method of control is to waylay the wasps before they get to the fruit, by setting a beer trap. Half fill a jar with stale beer, cider or anything else sweet. Cover the top with a piece of paper or plastic with a smallish hole in it. The wasps get into the jar, attracted by the smell, but once inside, they can't get out and they drown.

RED SPIDER MITE

These tiny mites will be a problem in very dry years. They can barely be seen with the naked eye, but the webs they form are visible. They suck the plant's sap, and affected leaves take on a characteristic mottled and yellowed appearance, eventually falling from the plant.

What to do

*As they thrive in dry conditions, avoid attacks by spraying regularly with water. If the attack is particularly bad, spray the plant with rotenone. See also greenhouse pests (*page 257*).*

Citrus fruit

The pests and diseases given below attack fruit grown outside. In the greenhouse, fruit may be affected by more general ailments such as red spider mite, scale insects and molds.

LITTLE LEAF

This problem is caused by a zinc deficiency. The leaves become mottled and crinkled and the fruit may be deformed.

What to do
Ensure that the soil contains the full complement of trace elements by applying a dressing of seaweed meal to the soil, or mulching round the tree with well-rotted compost or manure.

LEMON SCAB

A fungus disease that causes distortion of the fruits, making irregular corky ridges on the skin.

What to do
Spray with copper fungicide when half the petals have fallen.

CITRUS GALL WASP

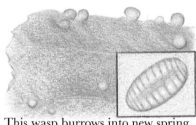

This wasp burrows into new spring growth to lay its eggs. When hatched, the larvae burrow within the shoot, causing round swellings, or galls, to appear.

What to do
There is no effective control. The only cure is to cut out all visible galls in summer and destroy them.

Soft tree fruit

This group contains all the tree fruits that have soft flesh surrounding a central stone, or pit. They are easily damaged by birds and wasps and are very prone to fungus diseases.

PLUM SAWFLY

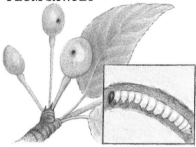

The caterpillars of this pest make holes in the fruit, rendering them inedible and causing them to drop from the tree.

What to do

As the pupae live in the soil beneath the tree, regular hoeing will expose them to insectivorous birds. If the caterpillar attack persists, spray the tree with rotenone after the petals have fallen.

BLACK APHID

This aphid attacks cherries in particular, though it is not generally a serious problem in the organic garden. It does, however, produce a sticky honeydew which attracts the growth of sooty mold.

What to do

Ensure your garden contains the plants that attract hover-flies, because their larvae eat aphids (see page 45). If attacks persist, spray with insecticidal soap (see page 53) in the evening to cover the pests but avoid insect predators.

BACTERIAL CANKER

This is a very serious and widespread disease of plums. The first signs are brown marks on the leaves. The leaf tissue than falls away, leaving what looks like caterpillar damage on the leaves. The branches then start to exude a sticky substance. The following spring, buds on infected branches fail to open or produce only small, yellow leaves.

What to do

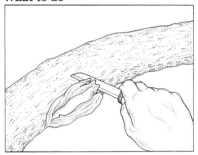

All infected wood should be cut away and destroyed. Spray the leaves with copper fungicide (see page 53) in mid summer and then twice more, leaving a month between each spraying.

PEACH-LEAF CURL

A fungus disease that attacks all the *Prunus* species. It causes red blisters on the leaves which eventually swell up. Spores are then produced, turning the leaf surface white. The leaves fall early and the vigor of the tree is affected.

What to do

Remove infected leaves as soon as you see them, but expect an infestation every year. To control it, spray with copper fungicide (see page 53) in mid winter and repeat every two weeks for at least four days. Spray again in autumn before the leaves fall. Protect fan-trained trees from rain, which carries the spores.

SILVER-LEAF

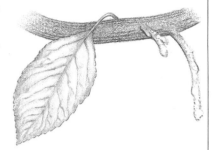

Many fruit trees suffer from this disease, but plums are the most susceptible, the variety *Victoria* especially. The leaves take on a silvery hue and may then turn brown. There is a progressive dieback of shoots and small purple, brown or white fungi appear on the dead wood. If you remove an infected branch, a brown or purple stain will be seen on the wood.

What to do

*Cut back all dead growth to at least 15cm (6in) past the affected point. As the fungus enters through open wounds, pruning should be done during the growing season when cuts heal quickly. As soon as the symptoms are seen, insert pellets of the parasitic fungus (*Trichoderma viride*) into 5cm (2in) holes in the trunk.*

PLUM RUST

This fungus disease causes yellow spots to appear on the upper surface of leaves and brown or orange pustules on the lower surface.

What to do

The disease occurs only in weak plants so feed those affected with blood, fish and bone meal at the rate of two handfuls per square meter/yard and mulch with well-rotted manure or compost. Hand water if the soil around the tree is dry.

Hard tree fruit

These fruits, which include apples and pears, are prone to attack by many pests and diseases, but organic methods and good husbandry will generally reduce problems to a minimum.

CODLING MOTH

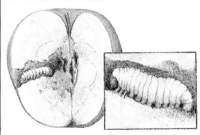

The female moths lay their eggs on developing apples and, as soon as the grubs hatch out, they enter the fruit. They are virtually impossible to see and the first sign is often a maggot inside the apple.

What to do

They can be controlled by hanging pheromone traps in the trees. These are triangular plastic boxes containing a sheet of sticky paper. In the center of the sheet is a capsule containing the phero-mone, which is the substance the female moth excretes at mating time to attract the male moth. The moths fly into the trap, stick to the paper and the female's eggs remain unfertilized. One trap for every five trees reduces the number of fertile eggs laid by about 80 per cent.

APPLE SAWFLY

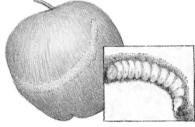

Before burrowing into the fruit, the sawfly larvae feed on the surface, causing a ribbon-like scar. Apples that have been attacked fail to ripen and fall from the tree in summer.

What to do

Pick and destroy the infected fruits as soon as you see any scarring. Spray the tree with ryania or rotenone a week after blossom fall.

BITTER PIT

Small, sunken areas appear in the fruit, with brown flesh immediately below the pits. Bitter pit appears during storage but may develop while the fruit is on the tree and is caused by a calcium deficiency and an imbalance of potassium or magnesium in the soil.

What to do

There is no effective treatment, but watering during dry periods and mulching with manure will help avoid it.

BROWN ROT

A fungus that turns fruit brown and makes the flesh decay. The fruit becomes covered with patches of white fungus spores and finally shrivels up, often falling off. Brown rot also attacks fruit in storage.

What to do

There is no totally effective control. Remove infected fruit and keep the soil around the trees clean. Check fruit for damage regularly whilst in storage.

APPLE APHIDS

The rosy apple aphid and the rosy leaf-curling aphid feed on shoots and leaves causing them to turn yellow or bright red and distort. The green apple aphid clusters round shoot tips and sucks the sap, causing stunting of growth.

What to do

Spray the tree with insecticidal soap, derris or rotenone and quassia when it is at the leaf cluster stage and again when the aphids are seen. Grow the plants that attract hover-flies (see page 45).

WOOLLY APHIDS

These insects suck sap from the shoots. They live in colonies and cover themselves with a white waxy coating, which makes them difficult to attack with sprays.

What to do

Paint small infestations of woolly aphids with methylated spirits, or simply scrape them off. Spray large areas with rotenone (see page 53) after petal fall, using a coarse, high-pressure spray. If this doesn't work, you may have to cut out the infestation.

PEAR SUCKER

These pests live in the blossom buds and cover the foliage with honey-dew, which attracts the fungus disease, sooty mold. Attacks gener-ally start in early spring and con-tinue through the summer.

What to do

Control them with insecticidal soap or rotenone (see page 53), applied three weeks after the petals have fallen.

WINTER MOTH

The female moths are wingless so they have to crawl up the tree to lay their eggs between autumn and spring. The caterpillars hatch in spring and feed until early summer, making holes in the leaves. They then make their way down into the soil to overwinter.

What to do

The most effective control is to tie a greaseband around the tree trunk during the egg-laying period. This prevents the females crawling up the tree to lay eggs.

APPLE SCAB

A fungus that appears as dark spots on leaves and fruit. It spreads to form large, unsightly patches.
What to do
Pick off spotty leaves and destroy them. Sweep up all the fallen leaves because fungus spores overwinter on them.

FIREBLIGHT

A bacterial disease that causes shoots to wilt from the top and the leaves to turn brown. It generally enters the tree through cuts or damage on the shoots and it can pass from one tree to another.
What to do
This is a complex disease. For latest information, consult your County Extension fruit specialists. Choose resistant pear varieties such as Seckel, Magness, Maxine, Moonglow, Orient.

CANKER

It starts as sunken, discolored patches on the bark, which soon extend. In summer, white pustules appear on the sunken patches and in winter small red fruiting bodies develop. If the fungus encircles a shoot, the shoot dies.
What to do

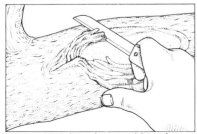

Diseased patches, shoots and branches must be cut out with a knife or chisel and destroyed immediately. It is important to cut right back to clean wood.

Soft fruit

All low-growing cane and bush fruits are classed as soft fruits. General garden pests and diseases affect many varieties of soft fruit. Birds are especially fond of them, particularly when the weather is hot and there is no other source of liquid. Soft fruits also have a number of specific pests and diseases.

RASPBERRY BEETLE

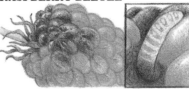

The larvae of this beetle feed on the ripening fruit, and are often first noticed when malformed fruits are seen. When they have finished feeding, the larvae fall into the soil and turn into pupae.
What to do

Hoe the soil to bring the pupae to the surface, where birds will eat them. Spraying with rotenone may be necessary. Spray raspberries when the first fruits turn pink, and hybrid berries immediately after flowering. Blackberries should be sprayed when their flowers first open. Unfortunately, this is when bees are active and rotenone kills bees, so spray blackberries with pyrethrum or quassia (see page 53) in the evenings when the bees are in their hives.

SAWFLY

The small, brown, spotted caterpillars of this pest attack leaves and can defoliate a plant within hours.
What to do
Birds, especially robins, will eat sawfly larvae, but they cannot control them totally. As soon as you see the first caterpillar, spray the bush with an insecticide like quassia or pyrethrum.

BIG BUD MITE

This gall mite attacks buds of blackcurrants, causing them to swell. It also carries a virus disease (*see below*). The mites attack the buds in early summer, and migrate to other buds the following spring.
What to do
Check the bushes in late winter and early spring. Remove and destroy big buds.

REVERSION

This virus disease is carried by the big bud mite. It is quite difficult to recognize – the mature leaves are narrower than usual and have less than five pairs of veins on the main lobe. The flower buds become bright magenta in color. The bushes lose their vigor and the yield is reduced.
What to do
There is no cure for this disease. Dig up affected bushes and destroy them.

SPUR BLIGHT

This fungus disease forms silver patches and fruiting bodies on raspberry canes and the briars of hybrid berries. The affected buds will eventually die.
What to do
Meticulous pruning of overcrowded canes should prevent infection. If the disease does occur, spray with copper fungicide when the buds first open and again when the flowers are showing white at the tips.

LEAF SPOT

Brown spots appear on leaves in spring; these spread and the leaf eventually falls off. This affects the vigor and reduces the yield.
What to do
Pick off any affected leaves and destroy them. If the disease persists, spray with copper fungicide at ten-day intervals.

THE HERB GARDEN

HERBS SHOULD ALWAYS BE included in the organic garden, for both practical and aesthetic reasons. They are generally not difficult to grow and most are extremely decorative plants which help attract useful predators to the garden, as well as those insects – such as bees – which are needed for pollination in the fruit garden (*see page 203*). They can be planted around shrubs as a ground cover to aid weed control, in mixed borders, or on their own in a traditional herb garden (*see opposite*). Some of the attractive lower-growing species – such as thyme, rosemary and parsley – are suitable for growing in tubs, window boxes and hanging baskets (*see* Container Gardening, *pages 126-31*). No matter where you choose to grow them, an assortment of herbs will add color and fragrance to the garden.

Most of the herbs I have suggested can be used in the kitchen to add subtle flavors to your food. Some can be made into herbal teas or pot-pourri. Others may be used in home-made cosmetics or as a means of dyeing fabric. Comfrey is an especially useful herb as it provides a fast-growing mulching material and can be made into high-potash liquid manure (*see page 244*). I have suggested a basic selection of herbs, but there are hundreds of different kinds with various culinary and decorative attributes, so you will doubtless want to experiment with others.

Planning a herb garden

It is worth planning a planting scheme on paper before you set about choosing and planting your herbs. In traditional herb gardens, the plants are arranged in formal patterns, with each herb or group of herbs enclosed by a low hedge like box (*Buxus sempervirens*) or lavender (*Lavandula* sp.). The main reason for these, often quite intricate, traditional designs is that most herbs are annuals or perennials, which die down completely in the winter, so you need to make the area look interesting all year round. Of course, herbs can also be grown very successfully in the flower garden and were one of the main constituents of the "real" old cottage gardens (*see page 89*).

Herbs like the variegated sages and the thymes make superb ground-cover plants, swamping weeds and providing a splash of color as well as attracting pollinating insects. It also pays to grow some of the "cultivated" forms of herbs especially for the flower garden. There are, for example, several varieties of giant chives with large, dramatic flowers. There are also golden and variegated balms and some highly attractive colored hops, all of which are as useful in the kitchen as their more commonly grown counterparts.

If you are opting for a traditional herb garden, remember to make the plants accessible by putting in pathways or stepping stones so that each plant can be reached without stepping off the path. Herbs will be harvested more regularly than most other plants, so good access is vital. Locate the herb garden in the sunniest part of the garden. Most herbs originate from the Mediterranean, so they thrive in warm sunshine. The few that prefer a little shade can be planted in the lee of one of the large sun-lovers.

SOIL PREPARATION FOR HERBS

Ideally, the soil in which herbs are grown should be well drained and light though, with good preparation, they will grow happily in heavier soils. Double dig the area (*see page 264*), breaking up the subsoil and working in plenty of well-rotted manure or compost, or one of the alternatives (*see pages 18-34*). Since most herbs like a soil pH of between 7.0 and 7.5, spent mushroom compost is ideal (*see page 30*).

The one thing most herbs cannot abide is bad drainage so, if your soil is wet and heavy and cannot be improved by deep digging or the inclusion of coarse grit and organic matter, it is best to build a raised bed (*see page 37*). If you can, use hard-wearing brick or stone to raise the sides, although wood can also be used. Old railway ties are ideal and they will raise the bed by about 30cm (12in), which is all that is needed.

If you are going to plant out pot-grown plants in the spring or summer, rake in two handfuls of blood, fish and bone meal per square meter/yard, about a fortnight before planting. Use a similar quantity of bone meal alone before planting out herbs in autumn.

SOWING AND PLANTING HERBS
The first essential is to ensure the soil is completely free of weeds. If there is so much as a sprig of ground elder root or a slip of couch grass, it will thrive unnoticed amongst the sprawling herbs. Then the only option is to lift the plants again and thoroughly clean the soil.

If you decide to grow your herbs in a special herb garden, delay planting for a year. Dig the area thoroughly, removing any trace of a weed, then cover the whole area with black plastic, its edges dug into the ground to prevent it blowing away, and leave it for a year.

Before sowing or planting, consider the potential height and spread of each plant, as well as its rate of growth and how much sun it prefers. Some, such as lovage, grow to enormous proportions and are only suitable for the back of a large herb garden. Plants like borage need a great deal of sun, while mint, for example, will thrive in semi-shade; both are fast spreading. Any special planting requirements are described in the individual entries on pages 241-45, and the maximum height of each herb is given overleaf.

MAINTAINING A HERB GARDEN
Feeding A mulch of well-rotted manure or compost applied over the top of the whole garden will maintain fertility. Spread a layer about 5-7.5cm (2-3in) thick in late winter to spring, but guard against slugs (*see page 50*).

Watering Some watering may be necessary in dry weather. Use a sprinkler for at least two hours to ensure that the water permeates through to the lower levels.

Weeding During the early stages of cultivation, it is important to remove weeds by hand. When the plants become established, they will spread and inhibit weeds themselves.

Pruning Some herbs, like lavender and thyme, must be trimmed back after flowering to keep them compact and within bounds. Regular harvesting will keep most herbs in check, but they will all respond well to being cut back from time to time. Mints can become rampant.

Thinning Some herbs need to be watched carefully and self-sown seedlings removed at an early stage. Plants like borage, balm and especially feverfew can completely take over if their seedlings are allowed to grow unchecked.

Propagation Perennial herbs can be lifted and divided (*see page 273*). The ideal time for this is in early to late autumn, though it can also be done in early spring. Propagate the shrubby herbs, like rosemary, bay and lavender, from softwood cuttings in early summer (*see page 274*).

An informal herb garden above
A herb garden can be both decorative and functional. Here, dramatic pink blooms are combined with sage and mint.

Herbs in a cottage garden right
Herbs form an integral part of this traditional walled garden. In the foreground is the perennial lemon balm and a tall bay tree stands beside the wooden bench.

A herb collection

Herbs are easy to grow, decorative and useful plants. They can be made into pot-pourri and used fresh, dried or frozen to add flavor to food. Plant them in the borders, in a special herb garden or in any odd space you have. This is a basic collection of nineteen herbs, but there are many more you could include. Cultivation details are given on pages 240-45.

CHIVES *Allium schoenoprasum*
Fast growing, reaches 20cm (8in). Lilac flowers.
For cultivation details, see page 242 and Perennials, page 115.

BORAGE *Borago officinalis*
Easy to grow, reaches 75cm (2ft 6in). Attracts bees.
For cultivation details, see page 241 and Annuals, page 116.

BALM *Melissa officinalis*
Robust and aromatic, reaches 90cm (3ft). Attracts bees.
For cultivation details, see page 242 and Perennials, page 115.

CHERVIL *Anthriscus cerefolium*
Fast growing, reaches 60cm (2ft). Prefers shade.
For cultivation details, see page 241 and Annuals, page 116.

SPEARMINT *Mentha spicata*
Fast growing, reaches 90cm (3ft). Prefers semi-shade.
For cultivation details, see page 242 and Perennials, page 115.

DILL *Anethum graveolens*
Fast growing, reaches 75cm (2ft 6in) in warm conditions.
For cultivation details, see page 241 and Annuals, page 116.

WINTER SAVORY *Satureia montana*
Evergreen shrub, reaches 30cm (12in). Attracts bees.
For cultivation details, see page 242 and Perennials, page 115.

SWEET BASIL *Ocimum basilicum*
Reaches 60cm (2ft), grown as annual in temperate areas.
For cultivation details, see page 241 and Annuals, page 116.

SORREL *Rumex acetosa*
Broad leaved, reaches 45cm (18in). Prefers semi-shade.
For cultivation details, see page 243 and Perennials, page 115.

Plant type — Tree · Shrub · Perennial · Annual · Biennial · Bulb · Climbing plants
Sun preference — Sun · Partial shade · Shade · Tolerant
Soil preference — Acid · Alkaline · Tolerant

FRENCH TARRAGON *Artemisia dracunculus*

Aromatic, reaches 60-90cm (2-3ft). Subtle flavor.
For cultivation details, see page 243 and Perennials, *page 115.*

FENNEL *Foeniculum vulgare*

Fast growing, reaches 1.5m (5ft). Decorative flowers.
For cultivation details, see page 243 and Perennials, *page 115.*

LOVAGE *Levisticum officinale*

Very tall, reaches 2.5m (8ft). Attractive seed heads.
For cultivation details, see page 243 and Perennials, *page 115.*

POT MARJORAM *Origanum onites*

Reaches 35cm (15in). Other types also grown.
For cultivation details, see page 244 and Perennials, *page 115.*

HORSERADISH *Armoracia rusticana*

Fast growing, reaches 60cm (2ft). Hot-flavored tap root.
For cultivation details, see page 244 and Perennials, *page 115.*

LEMON THYME *Thymus citriodorus*

Evergreen shrub, reaches 20cm (8in). Attracts bees.
For cultivation details, see page 244 and Shrubs, *page 112.*

SAGE *Salvia officinalis*

Hardy shrub, reaches 60cm (2ft). Decorative and aromatic.
For cultivation details, see page 245 and Shrubs, *page 112.*

ROSEMARY *Rosmarinus officinalis*

Aromatic evergreen, reaches 90cm (3ft). Attracts insects.
For cultivation details, see page 245 and Shrubs, *page 112.*

JUNIPER *Juniperus communis*

Tall conifer, reaches 3m (10ft). Blue-black berries.
For cultivation details, see page 245 and Shrubs, *page 112.*

BAY *Laurus nobilis*

Frost tender, reaches 6m (20ft). Prefers semi-shade.
For cultivation details, see page 245 and Shrubs, *page 112.*

Cultivating herbs

The range of plants you grow will depend on personal priorities. You may base your selection on culinary value, decorative qualities, or a combination of these and other factors. However, you must also consider the practicalities of your choice. A young specimen of fennel, for instance, may seem an attractive proposition, but bear in mind it will grow into a bushy plant about 1.5m (5ft) tall. If you wish to grow the tender species, like bay, in a temperate area, they must be planted in pots and brought into a frost-free greenhouse during winter. So, before you buy your seeds or young plants, ensure you can provide the space and conditions needed to grow them successfully.

Attracting pollinating insects *The decorative lilac-pink flowers of thyme attract bees and other insects which are necessary for the pollination of border plants.*

HARVESTING AND STORING HERBS

Many of the herbs in this chapter can be preserved by drying. This enables them to be used throughout the year and can sometimes actually improve the flavor. Pick leaves for drying before the plant flowers to get the best results. Most of the herbs are dried quite simply in the way described below. If a different method is required, this is explained under the relevant herb entry.

1 *The leaves of many herbs, including thyme (shown here), can be harvested fresh throughout the growing season. For drying purposes, though, cut them before the plant comes into flower, and only ever take young, healthy leaves. Do not harvest more stems than you have room to dry immediately, and avoid handling the individual leaves.*

2 *Tie the stems in small bunches and hang them in a dry, airy shed. Do not tie large bunches together as this will slow down the drying process by restricting air circulation. Any damage to the leaves causes essential oils to be lost and has a detrimental effect on the aroma and flavor of the herbs, so be very careful when handling them. Crumble the dried leaves into an airtight jar.*

3 *If you wish to save the seeds, harvest stems just as the seeds ripen and hang them upside down in small bunches, in a dry, airy shed. Place a cloth or bowl beneath the hanging plants to catch the seeds as they fall. Apart from the seeds used in cooking – such as lovage (shown here) – remember to save those of annual herbs for sowing the following year.*

Borage

This hardy annual will freely seed itself each year. The arching sprays of deep-blue flowers make borage worth growing in the border for its decorative value alone, but it is also an excellent bee attractor.

SOIL AND SITE

Borage prefers a sunny, open position and will not do well in shade. It is tolerant of a wide range of soil conditions.

SOWING

Sow seeds in the open ground in mid spring and thin to 35cm (15in) apart. The herb will die down in the autumn after seeding itself, and the seedlings will grow the following year. Remove any seedlings that start to grow where they are not wanted.

MAINTENANCE

This herb needs no further encouragement to grow well, but it will need regular trimming to keep it in check.

HARVESTING AND STORING

Pick young leaves during the summer. They freeze successfully but do not dry well. The flowers can be crystallized by painting them with egg-white and then dipping them in caster sugar.

Chervil

This self-seeding hardy annual is not a very attractive herb, looking rather like a weedy version of parsley, but it is one of the most useful in the kitchen. It has a spicy, aniseed flavor.

SOIL AND SITE

It is essential that you give chervil a shaded position in moist soil, or it will run to seed as soon as the sun shines.

SOWING

Sow seeds in early or mid spring, 23cm (9in) apart. Either allow them to reseed themselves, thinning to 23cm (9in), or let one or two plants run to seed, harvest the seeds then resow in late summer or early autumn. These late sowings will have to be covered with cloches (see page 140) to protect them against the cold in all but the mildest areas.

MAINTENANCE

Keep the plants well watered in dry weather and pick off flowers as they form, to delay seeding until the last flush of flowering.

HARVESTING AND STORING

Take fresh leaves from the outside of the plants to encourage continued production from the centers. The leaves can be frozen or dried (see opposite).

Dill

This attractive hardy annual may sometimes seed itself but, in cold areas, it is worth saving seed for resowing. Its feathery leaves and delicate yellow flowers make dill a suitable plant for the border, and it is also a widely used culinary herb.

SOIL AND SITE

A well-drained soil and sunny position will suit dill best.

SOWING AND PLANTING

Sow seeds in short rows 30cm (12in) apart outside in mid spring, and thin the plants to 30cm (12in) apart. Make a single sowing if you only require the seeds but, for leaves, sow successively at monthly intervals until mid summer. If you buy plants or grow them in pots, plant them out 30cm (12in) apart. Do not sow dill near fennel (see page 243) as the two may cross-pollinate.

MAINTENANCE

Keep plants free from weeds and well watered in dry weather.

HARVESTING AND STORING

Pick fresh leaves as they are required. The leaves and the seeds can be dried and stored as described opposite.

Basil

Basil is grown as a perennial in warm climates, and an annual in areas where it is liable to get killed by frost. There are two types: sweet and bush. Sweet basil is taller, has larger leaves and a better flavor.

SOIL AND SITE

Plant basil in a sunny, sheltered place in the best possible soil.

SOWING AND PLANTING

Sow in small pots inside in early spring. Harden off in a cold frame (see page 256) and plant out 30cm (12in) apart when all danger of frost has passed.

MAINTENANCE

Keep the plants well watered at all times and pinch off the flower buds as they appear, to maintain the rate of growth.

HARVESTING AND STORING

Harvest the fresh leaves throughout the summer. Leaves can be dried in the sun and stored in airtight jars, but will not be as flavorsome as when fresh. They can also be frozen. (w/ olive oil)

Parsley

There are several varieties of this popular herb: the crisp type (Petroselinum crispum) or the plain-leaved "Italian" parsley are generally grown. They are biennials, but should be grown as annuals to prevent seeding at the end of the first year. The plants grow up to a maximum height of about 30cm (12in).

SOIL AND SITE

Parsley prefers some shade and a soil enriched with well-rotted manure or compost.

SOWING

Sow an early crop inside in late winter and transfer to the open ground in mid spring, planting out seedlings 15cm (6in) apart. Alternatively, sow direct outside in mid spring and again in mid summer for a continuous supply. You can also sow another mid summer crop in pots for growing inside during the winter. The seeds take a long time to germinate, so be prepared to wait for signs of growth. Leaf harvest can extend into autumn and winter.

MAINTENANCE

There is little to do except remove weeds and water during dry weather.

HARVESTING AND STORING

Cut the leaves as and when they are required, but do not completely defoliate plants to allow them to regrow. Leaves can be dried quickly in a warm oven or frozen in ice-cubes.

Chives

This well-known and much valued hardy perennial herb makes an attractive border edging because of its distinctive globular flowers. The fresh leaves are usually chopped over potato or egg dishes or in cheeses. The bulbs can also be pickled in wine vinegar. There are several different forms that have great decorative merit.

SOIL AND SITE

Chives have no specific light requirements, but prefer moist soil conditions.

SOWING AND PLANTING

Sow seeds outside 30cm (12in) apart, in early spring. Alternatively, divide established plants and plant divisions 30cm (12in) apart in spring or autumn.

MAINTENANCE

Lift the clumps every three years in early or mid autumn, divide them with a knife and replant them in fresh soil as described for all perennials (*see page 273*). If you want to keep the plants in the same place, lift them, heel them into a spare piece of land (*see page 113*), dig over the soil – incorporating well-rotted manure or compost – and replant.

HARVESTING AND STORING

The plants thrive on being cut back, so cut off the leaves with scissors to leave about 1cm ($\frac{1}{2}$in). They can be frozen into ice-cubes, but do not dry well.

Balm

This perennial herb has a pleasant lemon flavor and can be planted in the flower border to attract bees to the garden. Decorative variegated and yellow varieties are available.

SOIL AND SITE

Balm prefers a water-retentive soil enriched with organic matter. Plant it in a sunny or semi-shaded place, as the leaves tend to blanch in deep shade.

SOWING AND PLANTING

Sow seeds outside in mid or late spring, 45cm (18in) apart, or divide established plants and plant at the same distances.

MAINTENANCE

Keep plants trimmed back to maintain the bushy habit and retain the color of variegated and yellow varieties. Lift and divide established plants every three years (*see page 273*).

HARVESTING AND STORING

Cut fresh leaves throughout the summer. Balm leaves do not dry well, but they can be frozen in plastic bags or in ice-cubes.

Mint

There are several types of mint, but apple mint and spearmint are best for cooking. Apple mint is perhaps preferable as it has some resistance to mint-rust disease. Mint is a hardy perennial and easy to grow, though it can also be invasive.

SOIL AND SITE

Mint will grow very well in practically any soil, but prefers a semi-shaded position.

STORING MINT

As an alternative to potting up mint, you can store the herb to ensure a fresh winter supply.

1 *Dig up a clump of mint and carefully remove a few sprigs with roots. Replant the remainder.*

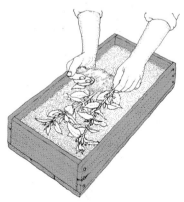

2 *Put a layer of moist compost in a wooden box. Lay the sprigs in the box and cover them with more compost.*

PLANTING

Plant root cuttings taken in autumn (*see page 274*). Mint is very invasive indeed, so plant it in a bucket or plastic tub sunk in the ground so that the rim of the bucket is above the soil level to prevent shoots rooting in over the edge. Plant it 60cm (2ft) away from other herbs.

MAINTENANCE

Mint needs little encouragement to grow. Water in dry weather and pick regularly to keep the plants in check.

HARVESTING AND STORING

Pick freely throughout spring and summer. At the end of the season, dig up a few roots and put them in pots in the greenhouse to ensure a supply of fresh mint during winter. This makes drying unnecessary. The leaves freeze well in ice-cubes or can be stored in moist compost (*see left*).

Savory

There are two types: summer savory is a rather floppy annual, while winter savory is a more erect perennial evergreen shrub. Both can be grown in the herb garden or the border, where they will attract bees.

SOIL AND SITE

Both types prefer a sunny position and a well-drained soil rich in organic matter.

SOWING AND PLANTING

Sow summer savory direct outside in mid or late spring, 15cm (6in) apart. Sow plenty, because the yield of each plant is not high. Increase the winter variety by taking cuttings (*see Softwood cuttings, page 274*) during summer, or by sowing seeds outside in late summer. Space the plants 45cm (18in) apart.

MAINTENANCE

Summer savory requires little attention except weeding and watering. Winter savory can become leggy, so keep pinching back – removing the top growth to encourage shoots at the base of the plant. In really cold weather, protect plants against frost by covering with cloches (*see page 140*). Replace savory plants every three to five years.

HARVESTING AND STORING

Pick leaves from summer savory throughout the season for immediate use and, for drying, just as the plant starts to flower. You can pick winter savory leaves fresh throughout the year.

Sorrel

There are two types of sorrel: the broad-leaved type shown on page 238, and the French variety. The latter has smaller leaves and is slightly lower growing than broad-leaved sorrel. Both are hardy perennials. Sorrel has a sharp taste, so use it sparingly.

SOIL AND SITE

Sorrel prefers partial shade and a moist soil enriched with plenty of organic matter.

SOWING AND PLANTING

The herb can be raised from seed but takes a long time to mature, so you may prefer to obtain an established root. Plant seeds or roots outside in the autumn about 30cm (12in) apart.

MAINTENANCE

Remove the flower heads as soon as they appear, to delay seeding until the final flush. Keep the plants weed free and make sure they never go short of water. Sorrel tends to deteriorate after a while, so lift, divide and replant the outer young offsets every three years (*see page 273*).

HARVESTING AND STORING

Pick fresh leaves throughout the season. The plants can be picked over quite hard and they will soon regenerate. Dry the leaves as shown below, and store them in airtight jars. They do not freeze well unless you make them into a purée first.

Drying sorrel *Lay fresh leaves flat on a wire cake tray. To hasten the drying process, ensure they are well spaced so air can circulate freely around each leaf.*

Tarragon

There are two types of tarragon: French shown on page 239 and Russian. Both are hardy perennials, though the Russian variety is more vigorous and hardy but has little, if any, flavor. Tarragon is a very useful culinary herb but only if you can obtain the French variety.

SOIL AND SITE

A sunny, sheltered position and good drainage are essential.

SOWING AND PLANTING

French tarragon cannot be grown from seed, so buy young plants and space them 45cm (18in) apart. Mature plants can be divided in spring (*see page 273*). Russian tarragon can easily be raised from seed sown 60cm (2ft) apart in spring.

MAINTENANCE

Weed and water as required. In winter, French tarragon in particular will need protecting from frost, so mulch with a light layer of straw or bracken. Lift, divide and replant both types of tarragon every four years to retain vigor and because the flavor of the leave deteriorates as the plant matures.

HARVESTING AND STORING

Pick fresh leaves throughout the season. The leaves can be preserved in bottles of vinegar. Simply rinse off before using. Use the vinegar on salads.

Fennel

Not to be confused with Florence fennel, which is grown for its swollen stem bases (*see page 181*), this is a vigorous hardy perennial herb. Fennel is a tall, stately plant with finely divided, feathery green leaves and bright-yellow flowers that will enhance the flower borders. A red-leaved variety is also available. The leaves and seeds both have a pleasant aniseed taste.

SOIL AND SITE

Fennel requires a fertile soil and plenty of sunshine.

SOWING AND PLANTING

Sow seeds 60cm (2ft) apart, in autumn or spring. Alternatively,

plant young plants or divided clumps in mid spring or autumn, 60cm (2ft) apart.

MAINTENANCE

Keep the plants trimmed down to provide a succession of young leaves, but allow some flowering heads to provide seeds. Keep fennel away from coriander, caraway and dill to avoid cross-pollination. Lift, divide and replant established plants every three years (*see page 273*).

HARVESTING AND STORING

Harvest fresh leaves as required. They can also be dried but tend to lose much of their flavor. Hang the plants up to dry the flower heads and collect the seeds as described on page 240.

Lovage

A shrubby, hardy perennial that dies down each year, lovage grows extremely tall and needs a lot of space, so is therefore best suited to the back of a large herb garden. It can also be used in the borders, since its foliage, large seed heads and clusters of yellow flowers are very attractive. All parts of the plant have a strong flavor, so experiment with the herb carefully.

SOIL AND SITE

Lovage will tolerate partial shade, but does better in a sunny location. It needs a moist soil with plenty of organic matter dug in.

SOWING AND PLANTING

Sow seeds in spring or plant divided clumps in early spring or autumn. You will probably only need one plant but, if you do plant more than one, set the plants 90cm (3ft) apart. Lovage dies down almost completely each winter.

MAINTENANCE

This herb needs no further encouragement to grow vigorously. It will reach full size in approximately four years. Lift, divide and replant established plants (*see page 273*).

HARVESTING AND STORING

Harvest the fresh leaves throughout the season. They can be dried as described on page 240.

Marjoram

Wild and pot marjoram are both hardy perennials, but sweet marjoram – the most flavorsome and aromatic of the three – is hardy only in warm areas and must be grown as a half-hardy annual elsewhere. All can be used widely in the kitchen.

SOIL AND SITE

All types of marjoram grow best in a sunny position. They prefer a well-drained soil but dislike dryness at the roots, so work in plenty of well-rotted organic matter before planting.

SOWING AND PLANTING

Plant young plants or divided clumps of wild and pot marjoram about 30cm (12in) apart. In temperate climates, sow sweet marjoram inside in early spring and plant out 20cm (8in) apart after all danger of frost has passed. In warmer areas, treat it like wild and pot marjoram, which can be sown directly outside in the spring.

MAINTENANCE

Pinch out regularly to ensure bushy, compact plants. Keep the plants weed free and water if necessary. Pot marjoram can be potted at the end of the summer and brought inside where it will continue to grow. Lift, divide and replant the perennials every three years (*see page 273*).

HARVESTING AND STORING

Pick fresh leaves from early summer onwards. Sweet marjoram dries well and its flavor will strengthen with drying (*see page 240*). However, with a supply of fresh leaves all summer and more from potted plants in winter, you may not consider it worthwhile. All types will also freeze well.

Horseradish

This vigorous hardy perennial is grown for its hot-flavored root. The name of the herb derives from "coarse radish".

SOIL AND SITE

Horseradish likes a rich soil and a sunny or semi-shaded position. If you want a large crop, the best way is to grow plants in a raised bed on a concrete path, raising the soil about 60cm (2ft) high (*see page 37*). That way you can be sure of containing the roots. Horseradish is a tap root, which means it is capable of reproducing from any small piece of the root left in the ground. It is very persistent if not kept in check.

PLANTING

Buy some roots, take cuttings about 15cm (6in) long, and plant them vertically 30cm (12in) apart in early spring.

MAINTENANCE

This herb needs no encouragement to grow vigorously.

HARVESTING AND STORING

Dig up the whole plant each year to prevent it overrunning the garden. Store the roots in boxes of damp sand or peat in a shed until required. Save some for replanting in spring.

Comfrey

This prolific perennial herb is a useful crop to cultivate as compost material. The foliage is very rich in potassium and contains some trace elements. English and Russian varieties are grown.

SOIL AND SITE

Comfrey prefers a soil rich in organic matter, a shady position and damp conditions.

SOWING AND PLANTING

Comfrey can be grown from seed but takes a long time to mature. It is better to buy an established plant and remove offsets from the outside of the root each autumn. Plant these 90cm (3ft) apart.

MAINTENANCE

This herb needs no further encouragement to grow vigorously. Lift, divide and replant clumps every three years (*see page 273*).

HARVESTING AND STORING

Cut the leaves with shears as required. To make a liquid manure high in potash, steep leaves of the Russian variety in a bucket and dilute the resulting liquid by about 10:1. The leaves – which can grow up to 30cm (12in) long – and the pretty, bell-shaped flowers can also be used for dyeing; they produce a yellow or orange color.

Thyme

There are several low- and high-growing varieties of thyme which make decorative garden plants and will attract pollinating insects. They can be used as edging for borders or as ground cover. Common and lemon thyme are the two most generally used in the kitchen.

SOIL AND SITE

Thyme likes a sunny position and well-drained soil. It prefers a soil pH of about 7.0, so add lime to neutralize acid soil if necessary (*see page 36*).

SOWING AND PLANTING

Common thyme can easily be raised from seed sown in mid spring outside, and both types from cuttings taken during summer, or by division (*see pages 273-4*). Thyme is often bought in pots, which can be planted out at any time. Sow or plant about 30cm (12in) apart. The plants will spread considerably, so plant them further apart if you are prepared to wait for ground cover a little longer.

MAINTENANCE

Pinch out regularly to prevent the plants becoming leggy (*see below*) and cut them back hard after flowering.

HARVESTING AND STORING

Pick the leaves fresh throughout the season, though this is one of the few herbs whose leaves have more flavor dry than fresh. Cut the sprigs before flowering and dry them in an airy shed, as described on page 240.

Pinching out thyme *You can encourage bushy growth and keep the plants compact by regularly pinching out the growing tips between your index finger and thumb.*

Sage

This is a hardy shrub that makes an attractive addition to the borders. It has pretty, velvety-gray and blue flowers. Several variegated forms and flowering cultivars are worth growing for their decorative qualities alone, but sage is also widely used as a culinary herb.

SOIL AND SITE
Sage likes a sunny position and a well-drained soil, so dig in plenty of organic matter (*see page 20*). Add grit to heavy soils to further improve drainage.

SOWING AND PLANTING
Sage can be grown from seed sown in spring, but often does not breed true. Alternatively, you can buy sage plants in containers or as bare-rooted shrubs and these should be planted 60cm (2ft) apart. It is also easy to propagate sage by layering (*see below and page 275*). Plants raised in this way can be potted up or re-planted in spring. A third option is to take softwood cuttings in early summer.

MAINTENANCE
Pinch back shoots as they grow to keep the plant compact. If shoots do get leggy, they can be layered as described below and left in place.

HARVESTING AND STORING
Pick young fresh leaves through-out the summer. These can be dried in an airy shed (*see page 240*), though they must be picked before flowering or the flavor will be impaired.

Layering sage *Peg down some shoots into the soil. When new roots develop at the point of contact, cut the shoots away from the parent plant.*

Rosemary

This attractive evergreen shrub makes a fine plant for the border, where its aromatic blue flowers attract insects. It is not winter-hardy in cold climates.

SOIL AND SITE
Rosemary prefers a sunny position and well-drained soil enriched with organic matter. Lighten heavy soils by incor-porating coarse grit (*see page 16*).

PLANTING
Plant container-grown plants at any time, setting them 60-90cm (2-3ft) apart. You can grow them from cuttings taken in early summer (*see page 274*). Rosemary can also be used for hedging, in which case the individual plants should be spaced closer together, with 45cm (18in) between them.

MAINTENANCE
Trim back the plants after flow-ering or the bushes will become leggy and will sprawl. Once they do, it is best to replace them.

HARVESTING AND STORING
This evergreen plant will provide fresh leaves all the year round, so there is really no point in pre-serving them. However, if you don't want to waste the prunings, dry them in an airy shed and crumble them into airtight jars (*see page 240*).

Juniper

This shrubby conifer has silvery-gray foliage which is aromatic when crushed. It needs plenty of room in the garden, and both male and female plants are needed to produce berries. Juni-per makes a good background for other plants and can be kept in check by clipping.

SOIL AND SITE
A sunny position will give the berries a fuller flavor. The plant likes a soil pH of about 7.0, so add lime if necessary (*see page 36*). A well-manured soil ensures rapid establishment.

SOWING AND PLANTING
Sow seeds outside in late winter or plant young plants or soft-wood cuttings (*see page 274*) in early summer.

MAINTENANCE
Make sure the plants are weeded, and fed with blood, fish and bone meal in late winter. Clip them in late summer if necessary.

HARVESTING AND STORING
Pick the berries when they are fully ripe, plump and black. They can be frozen, or dried on open trays at room temperature. It is important to dry them very slowly. When they are shrivelled and have lost their moisture, store them in airtight jars.

Bay

Bay is a frost-tender tree, so can only be grown in the soil in warm areas. Elsewhere, grow it in a tub and bring it inside in winter. Bay resembles laurel (*Kalmia* sp.), which is poisonous to eat, but it can be identified by its charac-teristic pungent smell, while laurel is practically odorless.

SOIL AND SITE
Bay prefers a dry, semi-shaded position. If you grow plants in tubs, use the soil-based compost recommended on page 252.

PLANTING
You can buy trees in containers or plant softwood cuttings taken in early summer (*see page 274*). One plant is all that is needed.

MAINTENANCE
Make sure the trees have ade-quate water at all times. Bay trees can be left to grow naturally or clipped into various shapes. If you choose to train your trees, regularly pinch out the tips of shoots that grow out of place during the summer to maintain the shape of the head.

Plants growing in tubs must be watered regularly. Let the top of the soil dry right out before rewatering and never let the pots become waterlogged. Feed once a month during the summer with liquid manure. In areas affected by frost, bring the tubs in for the winter or, if you leave them out-side, wrap the container in bur-lap and cover the top with a sheet of woven polypropylene.

HARVESTING AND STORING
Pick fresh leaves during the sum-mer. They can be dried in the sun and stored in airtight jars.

GREENHOUSE GARDENING

A GREENHOUSE IS A VERY useful addition to any garden. The major advantage of owning one is that it enables you to sow and harvest crops months earlier than would otherwise be possible in temperate or cold areas. The growing season is therefore considerably extended, which makes it possible to increase annual yields substantially. Indeed, with careful planning, certain crops can be harvested continuously, and many frost-tender plants can be "overwintered" – kept in the greenhouse during the winter months to protect them from the cold. A greenhouse therefore turns the cultivation of plants into a year-round activity.

The warmth and light provided by the greenhouse also make it possible for you to raise a great many plants from seed. Their growth will be much stronger and healthier than any you manage to raise on a very sunny windowsill in the house, where no more than fifty per cent of available light will actually reach the plants. By starting off young plants in the best possible environment, you can ensure that the seedlings are in peak condition when you plant them outside. Growing from seed allows you to choose any crop or variety you wish, rather than relying solely on the range of comparatively expensive young plants offered by a nursery. Provided you buy seed that has not been "dressed" with a fungicide, you can also be certain that your crops are completely untainted by chemicals.

A further benefit of greenhouse gardening is the opportunity of cultivating tender plants that can normally be grown outside only in sub-tropical or tropical conditions. This applies to many vegetable and fruit crops (*see pages 132-97 and 202-31*) as well as exotic decorative plants. Even if you garden in a warm climate, the relatively high temperature provided by a greenhouse increases the range of plants you can grow. In addition, the quality and yield of some crops, such as tomatoes and eggplants, which can be grown outside in temperate climates, will improve if they are cultivated in the greenhouse where they are protected from adverse weather conditions.

Always allow for a greenhouse in your plan (*see pages 72-3*) if you possibly can. The increased choice, quality and quantity of the plants you can grow in a greenhouse more than repays the initial cost, and the space taken up could not be put to better use. Bear in mind that it needs a sunny position and try to site it fairly close to the house, to make the connection of heating, water and electricity supplies easier and more economical.

Choosing a greenhouse

Greenhouses come in an assortment of shapes, sizes and materials. Of course, the appearance of the structure is important, but practicality should be the first consideration. There are many factors that will affect your choice and it is difficult to lay down strict guidelines. For example, conservatories (*see opposite*) are becoming increasingly popular. Despite the fact that they do not admit as much light as conventional greenhouses, and are therefore less efficient, they take up less space and are generally cheaper and more convenient to heat. Each person's priorities are different, so check the advantages and disadvantages of each greenhouse carefully before deciding which to buy.

SIZE
Even a tiny greenhouse can accommodate a large quantity of plants and produce, especially if you use it in conjunction with a cold frame or even with cloches (*see pages 254 and 140*). Buy the biggest you can afford, or consider one designed to take additional sections at a later date because, in my experience, a greenhouse of any size will always be full. If you cannot heat it all, a large greenhouse can easily be divided.

GREENHOUSE SHAPES

There are many different shapes of greenhouses available, ranging from the traditional rectangular structure to a modern, multi-faceted dome. You must balance the aesthetic and practical advantages and disadvantages of each. Whichever type you prefer, always ensure that the height to the eaves is sufficient to make working in the greenhouse comfortable, and that the design of the structure will not restrict the range of plants you wish to grow.

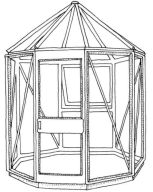

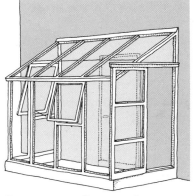

Traditional *The standard rectangular "barn" shape has four vertical sides and a span roof with a central ridge. It is a very popular and practical design, and enables you to make the best possible use of the available space. The walls may be glass or timbered to staging level.*

Circular *Round or lantern-shaped greenhouses usually have six, nine or twelve sides and are one of the most attractive designs. The working space inside is usually fairly limited, but they are very useful for small gardens.*

Conservatory *Conservatories, or "lean-to" greenhouses, also serve as an additional room in the house. Their location makes heating and regular plant care convenient, but means that light levels are reduced as light can only enter from three sides.*

MATERIALS

Greenhouse frames are usually made of aluminum or wood. Aluminum houses let in more light because the glazing bars can be thinner. This is important if you garden in a comparatively cold area, where light levels are low in the early spring. Wooden houses are perhaps slightly cheaper to heat, because the wood itself is warmer, and they certainly look more attractive. However, the wood must be painted regularly to protect it against decay – unless you choose cedar, which is particularly weather-resistant. Never use creosote as a greenhouse preservative as it gives off fumes toxic to plants.

Although glass is the most commonly used material for the walls and roof, greenhouses can also be made from sheet polyethylene stretched over metal hoops or a greenhouse-shaped frame. This is considerably cheaper than using glass, even though the material has to be replaced every couple of years.

VENTILATION

In order to maintain the best possible growing conditions, it is vital that the temperature inside the greenhouse can be accurately controlled. This is achieved by regulating the passage of air through vents in the roof or sides of the structure. Ensure that any house you choose has an adequate number of vents. A 2×2.5m (6×8ft) greenhouse should have at least two roof vents, and there should be proportionally more in larger houses. Plastic greenhouses can be difficult to ventilate. The plastic generates a great deal of condensation and it is impractical to install adjustable ventilation panels. Permanent ventilation has to be installed instead: plastic greenhouses up to about 3×8m (10×25ft) should have an open-mesh panel in the door; larger ones should have a mesh "skirt" running along the base of each side. This reduces condensation and allows the free passage of air in and out of the greenhouse. However, it also makes it impossible to control the temperature, so plastic greenhouses can only be used for crops which need no extra heating.

Using alternative materials *Polyethylene greenhouses have excellent light transmission qualities. They are usually reserved for crops that need no supplementary heating, but are valuable as "walk-in cloches" (see page 140). Although comparatively cheap, the plastic must be replaced regularly.*

THE GREENHOUSE

Whatever type of greenhouse you have, it will provide you with the space and environment to extend your gardening activities. Certain features will be included in the greenhouse you buy and others can be added, together with basic equipment, to enable you to get the best from it.

Shading Special compounds can be painted on to the outside of the glass in summer.

Ventilation Panels in the roof and walls control greenhouse temperatures.

Insulation Sheets of bubble polyethylene can be used to help prevent heat loss.

Capillary mat Plants can be watered automatically using absorbent matting.

Measuring temperature A maximum/minimum thermometer has two small markers which are forced up or down by the movement of the mercury and record the highest and lowest temperatures reached during a specific period. The thermometer is reset so a daily record can be maintained. The difference between the two extremes should be kept as small as possible.

Blinds These protect against sun scorch in hot weather.

A permanent water supply Keep a tank of water inside the greenhouse, under the staging if space is limited. Refill it after watering each day, so the water is always at greenhouse temperature.

Propagator Seeds can be germinated in a specially heated container.

Watering can Use a fine nozzle attachment when watering delicate seedlings.

Raising seedlings After germination, seedlings are grown in trays and pots on the greenhouse staging.

Greenhouse borders Many crops, such as lettuce, can be grown to maturity in the greenhouse borders.

Storage space The space below the staging is used to store greenhouse equipment.

Hot bed Fresh straw horse manure is used as an organic means of heating the soil around plants growing in the borders.

Staging Many greenhouse plants are cultivated on waist-high benches made from wood or aluminum. These raise the plants up nearer to the light, ensuring healthy growth.

Heating A variety of permanent and portable systems are available.

Potting bench Use a portable bench for messy jobs such as repotting.

Growing bags A range of plants can be grown in self-contained beds.

MAKING YOUR OWN STAGING

Ready-made staging is often included in the price of a greenhouse, or it can be bought separately from most manufacturers. A cheap and easy alternative is to make your own.

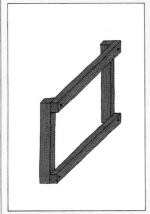

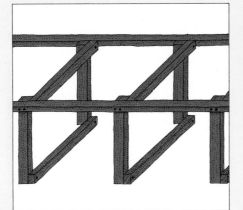

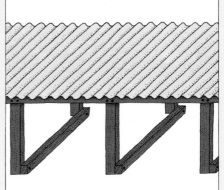

1 *Using 7.5×5cm (3× 2in) timber, make a series of rectangular frames for the "legs". Cut the wood to convenient lengths and join them with steel bolts, as shown here.*

2 *Space the "legs" about 1m (3ft) apart and bolt long wooden rails to the back and front of each to secure them. The staging will have to support a lot of weight, so it is important to ensure the basic framework is strong.*

3 *Fix a sheet of corrugated iron or aluminum on to the base and cover this with a layer of sand, which can be kept moist to supply the plants with water. Alternatively, make a lighter top with 3mm (⅛in) marine quality plywood and cover this with a sheet of capillary matting (see page 255).*

WORK SURFACES

In large commercial greenhouses, the high light levels mean that plants can be grown satisfactorily on the floor. But in a small greenhouse, and especially one that has a wooden or brick wall around the base, plants must be lifted up towards the light to avoid leggy growth. The raised surfaces on which many greenhouse plants are grown are collectively known as "staging". This consists of aluminum or timber benches, about 1m (3ft) high, with a maximum width of 1m (3ft) (*see above*).

Heating a greenhouse

The amount of heat you are prepared to use in the greenhouse will determine the range of plants you can grow in it. Even in an unheated greenhouse, yields will always be considerably earlier and therefore often heavier than from plants grown outside. However, in temperate climates, frost-tender plants can only be kept in a "cold" greenhouse from four to six weeks before the last frost is expected.

If you decide to provide just enough heat to keep frost at bay, the greenhouse becomes much more of an asset. Half-hardy perennials like fuchsias and geraniums can be housed over the winter, and tender plants can be planted much earlier than would otherwise be possible.

You can, theoretically, grow tropical plants in even the coldest area – as long as you provide enough heat. However, in practice, this is likely to be prohibitively expensive.

CONTROLLING TEMPERATURES

When heating your greenhouse, it is vital to keep a check on the temperature. The important statistics to know are the minimum temperature at night and the maximum reached during the day. To grow plants well, the variation between the two figures should be no more than about 10°C (18°F). However, if left to its own devices, the daily temperature variation in a closed greenhouse can be up to 35°C (64°F) in the spring. Such a fluctuation can be disastrous for young seedlings, so use a maximum/minimum thermometer to record the daily extremes of temperature, and try – by careful ventilation (*see page 247*) and heating adjustment – to even out the differences as much as possible.

Reducing heating costs

Unless you specialize in growing temperature-sensitive plants, it is not normally necessary to heat the greenhouse to high temperatures for more than a few months of the year. Even then, you will want to keep your costs as low as you can. Locate the house in a bright place so it can

METHODS OF HEATING

Connecting your greenhouse heating to a mains supply is initially expensive but more economical in the long run than using portable heaters. Most modern heaters, whether permanent or portable, are thermostatically controlled, so the temperature can be kept at a constant level.

Solid fuel
Various forms of solid fuel can be used to heat water pipes in the greenhouse. Coal, the most commonly used material, is cheap and efficient. However, it requires a considerable capital outlay for the boiler and the necessary piping. Frequent refuelling is also necessary.

Gas
Heating with gas is more expensive than using solid fuel, but very convenient. It can either be bought in portable propane or butane gas cylinders or piped to the greenhouse via the normal household supply.

Either way is efficient, since gas can be controlled with a thermostat and constant refuelling is not necessary. However, it requires a fairly large capital outlay and can emit fumes harmful to plants.

Oil and kerosene
The cost of heating with oil is liable to fluctuate frequently. A small kerosene heater requires very little capital outlay but thermostatic control is difficult and heaters can emit fumes harmful to plants. As with solid fuel, portable kerosene heaters require frequent refuelling. The wick must be adjusted according to the weather conditions and trimmed regularly to avoid the emission of harmful fumes.

Electricity
Using electricity is now one of the cheapest options, and certainly the most convenient. Capital outlay is not high and temperature control is very accurate (and therefore cost-effective). Portable fan or convection heaters keep the air in the greenhouse circulating well. Make sure the initial wiring of a permanent system is professionally installed as special waterproofing of the equipment is essential.

benefit from as much free solar heat as possible and, if you can also provide shelter from strong winds, do so. Inside the greenhouse, insulate to prevent heat loss and ensure you are heating the minimum area required.

USING A PROPAGATOR
A propagator helps reduce heating costs by restricting the area to which heat has to be supplied. Propagators are enclosed cases which contain some form of built-in heating element, and are used for germinating seeds at the start of the season. You can buy them or make your own (*see below*). A small container will accommodate all the seeds required by most gardens, and

a steady temperature of 18-21°C (65-70°F) can be provided to ensure rapid germination.

HEATING THE SOIL
Heating the roots of plants reduces the need to heat the air around them. Plants that grow in pots on the staging are usually heated from below, as heating is generally located low down, around the greenhouse walls or on the floor. However, those plants that grow in the borders do not receive the benefit of the rising warm air. A simple way to overcome this is to install an electric soil-heating cable, which will warm the root areas directly (*see below*). Alternatively, you can make a hot bed (*see page 253*).

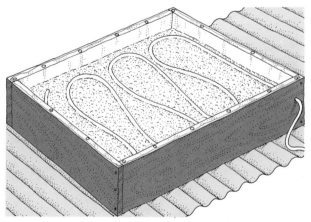

Using a home-made propagator *This simple propagator is very efficient and cheap to run. The timber case has been lined with plastic and filled with expanded polystyrene granules to retain heat. It has a clear perspex lid for maximum light transmission. One way of heating the propagator is with boiling water (left). Every morning and evening, the water is poured into a small can which stands inside a larger one in the center of the case. Alternatively, you can use an electric heating cable (above). This is installed in serpentine fashion between layers of polystyrene granules and connected to the mains supply through a hole in the box. Electric cables can also be used to heat the soil in the greenhouse borders.*

USING POLYETHYLENE INSIDE THE GREENHOUSE

Once the seedlings raised in the propagator are big enough to transfer to wider spacings in the trays, you need more room, though not usually the whole greenhouse. If you can manage with part of it, divide the greenhouse with a polyethylene curtain so that you only heat a small area.

The roof and sides can be lined with plastic sheeting too, to keep in the heat. The best material to use is bubble plastic, which consists of thousands of air-filled bubbles, so it acts as a double insulator.

Plastic sheeting of any kind reduces the amount of light admitted to the greenhouse quite considerably. Unfortunately, the insulation it provides is needed at the time of year when the light levels are most critical. Young seedlings need all the light they can get, and in the early spring the levels are low. One way to overcome this problem is with a "thermal screen" (*see below*) which can be drawn at night to retain the heat when it is most needed, and pulled back to admit light during the day.

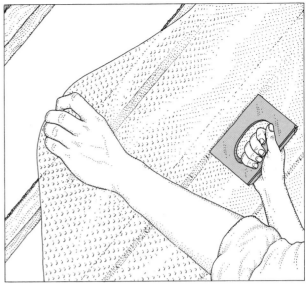

Insulating the greenhouse *You can cut heating costs by covering the inside of the greenhouse with bubble plastic, which is cheap and easy to use. Fix it to the greenhouse frame with staples or special clips, so that about 2.5cm (1in) of air is trapped between the plastic and the glass. Provided it is fitted correctly, bubble plastic insulation can cut heat loss by between 40 and 50 per cent.*

MAKING A THERMAL SCREEN

Dividing a heated greenhouse with a plastic screen that can be moved back and forth enables you to provide maximum sunlight during the day and save money by cutting heat loss at night.

1 *Run a length of wire along either side of the greenhouse, about 30cm (12in) from the sides, and at the height of the eaves. The wire will have to bear the weight of the screen, so make sure it is attached securely to the frame of the greenhouse.*

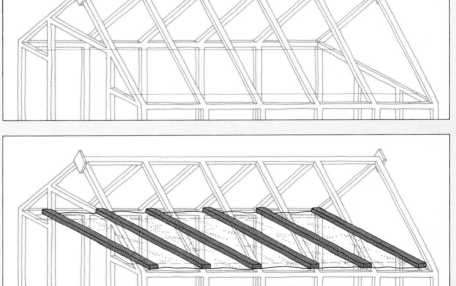

2 *Measure the length and width of the greenhouse and cut a large sheet of plastic to the same size. Cut some thin pieces of wood slightly narrower than the greenhouse. Fix these across the plastic at regular intervals, using glue or tacks, and position the sheet so it rests on the wires.*

3 *Pull the thermal screen towards the door at night and push it back again first thing in the morning – as soon after sunrise as possible, to avoid wasting valuable daylight hours.*

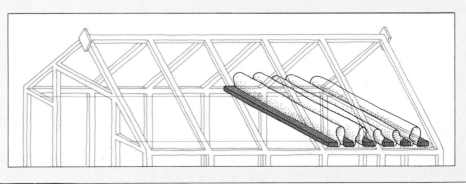

Caring for greenhouse plants

Plants grown in the greenhouse have different requirements from those cultivated outside and will need much more attention. As well as providing adequate ventilation and heating (*see pages 247 and 249*), you must feed and water regularly, decide on the most suitable growing medium, provide the necessary humidity, and keep the house clean (*see page 255*) in order to discourage pests and diseases.

Choosing potting mixtures

A number of organic potting or seed mixtures are commercially available, most consisting of peat mixed with animal manure, worm-worked material or seaweed. It is rather difficult to advise on proprietary media because they vary greatly. Trial and error is the only possible way to evaluate them so, once you have found a mixture that suits you and your plants, I recommend you stick with it.

MAKING SOIL-BASED POTTING MIXTURES

As an alternative to proprietary composts, it is quite possible to make your own. I have grown perfectly good plants in pure sphagnum peat moss, with the addition of 30g (1oz) of Dolomite lime (*see page 36*) to every 9-liter (2-gallon) bucket of the mixture.

Bear in mind that peat contains no nutrients at all, so you must add the trace elements as well as the major elements. Feed plants grown in this peat mixture with liquid seaweed (*see page 41*). Moisten the mixture prior to sowing with a half-strength solution and use it at the same dilution at the seedling stage. After potting up the young plants, change to full strength.

Alternatively, you can use worm-worked compost (*see page 81*), and mix it with peat, using two parts peat to one of worm-worked material. Add 30g (1oz) of lime to every 9-liter (2 gallon) bucket of this mixture.

MAKING SOIL-BASED POTTING MIXTURES

Many gardeners prefer to use a soil-based mixture and there are certainly some advantages. Soil retains moisture longer than peat and is much easier to rewet if it does dry out. Most good garden soils also contain a certain quantity of trace elements. Use soil-based mixture for plants grown in containers outside – where they tend to get forgotten and perhaps not watered as much as they would like. Some plants like chrysanthemums and fuchsias, seem to prefer the stability of loam-based mixtures. The problem is that not all garden soil is good enough. The loam must be fibrous and crumbly to be useful and this type is only obtained from freshly cultivated grassland or from stacked turf – so supplies are not always easy to come by. However, it is possible to make your own (*see below*).

For sowing, mix two parts of loam made from stacked turf (*see below*) with two parts of sphagnum peat and one part of coarse grit. To each 9-litre (2-gallon) bucketful, add 60g (2oz) of bone meal and 30g (1oz) of garden lime.

For potting, use seven parts of loam to three parts sphagnum peat and two of coarse grit. Add 30g (1oz) of garden lime and 150g (5oz) of blood, fish and bone meal to every bucketful.

Repotting plants

When the roots of a plant completely fill its pot, the plant must be "potted on" into a slightly larger container. Do this in the spring or summer – but not in the winter, if the plant is dormant Plants should not be moved into pots very much larger than the one they are in, as this simply surrounds the roots with a mass of cold, wet compost and is not conducive to root growth.

There is an easy way of repotting plants which prevents any damage to the root ball (*see opposite*). Water repotted plants and then leave them so the roots spread outwards in search of water.

MAKING LOAM FOR POTTING MIXTURE

Making a fibrous loam for soil-based potting mixture is very simple. Use the space between and around rows of raspberries, soft-fruit bushes, or even apple trees. Sow this ground with grass and use it as a path for at least a year. Then strip off the grass with a 2.5cm (1in) layer of soil and stack it, grass side down, for a year. Replace the soil you remove with the once-used mixture you throw out after the greenhouse crops have finished, and then resow it immediately with grass.

The process takes three years in all, so you need three plots to provide a succession.

I have never encountered any problems with my loam other than weeds, which are easily pulled by hand when they are very small. However, as a safeguard against soil-borne pests and diseases, you may choose to sterilize your loam. This can be done with an electric sterilizer or by heating in an ordinary oven to a temperature of 100°C (212°F) for 15 minutes.

MAKING A PLANT MOLD

The most convenient way of repotting plants is to pack fresh mixture around the discarded pot, forming a mold into which the root ball of the plant will fit, without risk of being damaged.

1 *Put some mixture into the new pot, to bring the top of the two pots level when the new one is placed inside. Remove the plant from its pot and place the empty pot in the center of the new one.*

2 *Fill the gap between the two pots with the mix. Firm it down and remove the inner pot, leaving a mold. Drop the plant into the new pot, tap it on the bench to settle it and water well.*

PLANT CONTAINERS

Many of the seedlings raised in the greenhouse are planted out in the garden, but others may be potted on into clay or plastic pots. Clay pots are porous and therefore "breathe" through the sides, giving a circulation of air around the roots. However, they also absorb moisture from the medium so plants grown in clay pots may need more watering, and they tend to harbor more disease as they are difficult to clean thoroughly (*see page 255*). I prefer to use clay pots for soil-based mixtures and plastic for peat-based ones, as peat dries out more quickly than soil. (*See also* Propagation, *pages 268-77*.)

Growing plants in greenhouse borders

Provided the soil is well prepared, with plenty of organic matter dug in (*see page 20*), the greenhouse border can be used to good effect.

There is a risk of encouraging the build-up of soil-borne pests and diseases if you grow the same crop year after year – tomatoes, for example, are especially at risk from root-rot. However, there are several ways in which you can avoid this. One is to grow varieties that have inbred resistance to disease. Another is to dig out the border soil each year and replace it with fresh soil from the garden. This involves a lot of hard work, so you may prefer to wait until trouble strikes, which might not be for several years. Then, simply grow a different crop in the borders and plant your tomatoes in growing bags on the other side of the house (*see right*).

MAKING A HOT BED

A hot bed heats the roots of plants by surrounding them with a horse manure mixture. It is a cheap, organic alternative to undersoil cable heating (*see page 250*).

1 *Break up the border soil and stack a 23cm (9in) layer of fresh straw horse manure. Cover this with a 5cm (2in) layer of soil and a dusting of lime.*

2 *Add two more layers of manure, with a second layer of soil and lime between. The lime has the effect of neutralizing the acid manure.*

3 *Make a series of holes, and fill them with soil-based potting mixture (see opposite). Cover the whole bed with a layer of soil.*

4 *Transplant young plants into the mixture-filled holes. The manure warms the roots and gets the plants off to a good start.*

Home-made growing bags *A cheap alternative to buying growing bags or other containers is to fill old plastic bags with worm-worked compost or animal manure. Tape up the end of the bag and cut holes in the top.*

THE COLD FRAME

A cold frame is an important piece of equipment, especially if you use the greenhouse to raise seedlings for planting outside.

If plants that have been raised in the warm, humid conditions of the greenhouse are put straight out in the open ground, their rate of growth will be considerably reduced. This is especially so in colder climates in the early spring. The plants need to be acclimatized gradually to lower temperatures and increased exposure, a process called "hardening off". The best way to do this is with a cold frame.

Most frames comprise a wooden, metal or brick box with a glass lid. The simplest – which you can build yourself – is a wooden box with a sheet of rigid plastic over the top. For a large garden, one with larger glass panes supported on old railway ties is a possibility. However, because all the plants in the cold frame must be at the same stage of hardening off, it may be more convenient to have two small frames than one large one.

Frames can also be used during the spring in colder climates to grow early vegetables of all kinds and such crops as melons. They also come in useful in the winter for growing vegetables that mature in spring, like lettuces.

Choosing a cold frame
The frame you choose must be deep enough to accommodate the range of plants you wish to grow, and let in plenty of light. Various designs are available in timber, metal and plastic.

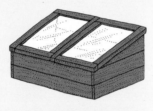

Using the cold frame

1 *A week or so before they are due to be planted out, bring greenhouse seedlings outside and put them into a closed cold frame. Leave it closed for the first 24 hours. During the second day, open the top slightly to begin acclimatizing the plants but close it again at night.*

2 *Gradually increase the opening until the top is off completely during the day but is still almost closed at night. Then start opening the frame more at night until the top is removed completely. The plants are then fully acclimatized and ready to be planted out.*

Feeding greenhouse plants

The base fertilizer contained in all composts will be used up by the plants within about eight weeks. This is because there is less soil life than outside to create and release nutrients (*see page 38*), and because constant watering tends to wash away any nutrients that are present more quickly. Greenhouse plants must therefore be provided with additional food. Use either the home-made animal-manure tea (*see page 42*) or a proprietary liquid seaweed or animal-manure feed (*see page 41*). I find seaweed ideal for most purposes because it contains the full range of nutrients needed for healthy plant growth.

Intervals between feeds will vary according to the crop; these are covered under the separate entries (*see* The Vegetable Garden, *pages 146-97 and* The Fruit Garden, *pages 216-31*). Always be sure to use fertilizers at the recommended strength and frequency; overfeeding can do more damage to plants than underfeeding. Generally, plants that are expected to grow and produce fruit at the same time – like tomatoes and cucumbers – are more demanding than most pot plants. At the height of the growing season these plants will need to be fed every time you water them.

Watering greenhouse plants

Plants that are grown inside rely on you for food and water, so you must be committed to giving them constant attention. In the summer the plants will need a lot of water, so install a hose-pipe that reaches inside the greenhouse and water them straight from the tap.

In the early spring, however, the water from the tap is likely to be much too cold for tender young seedlings. To avoid damaging the plants, fill the can after watering and leave it in the greenhouse so that the water has warmed to greenhouse temperature by watering time the next day. Better still, keep a tank inside the greenhouse and top it up with tap water as soon as the watering is finished.

Delicate young plants and seedlings must be sprayed with water using a fine nozzle to prevent damaging them. Use a hose with a plastic or brass lance attachment or a can with a spout long enough to reach to the back of the bench. Always water in the morning rather than later in the day. Watering "little and often" is not a good idea; most greenhouse plants do better if they are given a thorough soaking and then left for a while before the next watering.

AUTOMATIC WATERING

An automatic watering system will save you a lot of time. There are many types available but,

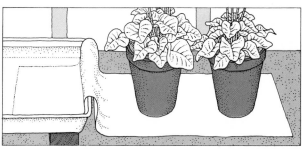

Watering with capillary matting above
Stand potted plants on the mat and place one end in a container of water. The water is gradually drawn out to moisten the whole mat and the plants take it up as required.

Watering with a trickle irrigation system left
The main hose leading from the overhead tank rests flat on the staging. From it, lengths of narrow-gauge tubing spaced at regular intervals are fixed into each pot with staples. The system can also be used to water plants grown in the border soil.

in my experience, the simplest is just as efficient as the most expensive.

For pot plants, put a sheet of plastic over the staging and cover it with a length of absorbent material known as a "capillary mat" (*see above*). If the mat is kept moist, the plants can take up water whenever they need it.

Alternatively, install a trickle irrigation line to water the plants individually. These are available from garden centers and consist of a series of nozzles fed through tubes leading from a water tank above the staging. The tank must be refilled regularly or connected to the mains supply through a valve and a ballcock. Trickle irrigation nozzles let a drop of water through at slow but regular intervals and can be adjusted to suit the requirements of the plants. They can be used for any greenhouse plants.

Maintaining a greenhouse

The environment inside the greenhouse must be routinely maintained to ensure the best possible growing conditions at all times. Controlling temperature and ventilation levels is very important (*see pages 247 and 249*) but other factors must also be considered.

KEEPING THE GREENHOUSE CLEAN
By keeping the greenhouse spotlessly clean, you will discourage pests and diseases that might otherwise thrive in the warm, humid environment. Make sure you remove any plant debris in which pests and diseases may hide and, at the end of the season, wash the house thoroughly with warm, soapy water, brushing it into every corner. If you empty the house for the winter, leave it open for the frost to help sterilize it. Always keep the glass clean, as dirty panes reduce the amount of light available to the plants.

Before re-using pots or seed trays, wash them thoroughly in boiling water to kill any disease spores or insect eggs that may be lurking. Plastic pots and trays are much easier to clean.

PROVIDING HUMIDITY
Most plants grown under glass require a moist, humid atmosphere. This is achieved by wetting the paths, the staging and often the plants themselves early in the morning, a process known as "damping down". Sometimes it may be necessary to repeat this process in the afternoon, but leaves should only be wetted in shaded houses or on dull days, to prevent sun-scorching. Use a fine mist sprayer when damping foliage.

Shading greenhouse plants

In the early spring you will need all the light you can get to produce strong, bushy plants but, in summer, the greenhouse must actually be shaded to reduce high light levels, which would otherwise scorch the plants and produce unacceptably high temperatures. The best method is to use roller blinds, which are simply pulled up or let down as required. A cheaper alternative is to paint the side of the house with a special shading material (*see overleaf*). Use one of the proprietary shading paints as they are designed to stay on in wet weather but wipe off easily with a dry cloth when no longer needed. Home-made shading is often washed off by rain and has to be replaced regularly, or else it is almost impossible to remove at the end of the season.

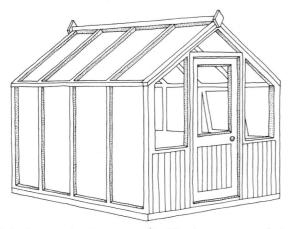

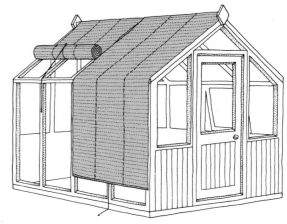

Painting on shading materials *The cheapest way to shade greenhouse plants is by coating the exterior glass with a special white compound which reflects light. This can usually be mixed to various concentrations, so you can provide light or heavy shading. The local climate and the nature of the plants you are growing will determine the appropriate strength of the shading.*

Using roller blinds *Slatted wooden blinds can be expensive but provide a permanent and controllable means of shading. They are best fitted on the outside of the greenhouse, as interior blinds are less effective at keeping down temperatures. Textile or plastic blinds are cheaper, but liable to blow away in strong winds. Remove the blinds each winter and store them indoors.*

Deciding what to grow

To make the best use of your greenhouse, you should keep it full for the major part of the year – if not all year round. To do this you must first decide on the range of plants you would like to raise and how much heat you are prepared to supply (*see page 249*), bearing in mind the cost of heating the house. If you wish to cultivate exotic species, for instance, it is perfectly possible to do so but considerably more expensive than just using the house "cold" or slightly heated to overwinter frost-tender plants.

The greenhouse is particularly valuable for raising fruit and vegetable plants for setting outside in spring. The propagation of these is covered in *The Vegetable Garden (see pages 132-201)* and *The Fruit Garden (see pages 202-35)*. All greenhouse plants are susceptible to the same range of pests and diseases (*see opposite*).

VEGETABLES
You can use the greenhouse to raise early crops of a range of vegetables, in exactly the way described for growing under cloches (*see page 140*). It is generally possible to sow or plant a week or two earlier if the house is heated (see below). However, there is little point in starting too soon since light levels are low in mid winter and this will have a marked effect on growth. In any case, the cost of heating will make growing the vegetables uneconomic.

Of course, if you decide to heat the greenhouse for raising seedlings, and there is excess space, it is sensible to fill the borders with early vegetables. Some, like radish and lettuce, can even be grown in pots. Grow them as described for cloches (*see page 140*) but start them off in mid

winter, or as soon as the heating is available.

Most vegetables are grown in unheated or slightly heated houses during the spring and summer and, in this way, early yields can be produced economically.

FRUIT
In cold areas the greenhouse can be used to produce high-quality, inexpensive fruit (*see pages 202-31*) which could not otherwise be grown. Most permanent fruit plants occupy little space, being confined to a wall or to the end or roof of the house. Some, like grape vines, may exclude light, but only during the summer – when it is likely that the glass would be shaded anyway. A vine or a peach is certainly worth considering in most houses as the fruits will be far superior to those produced outside.

DECORATIVE PLANTS
Many flowering and foliage plants can be cheaply raised from seed and used either as houseplants or to decorate the greenhouse itself. In cold climates you can grow tropical plants that you would not otherwise be able to grow in the garden or bring on bedding plants for planting outside (*see The Ornamental Garden, pages 74-125*). The range of possible plants is almost limitless and they will require no heat in most areas once frost danger is over. Grow your plants in the peat mixture fed with seaweed, in worm-worked sowing and potting mixture or in the soil-based medium, depending on your preference (*see page 252*). Feed them all with liquid seaweed or animal manure while they are growing vigorously.

Greenhouse pests and diseases

Greenhouse pests can build up rapidly because the warmth and humidity that are necessary for healthy plant growth are also ideal for pests and diseases. Try to prevent attacks by vigilance and scrupulous cleanliness (*see page 255*), removing any damaged plant material as soon as you see it. The following are general pests and diseases that attack a range of plants in the greenhouse. Specific problems are discussed in the relevant chapters (*see pages 198-201 and 232-35*).

TREATING COMMON GREENHOUSE PROBLEMS

VINE WEEVILS
These small grubs, which have white bodies and brown heads, invade potting mixtures and eat the roots of many plants. Severely affected plants may keel over.
What to do
Make up a solution of rotenone (see page 53) and immerse pots in it completely.

APHIDS
These small green or black flies are one of the most common and troublesome of all garden pests (*see also page 50*). Aphids weaken a wide range of plants by sucking the sap from their stems. They also transmit virus diseases (*see right*), and the sticky honeydew they secrete can attract sooty mold (*see page 52*), which spoils the appearance of the host plant.
What to do
There are certain flowers you can plant to attract hover-flies, which will eat the pests (see Companion planting, page 46). Spray with pyrethrum or insecticidal soap in severe cases (see page 53).

WHITEFLIES
Serious and persistent greenhouse pests, these small white flies weaken plants by sucking sap and are often found on the undersides of leaves (*see also page 50*).
What to do
The flies can be controlled with the parasitic wasp Encarsia formosa *(see Biological pest control, page 52). Alternatively, hang a grease-coated yellow card in the greenhouse. This attracts the flies and they stick to it. As a last resort, spray three times with rotenone (see page 53) at five-day intervals; do not spray if you have already introduced the* Encarsia *parasite.*

LEAF MINERS
This pest burrows into leaves, making characteristic yellow tunnels which are clearly visible.
What to do
Remove and destroy affected leave as soon as you see them or squash the grubs by squeezing the leaf.

RED SPIDER MITES
Although they are barely visible, these tiny pale green or red mites cover plants with webs and cause a fine mottling on leaves.
What to do
They are only a problem in a dry atmosphere, so increase the humidity as a safeguard (see page 255). If they persist, they can be controlled by encouraging the parasitic mite Phytoseiulus persimilis *(see Biological pest control, page 52). Deal with small infestations by spraying with rotenone (see page 53) three times at six-day intervals; do not spray if you have already introduced* Phytoseiulus.

SCALE INSECTS
These are small, disc-like insects that cling tenaciously to leaves and stems, sucking sap and secreting honeydew. Affected plants are weakened and turn yellow, and their leaves drop.
What to do
Scrape off the insects with a piece of wood as soon as you see them.

BOTRYTIS
Also known as gray mold, this is a common fungus diseases showing as a dirty white or gray-brown mold on leaves and stems. It affects plants both in the greenhouse and the garden (*see also page 52*).
What to do
It thrives in low temperatures and poor ventilation, so increase both. Remove and burn infected material immediately since it will not recover.

DAMPING OFF
Another fungus disease affecting seedlings, damping off shows as a blackened area at the base of the stem. Affected plants will topple over and die.
What to do
Sow seeds more thinly, water less, and increase the temperature in the greenhouse. Sometimes, the disease is carried in the soil, which will need to be sterilized by heating to kill it. Watering with copper fungicide (see page 53) will help prevent its spread.

MILDEW
Mildew is a white, powdery coating which forms on leaves, causing puckering and distortion (*see also page 52*).
What to do
Remove affected leaves immediately since they will not recover and will spread the disease to the rest of the crop. Mildew is more likely to attack when soil is dry, so make sure plants never go short of water. Spray with copper fungicide or dispersible sulfur in severe cases (see page 53).

BLIGHT
Brown marks on leaves, and sometimes fruit, may well be caused by blight. These marks are likely to spread and can later turn black.
What to do
Remove infected leaves immediately and, if the disease persists, spray with copper fungicide (see page 53).

VIRUS DISEASES
Affecting tomatoes, cucumbers and many other plants, virus diseases cause a variety of symptoms, among them yellow mottling of the leaves and a "ferny" appearance in young leaves. The leaves also wilt badly and appear to recover in the morning only to wilt again during the day. Affected plants lose vigor and the crop will be poor. Virus diseases are spread by insects, garden tools, by hand and by tobacco.
What to do
There is no cure, so dig up and burn all affected plants, and do not use them for propagation. Control aphids, which spread virus disease. If necessary, consult your local County Extension Service. Don't smoke in the greenhouse.

LEAF MOLD
Thriving in poor ventilation and overcrowded conditions, leaf mold causes yellow spots and a brown mold to appear on leaves.
What to do
Space plants further apart to give them more air and adjust greenhouse ventilation if necessary (see page 247) if the condition persists.

BASIC TECHNIQUES

THE BASIC TECHNIQUES of practical organic gardening draw much from traditional methods. The spade, for example, which has been with us since Roman times, remains the very best tool for digging; gardeners have been controlling weeds with the hoe ever since men started to cultivate the soil, and it is still the most effective and beneficial method of weed control in the garden.

It would, however, be foolish to ignore some of the results of modern research and technology. It may be manufactured, and it is certainly not organic in origin, but I would not like to be without polyethylene sheeting in the garden. Neither would I wish to revert to tying with old-fashioned hemp string if it had to last more than one season; I would rather use long-lasting nylon twine.

So, the organic techniques of today should combine the best of modern technology with tried and tested traditional methods, without us having to sacrifice our valued organic standards. We owe a lot to the research carried out for commercial growers, but it would be folly to copy their methods blindly because their requirements are very different.

Gardening is like many other types of activity, in that you need to have a basic core of information, perhaps gleaned from more experienced "old hands" or from books such as this, and, of course, the correct tools for the particular tasks you are undertaking. If you are new to gardening in general, or organic gardening in particular, you will almost certainly find that other gardeners are only too pleased to share their knowledge with you.

Choosing the right tools

If you are new to gardening, you might easily spend hundreds of dollars on a complete set of tools, or, by choosing the bare essentials, buy just what you need for relatively little money. Bear in mind, however, that it is a false economy to buy anything but the best. Cheap tools just don't last and, far worse than that, they make the work more difficult. So, if your budget is tight, buy slowly, one tool at a time, but buy the best quality you can afford. And, with all tools,

but the fork and the spade in particular, do not buy anything that is too large for you. You can do a lot more, much quicker, with a smaller fork that does not tire you out than with a larger one that you find difficult or awkward to use.

I have listed some of the more common tools below. Naturally there are many more that are useful, and many that are not. Beware of the "gimmicks" claimed to be indispensable: you can usually manage just as well without them.

Fork The digging fork is second only to the spade in usefulness in the garden, and invaluable for loosening the soil without inverting it. I have listed it first simply because, if you have no equipment at all, then you can use the fork in place of the spade for most digging jobs (and it will double as a rake, too). Buy a fork that is made of forged steel, fitted with a wooden or metal handle. Never buy a pressed-steel fork, since it will bend and distort as soon as you put it under pressure.

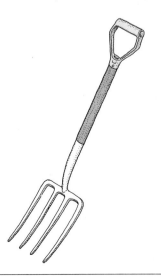

Spade You will probably use a spade more than any other tool, so it is worth buying a really good one. Stainless-steel spades are undoubtedly the best: soil, no matter how sticky, simply falls off the polished surface, making digging much easier. If you cannot afford stainless steel, buy a strong, forged-steel spade and always keep it clean. Once this type of spade is worked in (when the blade becomes sharp and the corners rounded) digging is much easier. Buy the size to suit you.

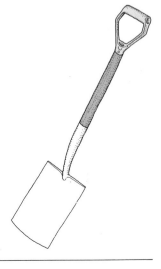

LARGE TOOLS

Rakes Once again, forged-steel rakes are the best. Those consisting of a metal strip with what look like nails driven through it tend to be awkward to use, as do rakes with more than about 12 teeth, unless you are very strong.

A spring-tine, or lawn, rake is useful for removing dead thatch from lawns in spring and autumn and for raking in grass seeds after sowing.

Hoes Ideally, you should have two hoes – a Dutch, or push, hoe and a swan-necked, or draw, hoe. Make sure the handles are long enough for you to work almost upright without straining your back.

With the Dutch hoe, you push it backwards and forwards while walking backwards, thus avoiding treading the weeds back into the soil again. Use the swan-necked hoe for hoeing weeds that have grown too large to hoe any other way, for earthing-up vegetables and making drills for sowing seeds.

A small "onion" hoe is ideal for working between closely planted subjects and particularly useful on

deep beds. A wheel hoe is a great time saver and it is invaluable on larger vegetable plots, though you will have to space your plants to allow for its width (*see page 57*). You would rarely use a wheel hoe in the ornamental garden because there is less space between plants.

Hollow-tined fork This is a useful tool for conditioning the lawn in the spring. It consists of a frame, attached to which are two or more tubes. When pushed into the lawn, a number of cores of soil are removed. You can fill these holes with grit, sand or compost to improve drainage or water retention.

Shovel A shovel is not simply a large spade: the blade is angled in quite a different way in order to make shovelling much quicker and easier. Its main use is for mixing compost or shifting a lot of soil in a new garden. Buy a builder's shovel with a metal handle and, if you ever use it for concreting, wash off every speck of cement. In this way it should last you for life.

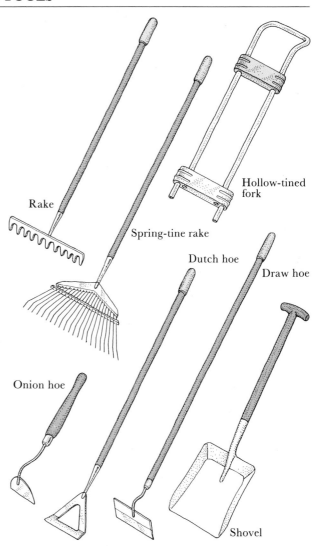

Rake

Spring-tine rake

Hollow-tined fork

Dutch hoe

Draw hoe

Onion hoe

Shovel

HAND TOOLS

Hand fork A small hand fork is not as useful as a trowel, but many gardeners use one for weeding and for tickling over the border soil to good effect.

Trowel Trowels are used extensively in the ornamental garden for planting and, to a lesser extent, in the vegetable garden. As with the spade, buy a stainless-steel one.

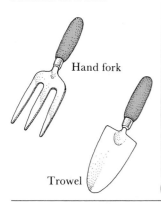

Hand fork

Trowel

Knives A pocket knife is just about the most used tool in the garden. Buy one that fits comfortably into your pocket and make sure that you keep it sharp. Use a small carborundum sharpening stone to touch up the edge of the blade regularly, particularly if you use it for cutting string, or anything similar, which tends to blunt the knife blade extremely quickly.

If you are going to do any budding, you need a special knife with a notch at the bottom of the blade.

Pruning saw This is a useful tool for cutting branches too large for even large pruners to handle. The saw is slightly curved with a narrow blade to allow you to cut in restricted spaces.

CUTTING TOOLS

Edging knife This is a half-moon-shaped tool for cutting out lawn edges. If you are the type of gardener who demands absolute precision, then it is essential. Personally, I have never used anything other than a spade for this job and the edges of my lawn look fine to me.

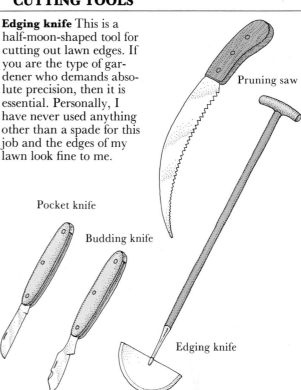

Pruning saw

Pocket knife

Budding knife

Edging knife

CUTTING TOOLS
(continued)

Pruners There are two types of pruners: the anvil type and the "parrot-bill" type. In my opinion they are both perfectly good for most pruning jobs and choice is largely a matter of personal preference. It is important, however, to ensure that you only use them on the size of wood they are designed for. Cutting branches that are too thick will damage them, and probably the branch being cut. For large fruit trees, you need a pair of long-handled pruners.

Shears You need two pairs of shears – a short-handled pair for cutting hedges and a long-handled pair for trimming the lawn edges. Neat edges make a lot of difference to the look of a lawn and it is not easy with short-handled shears. It is worth buying expensive shears that will hold a good, sharp edge.

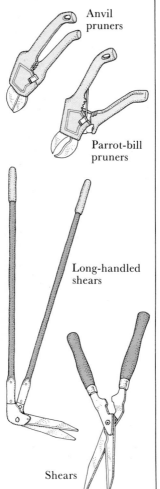

Anvil pruners

Parrot-bill pruners

Long-handled shears

Shears

WATERING EQUIPMENT

Watering can Buy the largest watering can you are able to carry comfortably, but remember that it will be a lot heavier when full of water. If you have a greenhouse, make sure the can has a long handle and spout so that you can water plants at the back of the staging. A fine nozzle for watering seedlings is essential.

Hose Watering in the garden needs to be thorough, so a hose is an essential piece of equipment. Buy the more expensive type that does not easily kink.

Ideally you should store your hose on a reel – preferably a through-feed type, which allows you to unroll just enough hose for your needs.

You may also find a seep hose useful. This slowly drips water along its length and you can leave it permanently in position underneath plastic mulches and simply turn it on whenever necessary (*see page 58*).

Sprinkler A sprinkler is essential because you can never put enough water on the garden if you have

to stand and hold a hose. Choose one with a fine spray pattern and one that has the sprinkler head mounted on a tall stand so that it is held well above the ground. In some areas, a license is needed for both hose and sprinkler.

Sprayer Although, as an organic gardener, you should always consider spraying a last resort, from time to time it will be necessary. If you buy a sprayer that breaks up the solution into small droplets and deposits it evenly, you need less chemical.

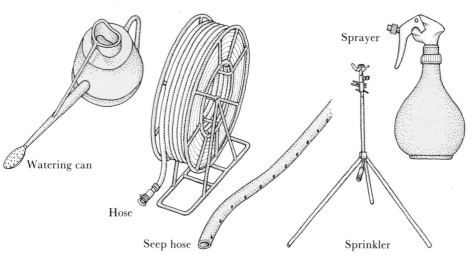

Sprayer

Watering can

Hose

Seep hose

Sprinkler

HOMEMADE TOOLS

Sieve A sieve with a 1.5mm ($\frac{1}{16}$ in) mesh is necessary for sprinkling a fine layer of medium over seeds after sowing. It is not expensive to make your own sieve; all you need to do is to nail a piece of plastic mesh on to a square or circular frame.

Planting board A planting board is simple to make and it is invaluable for the accurate spacing of plants. It should be about 3m (10ft) long, made from 8×2.5cm (3×1in) wood with a sawcut every 8cm (3in). Mark each 30cm (12in) division with an appropriate number of nails. If you grow vegetables on deep beds (*see page 136*), make a 1.25m (4ft) board as well. Mark this board with 15cm (6in) divisions.

Garden line Used for marking lines for drawing seed drills and marking off areas of soil for digging. It consists of two sticks, or pegs, and a length of thick nylon string. Always make at least two garden lines.

Dibber Used to transplant seedlings, you can make your own using a broken spade or fork handle. Cut it to 30cm (12in) and shave the end to a point.

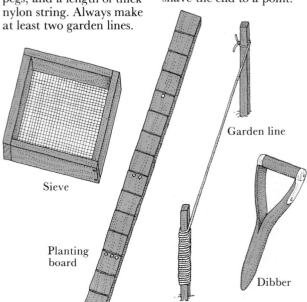

Sieve

Planting board

Garden line

Dibber

HOMEMADE TOOLS (continued)

Tool cleaner Cut a piece of wood to a spade shape and use it regularly when digging, to remove any soil sticking to the blade. It makes all the difference, especially when working heavy soil. Use it to clean all your tools before putting them away at the end of the day.

Firming board A firming board is a 1cm (½in) thick piece of wood cut slightly smaller than your seed trays with a handle screwed to one side. It is invaluable for levelling off potting medium when filling the trays and for firming it down evenly prior to sowing. Make one to fit each tray size.

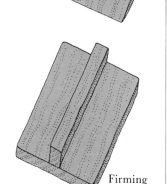

Tool cleaner

Firming board

CONTAINERS

Buckets Buy plastic rather than metal buckets; they are lighter to carry when full and last longer. All the "bucketful" measurements given in the book are based on a 9-liter (2-gallon) bucket.

Wheelbarrow The best type is a builder's wheelbarrow – which is often cheaper to buy from a builders' merchant than from a garden center. Choose the type with a pneumatic tire – it makes all the difference when wheeling a heavily laden barrow over rough ground. If you ever use it for concreting, make sure you wash off every speck of cement afterwards.

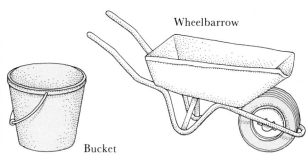

Wheelbarrow

Bucket

Choosing garden machinery

Power tools can be a great boon to the gardener, saving many hours of repetitious and exhausting work. They can, however, be expensive.

If machinery, such as a lawn mower or hedge trimmer, is likely to be used on a regular basis, then its purchase is easily justified. If, however, you have only an occasional need for machinery such as a power tiller then, unless you have an enormous garden, it is better to rent it. Make sure when renting machinery that it comes with full instructions, with all safety features fitted, and that it is fully operational.

Mowers There are two main types: a cylinder mower and a rotary grass cutter. A cylinder mower will generally produce a better finish than a rotary mower. Choose one with as many blades on the cylinder as possible.

Rotary mowers come into their own if you have areas of tall grass. You can use them on closer-cut lawns but they will not give a very fine finish.

You can buy petrol- or electric-powered mowers. Some petrol engines even have electric starting. Electric mowers are cheap to buy and easy to use, but you do need to drag a length of cable behind you, which can be a real disadvantage in a large garden. They are quite safe to use, since the machines are double insulated. It is advisable, though, to fit a device that instantly cuts off the current if you accidentally cut through the cable or if there is any other kind of electrical fault.

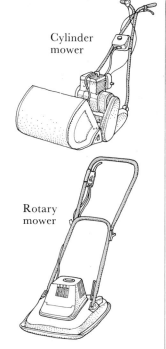

Cylinder mower

Rotary mower

Power tiller A power tiller is invaluable in a very large garden: you can make a very fine seed bed in half the time it takes to dig one by hand, and it is extremely useful for incorporating green manure, compost and other organic matter into the soil. However, you must hand dig at least part of your garden every year because constant power tilling can "glaze" the soil, creating an impermeable layer; most machines cultivate down to about 15cm (6in) and rarely deeper than about 23cm (9in).

There are various types of power tiller. Those that are driven through their wheels and have the blades at the back of the machine are easiest to use and the most controllable. Unfortunately, they also tend to be expensive.

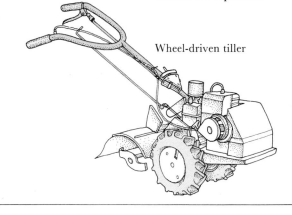

Wheel-driven tiller

GARDENING MACHINERY (continued)

Much cheaper are the models that are driven forwards solely by the rotor blades. This type can be difficult to control, particularly on hard ground, because it tends to run away with you. However, once you learn to push the rear skid into the ground, instead of pulling back on the handles, when it accelerates, it is not hard to use.

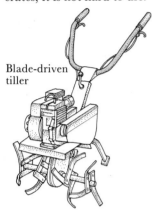

Blade-driven tiller

Strimmer A fairly recent development is the nylon-line strimmer. A short length of strong nylon line turns at speed and cuts grass without any danger of anything more substantial being damaged. This enables you to use them right up to walls or trees. Strimmers are available with petrol engines or electrically driven.

Shredder This is an electrically- or petrol-driven machine capable of shredding woody material extremely finely. It takes all the prunings from the garden that would otherwise only be destroyed. The resulting material is excellent for mulching and is a cheap alternative to chipped or composted bark (*see page 59*). The machines are expensive but useful.

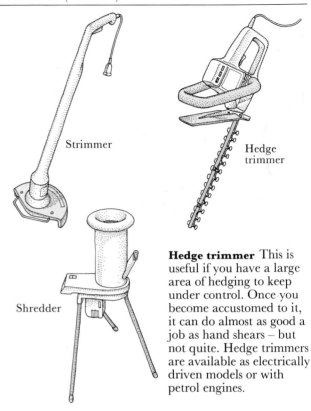

Strimmer

Hedge trimmer

Shredder

Hedge trimmer This is useful if you have a large area of hedging to keep under control. Once you become accustomed to it, it can do almost as good a job as hand shears – but not quite. Hedge trimmers are available as electrically driven models or with petrol engines.

Cultivation techniques

If you have difficult soil, either in a new garden or in your existing plot, and poor drainage seems to be responsible, then there is much you can do to alleviate the problem. You can bring about dramatic improvements in the condition of your soil by adopting the correct cultivation techniques and by the addition of plenty of organic matter and free-draining material. Soil management for the five main soil types is described in more detail in *The Soil* (*see pages 15-17*).

Improving drainage

Badly drained soil can be a problem. But a distinct lack of realism persists in relation to the subject of drainage. There is a great deal you can do to improve the soil drainage by digging and incorporating organic matter and grit. In some areas it is also possible to install a drainage system. However, there is no point in digging out and laying an elaborate system of drainage pipes unless you have somewhere to drain the water to. It is sometimes suggested that you dig a soakaway in one corner of the garden. This is a hole filled with gravel or other drainage material that will, in theory, absorb excess water from your land. In fact, a soakaway can only take

so much water and, once it is full, you are back to square one again.

The only possible way that a drainage system can be effective is if you are lucky enough to have a drainage ditch near the garden into which water can be drained and subsequently removed. It is sometimes possible to obtain local authority permission to run your drainage system into the public storm drains, but make sure you enquire *before* you start laying your drains.

INSTALLING A DRAINAGE SYSTEM
If you have an outlet for the water, a herring-bone system of drains is ideal (*see right*). The distance between the "arms" of the system will vary according to the soil – constantly wet soil needs the arms closer together than soil that has only a mild problem. On average, 2.5-3m (8-10ft) between arms is ideal.

Fill the arms with twiggy material or, better still, earthenware or perforated plastic pipes, available from agricultural merchants, then cover them with soil. Plastic pipes are no cheaper than the earthenware ones, but they are much easier to lay – just roll them out into the trenches. On land that lies very wet, this kind of effort will be amply rewarded. However, in reality, it is rarely necessary to go to these lengths.

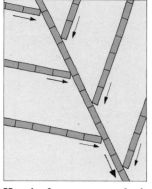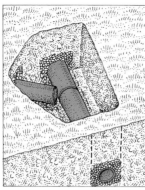

Herringbone pattern drains *Dig a series of trenches, about 45cm (18in) deep, that slope gently towards the outlet. Put a 15cm (6in) layer of stones or twiggy material in the bottom of each, then refill the remaining 30cm (12in) with soil. Better still, lay tile drains (short lengths of pipe) on a bed of gravel to form a continuous run. Cover the pipes with about 10cm (4in) of gravel and then refill the trench with soil. The water seeps in through the spaces left between the pipes.*

COMPACTED AND HEAVY SOIL

The most common reason for badly drained land is that there is an impervious layer of compacted soil beneath the surface. This is often caused during the building of a house. Immediately after construction, the builder covers compacted soil with extra soil, unfortunately often subsoil, which is guaranteed to cause wet conditions. You can usually solve the problem by digging to break up the compacted layer.

Sometimes the impervious layer is caused by constant ploughing to the same depth, so if you have a new house built on land that was farmed, dig deeply to investigate any hard layer of soil that might be present.

If, however, the problem is simply one of heavy soil, you can generally overcome this simply by using the correct cultivation methods without resorting to complicated drainage systems. Dig deeply, incorporating gravel and lots of organic matter, to raise the areas that will be cultivated. It is difficult to be precise because each piece of land requires slightly different amounts, but one or two bucketfuls each of gravel and organic matter per square meter/yard should be sufficient. Improvement will take some time to bring about, but just growing plants on heavy soil helps improve drainage by opening up the soil (*see pages 15–16*).

In the ornamental garden, if you raise the flower borders, your lawn will be at risk of constant dampness. To counter this, put down a 15cm (6in) layer of ash or gravel below the topsoil before sowing or turfing a new lawn.

Digging

Hand digging is the main method of cultivating the soil: it breaks up compacted land, introduces air and allows water to drain away and roots to penetrate. It also enables you to work

organic matter into the lower levels, increasing the depth of the topsoil. Prepare all new ground by double digging, then single dig every year in autumn for heavy soils and in spring for light soils (*see overleaf*).

DIGGING HEAVY SOILS

It is best if you dig heavy soils in the autumn, before the worst of the winter rains makes cultivation difficult. Choose your moment carefully, when the soil is neither too dry and hard nor too wet and sticky. If necessary, cover an area of soil with polyethylene to keep it dry.

When digging heavy soils in winter, throw the spadefuls forwards, leaving them rough and unbroken for the winter. This leaves the maximum amount of soil surface exposed to the drying winds and to the frosts. By the spring, the weather will have broken the surface down to a fine tilth that you will only have to rake to make suitable for sowing. Leaving the soil rough over winter also allows heavy rains and frost to kill weeds and pests, as well as making them more accessible to birds and other predators.

DIGGING LIGHT SOILS

Sandy and limy soils will crumble to a fine tilth more readily than heavy soils. The problem with light soils is that they drain easily, causing leaching of the nutrients. To minimize this, keep the ground covered for the winter by sowing a green-manure crop in autumn and digging it in a short time before sowing.

BASIC RULES OF DIGGING

Digging can cause severe back strain or it can be a healthy, invigorating and enjoyable exercise – it all depends on using your common sense.

● Never dig when the soil is wet enough to stick to your boots – you risk spoiling its structure.
● Start by using a spade and fork that are the correct size for you. You gain nothing by using oversized tools, which simply tire you quickly and slow you down.
● Never take spadefuls that are too big to handle comfortably. By taking smaller amounts, and not straining yourself, you can dig more for longer.
● Always take your time: there is no point in rushing. Adopt a rhythmic and methodical approach to digging, being conscious all the time of avoiding strain. As soon as you feel you have had enough or you begin to find it difficult to straighten up – stop! It is at this stage that you are likely to do damage to yourself. Above all, don't try to do all the digging at once. Leave plenty of time so that you can do it in stages.
● Finally, keep your tools in good, clean condition. Carry a scraper in your pocket and use it regularly to clean soil from your tools. When you finish, clean the tools thoroughly and rub them over with an oily cloth to prevent rust.

DOUBLE AND SINGLE DIGGING

You should double dig all new ornamental borders before planting, to work organic matter to the lower levels of soil. The vegetable plot also benefits from initial double digging and, subsequently, you should double dig at intervals of about five years, depending on soil type. The best way to achieve this is by digging at least one-fifth of your land each year, on a rotation basis.

With single digging it is only necessary to dig one spade deep and incorporate one layer of manure, and so there is no need to mark out trenches as carefully as for double digging.

Double digging

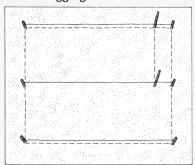

1 *Mark out the plot to be dug by setting up lines down either side. If it is a wide plot, divide it down the middle as well. Cut two 60cm (2ft) canes to mark the width of the trenches. Make each trench exactly the same size so you refill each one with the same amount of soil as you have taken out.*

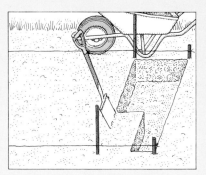

2 *Mark out the first 60cm (2ft) trench with the canes and dig out all the soil to the depth of the spade, putting it in a wheelbarrow. Take it to the other end of the plot, so it can be used to refill the last trench. If you are digging a wide plot divided into two halves, put the soil at the start of the other half.*

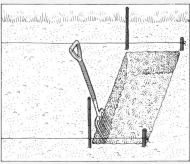

3 *Clean out the crumbs of soil from the bottom of the trench and then "fork" the soil to the depth of the fork. This is the subsoil and should not be inverted. Simply loosen it by digging it up and throwing it back as it came out.*

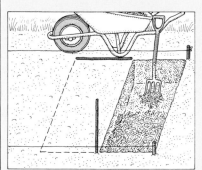

4 *Put a 5-8cm (2-3in) layer of organic matter in the bottom of the trench. Then, leaving one cane in the corner of the trench you have dug out, mark out the second trench, to the same size, with the other cane.*

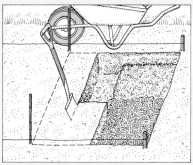

5 *Start digging out the new trench to the same depth, but throw the soil forward to cover the organic matter in the first trench. Spread another layer of organic matter in the first trench and cover it with the remaining soil from the second trench. This will raise the bed.*

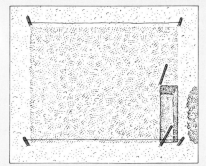

6 *Carry on working down the plot in this way and, when you get to the last trench, refill it with the soil you removed from the first trench. Cover the entire area with another layer of organic matter. It will soon be washed into the bed by the rain.*

Single digging

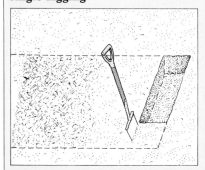

1 *Dig out the first trench one spade deep, taking no more than 10cm (4in) "bites". Throw all the soil behind you, spreading it out more or less evenly over the surface of the bed.*

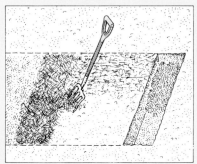

2 *Spread a layer of manure over the soil about 1 meter/yard behind you; there should be enough to fill up to three trenches with a 5-8cm (2-3in) layer of manure. Then, scrape some forward into the bottom of the first trench.*

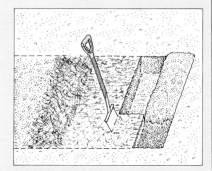

3 *Dig a second trench, throwing the soil forward to cover the organic matter in the first trench. Continue the process until all the organic matter has been dug in. Then spread another layer further down the plot and carry on.*

REMOVING WEEDS

Whenever you are digging, you should put any perennial weeds in a bucket and then burn them or throw them away. Annual weeds can go in the bottom of the trenches to add to the organic content of the soil. It is sometimes suggested that you can scrape annual weeds off the soil surface with a spade before starting to dig. In my experience, however, there are always a few perennials mixed with them and they can be difficult to recognize without their foliage. Thus, it is best to remove them by hand as you dig.

Raking

The soil must be raked level before you can start sowing. This is a technique that can be learned only through experience. There are a few basic rules. First, choose a rake that suits your body size; a large-headed rake in the hands of a small person will be difficult to control.

Second, try not to lunge forward with the rake, pulling back soil from some way away; it will result in a wavy, uneven surface. Instead, reach forward no more than about 30cm (12in) and keep the head of the rake nearly parallel to the surface of the soil.

Finally, take time to step back now and then, squat down and squint across the soil surface, looking for any high and low spots in the soil.

Hoeing

This is the principal organic method of weed control. There really is no need to resort to chemicals to keep your garden weed free.

Always hoe *before* it is necessary to do so. If you have perennial weeds, for example, cutting off their shoots below ground level, so depriving them of light, eventually starves them into submission. Annual weeds are not so much of a problem. Hoe them out when they are quite small – no larger than about 13mm ($\frac{1}{2}$in) – and certainly don't let them flower or seed.

Choose a hot, sunny day for hoeing. That way the weeds will lie on the surface where their roots will soon become dried out and die, returning their organic matter to the soil. If hot days are too infrequent, try to rake off as much of the weed as you can, then use a Dutch hoe to lift the root. Walk backwards to avoid treading on the hoed weeds and effectively transplanting them (*see also* Organic Weed Control, *page 57*).

Mulching

This is a technique that involves covering the surface of the soil – either with organic matter to condition the soil, or with plastic or paper to inhibit weed growth. Mulching with well-rotted manure or compost in the spring is more important than most people realize. In an organic garden, the regular addition of bulky organic matter is essential. A 5-7.5cm (2-3in) layer helps to retain moisture in the soil by preventing evaporation, and it can also help to control weeds (*see page 58*). The compost or manure adds vital nutrients and will eventually be incorporated into the soil by the action of the weather and soil organisms. In addition, it will help to prevent "capping" – the formation of a crust on the soil surface that stops rain entering and restricts the natural air flow.

MULCHING WITH ORGANIC MATERIAL

You can use any organic material. Manure is ideal, but it must be well rotted or it can scorch young shoots; even well-rotted manure should be kept away from direct contact with foliage.

Compost can do no harm at all, rotted or not; you can even use it green. Grass cuttings are the most convenient, but look rather conspicuous until they have rotted down to a dark brown colour. Never put grass cuttings on too thickly or they will rot down into a slimy mass.

Peat, although it contains no nutrients, makes a fine soil conditioner, but it is, unfortunately, quite expensive, while composted bark is perhaps even more costly. Nevertheless, its acid content makes it a superb weed inhibitor. Peat moss as a mulch tends to form an inpenetrable crust to moisture.

You will find more information about the nutrient values of organic materials in *Soil Improvement* (*see pages 18-34*). All organic mulches, with the exception of bark, improve conditions for soil pests (*see pages 49-50*).

MULCHING WITH POLYETHYLENE, PAPER OR GRAVEL

Plastic mulches add nothing to the soil and paper only a very small amount. They are, however, perfect weed controllers and minimize water loss through evaporation. They have the added advantage of keeping low-growing fruits clean by preventing soil splashing.

Either lay these materials between rows of crops, holding them down at the edges with stones or with piles of soil, or cover the ground completely, burying the edges in a shallow trench, and plant through slits in the material. Areas over about 1.2m (4ft) wide must have provision for watering; so lay a length of seep hose on the ground before laying the plastic.

In the ornamental garden, you could consider a permanent mulch of gravel. It will have excellent water retention and inhibit weed growth and, in the right setting, it looks extremely attractive. It adds nothing to the soil and you should not use it where regular surface dressing with organic matter is needed.

Watering plants

All plants require adequate supplies of water and there are always occasions when it is necessary to water artificially. However, watering is not simply a matter of pouring water on to the soil. This can, in fact, do more harm than good.

First, never add water in small amounts. It is essential to apply enough to get right down to the root zone where it is needed. Otherwise, roots will come to the surface in search of the water, and there they will be even more vulnerable to the effects of heat and lack of moisture.

Second, although large quantities of water are required, you must apply it carefully. Water applied in the form of large droplets or with great force will cause the soil "crumbs" to break down and form a hard surface crust. This prevents further water entering the soil and it also inhibits the free interchange of air and gases, with disastrous effects. On a seed bed, this crust can actually stop the tender young seedlings from pushing through the soil to the surface. To prevent this occurring, apply water through a sprinkler with a fine spray pattern of small droplets. When watering seed trays, use a can fitted with a fine nozzle. Pour the water to one side of the tray or pot, then pass the can over the seedlings, keeping the angle of the nozzle constant throughout. When you have finished, do not raise the can until it is clear of the tray or pot.

The size of droplets is not as important where the soil is covered with grass, so lawn sprinklers are not generally made with such attention to optimum droplet size. Consequently, if you want to buy one sprinkler only, buy one with a fine spray; it will be perfectly suitable for the lawn as well as the seed beds.

WHEN TO WATER
It is not necessary to keep the soil moist all the time – water when the soil is dry, but before the plants begin to suffer – and, provided you use a fine sprinkler, you can water at any time of day. However, timing is important. For example, watering when fruits or vegetables are swelling will greatly increase their overall weight. Once fruits, in particular, begin to color, though, extra water could invite a fungus attack, especially from botrytis (*see page 52*).

HOW MUCH WATER TO GIVE
It is, of course, not difficult to overwater, especially with plants in pots. Try to strike a balance between an aerated soil or medium and one with sufficient moisture. A cold, wet, airless medium will not do anything to encourage plant growth. If you are watering in the ornamental or vegetable garden, leave the sprinkler on for at least an hour each time.

WATERING NEW PLANTS
When you have just planted a plant, encourage it to search for water, thus increasing its root system. Water it thoroughly immediately after planting, then leave it to its own devices for a while, almost allowing the soil to dry out, before watering the plant again.

Supporting plants

Plants need supporting for a variety of reasons. New trees and shrubs, for example, must have their roots firmly anchored to stop them moving in the soil and breaking young roots. Trained fruit trees must be tied in at regular intervals, and so you need a framework to fix them to. Some naturally climbing plants need an artificial support or can be allowed to grow through trees and shrubs, while climbing vegetables must be provided with a framework. Tall herbaceous plants may also need support to stop them flopping over in the borders.

TREE STAKES
Newly planted young trees must be supported with a stake no more than one-third the length of the stem. If the tree is bare-rooted, a single stake driven into the planting hole before planting is enough. Make sure that the stake is thicker than the tree and that you drive it into the soil to a depth of at least 45cm (18in). Container-grown trees are best supported with a stake either side of the root ball, with a crossbar nailed to them. (*See also pages 82-3.*)

As the stakes will not be permanent, there is no need to treat them with preservative and they should be left in the ground until they rot. In both cases, fix the tree to the stake with a plastic tree-tie, nailed to the stake to prevent slipping.

SUPPORTING TRAINED TREES
Trained fruit trees and bushes – cordons, fans and espaliers – will need support throughout their lives. Because the support is permanent,

use pressure-treated timber or metal stakes. Use 2.5m (8ft) stakes, 7.5cm (3in) in diameter, or 5cm (2in) angle irons, and drive them at least 45cm (18in) into the ground, about 3m (10ft) apart. The end stakes need angled struts secured to the lower half. Galvanized wires are then fixed horizontally between the posts at various intervals; the distance depends on the method of training (*see pages 206-9*).

Start by straining the top wire and work downwards, since there is more leverage at the top of the stake. If you work the other way round, you will slacken the wires already in place. If you have a lot to do, it is worth hiring a special wire-strainer. Fix the wires to the stakes with staples or simply twist them round. Trees should not be tied directly to the wires because the wires will rub against the bark. Instead, tie canes to the wires and the plants to the canes. It is also possible to train fruit trees along wires against a wall or fence (*see also page 206*).

SUPPORTING HERBACEOUS PLANTS
Many herbaceous plants, such as poppies, have weak stems and need to be supported. The best technique is to install the support before the plant starts to grow too tall and allow it to grow through. There are special wire frames for this purpose or you could use old wide-mesh wire netting or even thin twigs bent over at the top. Tall herbaceous plants, such as delphiniums and dahlias, will need the support of single canes or posts. Tie them in regularly with soft string as they grow.

Alternatively, you can support climbers on a wooden archway, or "pergola", or on a single pillar of stout, pressure-treated timber. You must drive the stakes at least 45cm (18in) into the ground, so buy timber of an adequate length. Tie the plants to the uprights loosely, using soft string (*see page 114*).

SUPPORTING VEGETABLES
In the vegetable garden, the main methods of support are canes, strings and netting.

The best way to support beans is with a double row of 2.5m (8ft) bamboo canes pushed about 30cm (12in) into the ground. Set them 30cm (12in) apart in the row, making two rows with 60cm (2ft) between them. Tie the canes so that they meet in the middle of the row and tie a cross cane in the V at the top to provide support and rigidity. A cheaper way is to set two strong 5 × 5cm (2 × 2in) posts about 2.5m (8ft) tall at least 45cm (18in) into the ground, one at each end of the row. Then run a wire or strong nylon twine from post to post at the top and another about 30cm (12in) from the ground. Next, tie vertical strands of nylon twine at 30cm (12in) intervals from wire to wire.

You can also train beans, cucumbers and melons on to "cane" wigwams. You need four 2.5m (8ft) canes. Put them in the ground to form a 90cm (36in) square and then tie them together at the top. Plant at the base of the canes and tie in cucumbers or melons at regular intervals; beans will wind themselves around the canes naturally.

SUPPORTING PLANTS AGAINST WALLS

Climbing plants can be trained up a wooden or plastic trellis fixed to the wall and supported on wooden battens; ensure that there is a space between the trellis and the wall to allow for tying. Alternatively, you can use galvanized wires tied to vine eyes and spaced horizontally at 30cm (12in) intervals. For twining climbers, such as clematis or honeysuckle (*Lonicera* sp.), attach vertical wires, also about 30cm (12in) apart, to form a mesh pattern. Train fruit trees by fixing the wires at the required heights and the canes to the wires to prevent chafing.

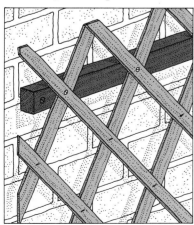

Wooden or plastic trellis *This can be screwed to wooden battens fixed on to the wall, so a gap is left to enable the plants to be tied in. The trellis itself is more decorative than a wire support.*

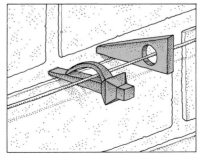

Vine eyes and wall ties *These are used to secure wire supports to a brick or stone wall and ensure that there is a gap between the wall and the wire. Vine eyes are small, flat steel tags with a hole at one end; wall ties are lead nails with a "tie" at one end. Both can be knocked into the wall quite easily and do not damage the mortar. Use brass eyes if the mortar is crumbly.*

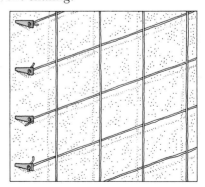

Horizontal wires *These can be fixed to the wall about every 30cm (12in) to help support climbing plants; tie the shoots into them as they grow. Twining plants may need a few vertical wires as well. Fix these at the same spacings to make a wide mesh.*

PROPAGATION TECHNIQUES

THE MODERN TREND is towards "convenience gardening", and a whole industry has developed to service this market. Instead of raising plants from seed and cuttings, for example, we are generally encouraged to buy young plants from the garden center or nursery – all we have to do is plant them.

For the organic gardener, however, there are some very sound reasons why this "convenience" method is not good enough. First and foremost, if you are interested enough to adopt an organic approach to gardening, you are likely to want to do the whole thing from start to finish. Second, it can be difficult to find plants that have been raised organically –

very few commercial growers can guarantee that their produce has been raised in organic soil without the "benefit" of chemical sprays or fertilizers. So, as an organic gardener you have no alternative but to raise all your plants yourself.

By following a few simple rules and taking sensible precautions, your success rate with home-raised seed, even using the minimum of equipment, will be gratifying; and by using other methods of propagation, such as division, cuttings, layering, budding and grafting, you can make sure of a constant and inexpensive supply of organically raised plants for the entire garden.

Growing from seed

The best way to ensure that everything in your garden has been cultivated organically is to grow as much as possible from seed. Either sow directly into your garden, or start seeds in the greenhouse or under fluorescent lights. Prepare the soil well for sowing outside and use a good mixture if sowing in containers (*see page 252*).

Sowing outside

The cheapest method of raising plants is by sowing seeds directly into prepared soil. This is the method you should adopt for most vegetables, hardy annuals and many herbaceous perennials. You can raise some trees this way but, since you need only a few, it is better to sow them in pots or boxes and plant out later.

SOIL PREPARATION

Normal, organic methods of soil preparation will produce a good, workable structure. Rake the soil down to make it level and then sprinkle fertilizer over the top at the recommended rate. A firm bed is usually required so, if your soil has been recently cultivated, compress it by walking over the surface with your weight on your heels.

Next, rake the soil down to a fine tilth. Never do this when the soil is wet enough to stick to your boots; you risk destroying the soil structure.

On deep beds, this consolidation is unnecessary and, indeed, you should never tread on the beds. Instead, leave them for three or four weeks after digging so the soil has a chance to settle.

WHEN TO SOW

The correct time to sow seeds varies from one plant to another and is normally shown on the back of the seed packet. I have given sowing times for different plants throughout the book where relevant. There is, however, no point in sowing too early. As a general rule, seeds sown in soil with a temperature below 7°C (45°F) will not germinate until the soil warms up. Seeds sown in mid spring will often germinate at the same time as, or even before, seeds sown in cold, wet soil. There are, of course, exceptions to this rule. Some alpine seeds, for example, and some trees require a period of freezing weather before they will germinate.

By sowing seeds under cloches you can start sowing outside in early spring. Place the cloches in position two weeks or so before sowing in order to warm the soil up (*see page 140*).

ENCOURAGING SEEDS TO GERMINATE

Some seeds have extremely hard coats. They germinate more successfully if you soak them overnight in water. Very hard seeds can first be filed with a nail file to assist the entry of the water into the seed coat.

Other seeds, such as beets, have a natural germination inhibitor within the seed coat to ensure premature germination does not take place. To speed up germination, remove the inhibitor by washing the seeds under the cold tap or by soaking them in water overnight.

DEPTH AND DISTANCE TO SOW

There is no doubt that the main cause of seeds failing to germinate is that they are sown too deeply. Seeds have a reserve of food which will enable the shoot to reach the surface and find the light. Until it does this, it cannot manufacture any more food. So, if the seed's reserve runs out before the shoot reaches the surface, the seedling will never appear. Of course, it is nonsense to suggest sowing seeds 6mm ($\frac{1}{4}$in) deep or less, since it is impossible to be that accurate when working with soil. I suggest making "shallow" drills, which means making a furrow as shallow as you can.

It is also important to space the seeds and drills correctly to avoid overcrowding. Some seeds can be thinned and transplanted later, others, such as those of root crops, will "fork" if transplanted. Recommended sowing distances are given in the book where relevant, but they will also be listed on the back of seed packets.

SOWING TECHNIQUES

Always aim to sow seed thinly. With the vast majority of seed varieties, between 60 and 90 per

THE STALE SEED BED

If the soil is prepared and in a condition for seeds to germinate, the weed seeds that are almost certainly lying there will soon be springing into life, too. Being native, they will germinate faster and grow quicker than most cultivated varieties. It is essential, therefore, to eliminate this competition before sowing.

The simple remedy is to cultivate the seed bed a few weeks before you need it. Let weed seeds that are lying dormant germinate, then hoe them out immediately before sowing. This way only seeds that appear later will cause problems, and these will not only be fewer in number but also lagging behind the cultivated varieties you have sown and will be easy to recognize.

cent of your seeds will germinate and, if they come up too thickly, they tend to compete for the available light, becoming thin and straggly in the process. Some gardeners become adept at sowing straight from the packet, but I find it much more accurate to hold the seeds in the palm of my hand and sow a pinch at a time.

Some seeds are large enough to sow singly or in "stations" (placing groups of two or three seeds at the required distances, then thinning if more than one seed germinates at any station). With deep beds you should adopt a block-sowing technique (*see page 136*).

Sowing in dry soil If your soil is very dry, water the drills before sowing. Use a can, more or less fill up the drill, allow the water to drain, then sow as directed. Never sow and then water afterwards, since this leads to "capping", where the soil forms a crust on top that can prevent the entry of further water or even prevent young

DRAWING SEED DRILLS

There are two different types of seed drill: narrow drills and wide bands. Both types should be as shallow as possible and of a uniform depth. Rake your soil to a fine tilth and tread down the soil firmly. Set up a tight planting line (*see page 260*), then make a furrow as described below.

Drawing a narrow drill *This is the most commonly used seed drill. Put one corner of a draw hoe in the ground and pull it towards you gently. Alternatively, many gardeners find it easier to draw a regular drill using a short stick.*

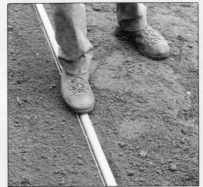

Making a narrow seed drill with a broom or rake handle *If you find it difficult to draw a drill using a hoe, place a broom handle or rake handle along the planting line and press it into the soil with your foot.*

Drawing a wide band *Put your hoe flat on the ground and pull it towards you. Make sure the furrow is of a uniform depth. Wide bands are used in deep-bed cultivation when sowing vegetable crops that are thinned selectively.*

seedlings breaking through to the light.

Covering after sowing Cover all seeds by running the back of your rake down the center of the row. Then, lightly tap down the soil with the back of the rake to ensure that the seed is in close contact with the soil.

Labelling rows of seeds Always use a proprietary plant label to mark the row clearly with the name of the plants. It is not good enough just to stick the seed packet on to a cane, as it always seems to blow away or becomes unreadable after heavy rain.

Pre-germinating seeds Sometimes it is an advantage to pre-germinate seeds inside and sow them outside only after they have started to grow. Examples of plants that benefit from this are parsnips, which take so long to germinate in the early spring that they often rot in the soil, and lettuce, which will not germinate in soil temperatures over 20°C (68°F), a temperature often reached in summer even in colder areas.

Sow the seeds on to a piece of moistened tissue in the bottom of a plastic container. If the seeds need heat to germinate, place the container in a warm place, such as the airing cupboard, until the first roots show through, and then sow as soon as possible. Do not let the roots grow longer than about 3mm ($\frac{1}{8}$in). If you cannot sow the seeds immediately, put the container in the refrigerator (not in the freezer compartment), where they can be kept for a few days.

You must sow the seeds without damaging the fragile roots. With large seeds this is not too difficult, since you can pick up each individual seed with tweezers. With small seeds, however, you need to fluid sow them. Suspend them in a special alginate gel or wallpaper paste and "sow" the mixture in a seed drill (*see page 140*). If your soil is dry, break the normal rule and water over the top immediately after sowing; otherwise the gel may set too hard and trap the seeds under the soil.

SOWING ALPINES AND TREES

Seeds of many alpine plants and trees require a cold period before they will germinate, so you must sow them outside. Since these seeds are often very small, and not used in large quantities, it is a good idea to sow them in pots. Fill the pots with a mixture made from equal parts of peat, soil and coarse grit for alpines or peat and coarse grit for trees, and sow the seeds thinly on top. Cover with a small quantity of coarse grit.

Do not use a can for watering but, instead, stand the pot up to its rim in a bowl of water. Leave it there until you see that the top of the mixture has darkened slightly, then remove it. The seeds will then be drawn down slightly into the mixture. Put the pots outside in a protected spot and cover them with a piece of wire netting as protection against birds and mice.

Sowing inside

By sowing seeds in trays or pots inside you can start much earlier in the year. Vegetables can be sown in mid winter and planted out under cloches in early spring. This way, you will have your first crop in late spring. A greenhouse is ideal for this purpose but you could put them on a windowsill indoors or, for reliable light, place them under fluorescent tubes. Check the recommended sowing temperature before you begin and ensure that you can provide it by starting the seeds off either in a heated propagator in the greenhouse or the airing cupboard or under lights.

Fill a pot or tray with moist seed mixture (*see page 252*) and firm it lightly. Peat-based mixtures require very little firming, so don't overdo it; merely push your fingers into the mixture. Then level the top of the mixture and firm the soil, with a firming board (*see page 261*) if you are using a tray, or with the bottom of another pot.

When you are sowing in containers it is very important to wet the mixture thoroughly before sowing. Spread some mixture on to your work bench, make a well in the center and pour some water into it. Gradually work the water into the mixture by rubbing it through your hands. Fill the container, then water again, since watering after sowing tends to wash the seeds into one spot, or even right out of the pot! Allow the mixture to drain for a few minutes and then sow the seeds as described below.

Cover all except very small seeds, such as those of begonias or lobelias, with their own depth of vermiculite. Then cover the pot or tray with a piece of opaque plastic and put it in a warm place. The airing cupboard is useful, but check the temperature first to ensure that it is suitable for the seeds you are sowing. The gentle heat of fluorescent tubes is ideal for seeds. Check the seeds every day and, as soon as the first one germinates and pushes to the surface, remove the whole container to a light place. Do not put the container in direct sunlight, and cover the seedlings with a sheet of newspaper if there is any chance of the sun scorching the delicate leaves.

If you are growing your seedlings on the windowsill, the fact that the light always comes from one direction only may make them long and spindly. You can reduce this effect to a minimum by making a "light box" out of an orange box, lined with kitchen foil to reflect available light all around the plants. If you use the light box in·winter, you should bring it into the warmth of the center of the room at night. You can cover the box with plastic at night, but remember to remove the cover in the morning, since it will greatly reduce the amount of light reaching your seedlings.

POTS AND CONTAINERS

Wood and clay are the traditional materials used for raising and maintaining plants. However, the plastic and styrafoam containers now available are much cheaper and, in some respects, give improved results.

Although there are proprietary trays and pots available (see below), in fact you can use any shallow container for sowing seed, from styrafoam meat trays to butter tubs or even the foil containers used for take-away food. Plastic yoghurt containers, styrafoam coffee cups and cut-off plastic bottles are ideal for sowing large seeds or for cuttings. Remember, though, if you do use any of these items, they must be thoroughly cleaned before use and they must have adequate drainage holes in the bottom.

Pots These are available in clay or plastic. Clay pots have two main advantages over plastic ones. They are porous and therefore "breathe" allowing the free flow of air around the plant's root ball and thus reducing the risk of overwatering. Conversely, of course, the mixes will dry out faster, so the plants may need watering more often. Clay pots are also heavier than plastic. This is important if you are growing tall, leafy plants that can become top heavy. The disadvantages of clay pots are that their porous nature makes them more likely to harbor disease, and more difficult to clean and sterilize, and that they are considerably more expensive than plastic.

Plants in plastic pots require less frequent watering than those in clay pots. This can be an advantage, particularly if you are using peat-based mixtures, which tend to dry out very quickly.

I recommend using clay pots and soil-based mixtures for plants such as alpines, which need very good drainage, and plastic pots and peat-based mixtures for most other plants.

Seed trays These are shallow trays, generally about 5-7cm (2-3in) deep and either 35×20cm (15× 9in) or 15×10cm (7× 4in). Traditional seed trays are made of thin wood. The disadvantage of wood is that, because it

is porous, it is difficult to clean and can harbor disease. Plastic seed trays, on the other hand, are very easy to sterilize with boiling water and are very much cheaper.

Styrafoam containers Though easily damaged, styrafoam can be particularly useful for seeds and cuttings because it retains warmth. You can buy styrafoam blocks divided into a number of small cells. Holes in the blocks of cells match pegs on a special styrafoam "presser" board. Seed is sown in the individual cells, and then, when it has germinated and developed a root system, the seedling and mixture can be pushed out with the presser board and planted or repotted. Because the roots are never disturbed, this eliminates growth check that sometimes follows transplanting. These styrafoam trays are particularly suitable for multiple sowing (see page 139).

Peat blocks You can buy small blocks of compressed peat mix for sowing. They are sold as small discs which, when immersed in water, swell up to form a cylinder of peat enclosed in nylon netting. Sow directly into the peat and transplant before too much root shows. You can also make them by pressing peat in a special clamp, but this is difficult and time consuming.

SOWING IN SEED TRAYS

Raising seed in trays inside means that vegetables and flowers can be started earlier in the year, without the risk of frost damage. Do not sow plants which fork when transplanted, such as long root vegetables, in seed trays; they have to be sown directly into the soil.

1 *Fill the seed tray with moistened sowing mixture. Remove the excess by running the side of a firming board across the top.*

2 *Press the sowing mixture into the edges of the tray with your fingers. Then consolidate it by pressing it down lightly with the firming board.*

3 *Pour some seed into your palm, then cup your hand slightly to form a channel in the side. Tap your hand with your finger to move the seeds along the channel; sow seeds around the edge of the tray, then work into the center.*

4 *Cover the seeds with their own depth of vermiculite or seed mixture. Vermiculite can be sprinkled over the seeds by hand. If using the mix, shake it over the seeds using a fine sieve.*

Sowing very small seeds *Put a small amount of silver sand into the seed packet to act as a spreading agent. Put the seed and silver sand mixture into your hand and sow as shown above. These seeds do not need to be covered.*

Sowing large seeds *Large seeds, such as beans or cucumbers, for example, should be sown two to a pot. Make holes in the mixture using a small stick, or dibber, and put the seeds in them on their sides. If both of the seeds germinate, carefully remove the weaker one (see overleaf).*

Thinning and transplanting seedlings

When seeds have germinated and are large enough to handle, they will need to be thinned to prevent overcrowding. Seeds that have been sown outside can be transplanted and thinned at the same time. You cannot, however, transplant all seedlings. Root crops will probably fork if seedlings are transplanted but most ornamentals and leaf vegetables can be moved.

SEEDLINGS GROWN OUTSIDE

Before either thinning out or transplanting, water the rows well. To thin seedlings, simply pull up unwanted seedlings, leaving the remaining plants at the required distance from each other. Put the thinnings into a seed tray and remove them to the compost heap. Left on the ground, the bruised stems attract pests.

If you need thinnings for transplanting, then you must take more care when handling the seedlings. Thin to leave one row of seedlings at the required spacing, then transplant the rest in new rows as recommended.

CONTAINER-GROWN SEEDLINGS

Container-sown seedlings need to be thinned, or transplanted, into a larger seed tray or pot when they are large enough to handle (*see below*). Before they are planted out, seedlings grown in the greenhouse must be acclimated to the colder conditions. Do this by placing them first into a closed, unheated cold frame. Then gradually open up the frame a little during the day and, finally, a little at night as well, until you leave it completely open (*see* Greenhouse Gardening, *pages 246-57*).

THINNING AND TRANSPLANTING

Whether grown outside in seed beds or in the greenhouse in seed trays, seedlings need to be thinned to prevent overcrowding. If you are thinning for transplanting, handle the seedlings by their leaves and not their stems because they bruise easily and could succumb to fungus attack. Transplanting from seed trays or pots into another container is known as "pricking out".

Transplanting outside

1 *Water the row of seedlings the day before you want to move them. Firm down the soil at the base of the plants that are to remain by straddling the stems with two fingers and pressing the soil down.*

2 *Lift the remaining seedlings either by placing your fingers under them and lifting carefully or by using a trowel, leaving as much root as possible on the plant. Then lay them in a seed tray.*

3 *Transplant the seedlings to new rows, using a planting board to calculate the spacing. Water the seedlings using a watering can with a fine nozzle.*

Pricking out

1 *Fill a larger seed tray with peat-based mixture. Water the seedlings thoroughly, then lift them out carefully by pushing a small dibber under the roots, handling the seedlings by the leaves only. Never touch the stems.*

2 *Use a small dibber to make holes in the new mixture. Put the seedlings in the holes and firm the mixture. After filling the new tray, water it well and put it in a light place out of direct sunlight.*

Thinning pot-grown seedlings

When growing two large seeds in the same pot, remove the weaker seedling when one reaches 5-7cm (2-3in), and leave the other to grow on. Firm down the roots of the seedling that is to remain while you remove the weaker one.

Other methods of propagation

Growing plants from seed is the most common method of propagation, but it is by no means the only one. Some plants will not produce their exact replicas from seed. Often, flower colors and sometimes even flower shapes will be different, so alternative, vegetative techniques of propagation are required. Of these, division is the simplest method but, for plants that you cannot divide, layering, cuttings, budding and grafting are methods that will ensure that the new plants are exactly the same as the parent.

Propagation by division

Division is a method used to increase perennials. It is perhaps the simplest and most effective method of propagation and it produces good, sizeable plants very quickly. Indeed, many perennials begin to lose vigor after a few years

and will benefit greatly from being lifted from the soil and divided.

For most perennials, this should be done in autumn. Cut back the old flower stems and lift the whole clump using a fork. Divide it in half and remove the young shoots from the outside of the clump (*see below*). The center of the clump is the older, less vigorous, part of the plant and you should discard it.

DIVIDING PLANTS WITH FLESHY ROOTS

Some plants, such as plantain lilies (*Hosta* sp.), have fleshy roots and should be treated differently. These are best lifted for division in spring, just before they start into growth. Then you will be able to see new buds and thus have an idea of where to cut. Each new piece should have at least one good bud. Cut through the root with a sharp spade or a large knife and replant the parts as soon as possible.

DIVIDING PERENNIALS

Perennial plants which form spreading clumps should be divided every few years to perpetuate the existing stocks and prevent overcrowding.

Small clumps can be divided by hand or with a trowel. Larger clumps or very old clumps, however, have to be pried apart using garden forks.

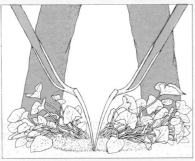

1 Lift the entire plant out of the border and divide it in half. If it has a large matted root system, stick two garden forks back to back into the center of the clump and force it apart.

2 Remove the young shoots from the outer side of the clump by breaking or cutting them off.

3 Cut all the leaves right back to within 2.5cm (1in) of the roots and replant immediately, or pot up in potting soil and put the pots in a shady area until you can replant them.

Taking cuttings

Most plants can be propagated by taking cuttings without too much difficulty. There are many different types of cuttings recommended for various plants, but I just take "hardwood" cuttings in autumn, when the wood is ripe, and "softwood" cuttings in summer, when the shoot is still growing. Most root using one of these methods, while half-hardy perennials require slight modification of the basic technique.

SOFTWOOD CUTTINGS

This method can be used to increase any shrubs. Softwood cuttings can be taken any time during

TAKING SOFTWOOD CUTTINGS

Take cuttings of soft, new plant growth, selecting healthy shoots about 10cm (4in) long. This method is suitable for most shrubs. Use the same method for conifer cuttings, but tear the leaves away from the shoots because the stems need to be bruised before they will root.

1 *Fill a tray with mixture of equal parts of peat and perlite. Trim cutting back by half, just below a leaf joint.*

2 *Carefully trim away all the side leaves, then dip the cutting in copper fungicide solution.*

Taking clematis cuttings

Take a cutting that is at least 30cm (12in) long. Make two cuts, the first one immediately above a leaf joint (see above) and the second about 4cm (1½in) below it (see below). Dip the cutting in copper fungicide and insert it into the mixture up to the leaves.

3 *If you want to use hormone rooting powder, dip the end of the cutting into the powder and shake off the excess. Then put the cutting in the seed tray. Space cuttings in rows 2.5cm (1in) apart each way.*

4 *Water using a copper fungicide solution. Wrap the tray in light plastic sheeting so that the sheeting touches the tops of the cuttings and is sealed under the tray. Put the tray into a softwood cuttings frame.*

TAKING CUTTINGS OF HALF-HARDY PERENNIALS

These are best taken in late summer or in early spring when the tubers produce new shoots. They root more readily than shrubs, but need a temperature of 13-15°C (55-60°F) at the roots.

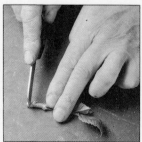

1 *Take a cutting that has at least three leaves and a new shoot. Then carefully cut away all the lower leaves.*

2 *Trim the stem of the cutting just below the lowest leaf joint. Then dip the stem in hormone rooting powder; tap off the excess powder.*

3 *Put the cutting in a pot filled with peat-based mixture. Make a hole with a small dibber, insert the cutting and firm down the mixture by pushing the dibber into it and pressing sideways towards the cutting.*

4 *Bend a piece of wire to form an arch over the cutting and place it in the pot. Cover with a plastic bag. Alternatively, put the pot in a plastic bag, blow up the bag with air and seal the top.*

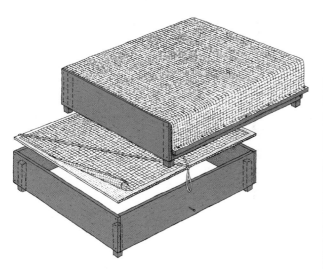

Making a softwood cuttings box *Make two wooden frames about 6in (15cm) deep and both exactly the same size. Make a lid for the first box from a sheet of corrugated plastic and use onion sacking as shading. Hold it in place with a thick rubber band, nailed on to one side and hooked to a nail on the other side. As the plants grow, the other frame can be set on top, and a new lid of sacking, weighted down at the front with a batten and nailed to the back, can be hung over the top.*

the summer, but the best time is early in the season. You do need a small amount of equipment, but this should cost you next to nothing, and the success rate should be about 80 per cent.

Some gardeners use hormone rooting powder to encourage cuttings to root quickly. It can be argued that this is not entirely organic because the hormones have been chemically synthesized. In fact, the hormones are synthesized in the same way as they would be in the plant, so rooting powder can be used in an organic garden provided it contains no additives.

Once the cuttings are potted up and in a cold frame or homemade softwood cuttings box (*see above*), providing the right amount of light is vital. The cuttings will be feeding through their leaves, so they need a certain amount of sunshine. Too much, on the other hand, will cause wilting. I use old onion nets, but a piece of greenhouse shade netting will do just as well. If the weather is likely to be very sunny during the day, cover the frame with two pieces of shading material. If it is only fairly sunny, use one piece. If it is dull, remove the shade altogether. Doing this makes all the difference between success and failure.

HARDWOOD CUTTINGS

This method is used to increase deciduous shrubs such as blackcurrants and gooseberries in the fruit garden, and many ornamental shrubs, such as dogwoods (*Cornus* sp.), mock orange (*Philadelphus* sp.) and Japanese rose (*Kerria* sp.), in autumn. It is worthwhile trying with most deciduous shrubs because it is simple and cheap and the plants will not suffer from the small amount of pruning required.

TAKING HARDWOOD CUTTINGS

Hardwood cuttings should be taken in the autumn, just after the plants have lost their leaves, although some, such as gooseberries, can be taken earlier in the season. Hardwood cuttings take some time to establish, but are worth the effort to increase a favorite or valuable shrub.

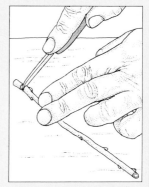

1 *Cut off a length of stem about 20-23cm (8-9in) long using a sharp knife. Trim it below the lowest bud and cut off the soft top growth by trimming just above a bud.*

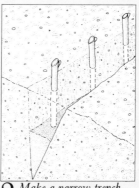

2 *Make a narrow trench and line the bottom with sharp sand. Place the cuttings in the trench, leaving 7.5cm (3in) of the top out of the ground. Refill the trench, firm in the cuttings and leave them for one year.*

3 *The following winter, plant them approximately 15-23cm (6-9in) apart in rows in a corner of the garden. Leave them for another year, then transplant them to their permanent position in the garden.*

Propagation by layering

This method of increasing plants involves putting part of the plant into the ground and leaving it attached to the parent until it has developed a root system sufficient to support itself. There are three different ways: tip layering, normal layering and serpentine layering.

TIP LAYERING

Use this method mainly for plants that root readily, particularly the briar fruits – blackberries, loganberries and other hybrid berries. In late summer, pull down as many shoots as you need and make a hole in the soil where the tip of the shoot rests. Place the tip in the hole and pin it in position using a forked stick. Cover the tip with soil and leave it until the leaves of the parent plant fall. You can then cut the layer from the parent, lift it and transplant the new plant to its permanent position.

NORMAL LAYERING
This method involves burying part of the shoot with the tip exposed, and leaving it to root. Layering is usually carried out in early spring for shrubs and early summer for climbers. It is suitable for plants that root less readily, such as rhododendron, clematis, abelia, some viburnum, magnolia, witch hazel (*Hamamelis* sp.), Mexican orange blossom (*Choisya* sp.), camellia and azalea. You may be able to cut the layer away from the parent plant by the following autumn, but some plants need longer to root. Rhododendrons, for example, can take two, even three years. You can tell when the layer has rooted by its more vigorous appearance.

SERPENTINE LAYERING
This method of propagation is suitable for certain types of climber, particularly clematis. Follow the instructions given for normal layering (*see below*), but alternately bury and expose parts of each stem, making many more plants from each. Wound the stem by slitting it

underneath and place that part underground. Then repeat the process further along the stem, making sure that there is at least one bud between the layers to provide the new shoot. The layers will produce shoots along the stem and, when the shoots start showing signs of growing, you can separate them from the parent plant and split them up to provide several new plants.

Grafting and budding

These are two similar techniques used to put new varieties on to existing plants, particularly fruit trees, and certain ornamental plants. They can be used either to change a variety, to put a variety on to a rootstock, or to put another variety on to a fruit tree to provide a pollinator.

Grafting is generally used to change a variety of an apple or pear tree completely, or to put a pollinator on to an existing tree. There is a risk with the latter because, if you don't use a new variety with the same vigor as the first tree, the

NORMAL LAYERING
By burying part of a shoot underground and leaving it to root, a new plant can be formed.

1 *Make a hole with one straight side by putting a spade or a trowel into the ground and pulling the soil towards you.*

2 *Carefully put the end of the shoot in the hole so that the tip is about 15cm (6in) out of the ground. Take care to avoid snapping the stem.*

3 *Pin the shoot into the ground with a forked stick or a wire pin, cover it with soil and put a large stone over the layer. This keeps the layer in the ground and conserves moisture in dry weather.*

4 *Very often, this is all you need do, but sometimes it is better if you damage the stem of the plant to encourage it to root. You can achieve this simply by twisting the stem fairly vigorously or by cutting a slit in the underside.*

CLEFT GRAFTING
Use this method to graft a new variety on to an existing tree in late winter or early spring.

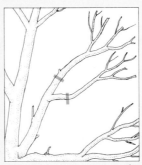

1 *In mid winter, prepare the limb where you will site the graft by cutting back two branches just above a fork.*

2 *Towards the end of winter or in early spring, just as the tree is starting its new growth, split each of the cut ends by driving a bill hook into each one with a hammer.*

3 *Prepare four lengths of stem (known as scions) from the required variety. Each scion should be of one-year-old growth and about 10-15cm (4-6in) long. Cut the base of each one to form a wedge shape.*

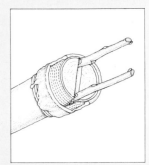

4 *Insert scions into each cut end, making sure the cambium layers (the layers just beneath the bark) correspond. Tie in the scions using raffia or string and cover the wounds with grafting wax.*

more vigorous variety may dominate. Cleft grafting is normally used to graft a new variety on to an existing tree; use the whip-and-tongue method if you want to graft a variety on to a rootstock. The latter technique is also used to graft varieties on to ornamental plants that do not respond to budding.

Grafting should be done in late winter or early spring, just as the tree is beginning its new growth, although the "limb" for grafting should be prepared in mid winter.

Budding is a modified form of grafting and a slightly easier method. It is most commonly used to put new varieties on to rootstocks. It involves making cuts in the bark of the tree or rootstock and inserting one or more buds from another variety into them. It should be done in early to mid summer, when the sap is running well and the bark will separate freely from the tree. It is generally possible to buy rootstocks from any nursery where they do their own budding. And, as they are sold bare rooted, plant them when dormant before you need them.

WHIP-AND-TONGUE GRAFTING

Use this method to graft a variety on to a rootstock. Several ornamental plants can also be grafted using this method.

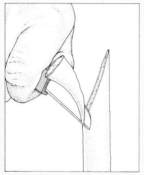
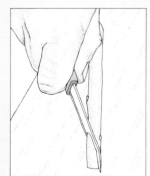

1 *Trim the rootstock right back and, with a sharp knife, make a long slanting cut in the top part of the stem to leave a long wedge shape.*

2 *Using a one-year-old scion as above, cut the end to form a corresponding wedge.*

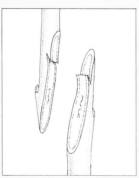
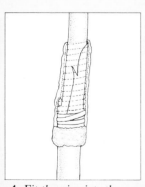

3 *Make two more cuts, one upwards in the rootstock and one downwards in the scion, to form two "tongues" that will fit together.*

4 *Fit the scion into the rootstock, making sure that the cambium layers correspond. Tie the graft with raffia and cover the wound with grafting wax.*

BUDDING ON TO A ROOTSTOCK

Budding is a form of grafting used to put new varieties on to rootstocks and is a relatively simple technique to carry out.

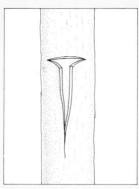

1 *In summer, cut a length of stem from the variety you want to bud. Leaving the leaf stalks on the cutting, remove all the leaves. (If you are budding a rose, remove the thorns first.) Immerse the whole stem in a bowl of water until it is needed.*

2 *With a sharp knife, cut a T-shaped slit in the bark of the rootstock and peel back the bark very slightly.*

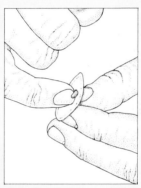

3 *Remove a bud from the prepared stem – insert a sharp knife into the stem below the bud and pull it upwards, keeping the knife just under the bud.*

4 *Examine the base of the bud carefully and you will see a sliver of wood in the center. Remove it with your fingernail.*

5 *Slide the bud into the T-shaped slit using the leaf stalk as a handle. When the bud is secure, cut away any excess bark to ensure a perfect fit and tie the bud on to the tree using raffia or a special rubber tie.*

6 *When the bud shows signs of having taken, carefully cut the raffia away; rubber ties can be left to rot. In the autumn, prune off the growth on the rootstock above the new shoot, and tie the shoot to the stub.*

THE GARDENING YEAR

GARDENING IS FAR from being an exact science, and the gardener who makes rules and sticks to them rigidly is bound to suffer disappointment and frustration. For there are almost always alternative methods to follow to reach desirable gardening goals, although new gardeners can't be expected to find much comfort in this truth. Of more concern to them, as well as to more experienced gardeners, are the existence of different regions with varying climatic conditions and soil types. These all affect plant growth, the kinds of plants that can be grown, and the timing of gardening operations.

In North America, there are many different climatic regions, as the map below shows. The gardening year is, in fact, more a state of mind than a reality in much of the country where frigid winters, often with long-lasting snow cover, stop outdoor gardening.

Assistance in coping with the regional aspects of gardening can come from several sources. Other gardeners in the area can be helpful, as can the Cooperative Extension Service, an organization of university-trained horticultural specialists with offices in nearly every county. New gardeners can also benefit from a guide such as the Calendar that follows. The Calendar is divided into seasons: spring, from March to end of May; summer, from June to the end of August; autumn, from September to the end of November and winter from December to the end of February.

CLIMATIC REGIONS OF THE USA

Region 1 Cool dry summers, often foggy. Heavy rainfall in winter.
Region 2 Drier and warmer than Region 1 in summer. Lowest temperature 10° to 20°F.
Region 3 Hot, dry summers and mild winters. Lowest temperature 22° to 24°F. Winter rainfall 8-10in.
Region 4 Conditions vary with altitude in this mountainous region.
Region 5 Coastal summers are cool and dry, with higher temperature inland. Rainfall 10in in valleys, 30in in mountains.
Region 6 Warm summers, with cool winters. Winter temperature 10° to 15°F. Highest rainfall in spring and winter.
Region 7 Warm summers with winter temperatures of 0° to 15°F. Rainfall 10-20in.
Region 8 A semi-arid region with hot summers and cold winters. Winter temperature −10° to 0°F.
Region 9 Hot summer days, frost at night. Cold winters.
Region 10 Very hot. Rainfall 3-10in.
Region 11 Very hot summer days, with frost at night. Cold winters.
Region 12 Rainfall and temperature vary with elevation and exposure.
Region 13 Rainfall and temperature vary with elevation and exposure, but temperatures about 7°F hotter than Region 12.
Region 14 Rainfall and temperature vary with elevation and exposure. Warmer than both Regions 12 and 13.
Region 15 Warm summers with very cold winters.
Region 16 Summers warmer than Region 15. Rainfall 12-22in.
Region 17 Hot and dry despite 12-22in rainfall, due to excessive evaporation.

Region 18 Humid summers with cold, dry winters.
Region 19 Hot winds in summer. Winter temperatures subject to sudden variations.
Region 20 Transition zone between the warm, dry areas to the west, and the humid climate of eastern Texas.
Region 21 Summers with 20-30in rainfall. Cold winters with drying winds.
Region 22 Flat prairie country with cold, drying winds in winter. Rainfall 30-40in.
Region 23 West of region has cold winters with drying winds. East of region is warmer and more humid due to proximity to water.
Region 24 Very humid atmosphere. Rainfall of 30-40in, spread throughout the year.

Region 25 Warm summers and moderate winters. Rainfall 40-50in, but still a risk of drought in summer.
Region 26 Long summer days, with cool nights. Winter brings heavy snowfalls.
Region 27 Heavy winter snows in colder areas. Rainfall 35-50in, falling throughout the year.
Region 28 A warmer zone than Region 27. Drought may occur at the end of summer. Winters moderate.
Region 29 Warm summers. High rainfall of 45-60in.
Region 30 Hot summers and short winters. Heavy rains in winter.
Region 31 Warm summers. Annual frosts may cause damage. Rainfall 50in.
Region 32 Only slight temperature variations throughout the year. No killing frosts. Rainfall 50-60in.

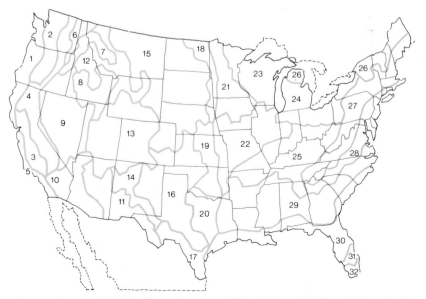

Spring

THROUGHOUT SPRING:
- **Heavy soils** Rake soil for sowing.
- **Light soils** Dig in overwintered green-manure crops early enough to allow land to settle before sowing.
- Start hoeing regularly from now on.
- Mulch between plants to control weeds and help water retention.
- Water regularly in dry weather, particularly newly planted subjects.
- Check the wormery; put it outside again if you over wintered it inside. If it was left outside and the worms have died over the winter, replace them and start filling it.
- Start spraying with insecticides or fungicides as necessary but never on open flowers.
- Construct a pond.
- Carry out grafting.

	EARLY SPRING	MID SPRING	LATE SPRING
THE ORNAMENTAL GARDEN **Throughout spring:** • Hoe carefully between ornamental plants. • Lightly fork over the soil to ready it for planting annuals. • Mulch vacant areas with organic matter.	• Rake the lawn with a spring-tine rake. • Start mowing lawn when the grass is growing well. • Sow grass seed in new lawns and resow bare patches. • Lay turf lawns. • Feed lawns and borders with general organic fertilizer. • Lift and divide perennials. • Lift, split and transplant snowdrops and early bulbs. • Prune hybrid bush roses, cutting away any frost damage. • Finish planting, bare-rooted deciduous trees, shrubs and hedging plants. • Start outside sowing of hardy annuals and many shrubs and climbers. • Start planting summer-flowering bulbs and perennials if ground is not frozen or water-logged. • Start sowing sweet peas. • Trim heathers (*Calluna* sp.). • Layer shrubs.	• Plant bare-rooted evergreen trees, shrubs and hedging plants. • Prune shrubs that flower on one-year-old wood immediately after flowering. • Prune shrubs that flower on wood made in the same season. • Prune heaths (*Erica* sp.) as they finish flowering. • Plant floating, submerged oxygenating and marsh plants in and around the pool. • Finish planting sweet peas. • Continue to plant perennials, and to lift and divide crowded clumps. • Continue to sow herbs and thin those sown in early spring. • Plant tubs and hanging baskets for spring and summer color. • Start spraying roses if black spot has been a problem. • Plant sweet peas sown inside.	• Finish planting bare-rooted evergreen plants. • Support tall perennials. • Trim spreading alpines after flowering. • When all danger of frost has passed, plant out half-hardy annuals and perennials. • If half-hardy annuals in seed trays look yellow, feed them with liquid seaweed fertilizer. • If space is needed, lift and heel in spring-flowering bulbs. • Start clipping fast-growing hedges. • Prune early flowering climbers. • Start tying in climbers. • Plant deep-water aquatic plants. • Sow hardy perennials and biennials in a seed bed. • Continue sowing herbs. • Start taking softwood cuttings. • Look out for caterpillars on roses and other ornamentals. • Control aphids.
THE VEGETABLE GARDEN **Throughout spring:** • Keep in mind which vegetables must be sown early and which ones need warmer soil. Timing is all-important. • Start successional sowing of lettuce, radish and spinach in early to mid spring.	• Sow peas and broad beans early – St Patrick's day is the traditional date in the North. • Feed spring cabbages with dried blood or seaweed meal. • Sow leeks, onions, broccoli and cabbages in a seed bed or in a cold frame. • Start sowing spinach outside. • Plant shallots, garlic, onion sets, potatoes and Jerusalem artichokes. • Plant out peas and early spinach sown in the greenhouse in late winter.	• Sow sweetcorn outside as the soil warms up. • Sow maincrop Florence fennel, peas, turnips, kohl-rabi, salsify and scorzonera, carrots, beets, autumn brassicas, Swiss chard and leeks outside. • Plant out broccoli, cabbage and onions sown inside and tomato, eggplant and pepper seedlings under cloches. • Plant globe artichoke seedlings or roots and asparagus crowns. • Set out poles for beans. • Sow heat-resistant lettuce.	• Finish planting squash and fruiting vegetables under cloches if nights are still frosty. Sow seeds for later crops. • Earth up potatoes. • Plant out leeks. • At the end of the period transplant celery and celeriac. • Pinch out tops of broad beans to thwart black fly.
THE FRUIT GARDEN **Throughout spring:** • In Northern regions, protect blossom of early flowering trees from frost with woven polypropylene. • Finish winter pruning and planting of fruit trees. • Prune fan-trained cherry and plum trees. • Start training in shoots of briar fruits. • Feed and mulch fruit trees and bushes. • If apple and pear scab or gooseberry mildew have been a problem, spray at fortnightly intervals.	• Feed currants with rock potash and blackcurrants with blood, fish and bone meal. • If you have protected figs for the winter, remove the straw and sacking, untie the shoots and retrain them. • Graft apples, pears and plums. • Hand-pollinate blossom covered with polypropylene.	• Continue hand-pollinating blossom. • Feed olive trees.	• Water fruit bushes and trees, if soil is dry. • Mulch under strawberry plants with straw to keep the fruits off the ground, and cover with netting to protect from birds. • Start tying in and pinching out wall-trained fruit. • Pull up unwanted shoots of raspberries that are growing into the paths. • Thin gooseberries to form large dessert fruits; use thinnings for cooking. • Put out codling moth traps. • Leave blossom uncovered during the day to allow insect pollination.
IN THE GREENHOUSE **Throughout spring:** • Ventilate the greenhouse on sunny days but close it at night. • Keep the atmosphere fairly dry.	• Sow the last of the ornamental half-hardy annuals. • Start sowing herbs. • Take cuttings of overwintered half-hardy perennials. • Sow peppers, eggplants and cucumbers for growing in a cold greenhouse and tomatoes for planting under cloches. • Sow okra and leeks. • Mulch around peaches. • Tie up roots of vines that were taken down for the winter.	• Start shading as necessary and increase ventilation. • Sow cucumbers, squash and melon seeds for planting under cloches. • Plant tomatoes in an unheated greenhouse in growing bags or in prepared soil in the borders. • Plant eggplant and pepper seedlings in a greenhouse or walk-in plastic shelter.	• Start summer pruning of grape vines. • Feed tomatoes and remove side-shoots. • Continue shading the greenhouse on very sunny days and increase ventilation.

Summer

THROUGHOUT SUMMER:
- Water the garden in dry weather.
- Continue hoeing; many weeds will now be seeding so this is very important. Cut down perennial weeds near your garden.
- Continue to mulch to control weeds and help moisture retention.
- Start a new compost bin if the first is full and not yet ready for use.
- Cover bare ground with compost as it becomes available.
- Sow vacant ground with a green-manure crop. Consult Cooperative Extension Service for recommendations.
- Top up wormery regularly as the worms work very fast now; water if necessary.
- Watch continually for signs of pests and diseases and treat immediately.
- This is the best season to take softwood cuttings and for budding.
- Start layering.

	EARLY SUMMER	MID SUMMER	LATE SUMMER
THE ORNAMENTAL GARDEN **Throughout summer:** • Mow lawn regularly, but not if the weather turns very dry, and remove rosetted weeds. • Water lawn as necessary. • Top up pool and soak marsh garden in dry weather. • Dead-head perennials, shrubs and roses to prolong flowering. • Tie in long-stemmed perennials. • Tie in climbers.	• Remove rose suckers. • Cut back early flowering perennials. • Continue to lift and heel-in spring-flowering bulbs; try to leave daffodils. • In cold areas, start to plant out half-hardy perennials and annuals. • Plant deep-water aquatic plants. • Transplant to nursery rows seedlings of perennials and biennials sown in early spring. • Continue sowing biennials. • Continue propagating climbers by layering. • Take cuttings of heaths (*Erica* sp.).	• Trim fast-growing hedges regularly. • Cut back perennials that have finished flowering, leaving lower foliage – shred woody stems before composting. Leave a few such as foxglove (*Digitalis* sp.) and delphinium to produce seed. • Transplant biennials and perennials raised from seed into nursery rows. • Buy and plant autumn-flowering bulbs. • Harvest herbs for drying before they come into full bloom.	• Lightly prune conifers. • Prune shrubs after flowering. • Dead-head annuals. • Cut down gladioli, leaving some foliage to build up food for next year's corms. • Continue transplanting perennials and biennials. • Order spring-flowering bulbs. • Start layering rhododendrons. • Take cuttings of half-hardy perennials. • Check over houseplants that have been summered outdoors. Bring them inside. • Store dried herbs and collect seeds. • Set earwig traps; if they are still troublesome, smear light grease below the affected blooms. • Take softwood cuttings of alpines, heathers and perennial herbs such as sage and rosemary.
THE VEGETABLE GARDEN **Throughout summer:** • Hoe weeds regularly. • Check all vegetable netting. • Continue successional sowing until late summer.	• In colder areas, sow tender vegetables such as sweetcorn. • Transplant autumn and winter brassicas and protect new plants from cabbage root maggot. • Finish sowing broccoli and transplanting leeks sown inside or in a seed bed. • Support asparagus tops with canes in exposed areas. • Harvest and store shallots. • Tie cucumbers to canes if growing them up tripod frames. • If growing sweetcorn under plastic, cut slits to allow the leaves through. • Sow chicory outside. • Earth up maincrop potatoes • Harvest early potatoes. • Put straw under bush tomatoes to keep the fruit clean.	• Early July is the last safe date for sowing squash in much of the North. • Start late sowings of vegetables such as turnips and carrots for maturing outside; use early varieties. • Draw soil away from onions to hasten ripening. • Earth up maincrop potatoes again. • Spray potatoes against blight at fortnightly intervals from now until you lift them.	• In mild winter regions, sow cabbages and other brassica crops for late winter and spring harvests. • Sow quick-maturing varieties of lettuce for a late crop. If frosts come early, sow in a cold frame. • Continue harvesting summer squash while fruits are small. Even with squash borers, plants continue to bear until frost in most regions. • Start lifting and storing onions.
THE FRUIT GARDEN **Throughout summer:** • Check all the fruit netting in the garden. • Tie in briar fruit and wall-trained fruit. • Spray aphids with insecticidal soap, if necessary. • Watch for sawfly larvae attacks on gooseberries; spray bushes with rotenone as soon as they are seen. • If apple or pear scab or mildew has been a problem, continue spraying at fortnightly intervals.	• Protect cherries against birds and pick fruit when ripe. • Start summer pruning trained soft fruit to encourage fruiting shoots. • Continue tying in and pinching out wall-trained trees. • Feed blackcurrants if necessary. • Peg down strawberry runners if you want them for forcing, or cut them off.	• After tree fruit has dropped naturally, thin fruit clusters. • Harvest raspberries, cut out fruited canes and weak new growth. Tie in new canes. Everbearers should bear crop at tip of new canes. • Harvest strawberries and cut old leaves down. Remove straw mulch. Dig up unwanted runners. • Start summer pruning soft fruit and trained pear trees. • Support heavily laden branches of tree fruit. • Towards the end of the period, tip layer briar fruit. • Thin fig trees. • Feed citrus fruit.	• Summer prune all trained forms of apples and pears. • Thin mulberry trees. • Tie in branches of festooned trees. • Prune plum and damson trees. • Pick early apples for eating immediately. • Continue summer pruning bush fruit. • Harvest briar fruits, then cut back fruited shoots. • Pot up rooted strawberry runners and leave them outside. • Plant new strawberry beds. • Continue spraying against pear and apple scab and mildew.
IN THE GREENHOUSE **Throughout summer:** • Feed all fruiting vegetables grown under glass at weekly intervals. • Damp down regularly.	• Paint shading on to greenhouse or let down blinds for the summer and increase ventilation. • Start pinching out, training and feeding fruiting vegetables. • Remove tomato side-shoots. • Summer prune vines.	• Make sure the greenhouse is in a good state of repair; renew cracked panes of glass and paint frame as necessary. • Continue feeding and removing side-shoots from tomatoes and cucumbers and start harvesting.	• Take fuchsia and geranium cuttings and sow cyclamen. • Start sowing winter lettuce in seed trays. • Maintain continual day and night ventilation.

Autumn

THROUGHOUT AUTUMN:
● **Heavy soils** Start digging soil, working in manure or compost as soon as land becomes vacant. Keep off all wet soil; cover an area with plastic so that you can cultivate it when the rest is wet.
● **Light soils** Sow green-manure crops to cover vacant land for winter.
● Dig in spring-grown green-manure crops.
● There will be an enormous amount of compost at this time. If bins are full, use some of the material as sheet compost.
● Start collecting leaves and compost them for leaf mold separately, or with the shredded prunings.
● Clean out debris under hedges.
● If you have ordered bare-rooted ornamental or fruit trees and bushes, cover a piece of ground with black plastic to prevent soil freezing. They can then be planted temporarily if the rest is frozen.
● Take the mower in for servicing.

LATE AUTUMN:
● Check all tree ties and stakes; renew or repair as necessary.
● Mulch around trees and bushes.
● Make sure compost bins are covered.
● Take up all garden stakes, clean and store for next year.
● Drain hoses, coil and store for winter.
● Carry out any "hard" landscaping provided ground is not frozen.

	EARLY AUTUMN	MID AUTUMN	LATE AUTUMN
THE ORNAMENTAL GARDEN **Throughout autumn:** ● Keep sprinkler going on lawns and borders for long periods if the weather is very dry. ● Start preparing empty borders for autumn planting. ● Lightly fork over any vacant ground in the borders and mulch with compost or manure.	● Do not cut the lawn if the weather turns very dry. ● If sowing a new lawn, prepare the soil and sow now. ● Plant spring-flowering bulbs as soon as they arrive from mail-order specialists. ● Continue to tie in stems of tall-growing autumn-flowering perennials. ● Prune climbing and rambling roses and weeping standards. ● Prepare trenches for planting new hedges. ● Continue trimming coniferous trees and hedges.	● Stop mowing the lawn. ● Lay turf lawns. ● Cover the pond with netting. ● Dig up, divide and replant perennials, if they are old, crowded or restricting shrubs. ● Lift and store half-hardy perennials and bulbs and tubers. ● Lift gladioli, remove old corms and store new ones. ● Replant tubs and hanging baskets for winter/spring. ● Dig up and compost annuals; replant with biennials. ● Start planting bare-rooted evergreen trees, shrubs and hedging plants. ● Plant lilies. ● Finish planting spring bulbs. ● Plant hardy perennials and heaths. ● Sow sweet peas in cold frame. ● Start taking hardwood cuttings. ● Pot up mint roots for winter.	● Start planting bare-rooted deciduous trees, shrubs and hedging. Continue planting conifers and broad-leaved evergreens, except in the far north. If ground is frozen or water-logged, heel them in. ● Lift a few perennials such as primroses for forcing in the greenhouse. ● Remove fallen leaves from the rock garden. ● Continue planting perennials if soil is not frozen or waterlogged. ● Continue to take hardwood cuttings. ● Pot up hyacinths, tulips and daffodils.
THE VEGETABLE GARDEN **Throughout autumn:** ● Keep leaves and vegetable debris tidied up to prevent spread of disease.	● Start lifting and storing root vegetables, except those that need frost to improve flavor. ● Move lettuce and endive plants into the cold frame, or be prepared to protect them against frost. ● Earth up celery, celeriac and leeks. ● Transplant spring cabbages in mild-winter regions. ● Lift and store maincrop onions. ● Lift and store potatoes; destroy the foliage if there has been any sign of blight. ● Remove any caterpillars on brassicas, especially broccoli.	● Transplant spring cabbages in mild-winter regions. ● Cut down peas and beans; leave the roots in the soil. ● Earth up celery, leeks and celeriac. ● Harvest chicory and store roots. ● Lift and store root vegetables except those that need frost. ● Force chicory roots inside. ● Remove all stumps of brassicas as they are harvested. ● Cut down Jerusalem artichokes. ● Blanch celery. ● Cut down asparagus foliage and mulch bed. Mulch rhubarb when the leaves have died down.	● Start sowing broad beans outside in mild-winter regions. ● Continue forcing crops in a warm place. ● Protect cauliflowers from frost by bending over the curds. ● Firm the stems of tall brassicas to prevent them rocking. ● Remove yellowing leaves of brassicas and compost them. ● Take up all stakes, clean them and store for next year. ● Finish earthing up celery. ● Lift and store a few parsnips and Hamburg parsley in case the ground freezes.
THE FRUIT GARDEN **Throughout autumn:** ● Continue to tie in new shoots of briar fruits. ● Check all tree ties and stakes; renew as necessary. ● Cut out damaged or diseased wood.	● Complete summer pruning of all trained trees. ● Mulch under autumn-fruiting strawberries with straw and cover with bird netting. Towards the end of the season, protect them with cloches. ● Continue planting strawberry beds. ● Pick blackberries and cut fruited shoots back. ● Take hardwood cuttings of currants and gooseberries. ● Cut off and destroy mildewed tips of fruit trees and bushes. ● Check apple, pear and quince trees for canker.	● Put greasebands around apple and cherry trees. ● Pick and store late apples, pears and quinces. ● Winter prune currants and gooseberries after leaf fall. ● Cut back foliage of autumn-fruiting strawberries after harvesting and remove straw mulch; compost everything.	● Plant bare-rooted trees and bushes and rootstocks for budding next spring. ● If the soil is frozen when trees arrive, cover the roots with peat and burlap, or heel the trees in. ● Start winter pruning of bush and standard trees and formative pruning of trained trees. ● Cover soft fruit bushes with bird netting. ● Finish storing tree fruit. ● Inspect fruit in storage and remove any showing signs of deterioration. ● Check fruit cage netting and repair if necessary.
IN THE GREENHOUSE **Throughout autumn:** ● Reduce ventilation and damping down.	● Continue sowing winter lettuce. ● Check that your heaters are working.	● Sow short-day lettuce in a cold greenhouse or cold frame. ● Check all plants; remove foliage or shoots that have been attacked by fungus disease. ● Start closing the cold frame and greenhouse at night; start heating if necessary.	● Transplant short-day lettuces. ● Plant vines, peaches and nectarines. ● If the greenhouse is heated and large enough, bring the wormery inside and the worms will keep going through the winter.

Winter

THROUGHOUT WINTER:
● **Heavy soils** Continue digging. Keep off the soil as much as possible, working from boards if necessary. Always keep off the soil if it is wet – cover some land with plastic so that you can continue cultivating when the rest is wet.
● Dig new deep beds and manure existing ones.
● **Light soils** Spread manure or compost over ground that is not sown with green manure.
● When the ground is frozen, try to keep off the soil and especially off the grass.
● If you have not already done so, check stakes and ties of all ornamental fruit trees; renew and repair as necessary.
● Protect roots of all plants in containers by wrapping the tubs or pots with burlap.
● Send for seed and bulb catalogues and plan next year's planting.
● Repair tools and machinery.
● Make any new tools.
● Repaint woodwork such as fences and gates. NEVER use creosote near plants.
MID WINTER:
● Sterilize pots and trays with boiling water, ready for sowing in late winter.
LATE WINTER:
● Start cleft and whip-and-tongue grafting.

	EARLY WINTER	MID WINTER	LATE WINTER
THE ORNAMENTAL GARDEN **Throughout winter:** ● Mulch between plants in borders after soil has frozen. ● Winter prune trees. ● Plant bare-rooted trees, shrubs and bushes when soil conditions are suitable. ● If there have been any frosts, check all newly planted shrubs to see if they have lifted. If they have, firm them back into the ground. ● Examine stored dahlia tubers: soak in warm water any that are shrivelled; if any show signs of rot, cut out the affected parts and dust the tuber with sulfur. ● Close the cold frame to protect sweet peas in very cold or wet weather.	● Replace any worn areas of lawn with turf in mild-winter regions. ● Lay turf lawns in mild-winter regions if ground is not frozen. ● Start winter pruning trees and shrubs. ● Sow alpines and tree seeds that need exposure to frost and leave them outside. ● Put container-grown, frost-in the greenhouse or other frost-free place, or leave outside and cover with woven polypropylene if winters are mild. ● Bulbs that have been potted up and covered outside should be brought into the house as soon as some of the buds are about 5cm (2in) high.	● Finish sowing plants and trees. ● Sow seeds of wax begonia, mealy cup sage (*Salvia farinacea*) and snap dragons (*Antirrhinum* sp.) and grow under fluorescent tubes.	● Spike badly drained areas of lawn with a hollow-tined fork and brush peat or grit into the holes. ● Start feeding the borders and lawn in late winter/early spring. ● Start pruning late-flowering climbers. ● Lift and divide mint and propagate from runners. ● Sow seeds of petunias, patience plants (*Impatiens*) and dusty-miller (*Artemisia stellerana*) and grow under fluorescent tubes.
THE VEGETABLE GARDEN **Throughout winter:** ● Put chicory roots and seakale into peat in a warm place for forcing every three to four weeks. ● Test soil pH and add lime if necessary. ● Continue digging and manuring when possible. ● Examine stored vegetables; remove any that show signs of deterioration.	● Order vegetable seeds from mail-order specialists.	● Continue sowing broad beans. ● Cover some soil with cloches to warm it up ready for sowing outside in a few weeks. ● Set up potato tubers to sprout if planting under plastic. ● Plant rhubarb if the soil is not waterlogged or frozen. Cover an established plant for early shoots.	● In mild-winter regions, feed spring cabbages. ● Start sowing early vegetable varieties under cloches and hardy varieties outside. ● Start planting early potatoes under cloches. ● Plant Jerusalem artichokes, shallots and garlic as soon as the soil is workable. ● Start planting out under cloches early sowings made in the greenhouse.
THE FRUIT GARDEN **Throughout winter:** ● Winter prune apple, pear and quince trees; cut out and destroy shoots showing signs of canker. ● Plant bare-rooted trees and bushes when weather conditions are suitable. ● Inspect fruit in storage; remove any showing signs of deterioration. ● Prune newly planted fruit trees and bushes.	● Cut back branches ready for grafting in the spring. ● In cold areas, protect fig shoots by tying them together and covering with straw and burlap.		● Feed and mulch fruit trees and bushes. ● Protect blossoms of early flowering wall-trained fruit from frost by covering with sheets of polypropylene; hand-pollinate flowers if necessary. ● Start training in new shoots of briar fruits. ● Prune autumn-fruiting raspberries. ● Put potted strawberry runners into the greenhouse for forcing. ● If peach-leaf curl has been a problem in the past, start spraying now.
IN THE GREENHOUSE **Throughout winter:** ● Ventilate whenever possible on sunny days. ● Keep atmosphere dry. ● Check maximum/minimum thermometer regularly and adjust heating as necessary.	● Take down greenhouse vines and lay them on the greenhouse borders. ● Wash down the greenhouse.	● Start heating the greenhouse if sowing early crops now. ● Mid to late winter: start sowing globe artichokes, peppers, cucumbers, onions, radishes, carrots, turnips, summer brassicas and spinach in a heated greenhouse.	● Start sowing seeds of flowering pot plants. ● Start sowing half-hardy annuals in late winter/early spring. ● Start sowing celery, tomatoes, eggplants, melons, cabbage, broccoli, cauliflower and early spinach. ● Start sowing tomatoes for growing under glass. ● Tie up rods of greenhouse vines as soon as they start new growth.

USEFUL ADDRESSES

SOURCES FOR SEEDS, PLANTS AND OTHER SUPPLIES

Bear Creek Nursery
P.O.B. 411
Northport, WA 99157
Cold- and drought-resistant fruit trees, other nursery stock, rootstocks and 'Consort' blackcurrant variety. Catalogue.

Biosystems
Box 162
Delta, PA 17314
Dehydrated seaweed. Catalogue.

W. Atlee Burpee Co.
900 Park Ave
Warminster, PA 18974
Seed (request untreated), plants, biological controls, organic pest controls, netting, cold frames. Catalogue.

Cape Cod Worm Farm
30 Center Ave.
Buzzards Bay, MA 02532
Red worms, worm castings.

Dalen Products, Inc.
11110 Gelbert Drive
Knoxville, TN 37932
Garden supplies, including perforated brown mulch (Miracle Mulch). Catalogue.

The Espoma Co.
6 Espoma Road
Millville, NJ 08332
Manufacturers of organic plant foods available in most garden centers. Brochures.

Dean Foster
Hartford, MI 49057
Fruits and general nursery stock. Catalogue.

Gardener's Supply Co.
128 Intervale Rd
Burlington, VT 05401
Tools and supplies, including organic pesticides. Catalogue.

Green River Tools
P.O.B. 1919
Brattleboro, VT 15301
Outdoor furniture from renewable resources, tools and natural pest controls. Catalogue.

Gurney Seed and Nursery Co.
Yankton, SD 57079
Seeds, plants, supplies. Catalogue.

Hoechst Fibers Industries
Spunbound Business group
P.O.B. 5887
Spartanburg, SC 29304
Earth blanket, a porous mulching material.

Johnny's Selected Seeds
Albion, ME 04910
Vegetable seeds including heirloom varieties and flower seeds, untreated except for corn. Supplies, including plastic mulch, wire and plastic for tunnel cloches and other protection, tools and organic pest controls and books. Catalogue.

Kinsman Garden Co.
River Rd
Point Pleasant, PA 18950
Imported tools, supplies, cold frames. Catalogue.

Mellinger Nursery Co.
2380 South Grange Rd
North Lima, OH 44452
Plants, general supplies, fertilizers and organic pest controls. Catalogue.

Memphis Worm Farms
650 Compress
Memphis, TN 38106
Red earthworms

Miller Nurseries
West Lake Drive
Canadaigua, NY 14424
Fruits and general nursery plants. Supplies, including natural beetle control (milky spore), plastic tree protectors, netting. Catalogue.

Natural Farm Products, Inc.
Spencer Rd.
Kalska, MI 49646
Natural fertilizers, including fish and seaweed products. Catalogue.

Nichols Garden Nursery
1190 North Pacific Highway
Albany, OR 97321
Vegetable and herb seeds and plants, supplies. Catalogue.

Organic Farm and Garden Supply
115 Warner Dr
Columbia, SC 29204
Organic fertilizers, supplies. Catalogue.

George W. Park Seed Co.
Greenwood
SC 29647-0001
Seeds, supplies, including fluorescent light lamps, cold frames. Catalogue.

Paradise Water Gardens
15 May St
Whitman, MA 02382
Water garden plants and supplies. Catalogue.

Pine Tree Garden Seeds
New Gloucester, ME 04260
Seeds, books, tools and bulbs. Catalogue.

Plantjoy
Box 1000
Trinidad, CA 95570
Peruvian seabird guano.

Plants of the Southwest
1812 Second St
Santa Fe
New Mexico 87501
Seeds, including ancient American vegetables and wildflowers, and regional books. Catalogue $1.

Rayner Bros. Inc.
Salisbury, MD 21801
Virus-free strawberry and other plants. Catalogue.

Reuter Laboratories
14540 John Marshall Highway
Gainesville, VA 22065
Natural pest controls and traps available in most garden centers.

Roses of Today and Yesterday
802 Brown's Valley Rd.
Watsonville, CA 95076-0398
Disease-resistant shrub roses, old and modern rose bushes. Catalogue $2.

Stark Bros.
Louisiana, MO 63353
Fruits including tayberry. Catalogue.

Stoke Seeds Inc.
P.O.B. 548
Buffalo, NY 14240-0548
Seeds including untreated pea, bean, corn, supplies for seed starting, organic fertilizers and pesticides. Catalogue.

Thompson and Morgan
P.O.B. 1308
Jackson, NJ 08527
Huge selection of seeds, mostly imports, plants and bulbs. Catalogue.

Otis S. Twilley Seeds Co. Inc.
P.O.B. 65
Trevose, PA 19047
Seeds including recommended varieties for states and regions, supplies, including bio-organic fertilizers. Catalogue.

Unique Insect Control
P.O.B. 15376
Sacramento, CA 95851
Ladybugs, mantis cases, trichogramma.

Vermont Bean Seed Co.
Garden Lane
Fairhaven, VT 05743-0250
Untreated seeds, including many heirloom vegetables, organic fertilizers and pesticides.

Don Walker
1209 North 44th St
Milwaukee, WI 53208
Fruits, insect traps for apple maggot, codling moth.

ORGANIZATIONS AND PUBLICATIONS

Cooperative Extension Service
Government funded organization associated with US Dept. of Agriculture and land grant universities, to assist home gardeners and farmers. Offices listed in telephone directory, often under County Government.

National Gardening Organization
Non-profit organization promoting gardening. Membership ($18 a year) includes monthly magazine, National Garden, which emphasizes food gardening without chemicals.

Seed Savers Exchange
Director: Kent Whealy
203 Rural Ave
Decorah, IA 52101
Organization dedicated to preserving heirloom food seeds of USA and Canada. Membership $10 a year. The Garden Seed Inventory, a listing of all non-hybrid vegetable seeds offered in USA and Canada is available for $12.

Control of Insects on Deciduous Fruits and Tree Nuts in the Home Orchard Without Insecticides: US Dept. of Agriculture Bulletin No. 211.
Available from Supt. of Documents, U.S. Government Printing Office, Washington D.C. for 90 cents.

Organic Gardening
Emmaus, PA 18099
Monthly organic gardening magazine.

INDEX

Page numbers in **bold** refer to illustrations and captions

Acknowledgments

Author's acknowledgments The material in this book is the result of ten years of trials and observation. This represents a great deal of work in growing plants and recording, collating and evaluating information. My thanks are due to my colleagues who did much of the work with skill, patience and dedication. To Carol Woods, Sue Jeal and Rod Biggs, the other three-quarters of the growing team at Barnsdale, I owe a major debt of gratitude.

My thanks are also due to the many manufacturers, growers and merchants who make up the British gardening industry for their unstinting support in supplying both materials and information.

Photographer Dave King was forced to break the habit of a lifetime and set out at dawn for my remote residence to take all the on-site photographs. The quality of his work needs no acclaim from me. It speaks for itself.

The editorial and design team of Jemima Dunne, Neville Graham, Sophie Mitchell, Tim Hammond, Derek Coombes and Joanna Martin, deserve not only my sincere thanks but a medal for fortitude and diplomacy. They have suffered gruelling hours plus my impatience and bad temper with commendable patience and humour.

My grateful thanks to a team of real professionals.

Geoff Hamilton, Barnsdale 1987.

Dorling Kindersley would like to thank: Vic Chambers and Tony Wallace without whom we would never have finished the book; Henrietta Winthrop for production; James Allen and Jonathan Hilton for editorial help; Tina Vaughan and Philip Lord for design help; Fred and Kathy Gill for proof reading; Richard and Hilary Bird for the index; Chris Cope for the black and white prints; Elizabeth Robinson for collecting the seaweed; Mr Grant at Whitkirk Produce Co. for the wool shoddy; Mr Don at Young's Brewery for the spent hops; Fulham Palace Road Garden Centre for plants and soil conditioners; Mrs Tree for reference photographs; Susan Watt for the mulberries; Mary Daniell and David Burnie for collecting weeds; Jim Keesing at The Royal Botanical Gardens, Kew; Dr Loveland at Rothamsted Experimental Station; Mrs Bench at Herb Nursery, Thistleton; Avon Bulbs; Hilliers of Winchester; Blooms of Bressingham; Hyam and Cockertons; and everyone at Barnsdale.

Illustrators
David Ashby
Vanessa Luff
Andrew Macdonald
John Woodcock
Brian Sayers

Jacket illustration
Jill Dow

Photography
Andreas Einsiedel – *Still-life photography*
Dave King – *Step-by-step and all other photography except:*
p6 (L) Andrew Butler, *(R)* Michael Warren; *p7 (L&R)* Karl Dietrich Buhler/Elizabeth Whiting and Associates; *p45 (B)* Heather Angel; *p65 (B)* Karl Dietrich Buhler/Elizabeth Whiting and Associates; *p67 (L&R)* Ann Kelly/Elizabeth Whiting and Associates; *p68* Michael Nicholson/Elizabeth Whiting and Associates; *p69 (TL)* Spike Powell/Elizabeth Whiting and Associates, *(BL)* Neil Holmes, *(BR)* Karl Dietrich Buhler/Elizabeth Whiting and Associates; *p70* Hugh Palmer/Good Housekeeping Magazine; *p71 (L&R)* Karl Dietrich Buhler/Elizabeth Whiting and Associates; *p76 (L)* Heather Angel, *(R)* Michael Warren; *p80 (T)* Stephen Hamilton; *p84 (CL)* Ardea, London, *(CR&BL)* Michael Warren, *(BR)* Heather Angel; *p85 (CR)* Ardea, London, *(BL)* Michael Warren; *p87 (TR)* Michael Warren, *(CR)* Heather Angel; *p91 (T)* Karl Dietrich Buhler/Elizabeth Whiting and Associates; *p92 (T&3rd down)* Michael Warren; *p93 (T)* Michael Warren; *p121 (TL)* Peter Steyn/Ardea, London, *(BL)* Heather Angel, *(TR&BR)* Michael Warren; *p125 (L)* Heather Angel, *(R)* Neil Holmes; *p127 (TR)* Karl Dietrich Buhler/Elizabeth Whiting and Associates; *p133 (T)* Andrew Butler; *p176* Andrew Butler; *p177* Neil Holmes; *p192 (T)* Neil Holmes; *p205 (T&R)* Neil Holmes; *p231* Neil Holmes; *p237 (L)* Karl Dietrich Buhler/Elizabeth Whiting and Associates, *(R)* Andrew Butler.

Key:
T = top   R = right
B = bottom   L = left

Filmsetting
Chambers Wallace Ltd, London

Headline setting
Airedale Graphics

Reproduction
Arnoldo Mondadori, Verona